THE O'LEARY SERIES

COMPLETE EDITION

Microsoft® PowerPoint 2010: A Case Approach

Timothy J. O'Leary

*Professor Emeritus,
Arizona State University*

Linda I. O'Leary

Mc Graw Hill

*Connect
Learn
Succeed*™

THE O'LEARY SERIES MICROSOFT® POWERPOINT 2010: A CASE APPROACH, COMPLETE

Published by McGraw-Hill, a business unit of The McGraw-Hill Companies, Inc., 1221 Avenue of the Americas, New York, NY, 10020. Copyright © 2011 by The McGraw-Hill Companies, Inc. All rights reserved. Printed in the United States of America. No part of this publication may be reproduced or distributed in any form or by any means, or stored in a database or retrieval system, without the prior written consent of The McGraw-Hill Companies, Inc., including, but not limited to, in any network or other electronic storage or transmission, or broadcast for distance learning.

Some ancillaries, including electronic and print components, may not be available to customers outside the United States.

This book is printed on acid-free paper.

1 2 3 4 5 6 7 8 9 0 RMN/RMN 1 0 9 8 7 6 5 4 3 2 1

ISBN   978-0-07-733130-6
MHID   0-07-733130-3

Vice president/Editor in chief: *Elizabeth Haefele*
Vice president/Director of marketing: *Alice Harra*
Publisher: *Scott Davidson*
Sponsoring editor: *Paul Altier*
Director, digital products: *Crystal Szewczyk*
Development editor II: *Alaina G. Tucker*
Development editor: *Alan Palmer*
Marketing manager: *Tiffany Russell*
Digital development editor: *Kevin White*
Director, Editing/Design/Production: *Jess Ann Kosic*
Project manager: *Marlena Pechan*
Senior buyer: *Michael R. McCormick*
Senior designer: *Srdjan Savanovic*
Senior photo research coordinator: *Jeremy Cheshareck*
Manager, digital production: *Janean A. Utley*
Media project manager: *Cathy L. Tepper*
Typeface: *10/12 New Aster LT STD*
Compositor: *Laserwords Private Limited*
Printer: *R. R. Donnelley*
Cover credit: © *Kjpargeter/Dreamstime.com*
Credits: The credits section for this book begins on page PPC.1 and is considered an extension of the copyright page.

Library of Congress Cataloging-in-Publication Data

O'Leary, Timothy J., 1947-
    Microsoft PowerPoint 2010 : a case approach / Timothy J. O'Leary, Linda I. O'Leary.—
 Complete ed.
       p. cm. — (The O'Leary series)
     Includes index.
     ISBN-13: 978-0-07-733130-6 (pbk.)
     ISBN-10: 0-07-733130-3 (pbk.)
     1. Microsoft PowerPoint (Computer file) 2. Presentation graphics software. I. O'Leary,
 Linda I. II. Title.
 P93.53.M534O44 2011
 005.5'8—dc23   2011017852

The Internet addresses listed in the text were accurate at the time of publication. The inclusion of a Website does not indicate an endorsement by the authors or McGraw-Hill, and McGraw-Hill does not guarantee the accuracy of the information presented at these sites.

www.mhhe.com

Brief Contents

Contents

LAB ② MODIFYING AND REFINING A PRESENTATION   PP2.1

We would like to extend our thanks to the professors who took time out of their busy schedules to provide us with the feedback necessary to develop the 2010 Edition of this text. The following professors offered valuable suggestions on revising the text:

Joan Albright
Greenville Technical College

Wilma Andrews
Virginia Commonwealth University

Robert M. Benavides
Collin College

Kim Cannon
Greenville Technical College

Paulette Comet
The Community College of Baltimore County

Michael Dunklebarger
Alamance Community College

Joel English
Centura College

Deb Fells
Mesa Community College

Tatyana Feofilaktova
ASA Institute

Sue Furnas
Collin College

Debbie Grande
The Community College of Rhode Island

Rachelle Hall
Glendale Community College

Katherine Herbert
Montclair State University

Terri Holly
Indian River State College

Mark W. Huber
University of Georgia

Joyce Kessel
Western International University

Hal P. Kingsley
Trocaire College

Diane Lending
James Madison University

Dr. Mo Manouchehripour
The Art Institute of Dallas

Sue McCrory
Missouri State University

Gary McFall
Purdue University

Margaret M. Menna
The Community College of Rhode Island

Philip H. Nielson
Salt Lake Community College

Craig Piercy
University of Georgia

Mark Renslow
Globe University/Minnesota School of Business

Ann Rowlette
Liberty University

Chakra Pani Sharma
ASA Institute

Eric Weinstein
Suffolk County Community College

Sheryl Wright
College of the Mainland

Laurie Zouharis
Suffolk University

We would like to thank those who took the time to help us develop the manuscript and ensure accuracy through painstaking edits: Brenda Nielsen of Mesa Community College–Red Mountain, Kaari Busick, Candice Spangler of Columbus State Community College, and Kate Scalzi.

Finally, we would like to thank team members from McGraw-Hill, whose renewed commitment, direction, and support have infused the team with the excitement of a new project. Leading the team from McGraw-Hill are Tiffany Russell, Marketing Manager; and Developmental Editor Alaina Tucker.

The production staff is headed by Marlena Pechan, Project Manager, whose planning and attention to detail have made it possible for us to successfully meet a very challenging schedule; Srdjan Savanovic, Designer; Michael McCormick, Production Supervisor; Kevin White, Digital Developmental Editor; Jeremy Cheshareck, Photo Researcher; and Betsy Blumenthal, copyeditor—team members on whom we can depend to do a great job.

About the Contributors

Sarah Clifford is an independent writer, editor, and educator based in the San Francisco Bay area. She has designed and delivered academic programs for large organizations in both the private and public sectors. Additionally, Sarah has served as a faculty member of Golden Gate University. Over the past 20 years, she has coauthored several texts on information technology for McGraw-Hill, including the Advantage Series of books, resources geared toward training college students and others in using and integrating personal computer applications. For the past six years, Sarah also has served as the curriculum director for Vita Academy, a private coeducational grammar school she helped found in Oakland, California.

Dr. Pat R. Graves is a Professor Emeritus in the School of Business at Eastern Illinois University. In the Computer Information Systems curriculum she taught courses such as Business Presentations and Document Design, Business Web Site Design and Development, and Managerial Communications. Dr. Graves received the Distinguished Professor award from the EIU School of Business and awards for Outstanding Teaching, Collaborative Learning, and Innovating Teaching. She received three University awards for Excellence in the Use of Technology, Achievement and Contribution Award in Research, and Faculty Excellence Award in Research. Dr. Graves has been an author of PowerPoint textbooks for McGraw-Hill Higher Education since 2002, having authored textbooks for Microsoft Office 2003, 2007, and 2010.

The 20th century brought us the dawn of the digital information age and unprecedented changes in information technology. There is no indication that this rapid rate of change will be slowing—it may even be increasing. As we begin the 21st century, computer literacy is undoubtedly becoming a prerequisite in whatever career you choose.

The goal of the O'Leary Series is to provide you with the necessary skills to efficiently use these applications. Equally important is the goal to provide a foundation for students to readily and easily learn to use future versions of this software. This series does this by providing detailed step-by-step instructions combined with careful selection and presentation of essential concepts.

Times are changing, technology is changing, and this text is changing too. As students of today, you are different from those of yesterday. You put much effort toward the things that interest you and the things that are relevant to you. Your efforts directed at learning application programs and exploring the Web seem, at times, limitless.

On the other hand, students often can be shortsighted, thinking that learning the skills to use the application is the only objective. The mission of the series is to build upon and extend this interest by not only teaching the specific application skills but by introducing the concepts that are common to all applications, providing students with the confidence, knowledge, and ability to easily learn the next generation of applications.

Instructor's Resource Center

The online **Instructor's Resource Center** contains access to a Computerized Test Bank, an Instructor's Manual, Solutions, and PowerPoint Presentation Slides. Features of the Instructor's Resource Center are described below.

- **Instructor's Manual** The Instructor's Manual, authored by the primary contributor, contains lab objectives, concepts, outlines, lecture notes, and command summaries. Also included are answers to all end-of-chapter material, tips for covering difficult materials, additional exercises, and a schedule showing how much time is required to cover text material.

- **Computerized Test Bank** The test bank, authored by the primary contributor, contains hundreds of multiple choice, true/false, and discussion questions. Each question will be accompanied by the correct answer, the level of learning difficulty, and corresponding page references. Our flexible EZ Test software allows you to easily generate custom exams.

- **PowerPoint Presentation Slides** The presentation slides, authored by the primary contributor, include lab objectives, concepts, outlines, text figures, and speaker's notes. Also included are bullets to illustrate key terms and FAQs.

Online Learning Center/Website

Found at **www.mhhe.com/oleary,** this site provides additional learning and instructional tools to enhance the comprehension of the text. The OLC/Website is divided into these three areas:

- **Information Center** Contains core information about the text, supplements, and the authors.

- **Instructor Center** Offers the aforementioned instructional materials, downloads, and other relevant links for professors.

- **Student Center** Contains data files, chapter competencies, chapter concepts, self-quizzes, additional Web links, and more.

Simnet Assessment for Office Applications

Simnet Assessment for Office Applications provides a way for you to test students' software skills in a simulated environment. Simnet is available for Microsoft Office 2010 and provides flexibility for you in your applications course by offering:

Pretesting options
Post-testing options
Course placement testing
Diagnostic capabilities to reinforce skills
Web delivery of tests
Certification preparation exams
Learning verification reports

For more information on skills assessment software, please contact your local sales representative, or visit us at **www.mhhe.com.**

O'Leary Series

The O'Leary Application Series for Microsoft Office is available separately or packaged with *Computing Essentials*. The O'Leary Application Series offers a step-by-step case-based approach to learning computer applications and is available in both introductory and complete versions.

Computing Concepts

Computing Essentials 2013 offers a unique, visual orientation that gives students a basic understanding of computing concepts. *Computing Essentials* encourages "active" learning with exercises, explorations, visual illustrations, and screen shots. While combining the "active" learning style with current topics and technology, this text provides an accurate snapshot of computing trends. When bundled with software application lab manuals, students are given a complete representation of the fundamental issues surrounding the personal computing environment.

Tim and Linda O'Leary live in the American Southwest and spend much of their time engaging instructors and students in conversation about learning. In fact, they have been talking about learning for over 25 years. Something in those early conversations convinced them to write a book, to bring their interest in the learning process to the printed page. Today, they are as concerned as ever about learning, about technology, and about the challenges of presenting material in new ways, in terms of both content and method of delivery.

A powerful and creative team, Tim combines his 30 years of classroom teaching experience with Linda's background as a consultant and corporate trainer. Tim has taught courses at Stark Technical College in Canton, Ohio, and at Rochester Institute of Technology in upstate New York, and is currently a professor emeritus at Arizona State University in Tempe, Arizona. Linda offered her expertise at ASU for several years as an academic advisor. She also presented and developed materials for major corporations such as Motorola, Intel, Honeywell, and AT&T, as well as various community colleges in the Phoenix area.

Tim and Linda have talked to and taught numerous students, all of them with a desire to learn something about computers and applications that make their lives easier, more interesting, and more productive.

Each new edition of an O'Leary text, supplement, or learning aid has benefited from these students and their instructors who daily stand in front of them (or over their shoulders). The O'Leary Series is no exception.

Dedication

We dedicate this edition to our parents—Irene Perley Coats, Jean L. O'Leary, and Charles D. O'Leary—for all their support and love. We miss you.

Objectives

After completing the Introduction to Microsoft Office 2010, you should be able to:

1. Describe the Office 2010 applications.

2. Start an Office 2010 application.

3. Use the Ribbon, dialog boxes, and task panes.

4. Use menus, context menus, and shortcut keys.

5. Use Backstage view.

6. Open, close, and save files.

7. Navigate a document.

8. Enter, edit, and format text.

9. Select, copy, and move text.

10. Undo and redo changes.

11. Specify document properties.

12. Print a document.

13. Use Office 2010 Help.

14. Exit an Office 2010 application.

What Is Microsoft Office 2010?

Microsoft's Office 2010 is a comprehensive, integrated system of programs designed to solve a wide array of business needs. Although the programs can be used individually, they are designed to work together seamlessly, making it easy to connect people and organizations to information, business processes, and each other. The applications include tools used to create, discuss, communicate, and manage projects. If you share a lot of documents with other people, these features facilitate access to common documents. If you are away on business or do not have your PC with you, you can use Office 2010 Web applications, browser versions of Word, Excel, PowerPoint, and OneNote, to edit documents and collaborate with others.

Microsoft Office 2010 is packaged in several different combinations of programs or suites. The major programs and a brief description are provided in the following table.

Program	Description
Word 2010	Word processor program used to create text-based documents
Excel 2010	Spreadsheet program used to analyze numerical data
Access 2010	Database manager used to organize, manage, and display a database
PowerPoint 2010	Graphics presentation program used to create presentation materials
Outlook 2010	Desktop information manager and messaging client
InfoPath 2010	Used to create XML forms and documents
OneNote 2010	Note-taking and information organization tools
Publisher 2010	Tools to create and distribute publications for print, Web, and e-mail
Visio 2010	Diagramming and data visualization tools
SharePoint Designer 2010	Web site development and management for SharePoint servers
Project 2010	Project management tools

The four main components of Microsoft Office 2010—Word, Excel, Access, and PowerPoint—are the applications you will learn about in this series of labs. They are described in more detail in the following sections.

Word 2010

Word 2010 is a word processing software application whose purpose is to help you create text-based documents such as letters, memos, reports, e-mail messages, or any other type of correspondence. Word processors are one of the most flexible and widely used application software programs.

WORD 2010 FEATURES

The beauty of a word processor is that you can make changes or corrections as you are typing. Want to change a report from single spacing to double spacing? Alter the width of the margins? Delete some paragraphs and add others from yet another document? A word processor allows you to do all these things with ease.

Edit Content

Word 2010 excels in its ability to change or **edit** a document. Basic document editing involves correcting spelling, grammar, and sentence-structure errors and revising or updating existing text by inserting, deleting, and rearranging areas of text. For example, a document that lists prices can easily be updated to reflect new prices. A document that details procedures can be revised by deleting old procedures and inserting new ones. Many of these changes are made easily by cutting (removing) or copying (duplicating) selected text and then pasting (inserting) the cut or copied text in another location in the same or another document. Editing allows you to quickly revise a document, by changing only the parts that need to be modified.

To help you produce a perfect document, Word 2010 includes many additional editing support features. The AutoCorrect feature checks the spelling and grammar in a document as text is entered. Many common errors are corrected automatically for you. Others are identified and a correction suggested. A thesaurus can be used to display alternative words that have a meaning similar or opposite to a word you entered. The Find and Replace feature can be used to quickly locate specified text and replace it with other text throughout a document. In addition, Word 2010 includes a variety of tools that automate the process of many common tasks, such as creating tables, form letters, and columns.

Format Content

You also can easily control the appearance or **format** of the document. Perhaps the most noticeable formatting feature is the ability to apply different fonts (type styles and sizes) and text appearance changes such as bold, italics, and color to all or selected portions of the document. Additionally, you can add color shading behind individual pieces of text or entire paragraphs and pages to add emphasis. Other formatting features include changes to entire paragraphs, such as the line spacing and alignment of text between the margins. You also can format entire pages by displaying page numbers, changing margin settings, and applying backgrounds.

To make formatting even easier, Word 2010 includes Document Themes and Styles. Document Themes apply a consistent font, color, and line effect to an entire document. Styles apply the selected style design to a selection of text. Further, Word 2010 includes a variety of built-in preformatted content that helps you quickly produce modern-looking, professional documents. Among these are galleries of cover page designs, pull quotes, and header and footer designs. While selecting many of these design choices, a visual live preview is displayed, making it easy to see how the design would look in your document. In addition, you can select from a wide variety of templates to help you get started on creating many common types of documents such as flyers, calendars, faxes, newsletters, and memos.

Insert Illustrations

To further enhance your documents, you can insert many different types of graphic elements. These include drawing objects, SmartArt, charts, pictures, clip art, and screenshots. The drawing tools supplied with Word 2010 can be used to create your own drawings, or you can select from over 100 adjustable shapes and modify them to your needs. All drawings can be further enhanced with 3-D effects, shadows, colors, and textures. SmartArt graphics allow you to create a visual representation of your information. They include many different layouts such as a process or cycle that are designed to help you communicate an idea. Charts can be inserted to illustrate and compare data. Complex pictures can be inserted in documents by scanning your own, using supplied or purchased clip art, or downloading images from the World Wide Web. Additionally, you can produce fancy text effects using the WordArt tool. Finally, you can quickly capture and insert a picture, called a screenshot, from another application running on your computer into the current document.

Collaborate with Others

Group collaboration on projects is common in industry today. Word 2010 includes many features to help streamline how documents are developed and changed by group members. A discussion feature allows multiple people to insert remarks in the same document without having to route the document to each person or reconcile multiple reviewers' comments. You can easily consolidate all changes and comments from different reviewers in one simple step and accept or reject changes as needed.

Two documents you will produce in the first two Word 2010 labs, a letter and flyer, are shown here.

A letter containing a tabbed table, indented paragraphs, and text enhancements is quickly created using basic Word features

January 27, 2012

Dear Adventure Traveler:

Imagine camping under the stars in Africa, hiking and paddling your way through the rainforests of Costa Rica, or following in the footsteps of the ancient Inca as you backpack along the Inca trail to Machu Picchu. Turn these thoughts of adventure into memories you will cherish forever by joining Adventure Travel Tours on one of our four new adventure tours.

To tell you more about these exciting new advent... area. These presentations will focus on the features and cu... of the places you will visit and activities you can participate... Plan to attend one of the following presentations:

Date	Time	Locati...
February 5	8:00 p.m.	Renaissan...
February 19	7:30 p.m.	Airport Pla...
March 8	8:00 p.m.	Crowne Co...

In appreciation of your past patronage, we are ple... of the new tour packages. You must book the trip at least... this letter to qualify for the discount.

Our vacation tours are professionally developed s... everything in the price of your tour while giving you the be... these features:

➤ All accommodations and meals
➤ All entrance fees, excursions, transfers and tips
➤ Professional tour manager and local guides

We hope you will join us this year on another spec... Travel Tours each day is an adventure. For reservations, pl... Travel Tours directly at 1-800-555-0004.

Be...

St...
Ad...

ADVENTURE TRAVEL TOURS

NEW ADVENTURES

Attention adventure travelers! Attend an Adventure Travel presentation to learn about some of the earth's greatest unspoiled habitats and find out how you can experience the adventure of a lifetime. This year Adventure Travel Tours is introducing four new tours that offer you a unique opportunity to combine many different outdoor activities while exploring the world.

Costa Rica Rivers and Rainforests

India Wildlife Adventure

Safari in Tanzania

Inca Trail to Machu Picchu

Presentation dates and times are January 5 at 7:00 p.m., February 3 at 7:30 p.m., and March 8 at 7:00 p.m. All presentations are held at convenient hotel locations. The hotels are located in downtown Los Angeles, in Santa Clara, and at the LAX airport.

Call Adventure Travel Tours at 1-800-555-0004 for presentation locations, a full color brochure, and itinerary information, costs, and trip dates. Student Name will gladly help with all of your questions.

A flyer incorporating many visual enhancements such as colored text, varied text styles, and graphic elements is both eye-catching and informative

Excel 2010 is an electronic spreadsheet, or **worksheet**, that is used to organize, manipulate, and graph numeric data. Once used almost exclusively by accountants, worksheets are now widely used by nearly every profession. Nearly any job that uses rows and columns of numbers can be performed using an electronic spreadsheet. Once requiring hours of labor and/or costly accountants' fees, data analysis is now available almost instantly using electronic spreadsheets and has become a routine business procedure. This powerful business tool has revolutionized the business world. Typical uses include the creation of budgets and financial planning for both business and personal situations. Marketing professionals record and evaluate sales trends. Teachers record grades and calculate final grades. Personal trainers record the progress of their clients.

EXCEL 2010 FEATURES

Excel 2010 includes many features that not only help you create a well-designed worksheet, but one that produces accurate results. The features include the ability to quickly edit and format data, perform calculations, create charts, and print the spreadsheet. Using Excel 2010, you can quickly analyze and manage data and communicate your findings to others. The program not only makes it faster to create worksheets, but it also produces professional-appearing results.

Enter and Edit Data

The Microsoft Excel 2010 spreadsheet program uses a workbook file that contains one or more worksheets. Each worksheet can be used to organize different types of related information. The worksheet consists of rows and columns that create a grid of cells. You enter numeric data or descriptive text into a cell. These entries can then be erased, moved, copied, or edited.

Format Data

Like text in a Word document, the design and appearance of entries in a worksheet can be enhanced in many ways. For instance, you can change the font style and size and add special effects such as bold, italic, borders, boxes, drop shadows, and shading to selected cells. You also can use cell styles to quickly apply predefined combinations of these formats to selections. Additionally, you can select from different document themes, predefined combinations of colors, fonts, and effects, to give your workbooks a consistent, professional appearance.

Unlike the Word application, Excel includes many formatting features that are designed specifically for numeric data. For example, numeric entries can be displayed with commas, dollar signs, or a set number of decimal places. Special formatting, such as color bars, can be applied automatically to ranges of cells to emphasize data based on a set of criteria you establish and to highlight trends.

Analyze Data

The power of a spreadsheet application is its ability to perform calculations from very simple sums to the most complex financial and mathematical formulas. Formulas can be entered that perform calculations using data contained in specified cells. The results of the calculations are displayed in the cell containing the formula. Predefined formulas, called functions, can be used to quickly perform complex calculations such as calculating loan payments or statistical analysis of data.

Analysis of data in a spreadsheet once was too expensive and time-consuming. Now, using electronic worksheets, you can use what-if or sensitivity analysis by changing the values in selected cells and immediately observing the effect on related cells in the worksheet. Other analysis tools such as Solver and Scenarios allow you to see the effects of possible alternative courses of action to help forecast future outcomes.

Chart Data

Using Excel, you also can produce a visual display of numeric data in the form of graphs or charts. As the values in the worksheet change, charts referencing those values automatically adjust to reflect the changes. You also can enhance the appearance of a chart by using different type styles and sizes, adding three-dimensional effects, and including text and objects such as lines and arrows.

Two worksheets you will produce using Excel 2010 are shown below.

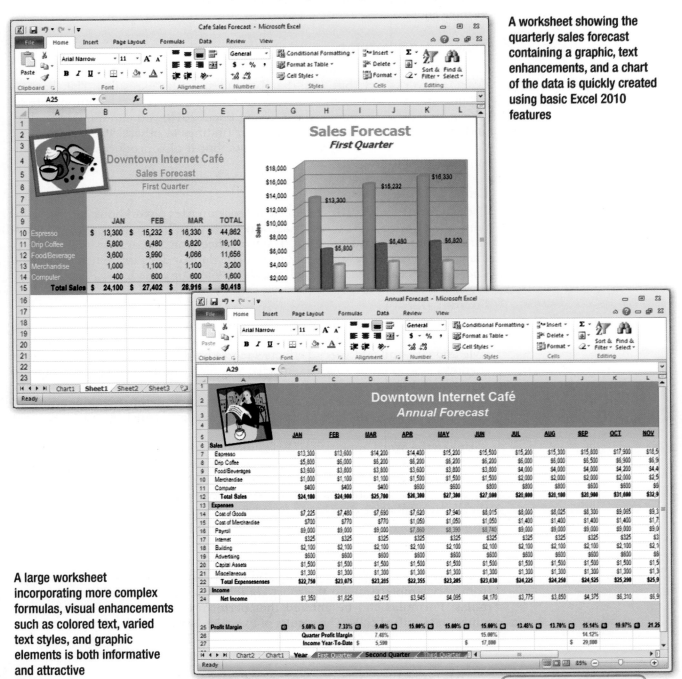

A worksheet showing the quarterly sales forecast containing a graphic, text enhancements, and a chart of the data is quickly created using basic Excel 2010 features

A large worksheet incorporating more complex formulas, visual enhancements such as colored text, varied text styles, and graphic elements is both informative and attractive

Access 2010 is a relational database management application that is used to create and analyze a database. A **database** is a collection of related data. **Tables** consist of columns (called **fields**) and rows (called **records**). Each row contains a record, which is all the information about one person, thing, or place. Each field is the smallest unit of information about a record.

In a relational database, the most widely used database structure, data is organized in linked tables. The tables are related or linked to one another by a common field. Relational databases allow you to create smaller and more manageable database tables, since you can combine and extract data between tables.

For example, a state's motor vehicle department database might have an address table. Each row (record) in the table would contain address information about one individual. Each column (field) would contain just one piece of information, for example, zip codes. The address table would be linked to other tables in the database by common fields. For example, the address table might be linked to a vehicle owner's table by name and linked to an outstanding citation table by license number (see example below).

Address Table

Name	License Number	Street Address	City	State	Zip
Aaron, Linda	FJ1987	10032 Park Lane	San Jose	CA	95127
Abar, John	D12372	1349 Oak St	Lakeville	CA	94128
Abell, Jack	LK3457	95874 State St	Stone	CA	95201

key fields linked   key fields linked

Owner's Table

Name	Plate Number
Abell, Jack	ABK241
Abrams, Sue	LMJ198
Abril, Pat	ZXA915

Outstanding Citation Table

License Number	Citation Code	Violation
T25476	00031	Speed
D98372	19001	Park
LK3457	89100	Speed

ACCESS 2010 FEATURES

Access 2010 is a powerful program with numerous easy-to-use features including the ability to quickly locate information; add, delete, modify, and sort records; analyze data; and produce professional-looking reports. Some of the basic Access 2010 features are described next.

Find Information

Once you enter data into the database table, you can quickly search the table to locate a specific record based on the data in a field. In a manual system, you can usually locate a record by knowing one key piece of information. For example, if the records are stored in a file cabinet alphabetically by last name, to quickly find a record, you must know the last name. In a computerized database, even if the records are sorted or organized by last name, you can still quickly locate a record using information in another field.

Add, Delete, and Modify Records

Using Access, it is also easy to add and delete records from the table. Once you locate a record, you can edit the contents of the fields to update the record or delete the record entirely from the table. You also can add new records to a table. When you enter a new record, it is automatically placed in the correct organizational location within the table. Creation of forms makes it easier to enter and edit data as well.

Sort and Filter Records

The capability to arrange or sort records in the table according to different fields can provide more meaningful information. You can organize records by name, department, pay, class, or any other category you need at a particular time. Sorting the records in different ways can provide information to different departments for different purposes.

Additionally, you can isolate and display a subset of records by specifying filter criteria. The criteria specify which records to display based on data in selected fields.

Analyze Data

Using Access, you can analyze the data in a table and perform calculations on different fields of data. Instead of pulling each record from a filing cabinet, recording the piece of data you want to use, and then performing the calculation on the recorded data, you can simply have the database program perform the calculation on all the values in the specified field. Additionally, you can ask questions or query the table to find only certain records that meet specific conditions to be used in the analysis. Information that was once costly and time-consuming to get is now quickly and readily available.

Generate Reports

Access includes many features that help you quickly produce reports ranging from simple listings to complex, professional-looking reports. You can create a simple report by asking for a listing of specified fields of data and restricting the listing to records meeting designated conditions. You can create a more complex professional report using the same restrictions or conditions as the simple report, but you can display the data in different layout styles, or with titles, headings, subtotals, or totals.

A database and a report that you will produce using Access 2010 are shown on the next page.

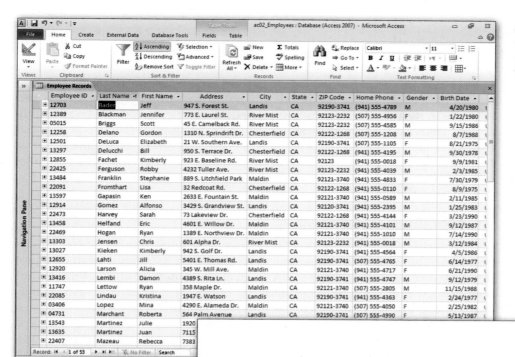

A relational database can be created and modified easily using basic Access 2010 features

Job Position Report
For **Landis**

Employee ID	First Name	Last Name	Position
12703	Jeff	Bader	Fitness Instructor
12389	Jennifer	Blackman	Sales Associate
05015	Scott	Briggs	Personal Trainer Director
12501	Elizabeth	DeLuca	Personal Trainer
12855	Kimberly	Fachet	Sales Associate
13484	Stephanie	Franklin	Food Service Server
12914	Alfonso	Gomez	Cleaning
22469	Ryan	Hogan	Personal Trainer
13303	Chris	Jensen	Greeter
13027	Kimberly	Kieken	Food Service Server
07650	Chris	Lamm	Sales Director
22085	Kristina	Lindau	Child Care Provider
13635	Juan	Martinez	Fitness Instructor
03225	Dan	Morgan	Food Service Director
99999	Student	Name	Human Resources Administrator
12420	Allison	Player	Maintenance
13005	Emily	Reilly	Assistant Manager
22297	Patricia	Rogondino	Greeter
07287	Anita	Roman	Child Care Director
12918	Carlos	Ruiz	Assistant Manager
00211	Chad	Schiff	Club Director
12583	Marie	Sullivan	Greeter
03890	Erona	Thi	Fitness Director
12380	Jessica	Thomas	Fitness Instructor

Saturday, December 01, 2012

Page 1 of 1

A professional-looking report can be quickly generated from information contained in a database

PowerPoint 2010 is a graphics presentation program designed to help you produce a high-quality presentation that is both interesting to the audience and effective in its ability to convey your message. A presentation can be as simple as overhead transparencies or as sophisticated as an on-screen electronic display. Graphics presentation programs can produce black-and-white or color overhead transparencies, 35 mm slides, onscreen electronic presentations called **slide shows**, Web pages for Web use, and support materials for both the speaker and the audience.

POWERPOINT 2010 FEATURES

Although creating an effective presentation is a complicated process, Power-Point 2010 helps simplify this process by providing assistance in the content development phase, as well as in the layout and design phase. PowerPoint includes features such as text handling, outlining, graphing, drawing, animation, clip art, and multimedia support. In addition, the programs suggest layouts for different types of presentations and offer professionally designed templates to help you produce a presentation that is sure to keep your audience's attention. In addition, you can quickly produce the support materials to be used when making a presentation to an audience.

Develop, Enter, and Edit Content

The content development phase includes deciding on the topic of your presentation, the organization of the content, and the ultimate message you want to convey to the audience. As an aid in this phase, PowerPoint 2010 helps you organize your thoughts based on the type of presentation you are making by providing both content and design templates. Based on the type of presentation, such as selling a product or suggesting a strategy, the template provides guidance by suggesting content ideas and organizational tips. For example, if you are making a presentation on the progress of a sales campaign, the program would suggest that you enter text on the background of the sales campaign as the first page, called a **slide**; the current status of the campaign as the next slide; and accomplishments, schedule, issues and problems, and where you are heading on subsequent slides.

Design Layouts

The layout for each slide is the next important decision. Again, PowerPoint 2010 helps you by suggesting text layout features such as title placement, bullets, and columns. You also can incorporate graphs of data, tables, organizational charts, clip art, and other special text effects in the slides.

PowerPoint 2010 also includes professionally designed themes to further enhance the appearance of your slides. These themes include features that standardize the appearance of all the slides in your presentation. Professionally selected combinations of text and background colors, common typefaces and sizes, borders, and other art designs take the worry out of much of the design layout.

Deliver Presentations

After you have written and designed the slides, you can use the slides in an onscreen electronic presentation or a Web page for use on the Web. An onscreen presentation uses the computer to display the slides on an overhead projection screen. As you prepare this type of presentation, you can use the rehearsal feature that allows you to practice and time your presentation. The length of time to display each slide can be set and your entire presentation can be completed within the allotted time. A presentation also can be modified to display on a Web site and run using a Web browser. Finally, you can package the presentation to a CD for distribution.

A presentation that you will produce using PowerPoint 2010 is shown below.

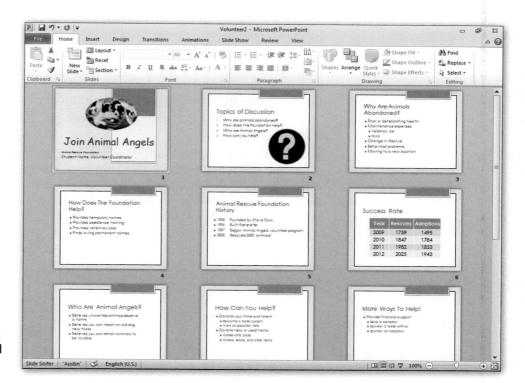

A presentation consists of a series of pages or "slides" presenting the information you want to convey in an organized and attractive manner

When running an on-screen presentation, each slide of the presentation is displayed full-screen on your computer monitor or projected onto a screen

As you follow the directions in the following hands-on section and in the application labs, you need to know the instructional conventions that are used. Hands-on instructions you are to perform appear as a sequence of numbered steps. Within each step, a series of bullets identifies the specific actions that must be performed. Step numbering begins over within each topic heading throughout the lab.

Three types of marginal notes appear throughout the labs. Another Method notes provide alternate ways of performing the same command. Having Trouble? notes provide advice or cautions for steps that may cause problems. Additional Information notes provide more information about a topic.

COMMANDS

Commands that are initiated using a command button and the mouse appear following the word "Click." The icon (and the icon name if the icon does not include text) is displayed following "Click." If there is another way to perform the same action, it appears in an Another Method margin note when the action is first introduced as shown in Example A.

When a feature has already been covered and you are more familiar with using the application, commands will appear as shown in Example B.

Example A

1

● **Select the list of four tours.**

● **Open the Home tab.**

● **Click** **B** **Bold in the Font group.**

Another Method
The keyboard shortcut is Ctrl + B.

Example B

1

● **Select the list of four tours.**

● **Click** **B** **Bold in the Font group of the Home tab.**

OR

1

● **Bold the list of four tours.**

Sometimes, clicking on an icon opens a drop-down list or a menu of commands. Commands that are to be selected follow the word "Select" and appear in black text. You can select an item by pointing to it using the mouse or by moving to it using the directional keys. When an option is selected, it appears highlighted; however, the action is not carried out. Commands that you are to complete appear following the word "Choose." You can choose a command by clicking on it using the mouse or by pressing the Enter key once it is selected. Initially these commands will appear as in Example A. Choosing a command carries out the associated action. As you become more familiar with the application, commands will appear as shown in Example B.

Example A

1

- Click **A ▼** Font Color in the Font group of the Home tab.

- Select Green.

- Choose Dark Blue.

Example B

1

- Click **A ▼** Font Color and choose Dark Blue.

FILE NAMES AND INFORMATION TO TYPE

Plain blue text identifies file names you need to select or enter. Information you are asked to type appears in blue and bold. (See Example C.)

Example C

1

- Open the document wd01_Flyer.

- Type **Adventure Travel presents four new trips**

Common Office 2010 Features

Now that you know a little about each of the applications in Microsoft Office 2010, you will take a look at some of the features that are common to all Office 2010 applications. In this hands-on section you will learn to use the common interface and application features to allow you to get a feel for how Office 2010 works. Although Word 2010 will be used to demonstrate how the features work, only features that are common to all the Office applications will be addressed.

COMMON INTERFACE FEATURES

All the Office 2010 applications have a common **user interface**, a set of graphical elements that are designed to help you interact with the program and provide instructions as to the actions you want to perform. These features include the use of the Ribbon, Quick Access Toolbar, task panes, menus, dialog boxes, and the File tab.

Starting an Office 2010 Application

To demonstrate the common features, you will start the Word 2010 application. There are several ways to start an Office 2010 application. The two most common methods are by clicking the ⊕ Start button to see a menu of available programs or by clicking a desktop shortcut for the program if it is available.

Additional Information

The procedure to start Excel, Access, and PowerPoint is the same as starting Word, except that you must select the appropriate program name or shortcut.

1

● **Click ⊞ Start to display the Start menu.**

● **Choose Microsoft Word 2010.**

Having Trouble?

If you do not see the program name on the Start menu, select All Programs, choose Microsoft Office, and then choose Microsoft Word 2010.

OR

1

● **Double-click the ▦ shortcut on the desktop.**

2

● **If necessary, click ▣ Maximize in the title bar to maximize the window.**

Your screen should be similar to Figure 1

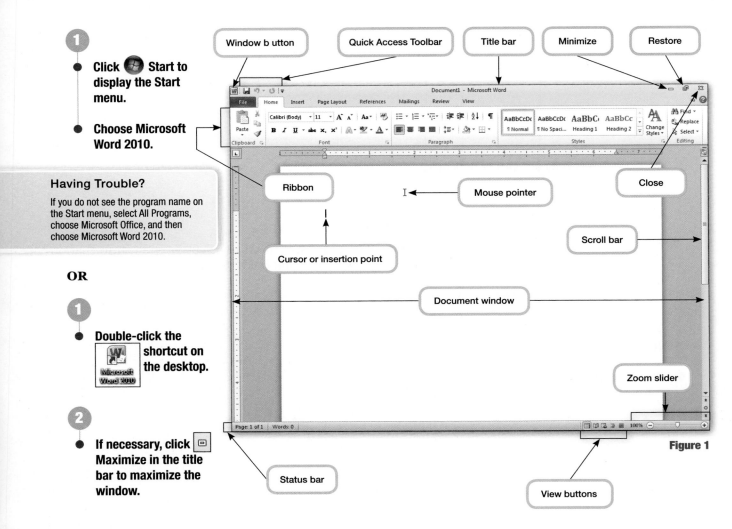

Figure 1

WWW.MHHE.COM/OLEARY

The Word 2010 program is started and displayed in a window on the desktop. All application windows display a title bar at the top of the window that includes the file name followed by the program name, in this case Microsoft Word. They also include the ⊟ Minimize, ⧉ Restore Down, and ⊠ Close buttons at the right end of the title bar. **Buttons** are graphical elements that perform the associated action when you click on them using the mouse. At the left end of the title bar is the W Window button. Clicking this button opens a menu of commands that allow you to size, move, and close the window just as the buttons on the right end of the title bar. To the right of the W Window button is the **Quick Access Toolbar** (QAT), which provides quick access to frequently used commands. By default, it includes the 🖫 Save, ↺ Undo, and ↻ Redo buttons, commands that Microsoft considers to be crucial. It is always available and is a customizable toolbar to which you can add your own favorite buttons.

Below the title bar is the **Ribbon**, which provides a centralized location of commands that are used to work in your document. The Ribbon has the same basic structure and is found in all Office 2010 applications. However, many of the commands found in the Ribbon vary with the specific applications. You will learn how to use the Ribbon shortly.

The large center area of the program window is the **document window** where open application files are displayed. When you first start Word 2010, a new blank Word document named Document1 (shown in the title bar) automatically opens, ready for you to start creating a new document. In Excel, a new, blank workbook named Book1 would be opened and in PowerPoint a new, blank presentation file named Presentation1 would be opened. In Access, however, a new blank database file is not opened automatically. Instead, you must create and name a new database file or open an existing database file.

The **cursor**, also called the **insertion point**, is the blinking vertical bar that marks your location in the document and indicates where text you type will appear. Across all Office applications, the mouse pointer appears as I I-beam when it is used to position the insertion point when entering text and as a ⇖ when it can be used to select items. There are many other mouse pointer shapes that are both common to and specific to the different applications.

On the right of the document window is a vertical scroll bar. A **scroll bar** is used with a mouse to bring additional information into view in a window. The vertical scroll bar is used to move up or down. A horizontal scroll bar is also displayed when needed and moves side to side in the window. The scroll bar is a common feature to all Windows and Office 2010 applications; however, it may not appear in all applications until needed.

At the bottom of the application window is another common feature called the **status bar**. It displays information about the open file and features that help you view the file. It displays different information depending upon the application you are using. For example, the Word status bar displays information about the number of pages and words in the document, whereas the Excel status bar displays the mode of operation and the count, average, and sum of values in selected cells. All Office 2010 applications include **View buttons** that are used to change how the information in the document window is displayed. The View buttons are different for each application. Finally, a **Zoom Slider**, located at the far right end of the status bar, is used to change the amount of information displayed in the document window by "zooming in" to get a close-up view or "zooming out" to see more of the document at a reduced view.

Displaying ScreenTips

You are probably wondering how you would know what action the different buttons perform. To help you identify buttons, the Office applications display ScreenTips when you point to them.

● **Point to the** 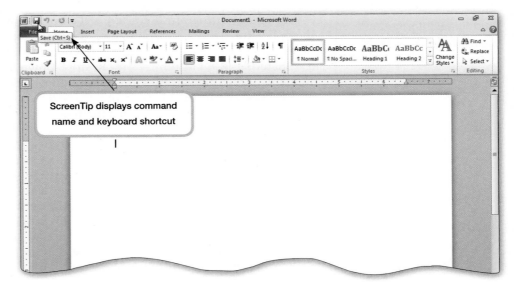 **Save button in the Quick Access Toolbar.**

ScreenTip displays command name and keyboard shortcut

Your screen should be similar to Figure 2

Figure 2

A **ScreenTip**, also called a **tooltip**, appears displaying the command name and the keyboard shortcut, Ctrl + S. A **keyboard shortcut** is a combination of keys that can be used to execute a command in place of clicking the button. In this case, if you hold down the Ctrl key while typing the letter S, you will access the command to save a file. ScreenTips also often include a brief description of the action a command performs.

Using Menus

Notice the small button ▼ at the end of the Quick Access Toolbar. Clicking this button opens a menu of commands that perform tasks associated with the Quick Access Toolbar.

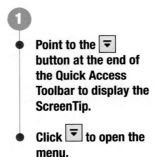

● **Point to the** ▼ **button at the end of the Quick Access Toolbar to display the ScreenTip.**

● **Click** ▼ **to open the menu.**

Click to open menu

Menu of commands for Quick Access Toolbar

Check indicates feature is on

Your screen should be similar to Figure 3

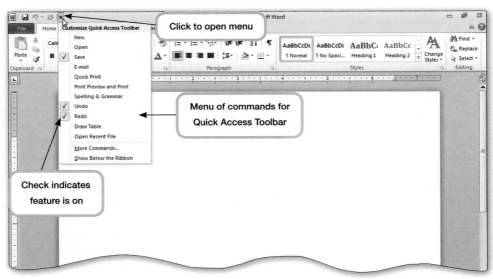

Figure 3

The first 11 items in the menu allow you to quickly add a command button to or remove a command button from the Quick Access Toolbar. Those commands that are already displayed in the Quick Access Toolbar are preceded with a checkmark. The last two commands allow you to access other command features to customize the Quick Access Toolbar or change its location.

Once a menu is open, you can select a command from the menu by pointing to it. As you do the selected command appears highlighted. Like buttons, resting the mouse pointer over the menu command options will display a ScreenTip. Then to choose a selected command, you click on it. Choosing a command performs the action associated with the command or button. You will use several of these features next.

2

● Point to the commands in the Quick Access Toolbar menu to select (highlight) them and see the ScreenTips.

● Click on the Open command to choose it and add it to the Quick Access Toolbar.

Your screen should be similar to Figure 4

Figure 4

The command button to open a document has been added to the Quick Access Toolbar. Next, you will remove this button and then you will change the location of the Quick Access Toolbar. Another way to access some commands is to use a context menu. A **context menu**, also called a **shortcut menu**, is opened by right-clicking on an item on the screen. This menu is context sensitive, meaning it displays only those commands relevant to the item or screen location. For example, right-clicking on the Quick Access Toolbar will display the commands associated with using the Quick Access Toolbar and the Ribbon. You will use this method to remove the Open button and move the Quick Access Toolbar.

3

- Point to the Open button on the Quick Access Toolbar and right-click.

- Click on the Remove from Quick Access Toolbar command to choose it.

- Right-click on any button in the Quick Access Toolbar again and choose the Show Quick Access Toolbar Below the Ribbon option.

Another Method

You also can type the underlined letter of a command to choose it or press (Enter) to choose a selected command.

Your screen should be similar to Figure 5

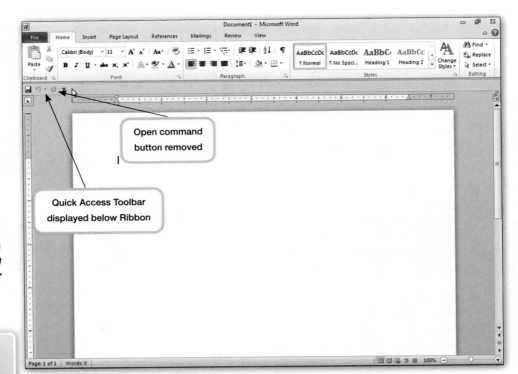

Figure 5

The Quick Access Toolbar is now displayed full size below the Ribbon. This is useful if you have many buttons on the toolbar; however, it takes up document viewing space. You will return it to its compact size.

4

- Display the Quick Access Toolbar menu.

- Choose Show Above the Ribbon.

Your screen should be similar to Figure 6

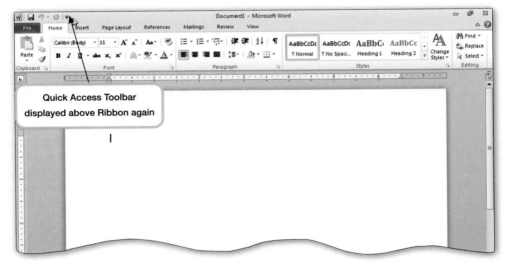

Figure 6

The Quick Access Toolbar is displayed above the Ribbon again.

Using the Ribbon

The Ribbon has three basic parts: tabs, groups, and commands (see Figure 7). **Tabs** are used to divide the Ribbon into major activity areas. Each tab is then organized into **groups** that contain related items. The related items are **commands** that consist of command buttons, a box to enter information, or a menu. Clicking on a command button performs the associated action or displays a list of additional options.

The Ribbon tabs, commands, and features vary with the different Office applications. For example, the Word Ribbon displays tabs and commands used to create a text document, whereas the Excel Ribbon displays tabs and commands used to create an electronic worksheet. Although the Ribbon commands are application specific, many are also common to all Office 2010 applications. In all applications, the Ribbon also can be customized by changing the built-in tabs or creating your own tabs and groups to personalize your workspace and provide faster access to the commands you use most.

Opening Tabs

The Word application displays the File tab and seven Ribbon tabs. The Home tab (shown in Figure 6), consisting of five groups, appears highlighted, indicating it is the open or active tab. This tab is available in all the Office 2010 applications and because it contains commands that are most frequently used when you first start an application or open a file, it is initially the open tab. In Word, the commands in the Home tab help you perform actions related to creating the text content of your document. In the other Office 2010 applications, the Home tab contains commands related to creating the associated type of document, such as a worksheet, presentation, or database. To open another tab you click on the tab name.

Click on the Insert tab.

Your screen should be similar to Figure 7

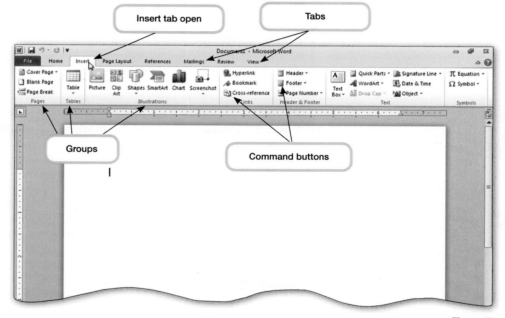

Figure 7

This Insert tab is now open and is the active tab. It contains seven groups whose commands have to do with inserting items into a document. As you use the Office applications, you will see that the Ribbon contains many of the same tabs, groups, and commands across the applications. For example, the Insert tab is available in all applications except Access. Others, such as the References tab in Word, are specific to the application. You also will see that many of the groups and commands in the common tabs, such as the Clipboard group of commands in the Home tab, contain all or many of the same commands across applications. Other groups in the common tabs contain commands that are specific to the application.

To save space, some tabs, called **contextual tabs** or **on-demand tabs**, are displayed only as needed. For example, when you are working with a picture, the Picture Tools tab appears. The contextual nature of this feature keeps the work area uncluttered when the feature is not needed and provides ready access to it when it is needed.

2

Click on each of the other tabs, ending with the View tab, to see their groups and commands.

Additional Information

If you have a mouse with a scroll wheel, pointing to the tab area of the ribbon and using the scroll wheel will scroll the tabs.

Your screen should be similar to Figure 8

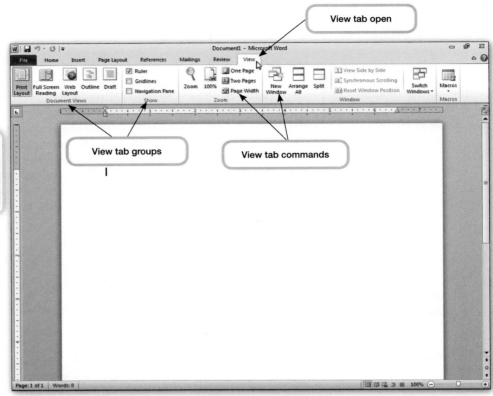

View tab open

View tab groups

View tab commands

Figure 8

Each tab relates to a type of activity; for example, the View tab commands perform activities related to viewing the document. Within each tab, similar commands are grouped together to make it easy to find the commands you want to use.

Displaying Enhanced ScreenTips

Although command buttons display graphic representations of the action they perform, often the graphic is not descriptive enough. As you have learned, pointing to a button displays the name of the button and the keyboard shortcut in a ScreenTip. To further help explain what a button does, many buttons in the Ribbon display **Enhanced ScreenTips**. For example, the ▢ Paste button in the Clipboard group of the Home tab is a two-part button. Clicking on the upper part will immediately perform an action, whereas clicking on the lower part will display additional options. You will use this feature next to see the Enhanced ScreenTips.

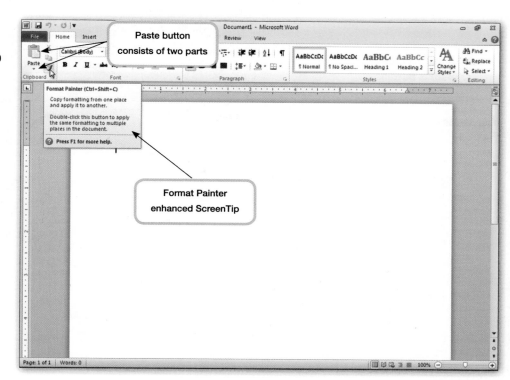

1

● Click on the Home tab to open it.

● Point to the upper part of the 🗐 Paste button in the Clipboard group.

● Point to the lower part of the ⌷Paste⌷ button in the Clipboard group.

● Point to 🖌 Format Painter in the Clipboard group.

Your screen should be similar to Figure 9

Figure 9

Additional Information

Not all commands have keyboard shortcuts.

Additional Information

You will learn about using Help shortly.

Because the 🗐 button is divided into two parts, both parts display separate Enhanced ScreenTips containing the button name; the keyboard shortcut key combination, Ctrl + V; and a brief description of what action will be performed when you click on that part of the button. Pointing to 🖌 Format Painter displays an Enhanced ScreenTip that provides more detailed information about the command. Enhanced ScreenTips may even display information such as procedures or illustrations. You can find out what the feature does without having to look it up using Office Help, a built-in reference source. If a feature has a Help article, you can automatically access it by pressing F1 while the Enhanced ScreenTip is displayed.

Using Command Buttons

Clicking on most command buttons immediately performs the associated action. Many command buttons, however, include an arrow as part of the button that affects how the button works. If a button includes an arrow that is separated from the graphic with a line when you point to the button (as in ⌷≣ ▾⌷ Bullets), clicking the button performs the associated default action and clicking the arrow displays a menu of options. If a button displays an arrow that is not separated from the graphic with a line when you point to it (as in ⌷≣▾⌷ Line Spacing), clicking the button immediately displays a menu of options. To see an example of a drop-down menu, you will open the ⌷≣ ▾⌷ Bullets menu.

1

● Click ⏷ in the ☰▾ Bullets button.

Your screen should be similar to Figure 10

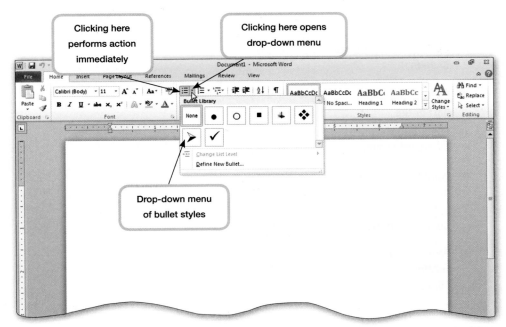

Clicking here performs action immediately

Clicking here opens drop-down menu

Drop-down menu of bullet styles

Figure 10

A drop-down menu of different bullet styles is displayed. The drop-down menu will disappear when you make a selection or click on any other area of the window.

2

● Click outside the Bullet menu to clear it.

● Click ⬆☰▾ Line and Paragraph Spacing.

Your screen should be similar to Figure 11

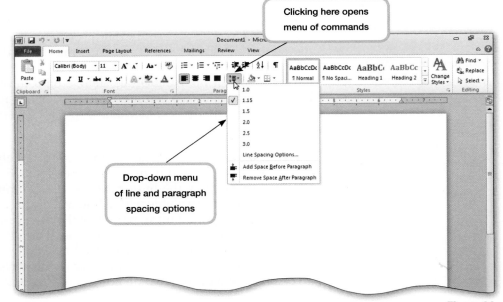

Clicking here opens menu of commands

Drop-down menu of line and paragraph spacing options

Figure 11

Another Method

You also can open tabs and choose Ribbon commands using the access key shortcuts. Press (Alt) or (F10) to display the access key letters in KeyTips over each available feature. Then type the letter for the feature you want to use.

The menu of options opened automatically when you clicked ⬆☰▾ Line and Paragraph Spacing.

Using the Dialog Box Launcher

Because there is not enough space, only the most used commands are displayed in the Ribbon. If more commands are available, a ⌷ button, called the **dialog box launcher**, is displayed in the lower-right corner of the group. Clicking ⌷ opens a dialog box or task pane of additional options.

1

- **Click outside the Line and Paragraph Spacing menu to clear it.**

- **Point to the ⌷ of the Paragraph group to see the ScreenTip.**

- **Click ⌷ of the Paragraph group.**

Your screen should be similar to Figure 12

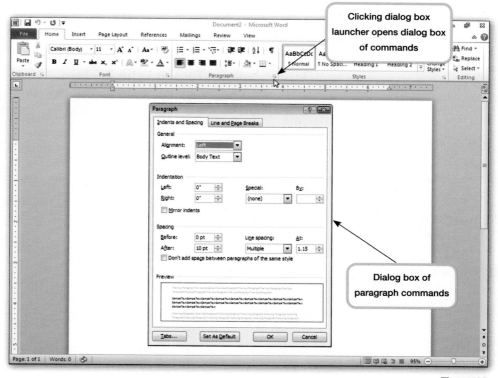

Figure 12

The Paragraph dialog box appears. It provides access to the more advanced paragraph settings options. Selecting options from the dialog box and clicking ⌷ OK will close the dialog box and apply the options as specified. To cancel the dialog box, you can click ⌷ Cancel or ⌧ Close in the dialog box title bar.

2

- **Click ⌧ to close the dialog box.**

- **Click ⌷ in the Clipboard group.**

Your screen should be similar to Figure 13

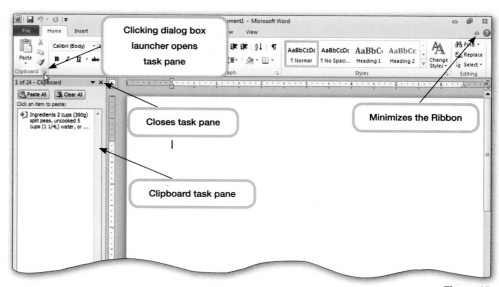

Figure 13

A task pane is open that contains features associated with the Clipboard. Unlike a dialog box, a task pane is a separate window that can be sized and moved. Generally, task panes are attached or docked to one edge of the application window. Also, task panes remain open until you close them. This allows you to make multiple selections from the task pane while continuing to work on other areas of your document.

● Click ⊠ Close in the upper-right corner of the task pane to close it.

Minimize and Expand the Ribbon

Sometimes you may not want to see the entire Ribbon so that more space is available in the document area. You can minimize the Ribbon by double-clicking the active tab.

● **Double-click the Home tab.**

Your screen should be similar to Figure 14

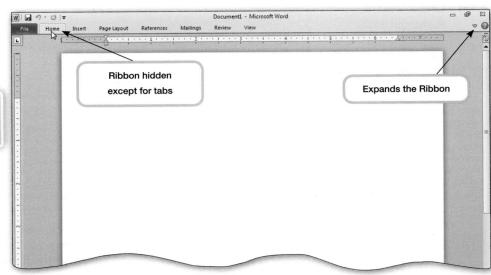

Ribbon hidden except for tabs

Expands the Ribbon

Figure 14

Now, the only part of the Ribbon that is visible is the tab area. Then, to expand the Ribbon, simply double click on the tab you want to make active. Another way to hide and redisplay the Ribbon is to click ⌃ Minimize the Ribbon or ⌄ Expand the Ribbon located at the far right end of the Ribbon tabs. You will unhide it using this feature.

● Click ⌄ Expand the Ribbon.

The full Ribbon reappears and the tab that was active when you minimized the Ribbon is active again.

Using Backstage View

To the left of the Home tab in the Ribbon is the File tab. Unlike the other tabs that display a Ribbon of commands, the File tab opens Backstage view. **Backstage view** contains commands that allow you to work *with* your document, unlike the Ribbon that allows you to work *in* your document.

Backstage view contains commands that apply to the entire document. For example, you will find commands to open, save, print, and manage your files and set your program options. This tab is common to all the Office 2010 applications, although the menu options may vary slightly.

1

● **Click the File tab to open Backstage view.**

Your screen should be similar to Figure 15

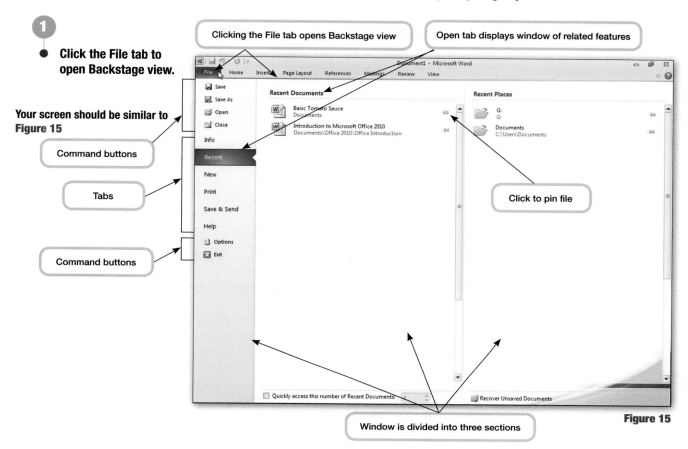

Clicking the File tab opens Backstage view

Open tab displays window of related features

Command buttons

Tabs

Command buttons

Click to pin file

Window is divided into three sections

Figure 15

The document window is hidden and the Backstage view window is open. The Backstage view window completely covers the document window and is divided into sections or panes. In all Office 2010 applications, the first (left) section always displays command buttons and tabs. You can select a tab or a button by pointing to it. As you do, the selected tab or button appears highlighted. Then to choose a selected tab or button, you click on it. Choosing a command button either opens a dialog box or immediately performs the associated action. Clicking a tab opens the tab and displays the related commands and features.

When you first open Backstage view and you have not yet opened a document or started to create a new document, the Recent tab is open. It displays a list of links to recently opened Word files in the second section, making it easy to quickly locate and resume using a file. The third section displays a list of folder locations that have been recently visited. In Excel, PowerPoint, and Access, the recently opened file list displays files for the associated application. The list of files and folders changes as you work to reflect only the most recent files and folder locations. The most recently used files and folder locations appear at the top of the list.

Next, you will try out some of these features by selecting and opening different tabs and command buttons.

2

● **Point to all the tabs and commands in the Backstage view menu.**

● **Click the New tab to make it active.**

Additional Information

The open tab is identified with a dark blue background.

Your screen should be similar to Figure 16

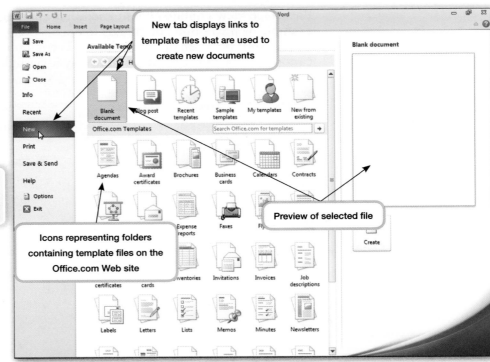

Figure 16

The second section of the New tab displays icons representing links to available templates on your computer or on the Office.com Web site. A **template** is a professionally designed document that is used as the basis for a new document. The Blank document icon is selected by default and is used to create a new Word document file from scratch. The third section displays a preview of the selected file. Icons in the Office.com area are links to different categories of template files that are contained in folders. Clicking on a folder icon opens the folder and displays file icons. Double-clicking on a file icon opens the file in Word. Again, the available templates are specific to the Office application you are using.

Additional Information

When you start the Word 2010 application, the Blank document template is automatically opened.

3

● **Click the Info tab.**

Your screen should be similar to Figure 17

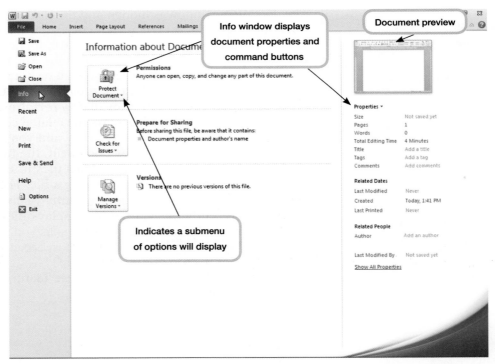

Figure 17

The Info tab displays information about your current document. The three buttons in the second section are used to define permissions, check for issues related to distribution, and manage document versions for the current document. A description of these buttons and the current document settings is shown to the right of the button. Notice that the buttons display a [▾]. This indicates that a menu of commands will be displayed when you click the button. The third section displays a preview picture of the current document and a list of the settings, called **properties**, associated with the document. The current properties displayed in the Info window show the initial or **default** properties associated with a new blank document.

Additional Information

You will learn more about document properties shortly.

4

● Click  to open the menu.

● **Point to Restrict Permission by People.**

Your screen should be similar to Figure 18

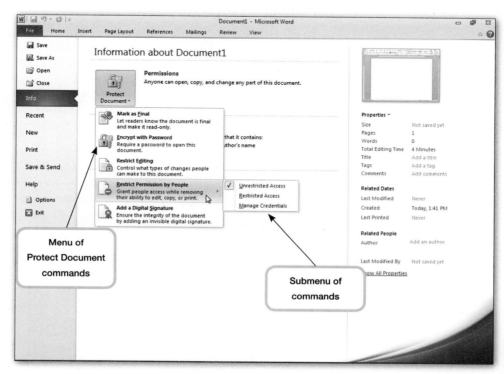

Figure 18

The Protect Document drop-down menu displays five commands. The highlighted command displays a submenu of additional commands. Next, you will clear the Protect Document menu and close Backstage view.

5

● Click  again to clear the submenu.

● **Click the Home tab to close Backstage view and open the Home tab again.**

Another Method

You also can press [Esc], click on the File tab or any other Ribbon tab, or click on the document preview in the Info screen to close the Backstage view window.

COMMON APPLICATION FEATURES

So far you have learned about using the Office 2010 user interface features. Next, you will learn about application features that are used to work in and modify documents and are the same or similar in all Office 2010 applications. These include how to open, close, and save files; navigate, scroll, and zoom a document; enter, select, edit, and format text; and document, preview, and print a file. To do this, you will open a Word document file and make a few changes to it. Then you will save and print the revised document. Once you have gained an understanding of the basic concepts of the common features using Word, you will be able to easily apply them in the other Office applications.

Opening a File

In all Office 2010 applications, you either need to create a new file using the blank document file or open an existing file. Opening a file retrieves a file that is stored on your computer hard drive or an external storage device and places it in RAM (random access memory) of your computer so it can be read and modified. There are two main methods that can be used to open an existing file. One is to select the file to be opened from the list of recently opened documents. If you have not recently opened the file you want to use, then you use the Open command in Backstage view.

1

- **Click the File tab to open Backstage view.**

- **Click**

Your screen should be similar to Figure 19

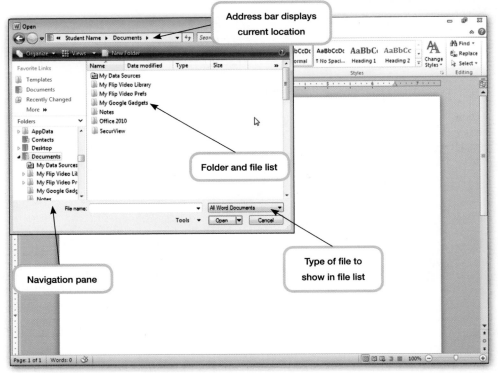

Figure 19

Additional Information

The Open dialog box is common to all programs using the Windows operating system. Your dialog box may look slightly different depending on the version of Windows on your computer.

The Open dialog box is displayed in which you specify the location where the file you want to open is stored and the file name. The location consists of identifying the hard drive of your computer or an external storage device or a remote computer followed by folders and subfolders within that location. The Address bar displays the default folder as the location to open the file. The file list displays folder names as well as the names of any Word documents in the current location. Only Word documents are listed because All Word Documents is the specified file type in the File Type list box. In Excel and Power-Point, only files of that application's file type would be displayed.

First you need to change the location to where your data files for completing these labs are stored. The file location may be on a different drive, in an external storage device, or in a folder or subfolder. There are several methods that can be used to locate files. One is to use the Address bar to specify another location by either typing the complete folder name or path or by opening the drop-down list of previously accessed locations and clicking a new location. Another is to use the Favorite Links list in the Navigation pane, which provides shortcut links to specific folders on your computer. A third is to use the Folders list in the navigation pane to navigate through the hierarchical structure of drives and folders on your computer. Clicking a link or folder from the list displays files at that location in the file list. Then, from the file list, you can continue to select subfolders until the file you want to open is located.

Change to the location where your student data files for this lab are located.

Your screen should be similar to **Figure 20**

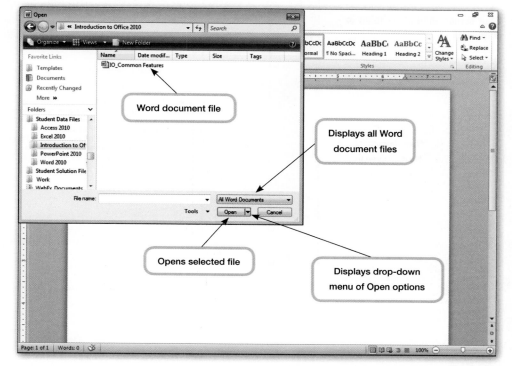

Figure 20

Now the file list displays the names of all Word files at that location. Next, you open the file by selecting it and clicking the [Open ▾] button. In addition, in the Office applications you can specify how you want to open a file by choosing from the [Open ▾] drop-down menu options described in the following table.

Open Options	Description
Open	Opens with all formatting and editing features enabled. This is the default setting.
Open Read-only	Opens file so it can be read or copied only, not modified in any way.
Open as Copy	Automatically creates a copy of the file and opens the copy with complete editing capabilities.
Open in Browser	Opens HTML type files in a Web browser.
Open with Transform	Opens certain types of documents and lets you change it into another type of document.
Open in Protected View	Opens files from potentially unsafe locations with editing functions disabled.
Open and Repair	Opens file and attempts to repair any damage.

Another Method

You could also press [Enter] to open a selected file or double-click on the file name.

You will open the file IO_Common Features. Clicking the [Open ▾] button opens the file using the default Open option so you can read and edit the file.

3

- **Select** IO_Common Features.

- **Click** [Open ▾].

Your screen should be similar to Figure 21

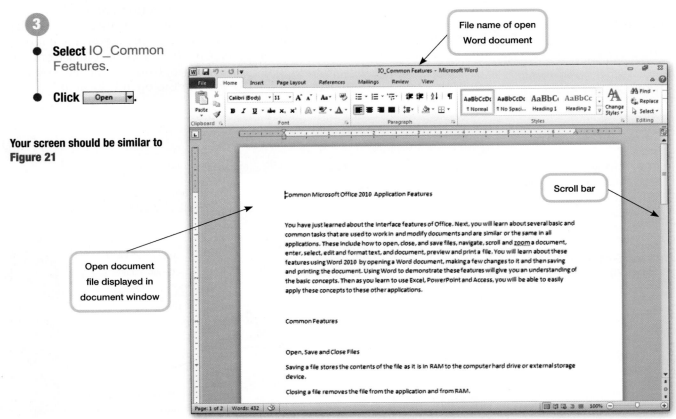

File name of open Word document

Scroll bar

Open document file displayed in document window

Figure 21

A Word document file describing the common Microsoft Office application features is displayed in the document window.

Scrolling the Document Window

As documents increase in size, they cannot be easily viewed in their entirety in the document window and much time can be spent moving to different locations in the document. All Office 2010 applications include features that make it easy to move around and view the information in a large document. The basic method is to scroll through a document using the scroll bar or keyboard. Both methods are useful, depending on what you are doing. For example, if you are entering text using the keyboard, using the keyboard method may be more efficient than using the mouse.

Additional Information

Scroll bars are also found in task panes and dialog boxes and operate similarly.

Additional Information

If you have a mouse with a scroll wheel, you can use it to scroll a document vertically.

The table below explains the basic mouse and keyboard techniques that can be used to vertically scroll a document in the Office 2010 applications. There are many other methods for navigating through documents that are unique to an application. They will be discussed in the specific application text.

Mouse or Key Action	Effect in:			
	Word	**Excel**	**PowerPoint**	**Access**
Click ▼ Or ↓	Moves down line by line.	Moves down row by row	Moves down slide by slide	Moves down record by record
Click ▲ Or ↑	Moves up line by line.	Moves up row by row	Moves up slide by slide	Moves up record by record
Click above/below scroll box Or Page Up / Page Down	Moves up/down window by window	Moves up/down window by window	Displays previous/next slide	Moves up/down window by window
Drag ▢ Scroll Box	Moves up/down line by line	Moves up/down row by row	Moves up/down slide by slide	Moves up/down record by record
Ctrl + Home	Moves to beginning of document	Moves to first cell in worksheet or beginning of cell entry	Moves to first slide in presentation or beginning of entry in placeholder	Moves to first record in table or beginning of field entry
Ctrl + End	Moves to end of document	Moves to last-used cell in worksheet or end of cell entry	Moves to last slide in presentation or to end of placeholder entry	Moves to last record in table or end of field entry

Additional Information

You also can scroll the document window horizontally using the horizontal scroll bar or the → and ← keys.

You will use the vertical scroll bar to view the text at the bottom of the Word document. When you use the scroll bar to scroll, the actual location in the document where you can work does not change, only the area you are viewing changes. For example, in Word, the cursor does not move and in Excel the cell you can work in does not change. To move the cursor or make another cell active, you must click in a location in the window. However, when you scroll using the keyboard, the actual location as identified by the position of the cursor in the document also changes. For example, in Word the cursor attempts to maintain its position in a line as you scroll up and down through the document. In Excel the cell you can work in changes as you move through a worksheet using the keyboard.

1

- Click ⊡ in the vertical scroll bar 10 times.

- Click at the beginning of the word Scroll in the Common Features section to move the cursor.

- Press ⬇ 10 times to scroll the window and move the cursor down 10 lines.

Your screen should be similar to Figure 22

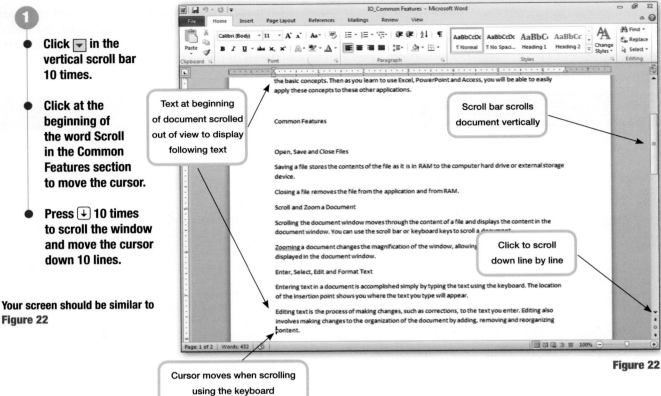

Text at beginning of document scrolled out of view to display following text

Scroll bar scrolls document vertically

Click to scroll down line by line

Cursor moves when scrolling using the keyboard

Figure 22

Having Trouble?

If your screen scrolls differently, this is a function of the type of monitor you are using.

The text at the beginning of the document has scrolled line by line off the top of the document window, and the following text is now displayed. In a large document, scrolling line by line can take a while. You will now try out several additional mouse and keyboard scrolling features that move by larger increments through the document.

2

- Click below the scroll box in the scroll bar.

- Press Ctrl + End to move to the end of the last line of the document.

- Drag the scroll box to the top of the scroll bar.

Your screen should be similar to Figure 23

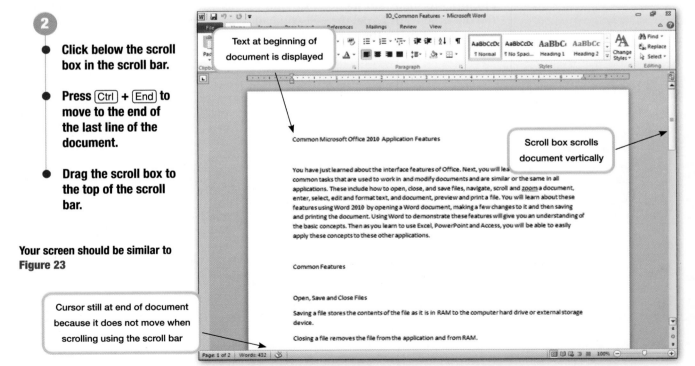

Text at beginning of document is displayed

Scroll box scrolls document vertically

Cursor still at end of document because it does not move when scrolling using the scroll bar

Figure 23

The document window displays the beginning of the document; however, the cursor is still at the end of the document. Using these features makes scrolling a large document much more efficient.

Using the Zoom Feature

Another way to see more or less of a document is to use the zoom feature. Although this feature is available in all Office 2010 applications, Excel and PowerPoint have fewer options than Word. In Access, the zoom feature is available only when specific features are used, such as viewing reports.

The Zoom Slider in the status bar is used to change the magnification. To use the Zoom Slider, click and drag the slider control. Dragging to the right zooms in on the document and increases the magnification whereas dragging to the left zooms out on the document and decreases the magnification. You also can change the zoom percentage by increments of 10 by clicking the ⊕ or ⊖ on each end of the slider control. In Word, the default display, 100 percent, shows the characters the same size they will be when printed. You can increase the onscreen character size up to five times the normal display (500 percent) or reduce the character size to 10 percent.

You will first "zoom out" on the document to get an overview of the file, and then you will "zoom in" to get a close-up look. When a document is zoomed, you can work in it as usual.

Additional Information

The degree of magnification varies with the different applications.

1

● **Click ⊖ in the Zoom Slider five times to decrease the zoom percentage to 50%.**

● **Press** Ctrl **+** Home **to move the cursor to the beginning of the document.**

● **Drag the Zoom Slider all the way to the right to increase the zoom to 500%.**

Your screen should be similar to Figure 24

Another Method

You can also hold down Ctrl while using the scroll wheel on your mouse to zoom a document.

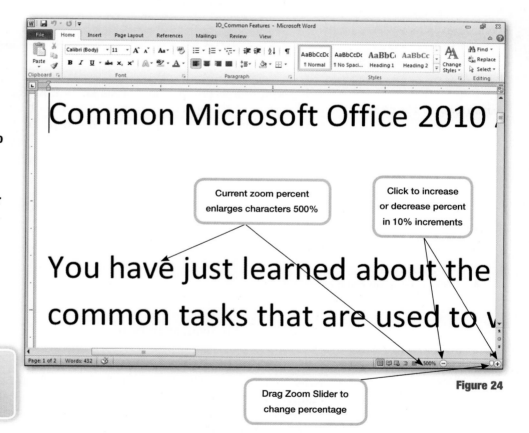

Figure 24

Another Method

You can also click on the zoom percentage in the status bar to open the Zoom dialog box.

Another way to change the magnification is to use the [Zoom] button in the View tab. This method opens the Zoom dialog box containing several preset zoom options, or an option that lets you set a precise percentage using the Percent scroll box. You will use this feature next to zoom the document. This method is available in Word only.

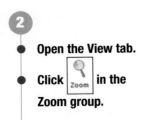

2

- Open the View tab.

- Click 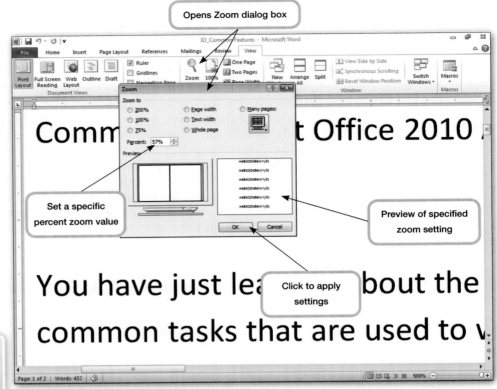 in the Zoom group.

- Click Whole Page and note that the percent value in the Percent text box and the preview area reflect the new percentage setting.

- Click the up scroll button in the Percent scroll box to increase the zoom percentage to 57.

Another Method

You could also type a value in the Percent text box to specify an exact percentage.

Your screen should be similar to Figure 25

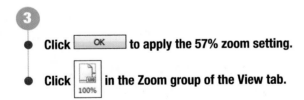

Figure 25

The Zoom dialog box preview areas show how the document will appear on your screen at the specified zoom percent. Not until you complete the command by clicking [OK] will the zoom percent in the document actually change. You will complete the command to apply the 57% zoom setting. Then, you will use the button in the Zoom group to quickly return to the default zoom setting.

3

- Click [OK] to apply the 57% zoom setting.

- Click in the Zoom group of the View tab.

The document is again at 100% magnification.

Entering and Editing Text

Now that you are familiar with the entire document, you will make a few changes to it. The keyboard is used to enter information into a document. In all applications, the location of the cursor shows you where the text will appear as you type. After text is entered into a document, you need to know how to move around within the text to edit or make changes to the text. Again, the process is similar for all Office applications.

Currently, in this Word document, the cursor is positioned at the top of the document. You will type your name at this location. As you type, the cursor moves to the right and the characters will appear to the left of the cursor. Then you will press [Enter] to end the line following your name and press [Enter] again at the beginning of a line to insert a blank line.

Additional Information

The effect of pressing [Enter] varies in the different Office applications. For example, in Excel, it completes the entry and moves to another cell. You will learn about these differences in the individual application labs.

Type your first and last name.

Press Enter **two times.**

Your screen should be similar to Figure 26

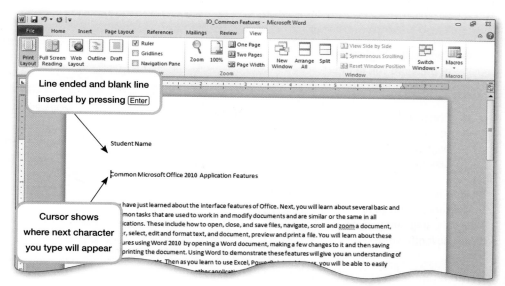

Line ended and blank line inserted by pressing Enter

Student Name

Common Microsoft Office 2010 Application Features

...have just learned about the interface features of Office. Next, you will learn about several basic and ...mon tasks that are used to work in and modify documents and are similar or the same in all ...ications. These include how to open, close, and save files, navigate, scroll and zoom a document, ...r, select, edit and format text, and document, preview and print a file. You will learn about these ...ures using Word 2010 by opening a Word document, making a few changes to it and then saving ...printing the document. Using Word to demonstrate these features will give you an understanding of ...ts. Then as you learn to use Excel, PowerPoint... ...you will be able to easily ...ther applicati...

Cursor shows where next character you type will appear

Figure 26

Additional Information

You can use the directional keys on the numeric keypad or the dedicated directional keypad area. If using the numeric keypad, make sure the Num Lock feature is off; otherwise, numbers will be entered in the document. The Num Lock indicator light above the keypad is lit when on. Press Num Lock to turn it off.

Additional Information

The mouse pointer also has other shapes whose meaning varies with the different applications. These specific features will be described in the individual application labs.

As you typed your name, to make space for the text on the line, the existing text moved to the right. Then, when you pressed Enter the first time, all the text following your name moved down one line. A blank line was inserted after pressing Enter the second time.

Next, you want to add a word to the first line of the first paragraph. To do this, you first need to move the cursor to the location where you want to make the change. The keyboard or mouse can be used to move through the text in the document window. Depending on what you are doing, one method may be more efficient than another. For example, if your hands are already on the keyboard as you are entering text, it may be quicker to use the keyboard rather than take your hands off to use the mouse.

You use the mouse to move the cursor to a specific location in a document simply by clicking on the location. When you can use the mouse to move the cursor, the mouse pointer is shaped as an ⌶ I-beam. You use the arrow keys located on the numeric keypad or the directional keypad to move the cursor in a document. The keyboard directional keys are described in the following table.

Key	Word/PowerPoint	Excel	Access
→	Right one character	Right one cell	Right one field
←	Left one character	Left one cell	Left one field
↑	Up one line	Up one cell	Up one record
↓	Down one line	Down one cell	Down one record
Ctrl + →	Right one word	Last cell in row	One word to right in a field entry
Ctrl + ←	Left one word	First cell in row	One word to left in a field entry
Home	Beginning of line	First cell in row	First field of record
End	End of line		Last field of record

Additional Information

Many of the keyboard keys and key combinations have other effects depending on the mode of operation at the time they are used. You will learn about these differences in the specific application labs as they are used.

In the first line of the first paragraph, you want to add the word "common" before the word "interface" and the year "2010" after the word "Office." You will move to the correct locations using both the keyboard and the mouse and then enter the new text.

Click at the beginning of the word You in the first paragraph.

Press [→] four times to move to the beginning of the second word.

Press [Ctrl] + [→] five times to move to the beginning of the seventh word.

Additional Information

Holding down a directional key or key combination moves quickly in the direction indicated, saving multiple presses of the key.

Type basic and press [Spacebar].

Having Trouble?

Do not be concerned if you make a typing error; you will learn how to correct them next.

Position the I-beam between the e in Office and the period at the end of the first sentence and click.

Press [Spacebar] and type 2010

Your screen should be similar to Figure 27

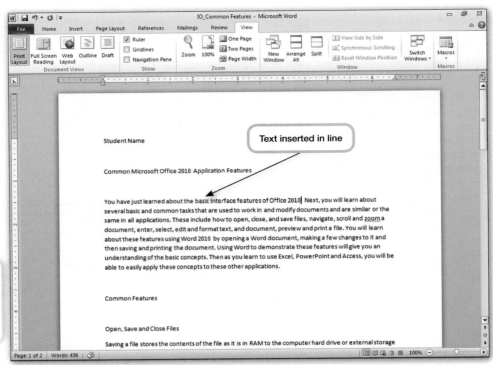

Figure 27

Next, you want to edit the text you just entered by changing the word "basic" to "common." Removing typing entries to change or correct them is one of the basic editing tasks. Corrections may be made in many ways. Two of the most basic editing keys that are common to the Office applications are the [Backspace] and [Delete] keys. The [Backspace] key removes a character or space to the left of the cursor. It is particularly useful when you are moving from right to left (backward) along a line of text. The [Delete] key removes the character or space to the right of the cursor and is most useful when moving from left to right along a line.

You will use these features as you make the correction.

3

- Move the cursor between the s and i in "basic" (in the first sentence).

- Press ⌜Del⌝ to remove the two characters to the right of the insertion point.

- Press ⌜Backspace⌝ three times to remove the three characters to the left of the cursor.

- Type **common**

- Correct any other typing errors you may have made using ⌜Backspace⌝ or ⌜Delete⌝.

Your screen should be similar to Figure 28

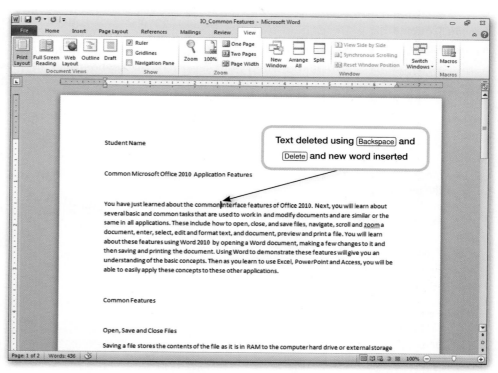

Figure 28

The word "basic" was deleted from the sentence and the word "common" was entered in its place.

Selecting Text

Additional Information

The capability to select text is common to all Office 2010 applications. However, many of the features that are designed for use in Word are not available in the other applications. Some are available only when certain modes of operation are in effect or when certain features are being used.

While editing and formatting a document, you will need to select text. Selecting highlights text and identifies the text that will be affected by your next action. To select text using the mouse, first move the cursor to the beginning or end of the text to be selected, and then drag to highlight the text you want selected. You can select as little as a single letter or as much as the entire document. You also can select text using keyboard features. The following table summarizes common mouse and keyboard techniques used to select text in Word.

To Select	Mouse	Keyboard
Next/previous space or character	Drag across space or character.	⌜Shift⌝ + ⌜→⌝/⌜Shift⌝ + ⌜←⌝
Next/previous word	Double-click in the word.	⌜Ctrl⌝ + ⌜Shift⌝ + ⌜→⌝/⌜Ctrl⌝ + ⌜Shift⌝ + ⌜←⌝
Sentence	Press ⌜Ctrl⌝ and click within the sentence.	
Line	Click to the left of a line when the mouse pointer is ⟋.	
Multiple lines	Drag up or down to the left of a line when the mouse pointer is ⟋.	
Text going backward to beginning of paragraph	Drag left and up to the beginning of the paragraph when the mouse pointer is ⟋.	⌜Ctrl⌝ + ⌜Shift⌝ + ⌜↑⌝
Text going forward to end of paragraph	Drag right and down to the end of the paragraph when the mouse pointer is ⟋.	⌜Ctrl⌝ + ⌜Shift⌝ + ⌜↓⌝
Paragraph	Triple-click on the paragraph or double-click to the left of the paragraph when the mouse pointer is ⟋.	
Multiple paragraphs	Drag to the left of the paragraphs when the mouse pointer is ⟋.	
Document	Triple-click or press ⌜Ctrl⌝ and click to the left of the text when the mouse pointer is ⟋.	⌜Ctrl⌝ + A

Having Trouble?

If you accidentally select the incorrect text, simply click anywhere in the document or press any directional key to clear the selection and try again.

You want to change the word "tasks" in the next sentence to "application features". Although you could use Delete and Backspace to remove the unneeded text character by character, it will be faster to select and delete the word. First you will try out several of the keyboard techniques to select text. Then you will use several mouse features to select text and finally you will edit the sentence.

1

- **Move the cursor to the beginning of the word "basic" in the second sentence.**

- **Press** Shift + → **five times to select the word basic.**

- **Press** Shift + Ctrl + → **to extend the selection word by word until the entire line is selected.**

- **Press** Shift + Ctrl + ↓ **to extend the selection to the end of the paragraph.**

Your screen should be similar to Figure 29

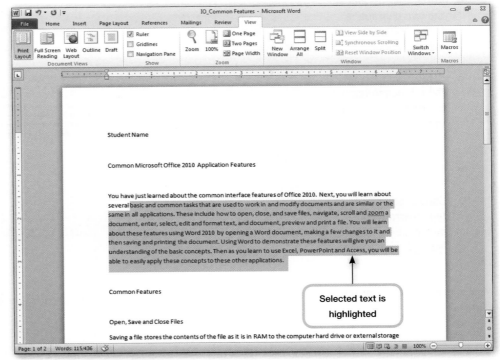

Selected text is highlighted

Figure 29

The text from the cursor to the end of the paragraph is selected. Next, you will clear this selection and then use the mouse to select text.

ce 2010

2

- Click anywhere in the paragraph to clear the selection.

- Click at the beginning of the word "basic" and drag to the right to select the text to the end of the line.

- Click in the left margin to the left of the fourth line of the paragraph when the mouse pointer is to select the entire line.

- Double-click in the margin to the left of the paragraph when the mouse pointer is to select the paragraph.

Your screen should be similar to Figure 30

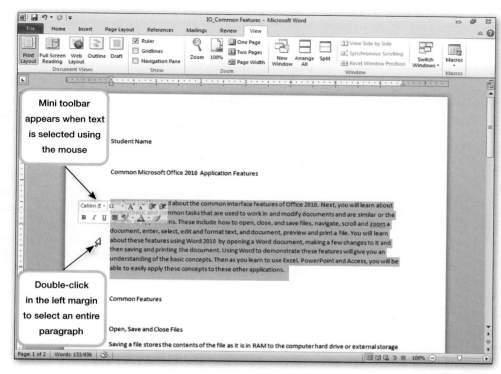

Figure 30

When you select text using the mouse, the **Mini toolbar** appears automatically in Word, Excel, and PowerPoint. You will learn about using this feature in the next section.

Text that is selected can be modified using many different features. In this case, you want to replace the word "tasks" in the second sentence with "application features".

Additional Information

When positioned in the left margin, the mouse pointer shape changes to ↗, indicating it is ready to select text.

3

- Double-click on the word "tasks" in the second sentence.

- Type **application features**

Your screen should be similar to Figure 31

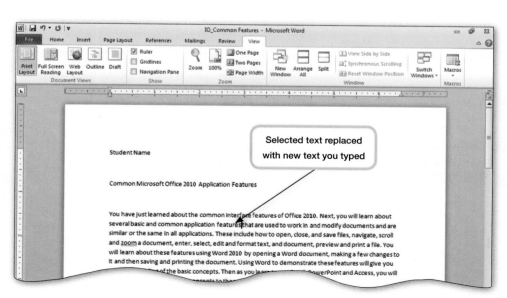

Figure 31

As soon as you began typing, the selected text was automatically deleted. The new text was inserted in the line just like any other text.

Formatting Text

An important aspect of all documents you create using Office 2010 is the appearance of the document. To improve the appearance you can apply many different formatting effects. The most common formatting features are font and character effects. A **font**, also commonly referred to as a **typeface**, is a set of characters with a specific design. The designs have names such as Times New Roman and Courier. Each font has one or more sizes. **Font size** is the height and width of the character and is commonly measured in points, abbreviated "pt." One point equals about 1/72 inch. **Character effects** are enhancements such as bold, italic, and color that are applied to selected text. Using font and character effects as design elements can add interest to your document and give readers visual cues to help them find information quickly.

First you want to change the font and increase the font size of the title of this document.

Additional Information

Font and text effects will be explained in more detail in each application lab.

1

● Click in the left margin next to the title line when the mouse pointer is ⬚ to select it.

● Open the Home tab.

● Open the
 Calibri (Body) ▾ Font
 drop-down menu in the Font group.

● Point to the Arial Black font option in the menu.

Your screen should be similar to Figure 32

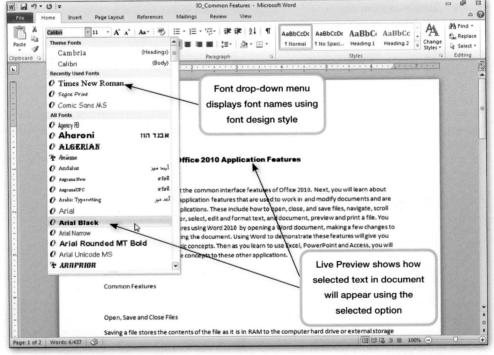

Font drop-down menu displays font names using font design style

Live Preview shows how selected text in document will appear using the selected option

Figure 32

Additional Information

Live Preview is also available in Excel, Access, and PowerPoint.

As you point to the font options, the **Live Preview** feature shows you how the selected text in the document will appear if this option is chosen.

2

● Point to several different fonts in the menu to see the Live Preview.

● Scroll the menu and click Segoe Print to choose it.

Your screen should be similar to Figure 33

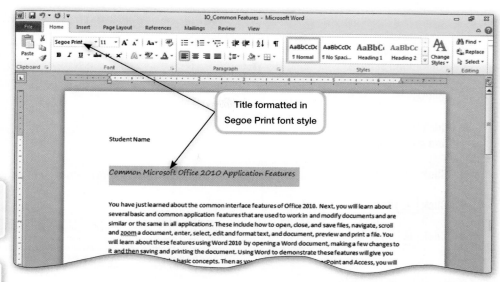

Figure 33

The title appears in the selected font and the name of the font used in the selection is displayed in the Segoe Print ▾ Font button. Next you want to increase the font size. The current (default) font size of 11 is displayed in the 11 ▾ Font Size button. You will increase the font size to 16 points.

3

● Open the 11 ▾ Font Size drop-down menu in the Font group of the Home tab.

● Point to several different font sizes to see the Live Preview.

● Click 16 to choose it.

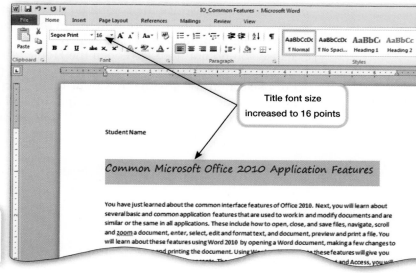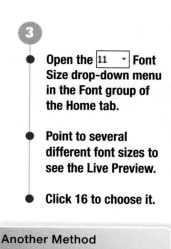

Figure 34

Your screen should be similar to Figure 34

Now the title stands out much more from the other text in the document. Next you will use the Mini toolbar to add formatting to other areas of the document. As you saw earlier, the Mini toolbar appears automatically when you select text. Initially the Mini toolbar appears dimmed (semi-transparent) so that it does not interfere with what you are doing, but it changes to solid when you point at it. It displays command buttons for often-used commands from the Font and Paragraph groups that are used to format a document.

4

- Select the line "Common Features" and point to the Mini toolbar.

- Click 11 ▾ Font Size and choose 14.

- Click **B** Bold.

- Click *I* Italic.

- Click <u>U</u> Underline.

Your screen should be similar to Figure 35

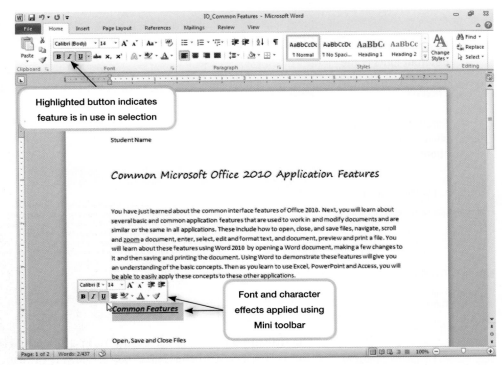

Figure 35

The increase in font size as well as the text effects makes this topic head much more prominent. Notice the command button for each selected effect is highlighted, indicating the feature is in use in the selection.

Using the Mini toolbar is particularly useful when the Home tab is closed because you do not need to reopen the Home tab to access the commands. It remains available until you clear the selection or press Esc. If you do nothing with a selection for a while, the Mini toolbar will disappear. To redisplay it simply right-click on the selection again. This will also open the context menu.

You will remove the underline effect from the selection next.

5

- Right-click on the selection to redisplay the Mini toolbar.

- Click **U** Underline on the Mini toolbar.

Your screen should be similar to Figure 36

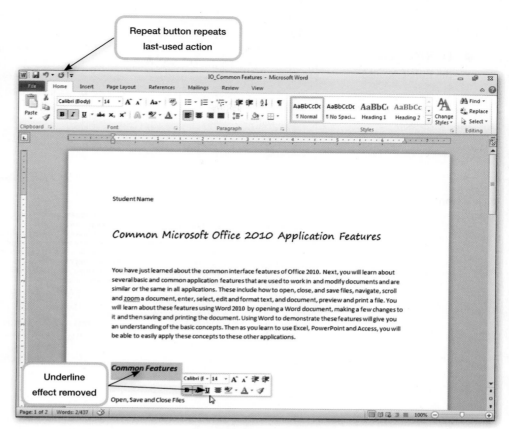

Repeat button repeats last-used action

Underline effect removed

Figure 36

The context menu and Mini toolbar appeared when you right-clicked the selection. The context menu displayed a variety of commands that are quicker to access than locating the command on the Ribbon. The commands that appear on this menu change depending on what you are doing at the time. The context menu disappeared after you made a selection from the Mini toolbar. Both the Mini toolbar and context menus are designed to make it more efficient to execute commands.

Also notice that the ⟳ Redo button in the Quick Access Toolbar has changed to a ⟳ Repeat button. This feature allows you to quickly repeat the last-used command at another location in the document.

Undoing and Redoing Editing Changes

Instead of reselecting the **U** Underline command to remove the underline effect, you could have used ↺ ▾ Undo to reverse your last action or command. You will use this feature to restore the underline (your last action).

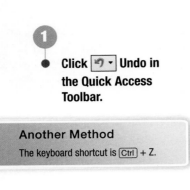

1

● Click Undo in the Quick Access Toolbar.

Another Method

The keyboard shortcut is Ctrl + Z.

Your screen should be similar to **Figure 37**

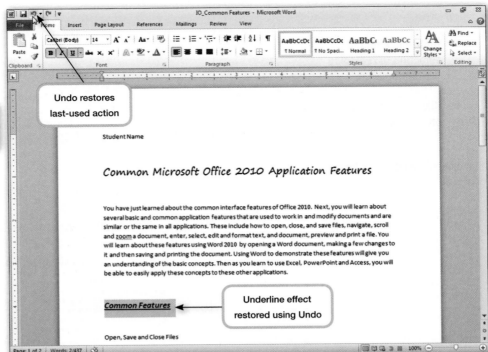

Undo restores last-used action

Student Name

Common Microsoft Office 2010 Application Features

You have just learned about the common interface features of Office 2010. Next, you will learn about several basic and common application features that are used to work in and modify documents and are similar or the same in all applications. These include how to open, close, and save files, navigate, scroll and <u>zoom</u> a document, enter, select, edit and format text, and document, preview and print a file. You will learn about these features using Word 2010 by opening a Word document, making a few changes to it and then saving and printing the document. Using Word to demonstrate these features will give you an understanding of the basic concepts. Then as you learn to use Excel, PowerPoint and Access, you will be able to easily apply these concepts to these other applications.

Common Features ← Underline effect restored using Undo

Open, Save and Close Files

Figure 37

Undo reversed the last action and the underline formatting effect was restored. Notice that the Undo button includes a drop-down menu button. Clicking this button displays a menu of the most recent actions that can be reversed, with the most-recent action at the top of the menu. When you select an action from the drop-down menu, you also undo all actions above it in the menu.

2

● Open the Undo drop-down menu.

● Choose Bold.

Your screen should be similar to **Figure 38**

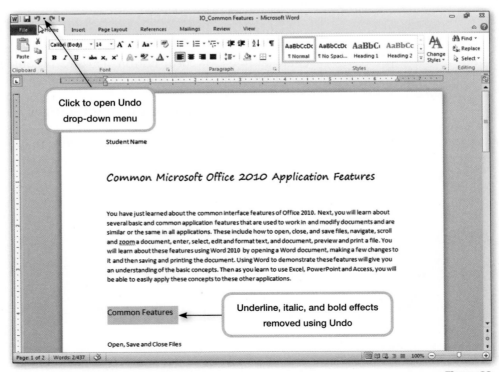

Click to open Undo drop-down menu

Student Name

Common Microsoft Office 2010 Application Features

You have just learned about the common interface features of Office 2010. Next, you will learn about several basic and common application features that are used to work in and modify documents and are similar or the same in all applications. These include how to open, close, and save files, navigate, scroll and <u>zoom</u> a document, enter, select, edit and format text, and document, preview and print a file. You will learn about these features using Word 2010 by opening a Word document, making a few changes to it and then saving and printing the document. Using Word to demonstrate these features will give you an understanding of the basic concepts. Then as you learn to use Excel, PowerPoint and Access, you will be able to easily apply these concepts to these other applications.

Common Features ← Underline, italic, and bold effects removed using Undo

Open, Save and Close Files

Figure 38

The underline, italic, and bold effects were all removed. Immediately after you undo an action, the Repeat button changes to the ⟳ Redo button and is available so you can restore the action you just undid. You will restore the last-removed format, bold.

Click ⟳ Redo.

Copying and Moving Selections

Common to all Office applications is the capability to copy and move selections to new locations in a document or between documents, saving you time by not having to recreate the same information. A selection that is moved is cut from its original location, called the **source**, and inserted at a new location, called the **destination**. A selection that is copied leaves the original in the source and inserts a duplicate at the destination.

When a selection is cut or copied, the selection is stored in the system **Clipboard**, a temporary Windows storage area in memory. It is also stored in the **Office Clipboard**. The system Clipboard holds only the last cut or copied item, whereas the Office Clipboard can store up to 24 items that have been cut or copied. This feature allows you to insert multiple items from various Office documents and paste all or part of the collection of items into another document.

First, you will copy the text "Office 2010" to two other locations in the first paragraph.

Select the text "Office 2010" in the title line.

Click 🗐 Copy in the Clipboard group of the Home tab.

Move to the beginning of the word "applications" (third line of first paragraph).

Click 📋 Paste in the Clipboard group.

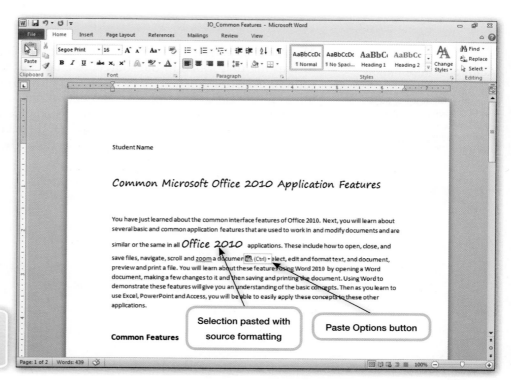

Figure 39

Your screen should be similar to Figure 39

The copied selection is inserted at the location you specified with the same formatting as it has in the title. The  Paste Options button appears automatically whenever a selection is pasted. It is used to control the format of the pasted item.

2

● **Click the**  **Paste Options button.**

Your screen should be similar to Figure 40

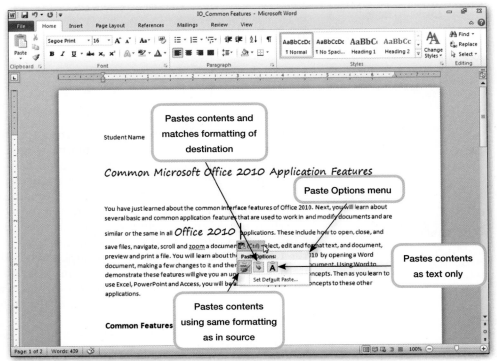

Figure 40

Additional Information

The Paste Options vary with the different applications. For example, Excel has 14 different Paste Options. The Paste Options feature is not available in Access and Paste Preview is not available in Excel.

The Paste Options are used to specify whether to insert the item with the same formatting that it had in the source, to change it to the formatting of the surrounding destination text, or to insert text only (from a selection that is a combination of text and graphics). The default as you have seen is to keep the formatting from the source. You want to change it to the formatting of the surrounding text. As you point to a Paste Options button, a **Paste Preview** will show how that option will affect the selection. Then you will copy it again to a second location.

3

● Click 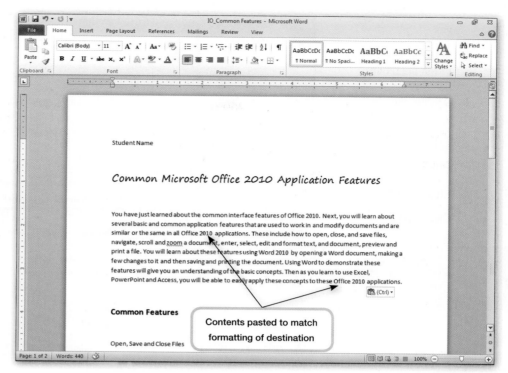 Merge Formatting.

● Select "other" in the last line of the first paragraph.

● Right-click on the selection and point to each of the Paste Options in the context menu to see the Paste Preview.

● Click Merge Formatting.

Your screen should be similar to Figure 41

Figure 41

The selected text was deleted and replaced with the contents of the system Clipboard. The system Clipboard contents remain in the Clipboard until another item is copied or cut, allowing you to paste the same item multiple times.

Now you will learn how to move a selection by rearranging several lines of text in the description of common features. You want to move the last sentence in the document, beginning with "Opening a file", to the top of the list. The Cut and Paste commands in the Clipboard group of the Home tab are used to move selections.

4

- Scroll to see the end of the document.

- Double-click in the left margin next to the last sentence in the document to select it.

- Click Cut in the Clipboard group.

Your screen should be similar to Figure 42

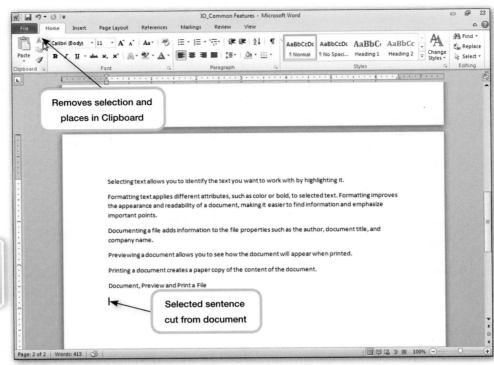

Figure 42

The selected paragraph is removed from the source and copied to the Clipboard. Next, you need to move the cursor to the location where the text will be inserted and paste the text into the document from the Clipboard.

5

- Move to the beginning of the word "Saving" at the top of the Common Features list.

- Press Ctrl + V.

Your screen should be similar to Figure 43

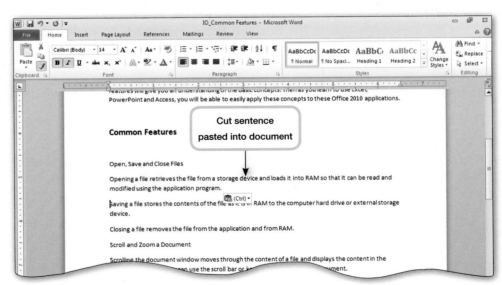

Figure 43

The cut sentence is reentered into the document at the cursor location. That was much quicker than retyping the whole sentence! Because the source has the same formatting as the text at the destination, the default setting to keep the source formatting is appropriate.

Using Drag and Drop

Another way to move or copy selections is to use the drag-and-drop editing feature. This feature is most useful for copying or moving short distances in a document. To use drag and drop to move a selection, point to the selection and drag it to the location where you want the selection inserted. The mouse pointer appears as as you drag, and a temporary insertion point shows you where the text will be placed when you release the mouse button.

Additional Information

You also can use drag and drop to copy a selection by holding down Ctrl while dragging. The mouse pointer shape is .

1

- **Select the last line of text in the document.**

- **Drag the selection to the beginning of the word "Documenting" (four lines up).**

Additional Information

You also can move or copy a selection by holding down the right mouse button while dragging. When you release the mouse button, a context menu appears with the available move and copy options.

Your screen should be similar to Figure 44

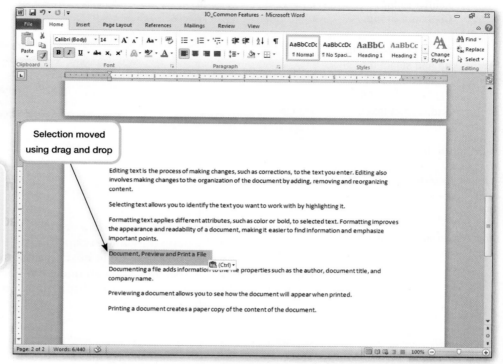

Figure 44

The selection moved to the new location. However, the selection is not copied and stored in the Clipboard and cannot be pasted to multiple locations in the document.

Copying Formats

Many times, you will find you want to copy the formats associated with a selection, but not the text. It is easy to do this using the Format Painter tool.

1

● Apply bold and italic effects and increase the font size to 14 of the currently selected text.

● Click Format Painter in the Clipboard group.

● Scroll the document up and select the topic line of text "Enter, Select, Edit and Format text".

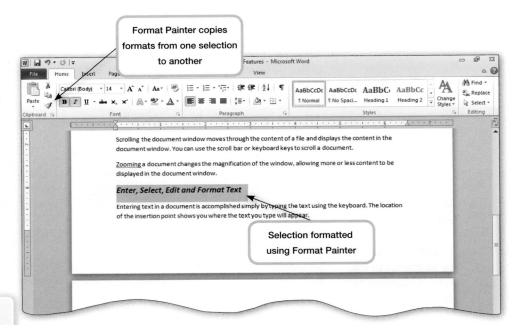

Format Painter copies formats from one selection to another

Selection formatted using Format Painter

Figure 45

Your screen should be similar to Figure 45

The text you selected is formatted using the same formats. This feature is especially helpful when you want to copy multiple formats at one time. Next, you want to format the other topic heads in the Common Features list using the same formats. To do this, you can make the Format Painter "sticky" so that it can be used to copy the format multiple times in succession.

2

● Double-click Format Painter in the Clipboard group.

● Select the remaining two topic heads in the Common Features list:

   Scroll and Zoom a Document

   Open, Save and Close Files

● Click Format Painter to turn off this feature.

● Clear the selection.

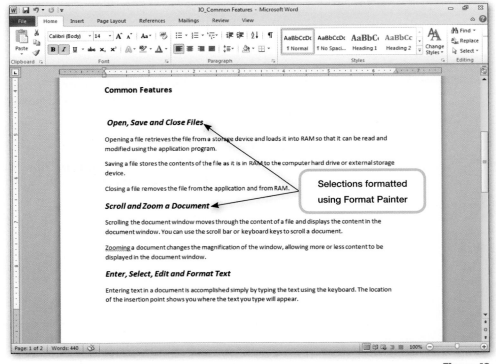

Selections formatted using Format Painter

Figure 46

Your screen should be similar to Figure 46

ce 2010

Specifying Document Properties

In addition to the content of the document that you create, all Office 2010 applications automatically include details about the document that describe or identify it called **metadata** or document **properties**. Document properties include details such as title, author name, subject, and keywords that identify the document's topic or contents (described below). Some of these properties are automatically generated. These include statistics such as the number of words in the file and general information such as the date the document was created and last modified. Others such as author name and tags or keywords are properties that you can specify. A **tag** or **keyword** is a descriptive word that is associated with the file and can be used to locate a file using a search.

By specifying relevant information as document properties, you can easily organize, identify, and search for your documents later.

Property	Action
Title	Enter the document title. This title can be longer and more descriptive than the file name.
Tags	Enter words that you associate with the presentation to make it easier to find using search tools.
Comments	Enter comments that you want others to see about the content of the document.
Categories	Enter the name of a higher-level category under which you can group similar types of presentations.
Author	Enter the name of the presentation's author. By default this is the name entered when the application was installed.

You will look at the document properties that are automatically included and add documentation to identify you as the author, and specify a document title and keywords to describe the document.

Open the File tab.

Click the "Show all properties" link at the bottom of the Properties panel in the Info window to display all properties.

Your screen should be similar to Figure 47

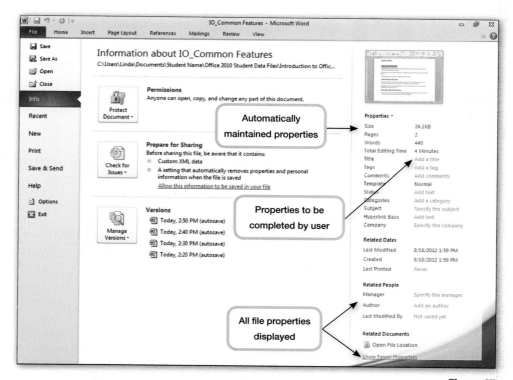

Figure 47

The Properties panel in the right section of the Info tab is divided into four groups and displays the properties associated with the document. Properties such as the document size, number of words, and number of pages are automatically maintained. Others such as the title and tag properties are blank waiting for you to specify your own information.

You will add a title, a tag, and your name as the author name.

2

● **Click in the Title text box and type Common Office Features**

● **In the same manner, enter common, features, interface as the tags.**

● **Click in the Add an Author text box and enter your name.**

Your screen should be similar to Figure 48

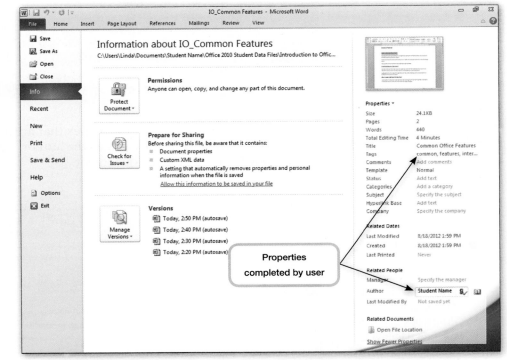

Figure 48

Once the document properties are specified, you can use them to identify and locate documents. You also can use the automatically updated properties for the same purpose. For example, you can search for all files created by a specified user or on a certain date.

Saving a File

As you enter and edit text to create a document in Word, Excel, and PowerPoint, the changes you make are immediately displayed onscreen and are stored in your computer's memory. However, they are not permanently stored until you save your work to a file on a disk. After a document has been saved as a file, it can be closed and opened again at a later time to be edited further. Unlike Word, Excel, and PowerPoint, where you start work on a new document and then save your changes, Access requires that you name the new database file first and create a table for your data. Then, it saves your changes to the data automatically as you work. This allows multiple users to have access to the most up-to-date data at all times.

As a backup against the accidental loss of work from power failure or other mishap, Word, Excel, and PowerPoint include an AutoRecover feature. When this feature is on, as you work you may see a pulsing disk icon briefly appear in the status bar. This icon indicates that the program is saving your work to a temporary recovery file. The time interval between automatic saving can be set to any period you specify; the default is every 10 minutes. After a problem has occurred, when you restart the program, the recovery file is automatically opened containing all changes you made up to the last time it was saved by AutoRecover. You then need to save the recovery file. If you do not save it, it is deleted when closed. AutoRecover is a great feature for recovering lost work but should not be used in place of regularly saving your work.

You will save the work you have done so far on the document. You use the Save or Save As commands to save files. The [💾 Save] command on the File tab or the 💾 Save button on the Quick Access Toolbar will save the active file using the same file name by replacing the contents of the existing disk file with the document as it appears on your screen. The [💾 Save As] command on the File tab is used to save a file using a new file name, to a new location, or as a different file type. This leaves the original file unchanged. When you create a new document, you can use either of the Save commands to save your work to a file on the disk. It is especially important to save a new document very soon after you create it because the AutoRecover feature does not work until a file name has been specified.

You will save this file using a new file name to your solution file location.

Additional Information

You can specify different AutoRecover settings by choosing Options/Save in Backstage view and specifying the AutoRecover settings of your choice.

Another Method

The keyboard shortcut for the Save command is [Ctrl] + S.

Additional Information

Saving a file is the same in all Office 2010 applications, except Access.

1

Click  in the left section of Backstage view.

Your screen should be similar to Figure 49

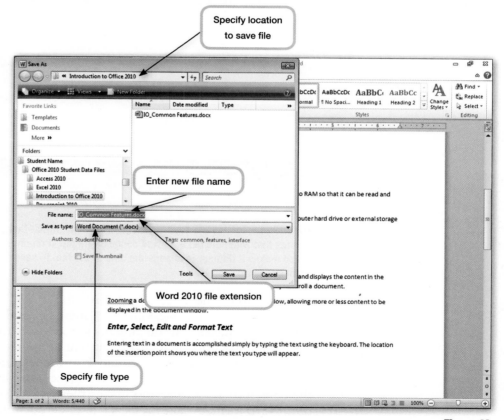

Figure 49

The Save As dialog box is used to specify the location where you will save the file and the file name. The Address bar displays the folder location from which the file was opened and the File name text box displays the name of the open file. The file name is highlighted, ready for you to enter a new file name. The Save as type box displays "Word Document.docx" as the default format in which the file will be saved. Word 2010 documents are identified by the file extension .docx. The file type you select determines the file extension that will be automatically added to the file name when the file is saved. The file types and extensions for the four Office 2010 applications are described in the following table.

Extensions	File Type
Word 2010	
.docx	Word 2007-2010 document without macros or code
.dotx	Word 2007-2010 template without macros or code
.docm	Word 2007-2010 document that could contain macros or code
.xps	Word 2007-2010 shared document (see Note)
.doc	Word 95–2003 document
Excel 2010	
.xlsx	Excel 2007-2010 default workbook without macros or code
.xlsm	Excel 2007-2010 default workbook that could contain macros
.xltx	Excel 2007-2010 template without macros
.xltm	Excel 2007-2010 template that could contain macros
.xps	Excel 2007-2010 shared workbook (see Note)
.xls	Excel 97–2003 workbook
PowerPoint	
.pptx	PowerPoint 2007-2010 default presentation format
.pptm	PowerPoint 2007-2010 presentation with macros
.potx	PowerPoint 2007-2010 template without macros
.potm	PowerPoint 2007-2010 template that may contain macros
.ppam	PowerPoint 2007-2010 add-in that contains macros
.ppsx	PowerPoint 2007-2010 slide show without macros
.ppsm	PowerPoint 2007-2010 slide show that may contain macros
.thmx	PowerPoint 2007-2010 theme
.ppt	PowerPoint 2003 or earlier presentation
Access	
.accdb	Access 2007-2010 database
.mdb	Access 2003 or earlier database

NOTE XPS file format is a fixed-layout electronic file format that preserves document formatting and ensures that when the file is viewed online or printed, it retains exactly the format that you intended. It also makes it difficult to change the data in the file. To save as an XPS file format, you must have installed the free add-in.

Office 2007 and 2010 save Word, Excel, and PowerPoint files using the XML format (Extensible Markup Language) and a four-letter file extension. This format makes your documents safer by separating files that contain macros (small programs in a document that automate tasks) to make it easier for a virus checker to identify and block unwanted code or macros that could be dangerous to your computer. It also makes file sizes smaller by compressing the content upon saving and makes files less susceptible to damage. In addition, XML format makes it easier to open documents created with an Office application using another application.

Previous versions of Word, Excel, and PowerPoint did not use XML and had a three-letter file extension. If you plan to share a file with someone using an Office 2003 or earlier version, you can save the document using the three-letter file type; however, some features may be lost. Otherwise, if you save it as a four-letter file type, the recipient may not be able to view all features. There also may be loss of features for users of Office 2007 (even though it has an XML file type) because the older version does not support several of the new features in Office 2010. Office 2010 includes a feature that checks for compatibility with previous versions and advises you what features in the document may be lost if opened by an Office 2007 user or if the document is saved in the 2003 format.

If you have an Office Access 2007 (.accdb) database that you want to save in an earlier Access file format (.mdb), you can do so as long as your .accdb database does not contain any multivalued lookup fields, offline data, or attachments. This is because older versions of Access do not support these new features. If you try to convert an .accdb database containing any of these elements to an .mdb file format, Access displays an error message.

First you may need to change the location to the location where the file will be saved. The same procedures you used to specify a location to open a file are used to specify the location to save a file. Then, you will change the file name to Common Features using the default Word document type (.docx).

2

- If necessary, select the location where you save your solution files.

- If necessary, triple-click or drag in the File Name text box to highlight the existing file name.

- Type **Common Features**

- Click   Save   .

Your screen should be similar to Figure 50

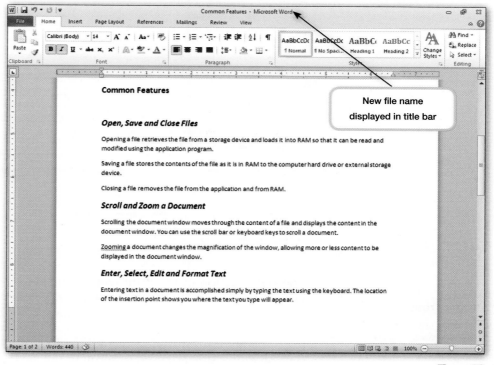

New file name displayed in title bar

Figure 50

The document is saved as Common Features.docx at the location you selected, and the new file name is displayed in the Word application window title bar.

Printing a Document

Once a document appears how you want, you may want to print a hard copy for your own reference or to give to others. All Office 2010 applications include the capability to print and have similar options. You will print this document next.

1 • **Open the File tab and choose Print.**

Another Method

The keyboard shortcut for the Print command is Ctrl + P.

Your screen should be similar to Figure 51

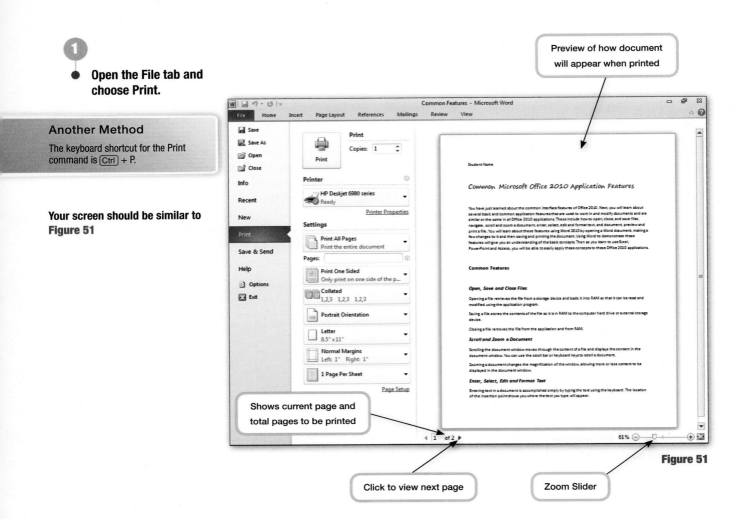

Preview of how document will appear when printed

Shows current page and total pages to be printed

Click to view next page

Zoom Slider

Figure 51

Having Trouble?

If necessary, use the Zoom Slider to change the preview zoom to 60%.

The right section of the Print window displays a preview of the current page of your document. To save time and unnecessary printing and paper waste, it is always a good idea to preview each page of your document before printing. Notice below the preview, the page scroll box shows the page number of the page you are currently viewing and the total number of pages. The scroll buttons on either side are used to scroll to the next and previous pages. Additionally, a Zoom Slider is available to adjust the size of the preview.

2

● Click ▶ to view the second page of the document.

● Increase the zoom to 70%.

Your screen should be similar to Figure 52

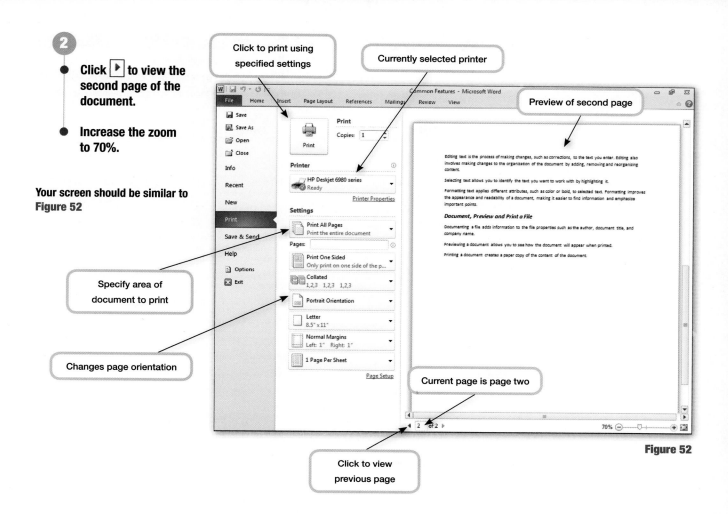

Figure 52

If you see any changes you want to make to the document, you would need to close the File tab and make the changes. If the document looks good, you are ready to print.

The second section of the Print window is divided into three areas: Print, Printer, and Settings. In the Print section you specify the number of copies you want printed. The default is to print one copy. The Printer section is used to specify the printer you will use and the printer properties such as paper size and print quality. The name of the default printer on your computer appears in the list box. The Settings area is used to specify what part of the document you want to print, whether to print on one or both sides of the paper or to collate (sort) the printed output, the page orientation, paper size, margins, and sheet settings. The Word print setting options are explained in the following table. The Print settings will vary slightly with the different Office applications. For example, in Excel, the options to specify what to print are to print the entire worksheet, entire workbook, or a selection. The differences will be demonstrated in the individual labs.

Option	Setting	Action
Print what	All	Prints entire document (default)
	Current page	Prints selected page or page where the cursor is located.
	Pages	Prints pages you specify by typing page numbers in Pages text box
	Selection	Prints selected text only (default)
Sides	One	Prints on one side of the paper.
	Both (short)	Prints on both sides by flipping the page vertically using a duplex printer
	Both (long)	Prints on both sides by flipping the page horizontally using a duplex printer
	Manually both	Reload the paper when prompted to print on the other side
Collate	Collated	Prints all of specified document before printing second or multiple copies; for example, pages 1,2 then 1,2 again (default)
	Uncollated	Prints multiple copies of each specified page sequentially (for example, pages 1,1 then 2,2)
Orientation	Portrait	Prints across the width of the paper (default)
	Landscape	Prints across the length of the paper
Paper	Size	Select the paper size (8.5 × 11 is default)
	Envelope	Select an envelope size
Margins	Normal	One-inch margins all around (default)
	Narrow, Wide	Select alternative margin settings
Sheet	One Page Per Sheet	Prints each page of the document on a separate sheet (default)
	Multiple pages per sheet	Specify number of pages to print on a sheet

NOTE Please consult your instructor for printing procedures that may differ from the following directions.

You will specify several different print settings to see the effect on the preview, then you will print using the default print settings.

3

If you need to change the selected printer to another printer, open the Printer drop-down menu and choose the appropriate printer (your instructor will tell you which printer to select).

Click [Print All Pages / Print the entire document] and choose Print Current Page from the drop-down menu.

Click [Portrait Orientation] and choose Landscape Orientation from the drop-down menu.

Your screen should be similar to Figure 53

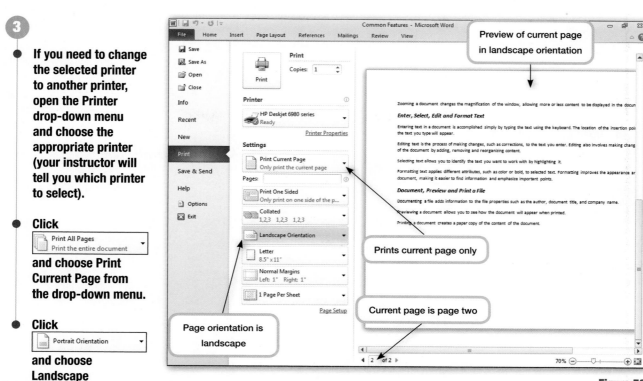

Figure 53

The preview window displays the current page in landscape orientation and the page indicator shows that page two of two will print. You will return these settings to their defaults and then print the document.

4

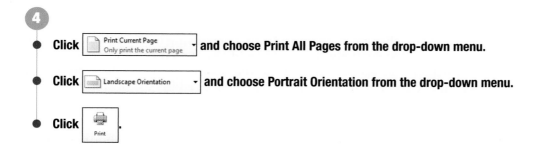

Click [Print Current Page / Only print the current page] and choose Print All Pages from the drop-down menu.

Click [Landscape Orientation] and choose Portrait Orientation from the drop-down menu.

Click [Print].

Your printer should be printing the document.

Closing a File

Finally, you want to close the document.

1

Open the File tab and click 📄 Close.

Another Method

The keyboard shortcut is [Ctrl] + [F4].

Your screen should be similar to Figure 54

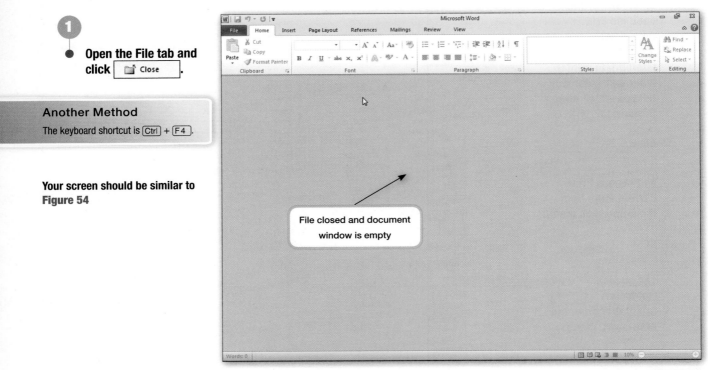

File closed and document window is empty

Figure 54

Additional Information

Do not click ⊠ Close in the window title bar as this closes the application.

Now the Word window displays an empty document window. Because you did not make any changes to the document since saving it, the document window closed immediately. If you had made additional changes, the program would ask whether you wanted to save the file before closing it. This prevents the accidental closing of a file that has not been saved first.

USING OFFICE HELP

Another Method

You also can press [F1] to access Help.

Notice the ⊙ in the upper-right corner of the Ribbon. This button is used to access the Microsoft Help system. The Help button is always visible even when the Ribbon is hidden. Because you are using the Microsoft Word 2010 application, Word Help will be accessed.

1

● Click 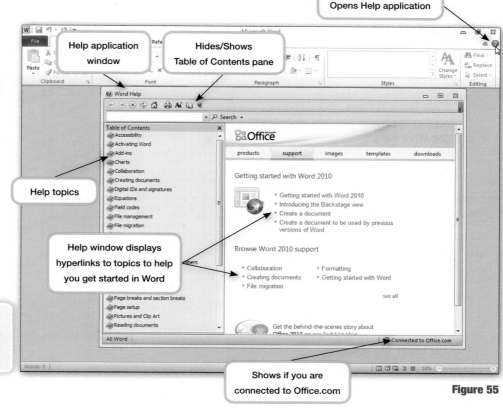 **Microsoft Word Help.**

● **If a Table of Contents pane is not displayed along the left side of the Help window, click** **Show Table of Contents in the Help window toolbar to open it.**

Your screen should be similar to Figure 55

Figure 55

The Word Help feature is a separate application and is opened and displayed in a separate window. The Help window on your screen will probably be a different size and arrangement than in Figure 56. A list of help topics is displayed in the Table of Contents pane along the left side of the window and the Help window on the right side displays several topics to help you get started using Word. If you are connected to the Internet, the Microsoft Office Online Web site, Office.com, is accessed and help information from this site is displayed in the window. If you are not connected, the offline help information that is provided with the application and stored on your computer is located and displayed. Generally, the listing of topics is similar but fewer in number.

Selecting Help Topics

There are several ways you can get help. The first is to select a topic from the listing displayed in the Help window. Each topic is a **hyperlink** or connection to the information located on the Office.com Web site or in Help on your computer. When you point to a hyperlink, it appears underlined and the mouse pointer appears as . Clicking the hyperlink accesses and displays the information associated with the hyperlink.

1
- Click "Getting started with Word 2010."
- Scroll the Help window and click "Basic tasks in Word 2010" in the Never Used Word Before area.

Your screen should be similar to Figure 56

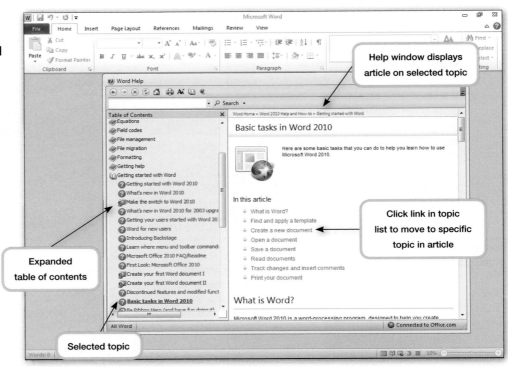

Figure 56

An article containing information about basic features of Word 2010 is displayed and the table of contents has expanded and current topic is underlined to show your location in Help. A topic list appears at the top of the article. You can either scroll the article to read it, or you can jump to a specific location in the article by clicking on a topic link.

2
- Click "Create a new document."

Your screen should be similar to Figure 57

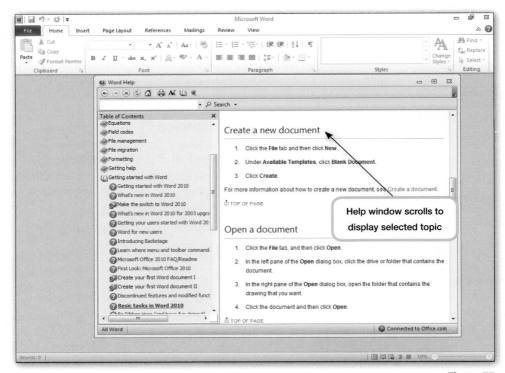

Figure 57

The information on the selected topic is displayed in the window. Notice, as you made selections in the Help window, that the Table of Contents pane shows your current location in Help.

Using the Help Table of Contents

Choosing a topic from the Table of Contents is another method of locating Help information. Using this method allows you to browse the entire list of Help topics to locate topics of interest to you. In this case, the Getting Started with Word topic has expanded to show the subtopics and the topic you are currently viewing is underlined, indicating it is selected. Notice the ⬚ Open Book and ⬚ Closed Book icons in the Table of Contents. The ⬚ Open Book icon identifies those chapters that are open. Clicking on an item preceded with a ⬚ Closed Book icon opens a chapter, which expands to display additional chapters or topics. Clicking on an item preceded with ⬚ displays the specific Help information.

● Click "Word for new users" in the Table of Contents list.

● Click "A tour of the Word user interface" in the Help window.

Your screen should be similar to Figure 58

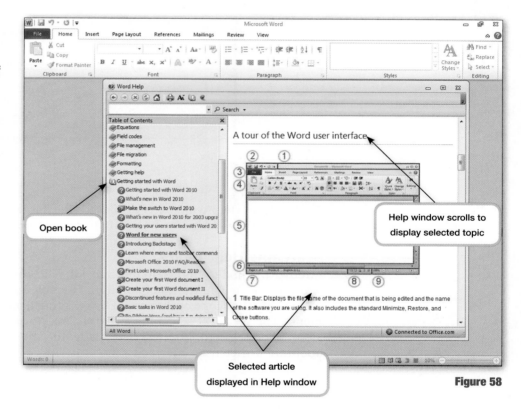

Figure 58

Now information about the user interface features of Word 2010 is displayed in the Help window. To move through previously viewed Help topics, you can use the ⬚ Back and ⬚ Forward buttons in the Help toolbar. You can quickly redisplay the opening Help window using ⬚ Home on the Help toolbar.

2

- Click ⬅ **Back to display the previous topic.**

- Click ⌂ **Home in the Help window toolbar.**

- Click **"Getting started with Word" in the Table of Contents pane to close this topic.**

Your screen should be similar to Figure 59

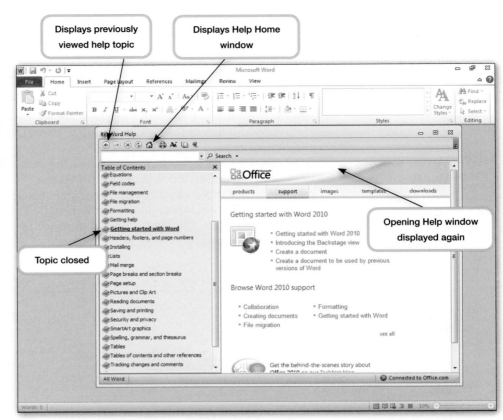

Displays previously viewed help topic

Displays Help Home window

Opening Help window displayed again

Topic closed

Figure 59

The opening Help window is displayed, the Table of Contents topic is closed, and the ➡ Forward button in the Help window toolbar is now available for use.

Searching Help Topics

Another method to find Help information is to conduct a search by entering a word or phrase you want help on in the Search text box. When searching, you can specify the scope of the search by selecting from the 🔍 Search ▾ drop-down menu. The broadest scope for a search, All Word under Content from Office .com, is preselected. You will use this feature to search for Help information about the Office user interface.

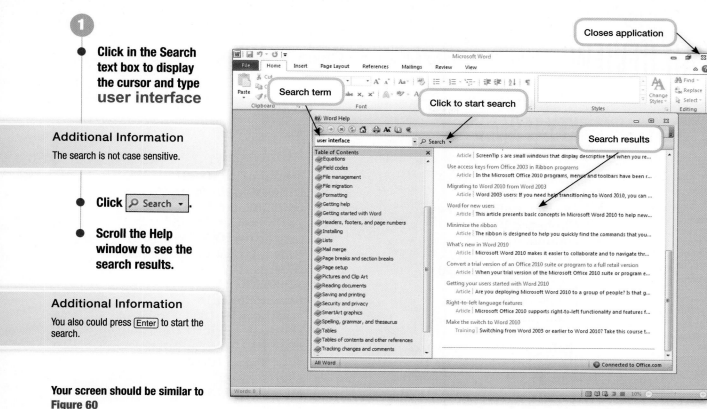

1

- Click in the Search text box to display the cursor and type **user interface**

Additional Information

The search is not case sensitive.

- Click [🔍 Search ▾].

- Scroll the Help window to see the search results.

Additional Information

You also could press [Enter] to start the search.

Your screen should be similar to Figure 60

Figure 60

The Help window displays links to articles that contain both the words "user" and "interface." The results are shown in order of relevance, with the most likely matches at the top of the list.

EXITING AN OFFICE 2010 APPLICATION

Now you are ready to close the Help window and exit the Word program. The [☒] Close button located on the right end of the window title bar can be used to exit most application windows. Alternatively, you can use the [☒ Exit] command on the File tab. If you attempt to close an application without first saving your document, a warning appears asking if you want to save your work. If you do not save your work and you exit the application, any changes you made since last saving it are lost.

1

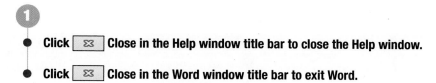

- Click [☒] Close in the Help window title bar to close the Help window.

- Click [☒] Close in the Word window title bar to exit Word.

Another Method

The keyboard shortcut for the Exit command is [Alt] + [F4].

The program window is closed and the Windows desktop is visible again.

LAB REVIEW

KEY TERMS

Backstage view IO.24
buttons IO.15
character effects IO.40
Clipboard IO.45
commands IO.18
context menu IO.17
contextual tabs IO.20
cursor IO.15
database IO.7
default IO.27
destination IO.45
dialog box launcher IO.23
document window IO.15
edit IO.3
Enhanced ScreenTip IO.20
fields IO.7
font IO.40
font size IO.40
format IO.3
groups IO.18
hyperlink IO.61
insertion point IO.15
keyboard shortcut IO.16
keyword IO.51
Live Preview IO.40
metadata IO.51

Mini toolbar IO.39
Office Clipboard IO.45
on-demand tabs IO.20
Paste Preview IO.46
properties IO.27, 51
Quick Access Toolbar IO.15
records IO.7
Ribbon IO.15
ScreenTip IO.16
scroll bar IO.15
shortcut menu IO.17
slide IO.10
slide shows IO.10
source IO.45
status bar IO.15
tables IO.7
tabs IO.18
tag IO.51
task pane IO.23
template IO.26
tooltip IO.16
typeface IO.40
user interface IO.14
View buttons IO.15
worksheet IO.5
Zoom Slider IO.15

COMMAND SUMMARY

Command/Button	Shortcut	Action
Quick Access Toolbar		
↺ ▾ Undo	Ctrl + Y	Restores last change
↻ Redo	Ctrl + Y	Restores last Undo action
↻ Repeat	Ctrl + Y	Repeats last action
❓ Microsoft Word Help	F1	Opens Microsoft Help

WWW.MHHE.COM/OLEARY

COMMAND SUMMARY (CONTINUED)

Command/Button	Shortcut	Action
File tab		
🖫 Save	Ctrl + S or 🖫	Saves document using same file name
🖫 Save As	F12	Saves document using a new file name, type, and/or location
📂 Open	Ctrl + O	Opens existing file
📁 Close	Ctrl + F4 or ✕	Closes document
Info		Displays document properties
Print/ 🖨 Print	Ctrl + P	Prints document using specified settings
✕ Exit	Alt + F4 or ✕	Exits Office program
View tab		
Zoom group		
🔍 Zoom		Changes magnification of document
Home tab		
Clipboard group		
📋 Paste	Ctrl + V	Inserts copy of Clipboard at location of cursor
✂ Cut	Ctrl + X	Removes selection and copies to Clipboard
📄 Copy	Ctrl + C	Copies selection to Clipboard
🖌 Format Painter		Duplicates formats of selection to other locations
Font group		
Calibri (Body) ▾ Font	Ctrl + Shift + F	Changes typeface
11 ▾ Font Size	Ctrl + Shift + P	Changes font size
B Bold	Ctrl + B	Adds/removes bold effect
I Italic	Ctrl + I	Adds/removes italic effect
U̲ Underline	Ctrl + U	Adds/removes underline effect

LAB EXERCISES   Hands-On Exercises

STEP-BY-STEP

EXPLORING EXCEL 2010

1. In this exercise you will explore the Excel 2010 application and use many of the same features you learned about while using Word 2010 in this lab.

   a. Use the Start menu or a shortcut icon on your desktop to start Office Excel 2010.

   b. What shape is the mouse pointer when positioned in the document window area? _____

   c. Excel has _____ tabs. Which tabs are not the same as in Word? _____

   d. Open the Formulas tab. How many groups are in the Formulas tab? _____

   e. Which tab contains the group to work with charts? _____

   f. From the Home tab, click the Number group dialog box launcher. What is the name of the dialog box that opens? _____ How many number categories are there? _____ Close the dialog box.

   g. Display ScreenTips for the following buttons located in the Alignment group of the Home tab and identify what action they perform.

   _____

   _____

   _____

   h. Open the Excel Help window. From the Help window choose "Getting started with Excel 2010" and then choose "Basic tasks in Excel 2010." Read this article and answer the following question: What is Excel used for? _____

   i. In the Table of Contents, open the "Worksheets" topic and then "Entering Data." Read the topic "Enter data manually in worksheet cells" and answer the following:

   • What is the definition of worksheet? Hint: Click on the grayed term "worksheet" to view a definition.

   _____

   • What four types of data can be entered in a worksheet? _____, _____, _____, _____

   j. Read the topic "Quick Start: Edit and enter data in a worksheet." If you have an Internet connection, click the Watch the video link and view the video. Close your browser window.

   k. Enter the term "formula" in the Search text box. Look at several articles and answer the following question: All formula entries begin with what symbol? _____

   l. Close the Help window. Exit Excel.

EXPLORING POWERPOINT 2010

2. In this exercise you will explore the PowerPoint 2010 application and use many of the same features you learned about while using Word 2010 in this lab.

   a. Use the Start menu or a shortcut icon on your desktop to start Office PowerPoint 2010.

   b. PowerPoint has _____ tabs. Which tabs are not the same as in Word?

   _____

   c. Open the Animations tab. How many groups are in this tab? _____

   d. Which tab contains the group to work with themes? _____

   e. Click on the text "Click to add title." Type your name. Select this text and change the font size to 60; add italic and bold. Cut this text. Click in the box containing "Click to add subtitle" and paste the cut selection. Use the Paste Options to keep the source formatting.

   f. Click on the text "Click to add title" and type the name of your school. Select the text and apply a font of your choice.

   g. Open the PowerPoint Help window. From the Help window, choose "Getting Started with PowerPoint 2010" and then choose "Basic tasks in PowerPoint 2010." Read the information in this article and answer the following questions:

   • In the "What is PowerPoint?" topic, what is the primary use of PowerPoint?_____.

   • In the "Save a presentation" topic, what is the default file format for a presentation?

   _____

   • What is the first tip in the "Tips for creating an effective presentation" topic?

   _____

   h. Enter the term "placeholder" in the Search text box. Look at several articles and write the definition of this term. Hint: Click on a word in an article that appears in light gray to view a definition.

   _____

   i. In the Table of Contents, open the "Delivering your presentation" topic. Choose "Create and print notes pages" and answer the following questions:

   • What are notes pages?

   _____

   • What is the Green Idea?

   _____

   j. Close the Help window. Exit PowerPoint and do not save the changes you made to the presentation.

LAB EXERCISES

EXPLORING ACCESS 2010

3. As noted in this Introduction to Microsoft Office 2010, when you start Access 2010 you need to either open an existing database file or create and name a new database. Therefore, in this exercise, you simply explore the Access 2010 Help information without opening or creating a database file.

   a. Use the Start menu or a shortcut icon on your desktop to start Office Access 2010.

   b. Open the Help tab in Backstage view and choose Microsoft Office Help.

   c. From the Help window, choose "Basic tasks in Access 2010." Read the information in this article and answer the following questions:

   - In the "What is Access?" topic, what are the two locations where you can keep your data? _____ and _____.

   - In the "Create a Database from Scratch" topic, what are the two choices? _____ or _____.

   d. In the Table of Contents pane, open the "Access basics" topic. Choose "Database basics" and answer the following questions:

   - In the "What is a database?" topic, define "database."
     _____

   - In "The parts of an Access database" topic, what are the six main parts? _____, _____, _____, _____, _____, _____.

   - In "The parts of an Access database" topic, how is data in a table stored? _____ and _____.

   - In "The parts of an Access database" topic, each row in a table is referred to as a _____.

   e. Enter the term "field" in the Search text box. Look at several articles and write the definition of this term. Hint: Click on a word in an article that appears in light gray to view a definition.
      _____

   f. Close the Help window. Exit Access.

ON YOUR OWN

EXPLORING WORD HELP

1. In addition to the Help information you used in this lab, Office 2010 Help also includes many interactive tutorials. Selecting a Help topic that starts a tutorial will open the browser program on your computer. Both audio and written instructions are provided. You will use one of these tutorials to learn more about using Word 2010.

   Start Word 2010. Open Help and choose "Getting started with Word" from the Help window. Click on the training topic "Create your first Word document I." Follow the directions in your browser to run the tutorial. When you are done, close the browser window, close Help, and exit Word 2010.

Objectives

After completing this lab, you will know how to:

1 Use a template to create a presentation.

2 View and edit a presentation.

3 Copy and move selections.

4 Move, copy, and delete slides.

5 Move, demote, and promote items.

6 Use a numbered list.

7 Check spelling.

8 Size and move placeholders.

9 Change fonts and formatting.

10 Insert and modify clip art.

11 Run a slide show.

12 Document a file.

14 Preview and print a presentation.

Animal Rescue Foundation

You are the volunteer coordinator at the local Animal Rescue Foundation. This nonprofit organization rescues unwanted pets from local animal shelters and finds foster homes for them until a suitable adoptive family can be found. The agency has a large volunteer group called the Animal Angels that provides much-needed support for the foundation.

The agency director has decided to launch a campaign to increase community awareness about the foundation. As part of the promotion, you have been asked to create a powerful and persuasive presentation to entice more members of the community to join Animal Angels.

The agency director has asked you to preview the presentation at the weekly staff meeting tomorrow and has asked you to present a draft of the presentation by noon today.

To help you create the presentation, you will use Microsoft PowerPoint 2010, a graphics presentation application that is designed to create presentation materials such as slides, overheads, and handouts. Using PowerPoint 2010, you can create a high-quality and interesting onscreen presentation with pizzazz that will dazzle your audience.

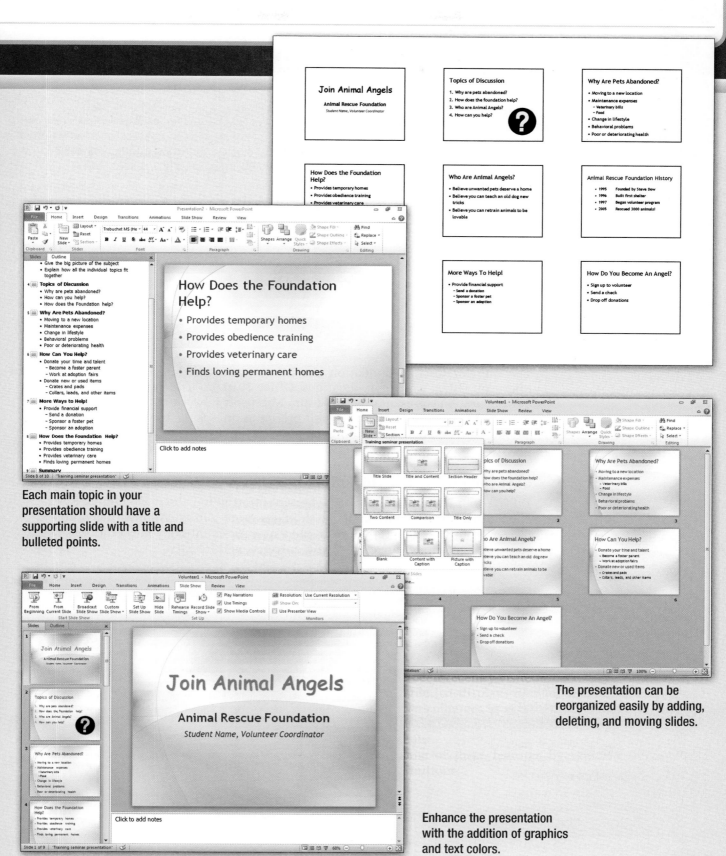

Each main topic in your presentation should have a supporting slide with a title and bulleted points.

The presentation can be reorganized easily by adding, deleting, and moving slides.

Enhance the presentation with the addition of graphics and text colors.

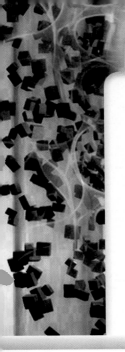

The following concepts will be introduced in this lab:

1 Slide A slide is an individual "page" of your presentation.

2 Spelling Checker The spelling checker locates all misspelled words, duplicate words, and capitalization irregularities as you create and edit a presentation, and proposes possible corrections.

3 AutoCorrect The AutoCorrect feature makes some basic assumptions about the text you are typing and, based on those assumptions, automatically corrects the entry.

4 Layout A layout defines the position and format for objects and text on a slide. A layout contains placeholders for the different items such as bulleted text, titles, charts, and so on.

5 Graphic A graphic is a nontext element or object such as a drawing or picture that can be added to a slide.

Starting a New Presentation

The Animal Rescue Foundation has just installed the latest version of the Microsoft Office suite of applications, Office 2010, on its computers. You will use the graphics presentation program, Microsoft PowerPoint 2010, included in the Office suite, to create your presentation. Using this program, you should have no problem creating the presentation in time for tomorrow's staff meeting.

DEVELOPING A PRESENTATION

During your presentation, you will present information about the Animal Rescue Foundation and why someone should want to join the Animal Angels volunteer group. As you prepare to create a new presentation, you should follow several basic steps: plan, create, edit, enhance, and rehearse.

Step	Description
Plan	The first step in planning a presentation is to understand its purpose. You also need to find out the length of time you have to speak, who the audience is, what type of room you will be in, and what kind of audiovisual equipment is available. These factors help to determine the type of presentation you will create.
Create	To begin creating your presentation, develop the content by typing your thoughts or notes into an outline. Each main idea in your presentation should have a supporting slide with a title and bulleted points.
Edit	While typing, you will probably make typing and spelling errors that need to be corrected. This is one type of editing. Another type is to revise the content of what you have entered to make it clearer, or to add or delete information. To do this, you might insert a slide, add or delete bulleted items, or move text to another location.
Enhance	You want to develop a presentation that grabs and holds the audience's attention. Choose a design that gives your presentation some dazzle. Wherever possible, add graphics to replace or enhance text. Add effects that control how a slide appears and disappears and that reveal text in a bulleted list one bullet at a time.
Rehearse	Finally, you should rehearse the delivery of your presentation. For a professional presentation, your delivery should be as polished as your materials. Use the same equipment that you will use when you give the presentation. Practice advancing from slide to slide and then back in case someone asks a question. If you have a mouse available, practice pointing or drawing on the slide to call attention to key points.

After rehearsing your presentation, you may find that you want to go back to the editing phase. You may change text, move bullets, or insert a new slide. Periodically, as you make changes, rehearse the presentation again to see how the changes affect your presentation. By the day of the presentation, you will be confident about your message and at ease with the materials.

EXPLORING THE POWERPOINT DOCUMENT WINDOW

During the planning phase, you have spoken with the foundation director regarding the purpose of the presentation and the content in general. The purpose of your presentation is to educate members of the community about the organization and to persuade many to volunteer. In addition, you want to impress the director by creating a professional presentation.

Start the PowerPoint 2010 application.

If necessary, maximize the window.

Having Trouble?

See "Common Office 2010 Interface Features," page IO.14, for information on how to start the application and use features that are common to all 2010 Office applications.

Your screen should be similar to Figure 1.1

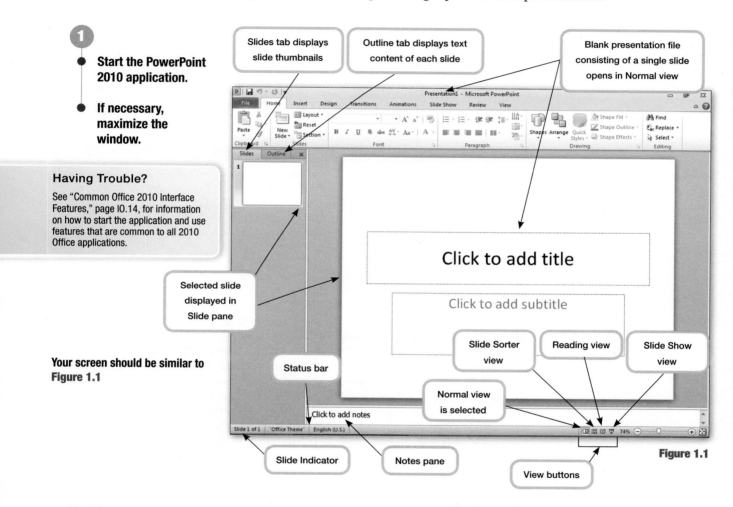

Figure 1.1

Additional Information

Because the Office 2010 applications remember settings that were on when the program was last exited, your screen may look slightly different.

When you first start PowerPoint, a new blank presentation file, named Presentation1, is opened and displayed in the document window. It is like a blank piece of paper that already has many predefined settings. These default settings are generally the most commonly used settings and are stored in the Blank Presentation template file.

Many other templates that are designed to help you create professional-looking presentations are also available within PowerPoint and from the Microsoft Office Online Web site. They include design templates, which provide a design concept, fonts, and color scheme; and content templates, which suggest content for your presentation based on the type of presentation you are making. You also can design and save your own presentation templates.

The Blank Presentation template consists of a single slide that is displayed in the document window.

Concept 1 Slide

A **slide** is an individual "page" of your presentation. The first slide of a presentation is the title slide, which is used to introduce your presentation. Additional slides are used to support each main point in your presentation. The slides give the audience a visual summary of the words you speak, which helps them understand the content and keeps them engaged. The slides also help you, the speaker, organize your thoughts and prompt you during the presentation.

When you first start PowerPoint, it opens in a view called Normal view. **A view** is a way of looking at a presentation and provides the means to interact with the presentation. PowerPoint provides several views you can use to look at and modify your presentation. Depending on what you are doing, one view may be preferable to another.

View	Button	Description
Normal		Provides four working areas of the window that allow you to work on all aspects of your presentation in one place.
Slide Sorter		Displays a miniature of each slide to make it easy to reorder slides, add special effects such as transitions, and set timing between slides.
Reading View		Displays each slide in final form within the PowerPoint window so you can see how it will look during a presentation but still have access to the Windows desktop.
Slide Show		Displays each slide in final form using the full screen space so you can practice or present the presentation.

Normal view is displayed by default because it is the main view you use while creating a presentation. Normal view has four working areas: Outline tab, Slides tab, Slide pane, and Notes pane. These areas allow you to work on all components of your presentation in one convenient location. The **Outline tab** displays the text content of each slide in outline format, and the **Slides tab** displays a miniature version or **thumbnail** of each slide. You can switch between the Slides and Outline tabs by clicking on the tab. The **Slide pane** displays the selected slide. The **Notes pane** includes space for you to enter notes that apply to the current slide.

Below the document window is the status bar, which displays the slide indicator, messages and information about various PowerPoint settings, buttons to change the document view, and a window zoom feature. The **slide indicator** identifies the number of the slide that is displayed in the Slide pane, along with the total number of slides in the presentation. You will learn about the other features of the status bar shortly.

You decide to try to create your first presentation using the Blank Presentation template. It is the simplest and most generic of the templates. Because it has minimal design elements, it is good to use when you first start working with PowerPoint, as it allows you to easily add your own content and design changes.

Notice the slide contains two boxes with dotted borders. These boxes, called **placeholders**, are containers for all the content that appears on a slide. Slide content consists of text and **objects** such as, graphics, tables and charts. In this case, the placeholders are text placeholders that are designed to contain text and display standard **placeholder text** messages that prompt the user to enter a title and subtitle.

ENTERING AND EDITING TEXT

As suggested, you will enter the title for the presentation. As soon as you click on the placeholder, the placeholder text will disappear and will be replaced by the text you want to appear in the slide.

Click the "Click to add title" placeholder.

Your screen should be similar to Figure 1.2

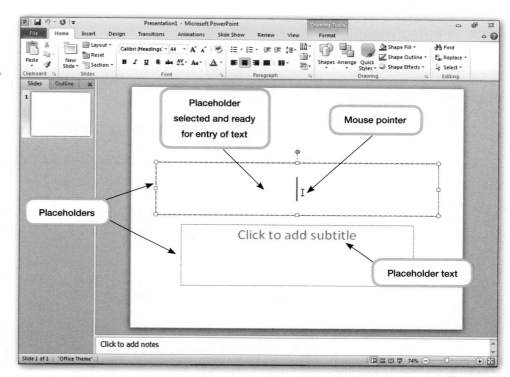

Figure 1.2

Additional Information

A solid border indicates that you can format the placeholder box itself. Clicking the dashed-line border changes it to a solid border.

Notice that the placeholder is surrounded with a dashed-line border. This indicates that you can enter, delete, select, and format the object inside the placeholder. Because this placeholder contains text, the cursor is displayed to show your location in the text and to allow you to select and edit the text. Additionally, the mouse pointer appears as a I to be used to position the cursor.

Next you will type the title text you want to appear on the slide. Then you will enter the subtitle.

Having Trouble?

See the section "Entering and Editing Text" in the Introduction to Microsoft Office 2010 to review this feature.

②

Type Join Animal Angels

Having Trouble?
If you make a typing error, press ⌈Backspace⌋ to delete the characters back to the error and retype the entry.

● **Click in the "Click to add subtitle" placeholder and type** Animal Rescue Foundation

Your screen should be similar to Figure 1.3

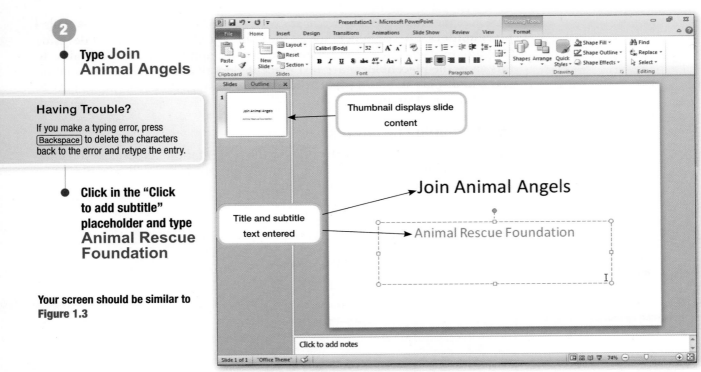

Figure 1.3

The content for the first slide is complete. Notice that the thumbnail of the slide in the Slides tab now displays the text you just entered.

INSERTING A SLIDE

Next you want to add the content for a second slide. To continue creating the presentation, you need to add another slide.

①

● **If necessary, click the Home tab to open it.**

● **Click** New Slide **in the Slides group.**

Another Method
You also can use the keyboard shortcut ⌈Ctrl⌋ + M to insert a new slide.

Your screen should be similar to Figure 1.4

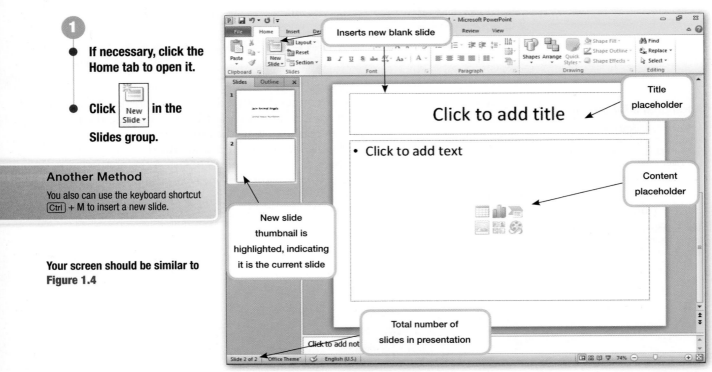

Figure 1.4

A new slide with a slide title placeholder and a content placeholder was added to the presentation. It is displayed in the Slide pane and is the **current slide**, or the slide that will be affected by any changes you make. The Slides tab displays a second slide thumbnail. It is highlighted, further indicating it is the current slide. The status bar displays the number of the current slide and the total number of slides in the presentation.

Now you could add text to the new slide and continue adding slides to create the presentation.

OPENING A PRESENTATION TEMPLATE

Although the Blank presentation template is opened automatically when you start PowerPoint, it is not the only method that can be used to create a presentation. Another is to use one of the many supplied design templates. A third is to save the design elements of an existing presentation as a custom template, which you would then use as the basis for your new presentation. Finally, you can open an existing presentation and modify the design and content as needed for the new presentation.

Because you have not decided exactly what content should be presented next in the presentation, you decide that it might be easier to use one of the templates that will suggest the content to include. You will close this file without saving it and then open a presentation template file.

Open the File tab and click ☐ Close **.**

Click Do_n't Save **.**

Open the File tab and choose New.

Your screen should be similar to Figure 1.5

Having Trouble?

To complete steps 2 and 3 you need an Internet connection. If you are not connected to the Internet, choose New from Existing, change to the location containing your data files, and double-click on the file pp01_Training. Then skip to the next section, Viewing the Presentation.

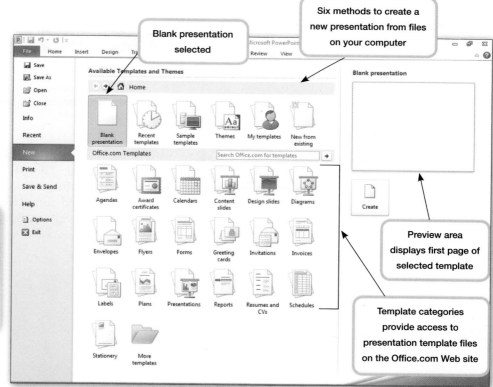

Figure 1.5

The Available Templates and Themes window of Backstage view is open. The upper section of this window displays six options from which you can choose to start a new presentation from files that are stored on your computer. The Blank presentation template is selected, as this is the default template that is opened when you first start PowerPoint. The five other choices provide the means of starting a presentation from recent templates you have opened, templates you have created, or other existing presentations.

The lower section of the window displays categories of templates that are available online from Microsoft. When you choose a category, folders of additional subcategories are displayed that contain the available presentation template files. For this presentation, you want to look at the online templates.

- **Choose Presentations from the Office.com Templates category.**

- **Choose the Training folder.**

- **Scroll the list of template files in the Training folder and select "Employee Training Presentation".**

Your screen should be similar to Figure 1.6

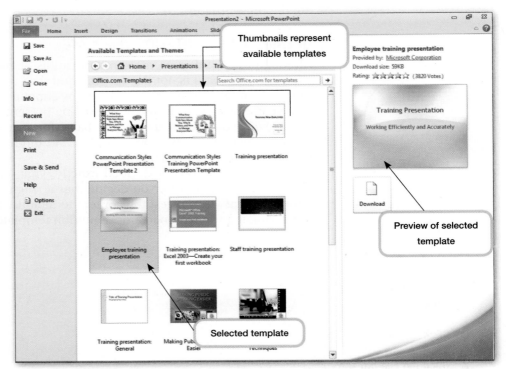

Figure 1.6

Thumbnail images representing the first slide in each template file are displayed in alphabetical order by name. The preview area displays a larger image of the selected thumbnail and information about the template.

You think the design of the selected template looks good and decide to begin your presentation for the volunteers using the content in this template as a guide.

Click 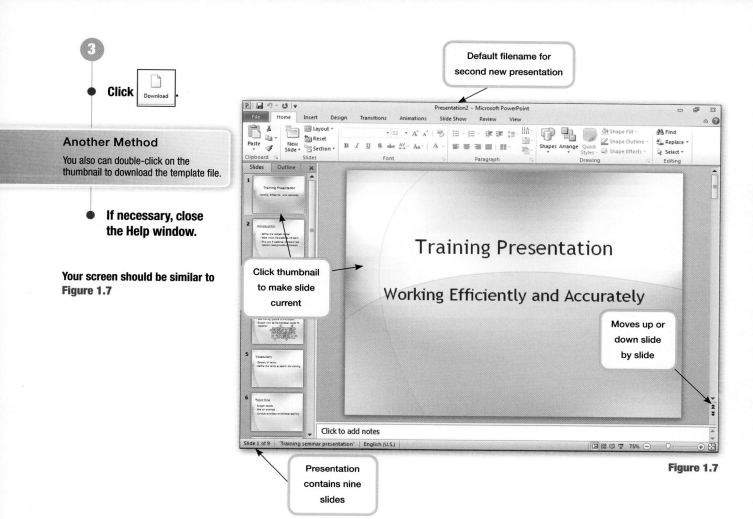 .

Another Method

You also can double-click on the thumbnail to download the template file.

● **If necessary, close the Help window.**

Your screen should be similar to Figure 1.7

Default filename for second new presentation

Click thumbnail to make slide current

Moves up or down slide by slide

Presentation contains nine slides

Figure 1.7

The template file is downloaded and opened in PowerPoint. It contains a total of nine slides. Because this is the second new presentation you have worked on since starting PowerPoint 2010, the default file name is Presentation2.

MOVING AMONG SLIDES

You want to look at the slides in the presentation to get a quick idea of their content. There are many ways to move from slide to slide in PowerPoint. Most often, the quickest method is to click on the slide thumbnail in the Slides tab. Clicking on a slide in the Slides tab displays it in the Slide pane and makes it the current slide. However, if your hands are already on the keyboard, you may want to use the keyboard directional keys. The following table shows both keyboard and mouse methods to move among slides in Normal view.

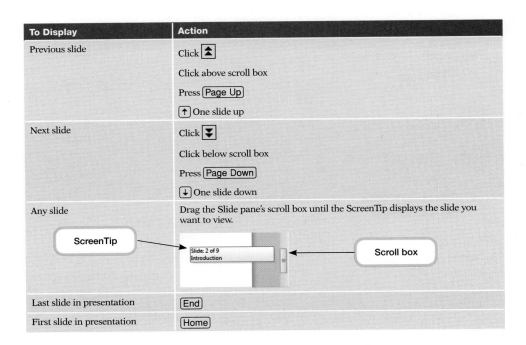

To Display	Action
Previous slide	Click [⤒] Click above scroll box Press [Page Up] [↑] One slide up
Next slide	Click [⤓] Click below scroll box Press [Page Down] [↓] One slide down
Any slide	Drag the Slide pane's scroll box until the ScreenTip displays the slide you want to view.
Last slide in presentation	[End]
First slide in presentation	[Home]

You will try out several of these methods as you look at the slides in the presentation. First you will use the Slides tab. This tab makes it easy to move from one slide to another. You also will increase the width of the Slide tab pane to make the slide thumbnails larger and easier to see.

1

- **Point to the splitter bar between the Slide pane and the Slides tab pane and when the mouse pointer is shaped as ◄┃┃► drag to the right to increase the width of the pane as in Figure 1.8.**

- **Press [↓] or [Page Down] to move to the next slide.**

- **Scroll the Slides tab to display slides 4 to 7.**

- **Click on slide 4.**

Your screen should be similar to Figure 1.8

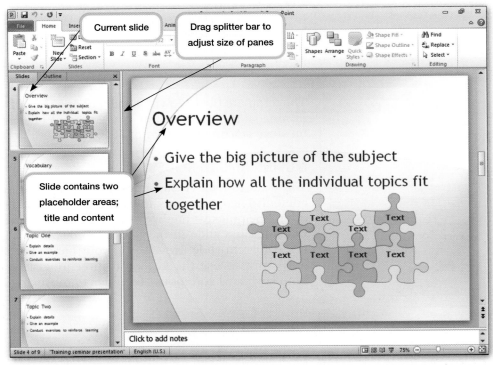

Figure 1.8

Slide 4 is the current slide and is displayed in the Slide pane. This slide contains two placeholders: title and content. The content placeholder consists of two bulleted items as well as a graphic. Next you will use the Slide pane scroll bar to display the next few slides.

● Click ⬇ Next Slide to display slide 5.

Having Trouble?
The ⬆ Previous Slide and ⬇ Next Slide buttons are located at the bottom of the Slide pane's vertical scroll bar.

● Drag the scroll box and stop when the ScreenTip displays Slide 6 of 9.

● Click below the scroll box to display slide 7.

● Press End to display the last slide.

Your screen should be similar to Figure 1.9

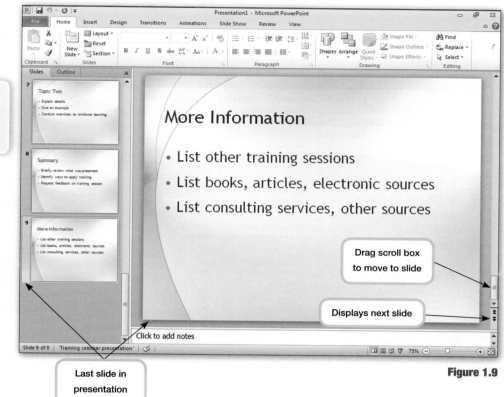

Last slide in presentation

Figure 1.9

You can see this template will help you to create your presentation because the content provides some basic guidance as to how to organize a presentation.

Editing a Presentation

Now you need to edit the presentation to replace the sample content with the appropriate information for your presentation. Editing involves making text changes and additions to the content of your presentation. It also includes making changes to the organization of content. This can be accomplished quickly by rearranging the order of bulleted items on slides as well as the order of slides.

USING THE OUTLINE TAB

You have already entered text in a slide in the Slide pane. Another way to make text-editing changes is to use the Outline tab in Normal view. The Outline tab displays the content of the presentation in outline form, making it easy to see the organization of your presentation as you enter and edit content. The first change you want to make is to enter a title for the presentation on slide 1. First, you will open the Outline tab and select the sample title text on the slide and delete it.

- **Click the Outline tab to open it.**

- **Scroll the Outline tab to the top to display the text for slide 1.**

- **Click anywhere on the text for slide 1 in the Outline tab to make it the current slide.**

- **Select the text "Training Presentation".**

Having Trouble?

Refer to the topic "Selecting Text" in the Introduction to Microsoft Office 2010 to review these features.

- **Press** Delete.

Your screen should be similar to Figure 1.10

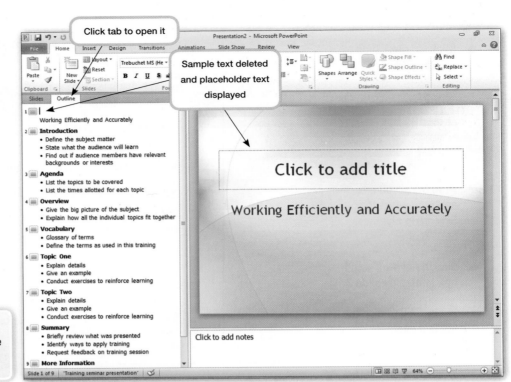

Figure 1.10

The sample text is deleted. As you change the text content in the Outline tab, it also appears in the slide displayed in the Slide pane. Notice that although you deleted the sample text, the slide still displays the title placeholder text.

You will enter the title and subtitle for the presentation next.

2

● **Type** Join
Animal Angels

Having Trouble?

If you make a typing error, use
[Backspace] or [Delete] to correct the
errors.

● **Select the text
"Working Efficiently
and Accurately"
on the second line
of slide 1 in the
Outline tab and type**
Animal Rescue
Foundation

**Your screen should be similar to
Figure 1.11**

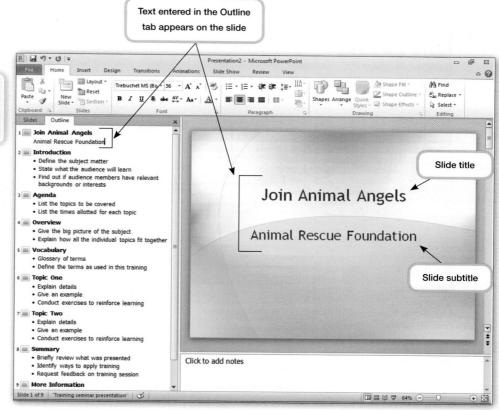

Figure 1.11

Additional Information

If you click the slide icon to the right of
the slide number in the Outline tab, all
text on the slide is selected.

As soon as you pressed a key, the selected text was deleted and replaced with
the text you typed. When entering the title for a slide, it is a common practice
to use title case, in which the first letter of most words is capitalized.

The next change you want to make is in the Introduction slide. The sample
text recommends that you define the subject of the presentation and what the
audience will learn. You will replace the sample text next to the first bullet
with the text for your slide. In the Outline tab, you can select an entire paragraph and all subparagraphs by pointing to the left of the line and clicking
when the mouse pointer is a ✥.

3

● **Click on the first bullet of slide 2 in the Outline tab when the mouse pointer is a** .

Having Trouble?

If you accidentally drag selected text, it will move. To return it to its original location, immediately click ↶ ▾ Undo on the Quick Access Toolbar.

● **Type Your Name, Volunter (this word is intentionally misspelled) Coordinator**

Your screen should be similar to Figure 1.12

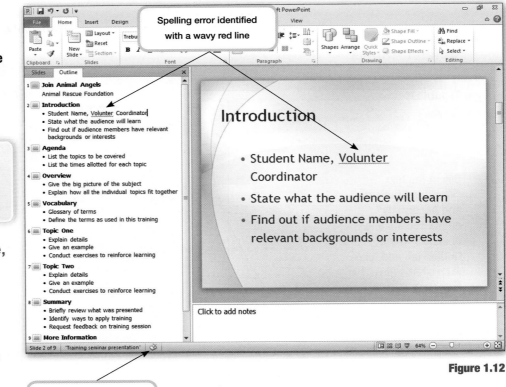

Spelling error identified with a wavy red line

Introduction

- Student Name, <u>Volunter</u> Coordinator
- State what the audience will learn
- Find out if audience members have relevant backgrounds or interests

Figure 1.12

Indicates document contains a spelling error

Having Trouble?

Do not be concerned if the spelling checker identifies your name as misspelled.

The sample text has been replaced with the text you typed. Depending on the length of your name, the text in this bullet may not have wrapped to a second line.

CORRECTING ERRORS

As you enter text, the program checks each word for accuracy. In this case, a spelling error was located. PowerPoint identified the word as misspelled by underlining it with a wavy red line. The Spelling indicator ✎ in the status bar also shows a spelling error has been detected in the document.

Having Trouble

If the Spelling indicator is not displayed, right click on the status bar and choose Spell Check from the context menu.

Concept **2** Spelling Checker

The **spelling checker** locates all misspelled words, duplicate words, and capitalization irregularities as you create and edit a presentation, and proposes possible corrections. This feature works by comparing each word to a dictionary of words. If the word does not appear in the main dictionary or in a custom dictionary, it is identified as misspelled. The **main dictionary** is supplied with the program; a **custom dictionary** is one you can create to hold words you commonly use, such as proper names and technical terms, that are not included in the main dictionary.

If the word does not appear in either dictionary, the program identifies it as misspelled by displaying a red wavy line below the word. You can then correct the misspelled word by editing it. Alternatively, you can display a list of suggested spelling corrections for that word and select the correct spelling from the list to replace the misspelled word in the presentation.

To quickly correct the misspelled word, you can select the correct spelling from a list of suggested spelling corrections displayed on the shortcut menu.

1

Right-click on the misspelled word in the Outline tab to display the shortcut menu.

Your screen should be similar to Figure 1.13

Additional Information

Sometimes the spelling checker cannot suggest replacements because it cannot locate any words in its dictionary that are similar in spelling. Other times the suggestions offered are not correct. If either situation happens, you must edit the word manually.

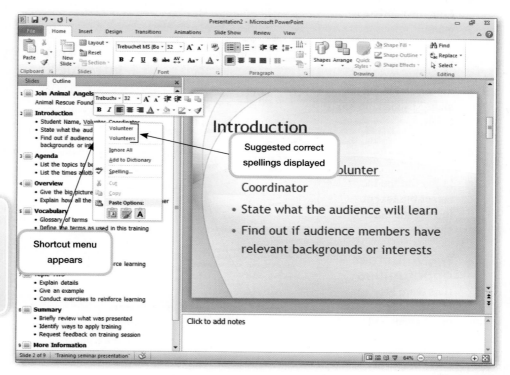

Figure 1.13

The shortcut menu displays two suggested correct spellings. The menu also includes several related menu options described below.

Additional Information

The spelling checker works just as it does in the other Microsoft Office 2010 applications.

Option	Effect
Ignore All	Instructs PowerPoint to ignore the misspelling of this word throughout the rest of this session.
Add to Dictionary	Adds the word to the custom dictionary list. When a word is added to the custom dictionary, PowerPoint will always accept that spelling as correct.
Spelling	Opens the Spelling dialog box to check the entire presentation.

You will replace the word with the correct spelling and then enter the information for the second bullet.

2

- Choose "Volunteer" from the shortcut menu.

- In the Outline tab, select the text in the second bullet on slide 2 by clicking the bullet.

- Press Delete.

- In the Outline tab, select the text in the second bullet on slide 2.

- Type **volunteer oppotunities** (this word is intentionally misspelled) and press Spacebar.

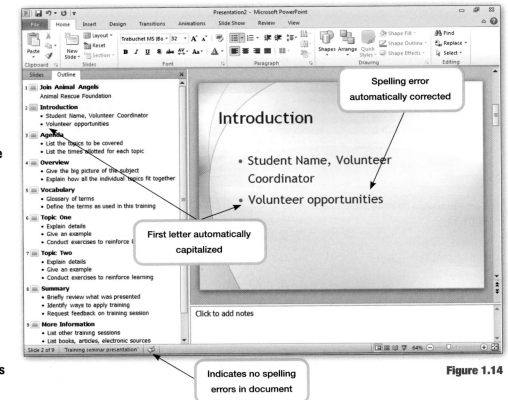

Figure 1.14

Your screen should be similar to Figure 1.14

Additional Information

Bulleted items in a presentation are capitalized in sentence case format. Ending periods, however, are not included.

Notice that the first letter of "volunteer" was automatically capitalized. Also notice that the incorrect spelling of the word "oppotunities" was corrected. These corrections are part of the AutoCorrect feature of PowerPoint.

Concept 3 AutoCorrect

The **AutoCorrect** feature makes some basic assumptions about the text you are typing and, based on those assumptions, automatically corrects the entry. The AutoCorrect feature automatically inserts proper capitalization at the beginning of sentences and in the names of days of the week. It also will change to lowercase letters any words that were incorrectly capitalized due to the accidental use of the Caps Lock key. In addition, it also corrects many common typing and spelling errors automatically.

One way the program makes corrections automatically is by looking for certain types of errors. For example, if two capital letters appear at the beginning of a word, the second capital letter is changed to a lowercase letter. If a lowercase letter appears at the beginning of a sentence, the first letter of the first word is capitalized. If the name of a day begins with a lowercase letter, the first letter is capitalized.

Another way the program makes corrections is by automatically replacing a misspelled word with the correct spelling in situations where the spelling checker offers only one suggested spelling correction. AutoCorrect also checks all words against the AutoCorrect list, a built-in list of words that are commonly spelled or typed incorrectly. If it finds the entry on the list, the program automatically replaces the error with the correction. For example, the typing error "aboutthe" is automatically changed to "about the" because the error is on the AutoCorrect list. You also can add words to the AutoCorrect list that you want to be corrected automatically. Any such words are added to the list on the computer you are using and will be available to anyone who uses the machine after you.

COPYING AND MOVING SELECTIONS

You are now ready to enter the text for the next slide in your presentation by entering the three main topics of discussion. You want to enter a new slide title, Topics of Discussion, with three bulleted items describing the topics to be discussed. Two placeholder bullets with sample text are displayed. You will edit these and then add a third bulleted item.

1

- Move to slide 3.

- In the Outline tab, replace the sample title, Agenda, with **Topics of Discussion**

- Select and replace the text in the first bullet with **Why are pets abandoned?**

- Select and replace the text in the second bullet with **How can you help?**

- Press Enter.

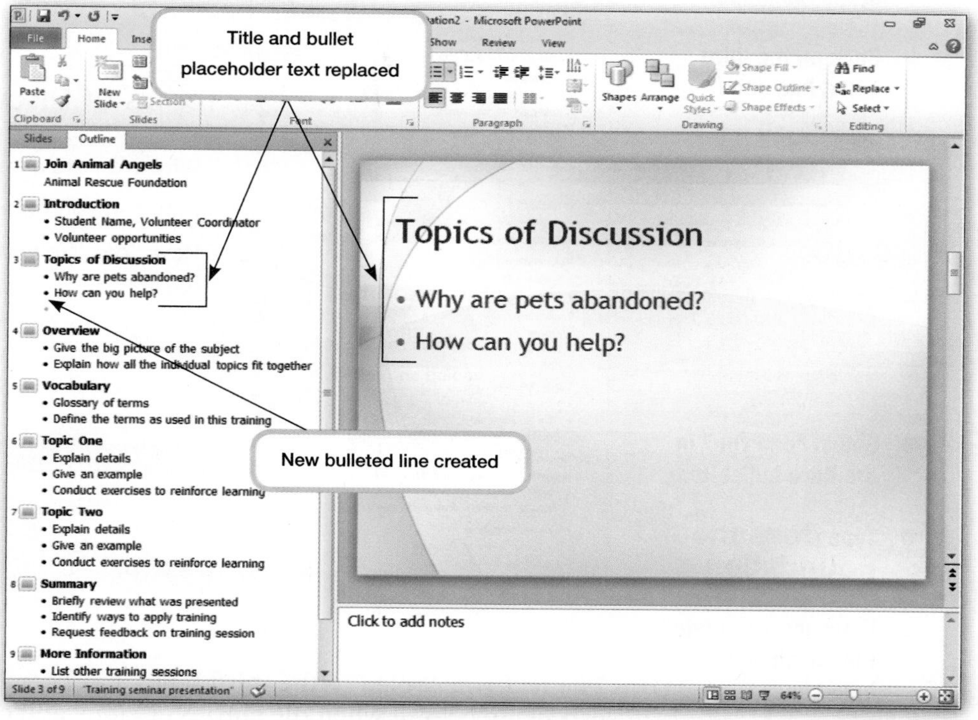

Having Trouble?

If you accidentally insert an extra bullet and blank line, press Backspace twice to remove them.

Your screen should be similar to Figure 1.15

Figure 1.15

Having Trouble?

Refer to "Copying and Moving Selections" in the Introduction to Microsoft Office 2010 to review this feature.

A new bulleted line is automatically created whenever you press Enter at the end of a bulleted item. Because the text you want to enter for this bullet is similar to the text in the second bullet, you decide to save time by copying and pasting the bullet text. Then you will modify the text in the third bullet.

● Select the second bulleted item.

● Click 📋 ▾ Copy in the Clipboard group of the Home tab.

● Click on the third bullet line and click [Paste].

Another Method

You also can press [Ctrl] + C to copy a selection and [Ctrl] + V to paste a selection.

● Select "can you" in the third bullet item.

● Type **does the Foundation**

● If necessary, delete the fourth blank bullet line.

Your screen should be similar to Figure 1.16

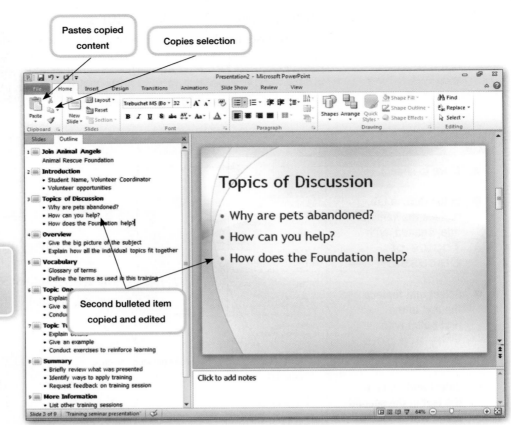

Pastes copied content

Copies selection

Second bulleted item copied and edited

Figure 1.16

The text you copied to the third bullet has been quickly modified. Copying is especially helpful when the entries are long and complicated.

As you review what you have entered so far in your presentation, you decide that it would be better to introduce yourself on the first slide. Rather than retyping this information, you will move your introduction from slide 2 to slide 1. You will do this using drag and drop.

3

- In the Outline tab, press [Enter] at the end of the subtitle in slide 1 to create a blank line.

- Select the first bulleted item on aslide 2.

- Drag the selection to the blank line on slide 1.

Another Method

You can also use ✂ Cut or [Ctrl] + X to cut a selection and then paste it to the new location.

- Move to the blank line at the end of slide 1 and press [Backspace] to delete it.

Your screen should be similar to Figure 1.17

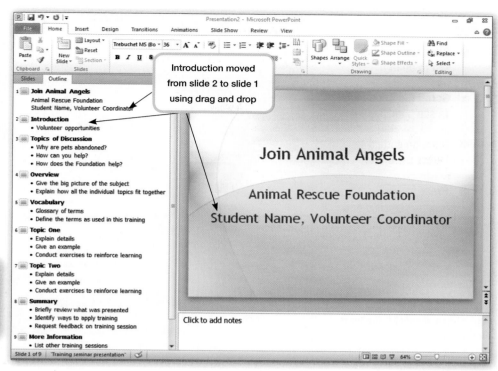

Figure 1.17

Additional Information

You can also delete and move slides in the Outline tab by clicking on the slide icon next to the slide number to select the entire slide and then use the appropriate command.

Because the Outline tab lets you see the content in multiple slides at once, it makes it easy to see the organization of the presentation and to quickly make text changes within and between slides.

MOVING, COPYING, AND DELETING SLIDES

As you continue to plan the presentation content and organization, you decide you will not use the Vocabulary slide and want to delete it. You also think a more appropriate location for the Overview slide may be above the agenda. Finally, you plan to have three slides to present the three main topics you plan to cover in the presentation. For this purpose, you want to add a third topic slide. Because you are not working with slide content, you will use the Slides tab to make these changes.

First you will delete slide 5, Vocabulary.

1

- **Click on the Slides tab to open it.**

- **Scroll the Slides tab to see slide 5.**

- **Click on slide 5 to select the slide.**

- **Press** Delete.

Another Method

You can also choose Delete Slide from the selected slide's context menu.

Your screen should be similar to Figure 1.18

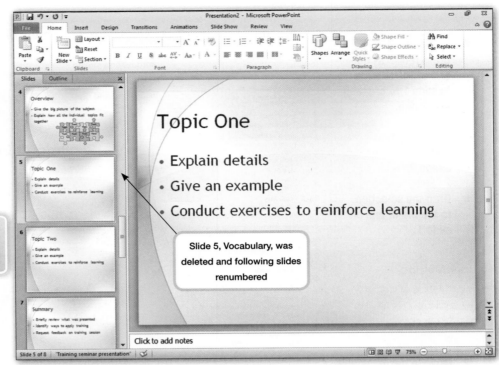

Figure 1.18

The slide has been deleted and all subsequent slides renumbered. Next, you will move the Overview slide (4) above slide 3 using drag and drop

2

- **Select slide 4 in the Slides tab.**

- **If necessary, scroll the Slides tab to show slide 3.**

- **Drag slide 4 above slide 3 in the Slides tab.**

Additional Information

A solid horizontal line identifies the location where the slide will be placed when you stop dragging.

Your screen should be similar to Figure 1.19

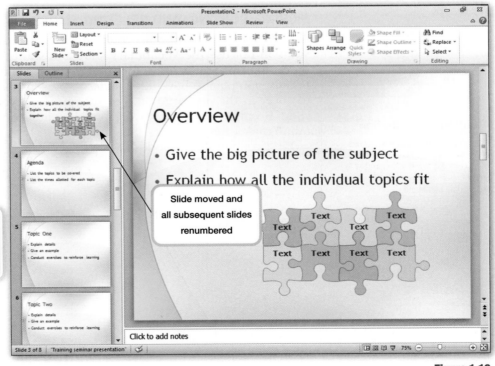

Figure 1.19

The Overview slide is now slide 3 and, again, all following slides are appropriately renumbered. Finally, you will make a copy of slide 6.

3

- Select slide 6 in the Slides tab.

- Open the [ ] drop-down menu and choose Duplicate.

Another Method

You could also copy and paste the slide to duplicate it or use [New Slide] in the Slides group and choose Duplicate Selected Slides from the drop-down menu.

- Scroll the Slides tab to see slides 5 to 7.

Your screen should be similar to Figure 1.20

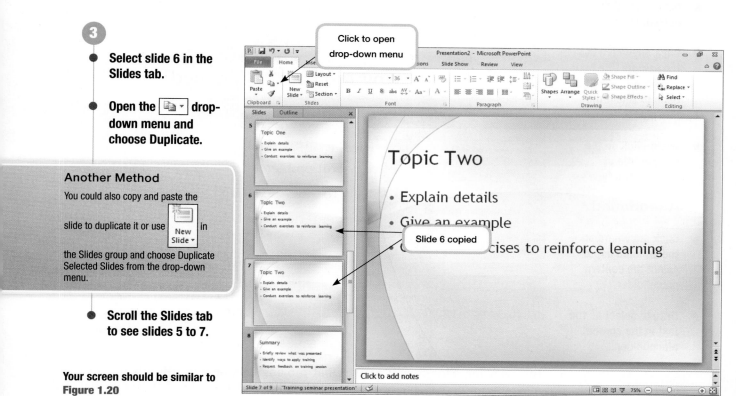

Figure 1.20

There are now three topic slides. The duplicate slide was inserted directly below the slide that was copied and is the selected slide.

MOVING, DEMOTING, AND PROMOTING BULLETED ITEMS

Now you are ready to enter the text for the three topic slides. You decide to enter the text for these slides using the Slide pane rather than the Outline tab. Simply clicking in an area of the slide in the Slide pane will make it the active area.

1

- Make slide 5 the current slide.

- Click anywhere in the sample title text of slide 5 in the Slide pane to select the title placeholder.

- Triple-click on the sample title to select it and type **Why Are Pets Abandoned?**

- Click anywhere on the bulleted list to select the content placeholder.

- Drag to select all the text in the content placeholder.

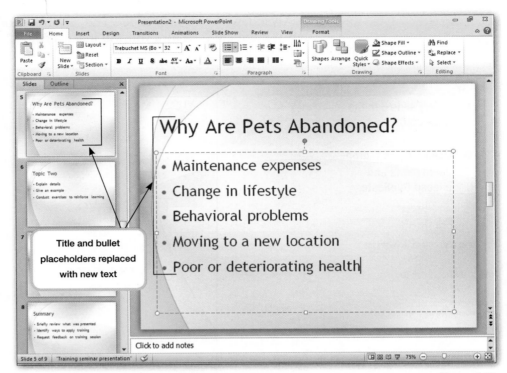

Figure 1.21

Another Method

You also can click [🗔 Select ▾] in the Editing group of the Home tab and click [🗔 Select ▾] or use the shortcut key [Ctrl] + A to select everything in a placeholder box.

In reviewing slide 5, you realize that moving to a new location is one of the most common reasons for pets to be abandoned, so you decide to move that to the top of the list. You can rearrange bulleted items in the Slide pane by selecting the item and dragging it to a new location in the same way you moved selections in the Outline tab.

- Enter the following bulleted items (Press [Enter] after each line, except the last, to create a new bullet):

Maintenance expenses

Change in lifestyle

Behavioral problems

Moving to a new location

Poor or deteriorating health

Your screen should be similar to Figure 1.21

2

- Select all the text in the fourth bulleted item in the Slide pane.

- Drag the selection to the beginning of the first bulleted item.

Your screen should be similar to Figure 1.22

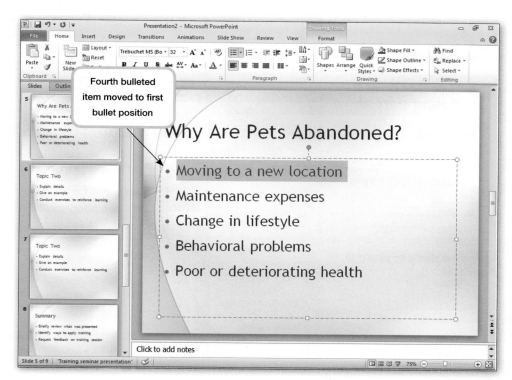

Figure 1.22

The fourth bullet is now the first bulleted item in the list.

In the next slide, you will enter information about how people can help the Animal Rescue Foundation.

3

- Make slide 6 the current slide.

- Replace the sample title text with **How Can You Help?**

- Select all the text in the bulleted text placeholder.

- Type **Donate your time and talent**

- Press Enter.

Your screen should be similar to Figure 1.23

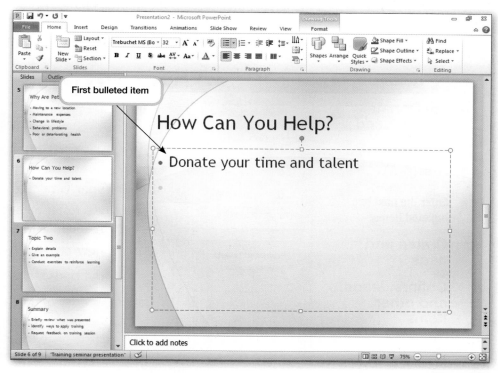

Figure 1.23

You want the next bulleted item to be indented below the first bulleted item. Indenting a bulleted point to the right **demotes** it, or makes it a lower or subordinate topic in the outline hierarchy.

● Press Tab.

● Type **Become a foster parent**

● Press Enter.

● Type **Work at adoption fairs**

● Press Enter.

Your screen should be similar to Figure 1.24

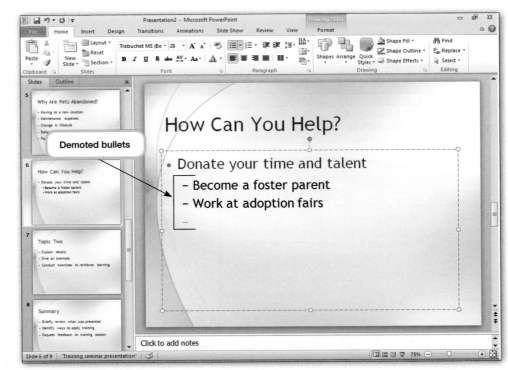

Figure 1.24

When you demote a bulleted point, PowerPoint continues to indent to the same level until you cancel the indent. Before entering the next item, you want to remove the indentation, or **promote** the line. Promoting a line moves it to the left, or up a level in the outline hierarchy.

● Press Shift + Tab.

● Type **Donate new or used items**

● Press Enter.

● Enter the next two bulleted items:

Crates and pads

Collars, leads, and other items

Your screen should be similar to Figure 1.25

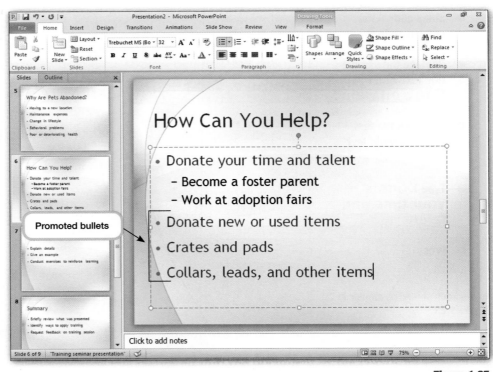

Figure 1.25

You also can promote or demote bulleted items after the text has been entered. The insertion point must be at the beginning of the line to be promoted or demoted, or all the text must be selected. You will demote the last two bulleted items.

6
- Select the two bulleted items "Crates and pads" and "Collars, leads, and other items".
- Press Tab.
- Move to the end of "Collars, leads, and other items".
- Press Enter.

Your screen should be similar to Figure 1.26

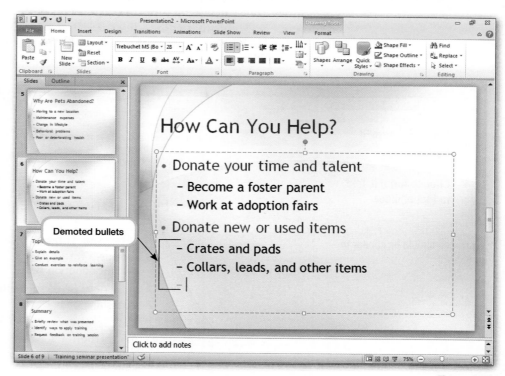

Figure 1.26

The last two items have been demoted. Next you will add more items to the bulleted list.

7
- Type Provide financial support
- Press Enter.
- Enter the following three bulleted items:

Send a donation

Sponsor a foster pet

Sponsor an adoption

- Promote the "Provide financial support" bullet.

Your screen should be similar to Figure 1.27

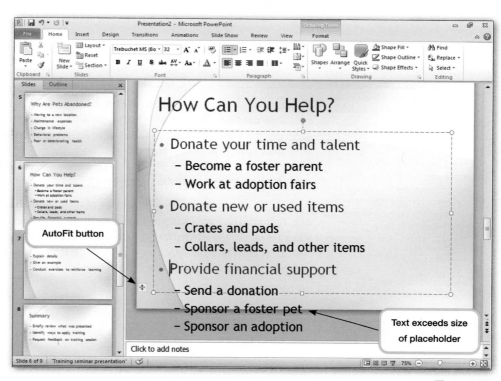

Figure 1.27

As you entered more bulleted items, the slide's text exceeds the size of the placeholder. When this happens a ⊟ AutoFit Options button appears at the bottom left corner of the placeholder. It provides options that allow you to control the AutoFit feature and to handle any overspilling text. The AutoFit feature will automatically adjust the line spacing and text size as needed to display the content inside the placeholder appropriately. Currently, this feature is off in this template.

- Click ⊟ AutoFit Options.

- Choose AutoFit Text to Placeholder.

Your screen should be similar to Figure 1.28

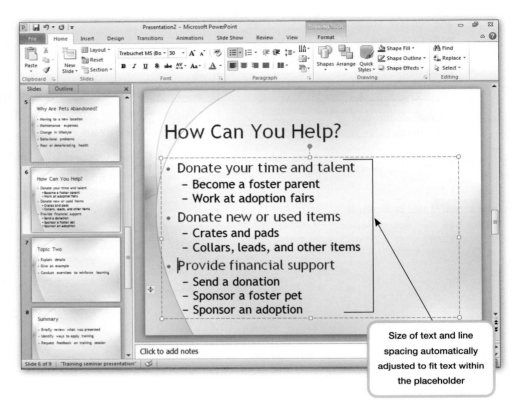

Figure 1.28

Now that the AutoFit Text to Placeholder option is on, the text size and line spacing of the bulleted items have been reduced to display the text more comfortably on the slide. If you were to add more text or increase or decrease the size of the placeholder, the AutoFit feature would continue to adjust the text size and spacing.

SPLITTING TEXT BETWEEN SLIDES

Although using AutoFit solved the problem, you decide that 10 bulleted items are too many for a single slide. Generally, when creating slides, it is a good idea to limit the number of bulleted items on a slide to six. It also is recommended that the number of words on a line should not exceed five. You decide to split the slide content between two slides.

1

● With the bullet placeholder in slide 6 still selected, click AutoFit Options and choose Split Text Between Two Slides.

● If necessary, scroll the Slides tab so that slides 6 and 7 are visible.

Your screen should be similar to Figure 1.29

Having Trouble?

You may have noticed that slide 6 in the Slides tab still displays all the bulleted items. Do not be concerned. The five bullets have been removed; however, the Slides tab has not updated to reflect the change.

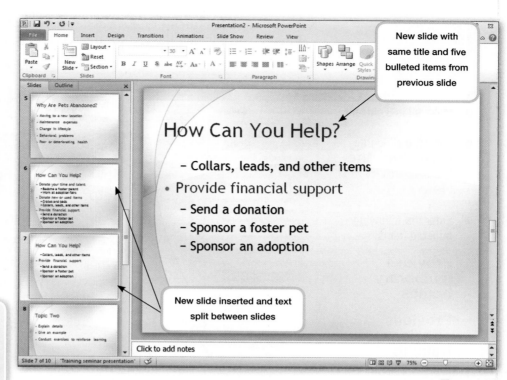

Figure 1.29

A new slide containing the same title as the previous slide and five of the bulleted items from the previous slide is inserted into the presentation. Often when splitting text between slides, the content may not split appropriately and you may still need to make adjustments to the slides. You will move the first bulleted item on slide 7 to the last item on slide 6 using the keyboard shortcuts for the Cut and Paste commands. You also will edit the slide title of slide 7.

2

● On slide 7, replace the title text with **More Ways to Help!**

● Select the first bulleted item on slide 7 and press Ctrl + X to cut the selection.

● Move to the end of the last item on slide 6 and press Enter.

● Press Ctrl + V to paste the item.

● If necessary, delete the new blank bullet line.

Your screen should be similar to Figure 1.30

Figure 1.30

Editing a Presentation **PP1.29**

Now the number of items on each slide seems much more reasonable. Finally, you will add the text for the third topic slide.

3

- **Make slide 8 current.**

- **Enter the slide title How Does the Foundation Help?**

- **Enter the following bulleted items:**

  Provides temporary homes

  Provides obedience training

  Provides veterinary care

  Finds loving permanent homes

- **Open the Outline tab and scroll the tab to see slides 4 through 8.**

Your screen should be similar to Figure 1.31

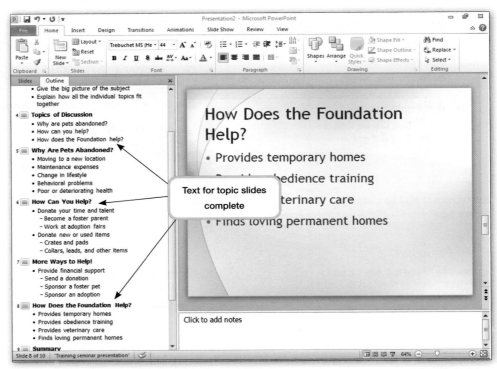

Figure 1.31

The text for the three topic slides reflects the order of the topics in the Topics of Discussion slide.

CREATING A NUMBERED LIST

After looking at slide 4, you decide that it would be better if the topics of discussion were a numbered list. You can easily change the format of the bulleted items to a numbered list using the ⊞ ▾ Numbering command in the Paragraph group on the Home tab.

1

● Open the Slides tab and make slide 4 current.

● Click anywhere in the bulleted items placeholder on slide 4.

● Click on the dashed-line border of the placeholder box to change it to a solid line.

● Click ≣▾ Numbering in the Paragraph group on the Home tab.

Your screen should be similar to Figure 1.32

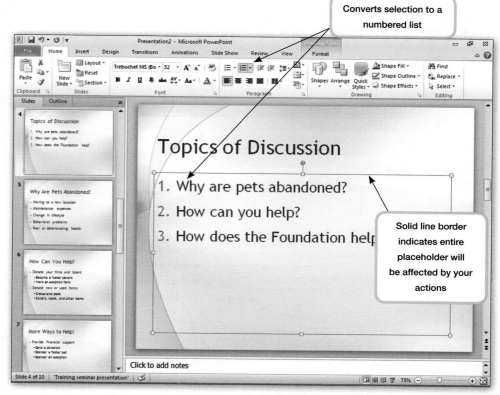

Figure 1.32

Notice the cursor does not appear in the placeholder box. This is because a solid line around the placeholder indicates your action will affect the entire placeholder rather than individual parts, such as the text, of the placeholder. The bullets have been replaced with an itemized numbered list.

MOVING, DEMOTING, AND PROMOTING NUMBERED ITEMS

Now it is obvious to you that you entered the topics in the wrong order. You want to present the information about the Foundation before information about how individuals can help. Just like a bulleted item, an item in a numbered list can be moved easily by selecting it and dragging it to a new location.

1

- Select the third item in the placeholder on slide 4.

- Drag the selection up to the beginning of the second line.

Your screen should be similar to Figure 1.33

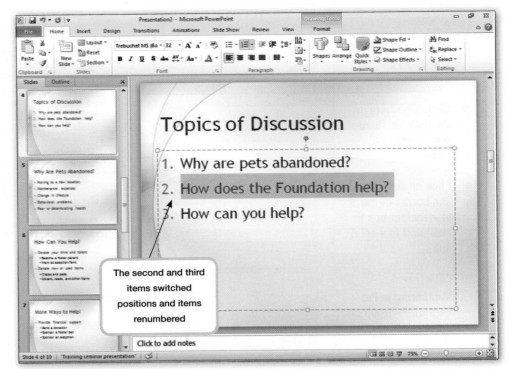

Figure 1.33

As soon as you clicked inside the placeholder, the cursor appeared and the solid-line border changed to a dashed-line border, indicating you can edit the contents of the placeholder. The third item in the numbered list is now the second item, and PowerPoint automatically renumbered the list for you.

Because you don't want to miss anything, you decide to go back and review the information you've entered so far. As you go back through the slides, you realize that you forgot to include the Animal Angels volunteer group as a topic to be discussed. You will add it to the Topics of Discussion slide as a subtopic below the "How can you help?" topic.

2

- Open the Outline tab to review the slide content.

- Click at the end of the third numbered list item on slide 4 and press Enter.

- Press Tab and type **Who are Animal Angels?**

Your screen should be similar to Figure 1.34

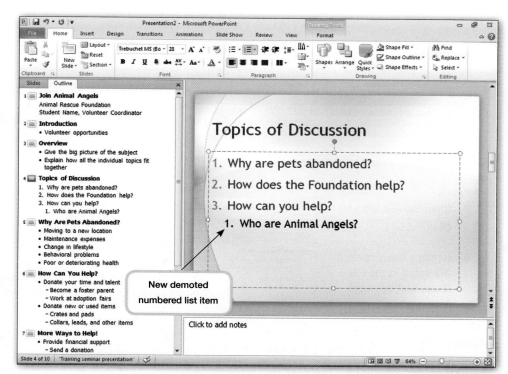

Figure 1.34

The numbering for the subtopic begins with one again. The new item is too important to be demoted on the list, so you decide to promote it and move it higher on the list.

3

- Select the entire fourth line.

- Press Shift + Tab to promote the fourth line.

- Drag the selected item to the beginning of the third line.

Your screen should be similar to Figure 1.35

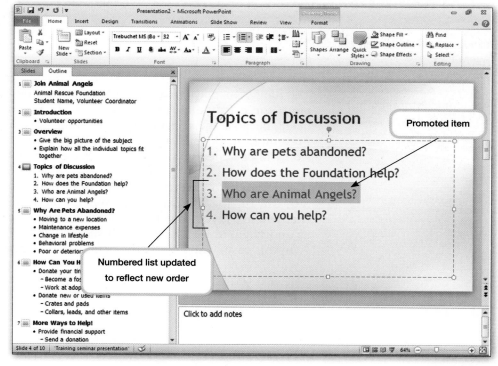

Figure 1.35

The numbered list has again been appropriately adjusted.

SAVING A PRESENTATION

You have just been notified about an important meeting that is to begin in a few minutes. Before leaving for the meeting, you want to save the presentation so that you don't lose your work.

The Save or Save As commands on the File tab are used to save files. When a presentation is saved for the first time, either command can be used to display the Save As dialog box, in which you specify the location to save the file and the file name.

Having Trouble?

See "Saving a File," in the Introduction to Microsoft Office 2010 to review this feature.

1

- Open the File tab and click ![Save As].

- Replace the proposed file name in the File Name text box with **Volunteer**

Having Trouble?

If you used the student data file pp01_ Training for this lab, choose Save As from the File tab. The file name in the Save As dialog box will be the name of the file you opened.

- Select the location where you will save your solution files.

Your screen should be similar to Figure 1.36

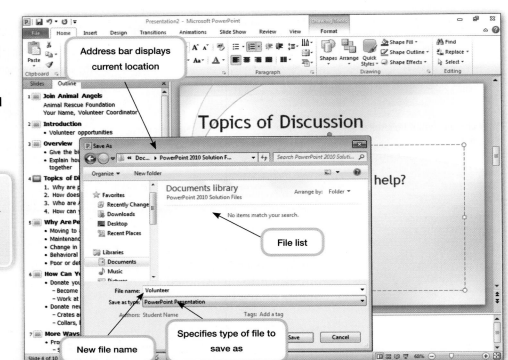

Figure 1.36

Additional Information

The file extensions may or may not be displayed, depending upon your Windows folder settings.

The file list displays folder names as well as the names of PowerPoint files (if any) stored in the current location. Only PowerPoint presentation files are listed, because the selected file type in the Save As Type list box is PowerPoint Presentation. Depending on what file type you choose, a different file extension will be added to the file name. Presentation files have a default file extension of .pptx.

You can also save PowerPoint presentations as an image file using the .gif, .tif, or .jpg file extension. When you save a presentation as an image file, you are given the choice to save the Current Slide Only or Every Slide as an image, in which case each slide will be saved as a separate image file.

In this case, you will use the default presentation file type (.pptx).

Click Save.

Your screen should be similar to Figure 1.37

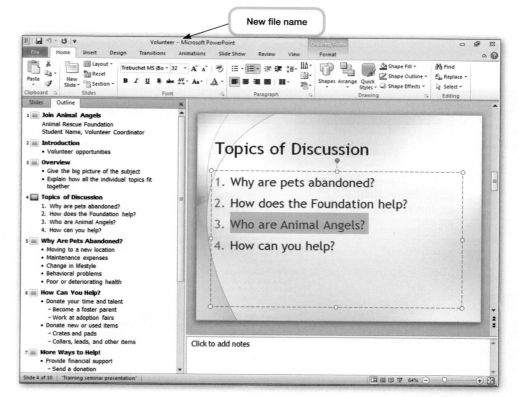

New file name

Figure 1.37

The presentation is now saved to the location you specified in a new file named Volunteer and the new file name is displayed in the application window title bar. The view in use at the time the file is saved also is saved with the file.

You are now ready to close the file.

Open the File tab and click  Close.

The presentation is closed, and an empty workspace is displayed. Always save your slide presentation before closing a file or leaving the PowerPoint program. As a safeguard against losing your work if you forget to save the presentation, PowerPoint will remind you to save any unsaved presentation before closing the file or exiting the program.

Opening an Existing Presentation

Additional Information

If you are ending your lab session now, open the File tab and click 🗙 Exit to exit the program.

After returning from your meeting, you continued to work on the presentation. You revised the content of several of the slides and added information for several new slides. Then you saved the presentation using a new file name. You will open this file to see the changes and will continue working on the presentation.

1

Open the File tab and click Open.

Another Method

The keyboard shortcut to open a file is Ctrl + O.

● If necessary, select the location containing your data files.

● Select pp01_Volunteer1.

Additional Information

You also can quickly open a recently used file by selecting it from the Recent Documents list in the File tab.

● Click Open ▾.

Another Method

You also could double-click the file name to both select it and choose Open ▾.

● Open the Outline tab.

● Replace "Your Name" in slide 1 with your name.

● Scroll the Outline tab to see the additional content that has been added to the presentation.

Your screen should be similar to Figure 1.38

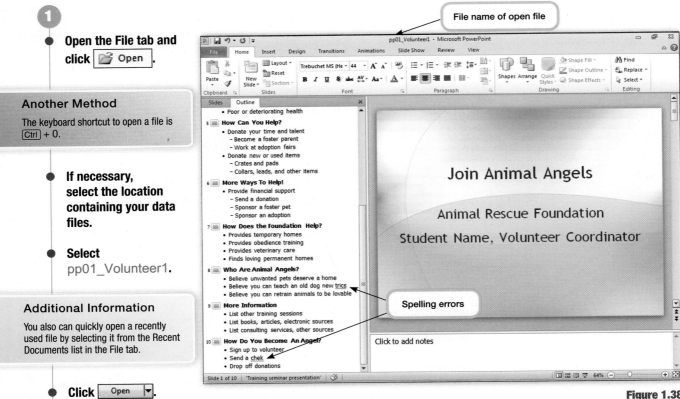

Figure 1.38

The presentation now contains 10 slides, and all the sample text has been replaced with text for the volunteer recruitment presentation, except for slide 9.

Using Spelling Checker

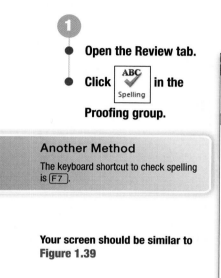

Additional Information

Unlike Word 2010, Powerpoint does not check for grammar errors.

As you entered the information on the additional slides, you left some typing errors uncorrected. To correct the misspelled words, you can use the shortcut menu to correct each individual word or error, as you learned earlier. However, in many cases, you may find it more efficient to wait until you are finished writing before you correct any spelling or grammatical errors. Rather than continually break your train of thought to correct errors as you type, you can check the spelling on all slides of the presentation at once by running the spelling checker.

1

● **Open the Review tab.**

● **Click** **[ABC Spelling]** **in the Proofing group.**

Another Method

The keyboard shortcut to check spelling is **[F7]**.

Your screen should be similar to Figure 1.39

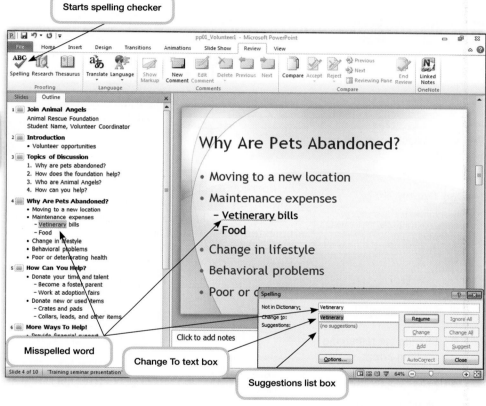

Figure 1.39

Additional Information

The spelling checker identifies many proper names and technical terms as misspelled. To stop this from occurring, use the Add Words To option to add those names to the custom dictionary.

The program jumps to slide 4; highlights the first located misspelled word, "Vetinerary," in the Outline pane; and opens the Spelling dialog box. The Spelling dialog box displays the misspelled word in the Not in Dictionary text box. The Suggestions list box typically displays the words the spelling checker has located in the dictionary that most closely match the misspelled word.

In this case, the spelling checker does not display any suggested replacements because it cannot locate any words in the dictionaries that are similar in spelling. If there are no suggestions, the Not in Dictionary text box simply displays the word that is highlighted in the text. When none of the suggestions is correct, you must edit the word yourself by typing the correction in the Change To text box.

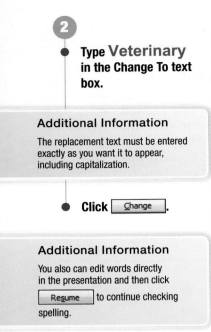

2

Type **Veterinary** in the Change To text box.

Additional Information

The replacement text must be entered exactly as you want it to appear, including capitalization.

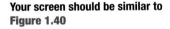

Click ___Change___.

Additional Information

You also can edit words directly in the presentation and then click ___Resume___ to continue checking spelling.

Your screen should be similar to Figure 1.40

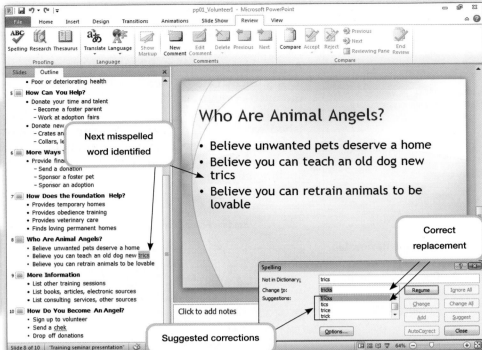

Figure 1.40

Having Trouble?

If necessary, move the dialog box by dragging its title bar to see the located misspelled word.

The corrected replacement is made in the slide. After the Spelling dialog box is open, the spelling checker continues to check the entire presentation for spelling errors. The next misspelled word, "trics," is identified. In this case, the suggested replacement is correct.

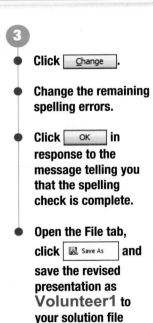

3

Click ___Change___.

Change the remaining spelling errors.

Click ___OK___ in response to the message telling you that the spelling check is complete.

Open the File tab, click ___Save As___ and save the revised presentation as **Volunteer1** to your solution file location.

Your screen should be similar to Figure 1.41

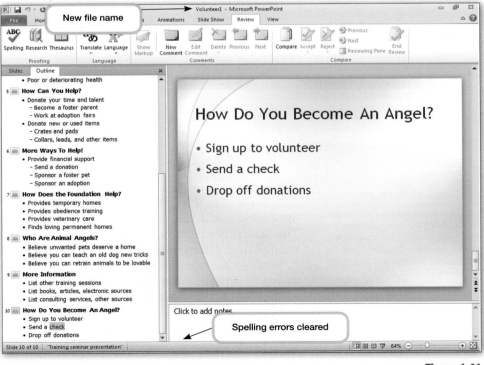

Figure 1.41

The Spelling indicator in the Status bar shows that all spelling errors have been resolved.

Using Slide Sorter View

To get a better overall picture of the presentation, you will switch to Slide Sorter view. This view displays thumbnail images of each slide in the work area and is particularly useful for rearranging slides to improve the flow and organization of the presentation. Clicking on a thumbnail selects the slide and makes it the current slide.

1

● **Click ⊞ Slide Sorter in the status bar.**

Having Trouble?

Pointing to a view button displays its name in a ScreenTip.

Another Method

You also could switch to Slide Sorter view by clicking [Slide Sorter] in the Presentation Views group of the View tab.

● **Set the zoom to 90%.**

● **Click on slide 1.**

Your screen should be similar to Figure 1.42

Having Trouble?

Do not be concerned if your screen displays a different number of slides per row. This is a function of the size of your monitor and your monitor settings.

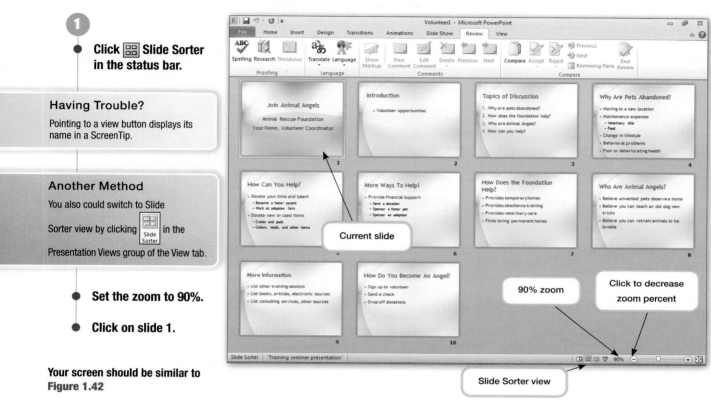

Figure 1.42

The currently selected slide, slide 1, appears with a yellow border around it. Viewing all the slides side by side helps you see how your presentation flows. You realize that the second slide is no longer necessary because you added your name to the opening slide. You also decide to delete slide 9 because you plan to add any necessary information to other slides. As you continue to look at the slides, you can now see that slides 7 and 8 are out of order and do not follow the sequence of topics in the Topics of Discussion slide.

SELECTING AND DELETING SLIDES

You will delete slides 2 and 9. In this view, it is easy to select and work with multiple slides at the same time. To select multiple slides, hold down Ctrl while clicking on each slide to select it.

- Select slide 2, hold down Ctrl, and click on slide 9.

- Press Delete.

- Increase the zoom to 100%.

Additional Information

You can use Delete to delete a slide in Slide Sorter view and in the Slides tab. However, in the Slide pane, using Delete deletes text or placeholder content.

Additional Information

The zoom setting for each view is set independently and remains in effect until changed to another zoom setting.

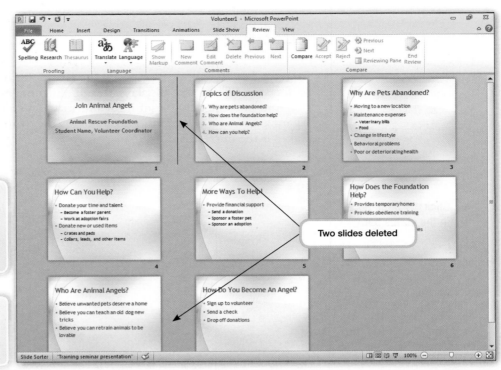

Figure 1.43

Your screen should be similar to Figure 1.43

The slides have been deleted, and all remaining slides have been appropriately renumbered.

MOVING SLIDES

Now you want to correct the organization of the slides by moving slides 6 and 7 before slide 4. To reorder a slide in Slide Sorter view, you drag it to its new location using drag and drop. As you drag the mouse, an indicator line appears to show you where the slide will appear in the presentation. When the indicator line is located where you want the slide to be placed, release the mouse button. You will select both slides and move them at the same time.

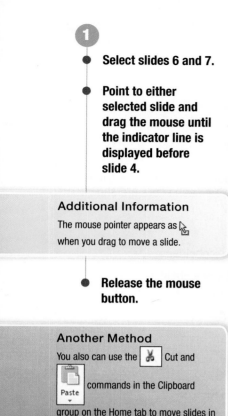

● **Select slides 6 and 7.**

● **Point to either selected slide and drag the mouse until the indicator line is displayed before slide 4.**

Additional Information

The mouse pointer appears as ⬚ when you drag to move a slide.

● **Release the mouse button.**

Another Method

You also can use the ✂ Cut and 📋 Paste commands in the Clipboard group on the Home tab to move slides in Slide Sorter view.

Your screen should be similar to Figure 1.44

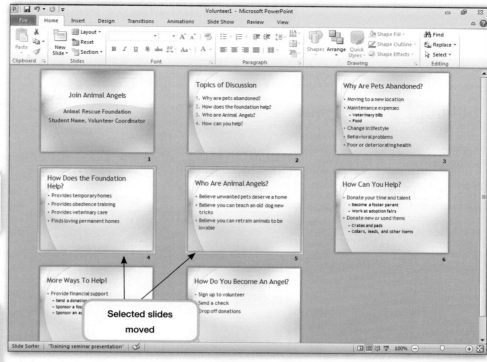

Figure 1.44

The slides now appear in the order in which you want them.

SELECTING A SLIDE LAYOUT

During your discussion with the foundation director, it was suggested that you add a slide showing the history of the organization. To include this information in the presentation, you will insert a new slide after slide 4.

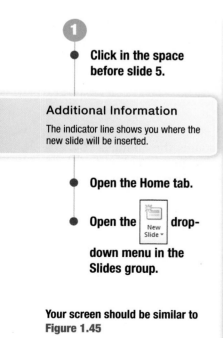

● **Click in the space before slide 5.**

Additional Information

The indicator line shows you where the new slide will be inserted.

● **Open the Home tab.**

● **Open the New Slide drop-down menu in the Slides group.**

Your screen should be similar to Figure 1.45

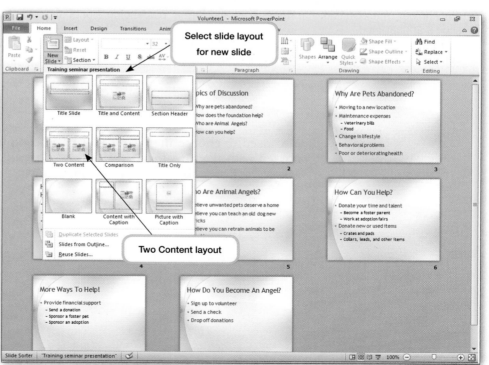

Figure 1.45

The drop-down menu displays 9 built-in slide layouts. The number of available layouts varies with the template you are using.

Concept 4 Layout

A layout defines the position and format for objects and text on a slide. Layouts provide placeholders for slide titles and slide content such as text, tables, diagrams, charts, or clip art. Many of these placeholders are shown in the following diagram.

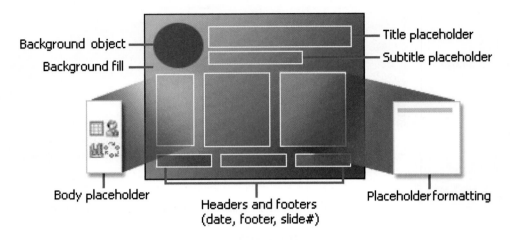

You can change the layout of an existing slide by selecting a new layout. If the new layout does not include placeholders for objects that are already on your slide (for example, if you created a chart and the new layout does not include a chart placeholder), you do not lose the information. All objects remain on the slide, and the selected layout is automatically adjusted by adding the appropriate type of placeholder for the object. Alternatively, as you add new objects to a slide, the layout automatically adjusts by adding the appropriate type of placeholder. You also can rearrange, size, and format placeholders on a slide any way you like to customize the slide's appearance.

To make creating slides easy, use the predefined layouts. The layouts help you keep your presentation format consistent and, therefore, more professional.

You need to choose the layout that best accommodates the changes you discussed with the director. Because this slide will contain two columns of text about the history of the organization, you will use the Two Content layout.

● **Choose Two Content.**

● **Double-click on the slide to switch back to Normal view.**

Additional Information
The current slide does not change when you switch views.

● **Open the Slides tab.**

Your screen should be similar to Figure 1.46

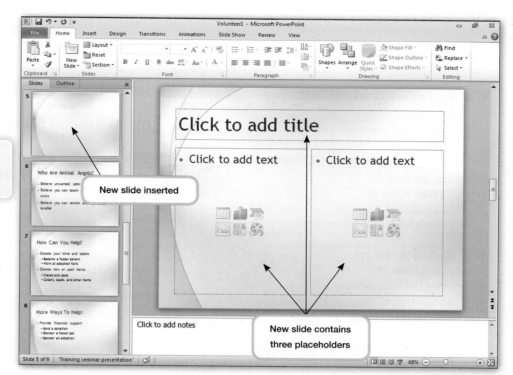

Figure 1.46

A new Two Content slide is inserted with the same design elements as the other slides in the presentation. The Two Content layout contains three place-holders, but unlike the template slides, the placeholders on the inserted slide do not contain sample text. When you select the placeholder, you can simply type in the text without having to select or delete any sample text.

CHANGING A PLACEHOLDER

You will add text to the slide presenting a brief history of the Animal Rescue Foundation. First, you will enter the slide title and then the list of dates and events.

1

- Click in the title placeholder.

- Type **Animal Rescue Foundation History**

- Use the AutoFit Options menu to fit the title to the placeholder.

- Click in the left text placeholder and enter the information shown below. Remember to press [Enter] to create a new line (except after the last entry).

   1995

   1996

   1997

   2005

- In the same manner, enter the following text in the right text placeholder:

   Founded by Steve Dow

   Built first shelter

   Began volunteer program

   Rescued 3000 animals!

Your screen should be similar to Figure 1.47

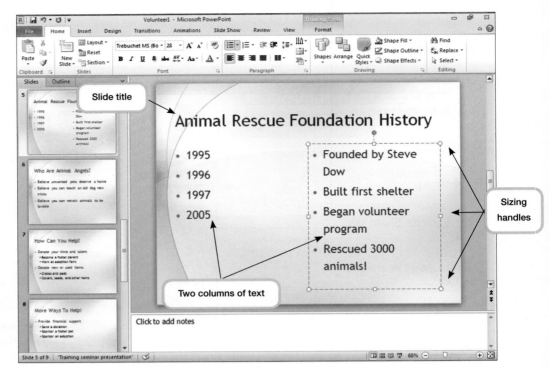

Figure 1.47

The left placeholder is too big for its contents and the right is too small, forcing some items to wrap to a second line. To correct the size, you can adjust the size of the placeholders.

SIZING A PLACEHOLDER

The four circles and squares that appear at the corners and sides of a selected placeholder's border are **sizing handles** that can be used to adjust the size of the placeholder. Dragging the corner sizing handles will adjust both the height and width at the same time, whereas the center handles adjust the associated side borders. When you point to the sizing handle, the mouse pointer appears as ⤢, indicating the direction in which you can drag the border to adjust the size.

1

- On the right placeholder, drag the left-center sizing handle to the left until each item appears on one line.

- Select the left text placeholder and drag the right-center sizing handle to the left (see Figure 1.48).

- With the left placeholder still selected, hold down [Shift] while clicking on the right placeholder border to select both.

- Use the bottom-middle sizing handle to decrease the height of the placeholders to fit the text.

Your screen should be similar to Figure 1.48

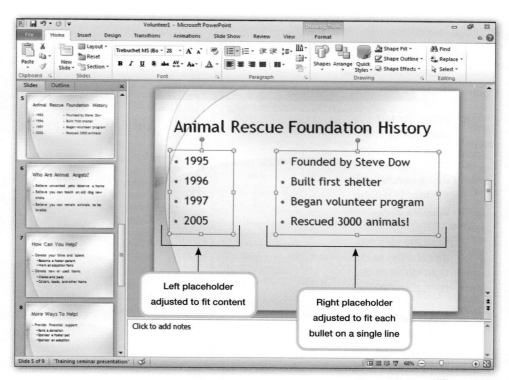

Figure 1.48

MOVING A PLACEHOLDER

Next, you want to decrease the blank space between the two columns. Then you want to move both placeholders so they appear more centered in the space. An object can be moved anywhere on a slide by dragging the placeholder's border. The mouse pointer appears as ✛ when you can move a placeholder. As you drag the placeholder, an opaque white copy of the placeholder is displayed to show your new location.

1

- Click outside the placeholders to clear the selection.

- Select the left placeholder and point to the edge of the placeholder (not a handle) until the mouse pointer appears as .

- Drag the selected placeholder to the right closer to the right placeholder.

- Select both placeholders and drag to center them horizontally in the slide as shown in Figure 1.49.

- Save your changes to the presentation.

Your screen should be similar to Figure 1.49

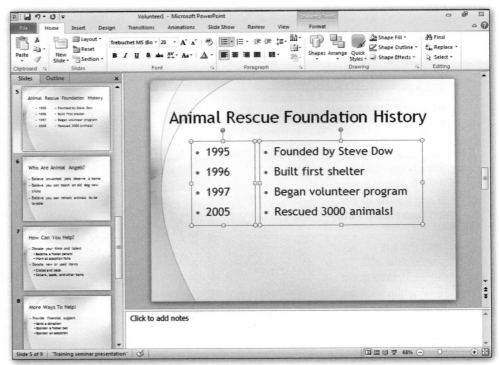

Figure 1.49

ADDING AND REMOVING BULLETS

Next, you want to remove the bullets from the items on the history slide. You can quickly apply and remove bullets using ⬚▾ Bullets in the Paragraph group on the Home tab. This button applies the bullet style associated with the design template you are using. Because the placeholder items already include bullets, using this button will remove them.

1

- With both text placeholders still selected, click ⬚▾ Bullets from the Paragraph group in the Home tab to remove all bullets.

Your screen should be similar to Figure 1.50

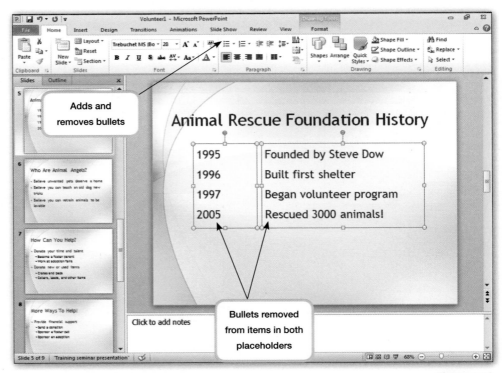

Figure 1.50

The bullets are removed from all the items in both placeholders. Now, however, you think it would look better to add bullets back to the years in the first column.

2

● Select the four years in the left column.

● Click ☰ ▾ **Bullets** from the Paragraph group in the Home tab.

● Click outside the selected placeholder to deselect it.

● Save the presentation again.

Your screen should be similar to Figure 1.51

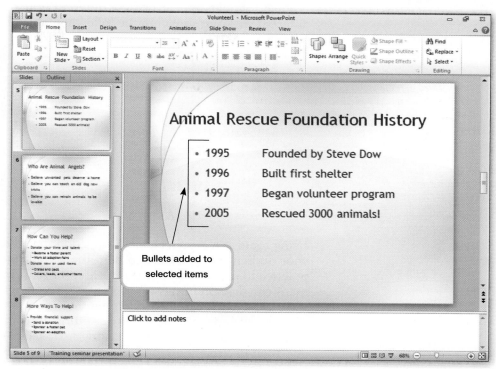

Figure 1.51

Bullets appear before the selected text items only.

Formatting Slide Text

The next change you want to make to the presentation is to improve the appearance of the title slide. Although the design template you are using already includes many formatting features, you want this slide to have more impact.

Applying different formatting to characters and paragraphs can greatly enhance the appearance of the slide. **Character formatting** features affect the selected characters only. They include changing the character style and size, applying effects such as bold and italics, changing the character spacing, and adding animated text effects. **Paragraph formatting** features affect an entire paragraph. A paragraph is text that has an [Enter] at the end of it. Each item in a bulleted list, title, and subtitle is a paragraph. Paragraph formatting features include the position of the paragraph or its alignment between the margins, paragraph indentation, spacing above and below a paragraph, and line spacing within a paragraph.

CHANGING FONTS

First, you will improve the appearance of the presentation title by changing the font of the title text. There are two basic types of fonts: serif and sans serif. **Serif fonts** have a flair at the base of each letter that visually leads the reader to the next letter. Two common serif fonts are Roman and Times New Roman.

Having Trouble?

Refer to the section "Formatting Text" in the Introduction to Microsoft Office 2010 to review this feature.

Serif fonts generally are used for text in paragraphs. **Sans serif fonts** do not have a flair at the base of each letter. Arial and Helvetica are two common sans serif fonts. Because sans serif fonts have a clean look, they are often used for headings in documents.

Each font can appear using a different font size. Several common fonts in different sizes are shown in the following table.

Font Name	Font Type	Font Size
Calibri	Sans serif	This is 10 pt. This is 16 pt.
Courier New	Serif	This is 10 pt. This is 16 pt.
Garamond	Serif	This is 10 pt. This is 16 pt.

Using fonts as a design element can add interest to your presentation and give your audience visual cues to help them find information quickly. It is good practice to use only two or three different fonts in a presentation, because too many can distract from your presentation content and can look unprofessional.

To change the font before typing the text, use the command and then type. All text will appear in the specified setting until another font setting is selected. To change a font setting for existing text, select the text you want to change and then use the command. If you want to apply font formatting to a word, simply move the insertion point to the word and the formatting is automatically applied to the entire word.

Additional Information

The font used in the title is Trebuchet MS (Headings), as displayed in the `Trebuchet MS (He ▾)` Font button. It is automatically used in all headings in this template.

The `Trebuchet MS (He ▾)` Font button in the Font tab or on the Mini toolbar that appears when you select text is used to change the font style. As you select a font from the drop-down menu, a live preview of how the selected font will appear is displayed in the document.

1

- Select the text "Join Animal Angels" in the Slide pane on slide 1.

- Open the Font drop-down list in the Mini toolbar.

- Point to several fonts to see the live preview.

Having Trouble?

Refer to the section "Using the Mini Toolbar" in the Introduction to Microsoft Office 2010 to review this feature.

Additional Information

The Live Preview feature is also available with many other formatting features.

Your screen should be similar to Figure 1.52

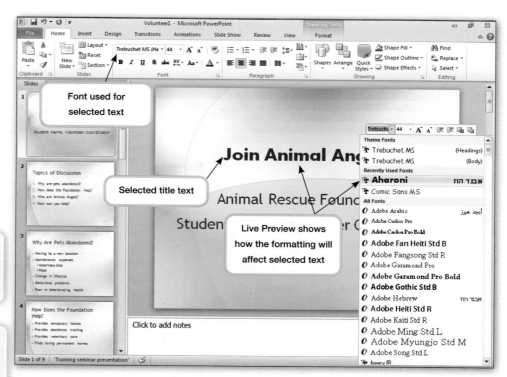

Figure 1.52

The selected text in the document appears in the font style you have selected in the menu. With Live Preview, you can see how the text will look with the selected font before you click the one that you want. You want to change the font to a design that has a less serious appearance.

2

- Scroll the menu and choose Comic Sans MS.

Another Method

You also could use Trebuchet MS (He ▾) Font in the Font group of the Home tab to change the font.

Your screen should be similar to Figure 1.53

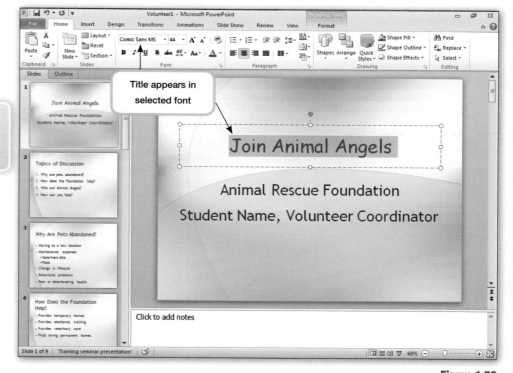

Figure 1.53

The text has changed to the new font style, and the Font button displays the font name used in the current selection.

CHANGING FONT SIZE

The title text is also a little smaller than you want it to be.

- Open the `44` Font Size drop-down list on the Mini toolbar.

Having Trouble?
If the Mini toolbar is no longer displayed, right click on the selection to display it again.

- Point to several different sizes to see how the font size changes using Live Preview.

- Scroll the list and choose 60.

Another Method
You also could use `44` Font Size in the Font group.

Another Method
Using `A` Increase Font Size in the Font group or the Mini toolbar will incrementally increase the font size. The keyboard shortcut is Ctrl + Shift + >.

Your screen should be similar to Figure 1.54

Additional Information
Use `A` Decrease Font Size or Ctrl + Shift + < to incrementally decrease the point size of selected text.

Additional Information
If a selection includes text in several different sizes, the smallest size appears in the Font Size button followed by a plus sign.

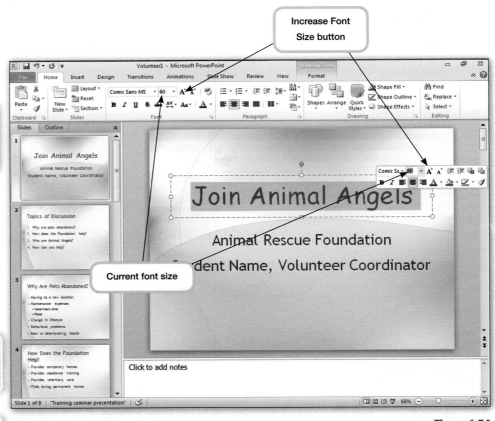

Figure 1.54

The font size increased from 44 points to 60 points. The Font Size button displays the point size of the current selection.

APPLYING TEXT EFFECTS

Next, you want to further enhance the title slide by adding **text effects** such as color and shadow to the title and subtitle. The table below describes some of the effects and their uses. The Home tab and the Mini toolbar contain buttons for many of the formatting effects.

Format	Example	Use
Bold, italic	***Bold Italic***	Adds emphasis
Underline	<u>Underline</u>	Adds emphasis
Superscript	"To be or not to be."[1]	Used in footnotes and formulas
Subscript	H_2O	Used in formulas
Shadow	**Shadow**	Adds distinction to titles and headings
Color	**Color Color Color**	Adds interest

You decide to add color and a shadow effect to the main title first.

1

- If necessary, select the title text.

- Click **S** Text Shadow in the Font group.

Additional Information

Many formatting commands are toggle commands. This means the feature can be turned on and off simply by clicking on the command button.

- Open the **A ▾** Font Color menu to display a gallery of colors.

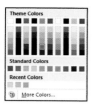

- Choose Green, Accent 1, Darker 25% in the Theme Colors section.

Additional Information

A ScreenTip displays the name of the color when selected.

Additional Information

You will learn about themes in Lab 2.

- Click the subtitle placeholder to select it.

Your screen should be similar to Figure 1.55

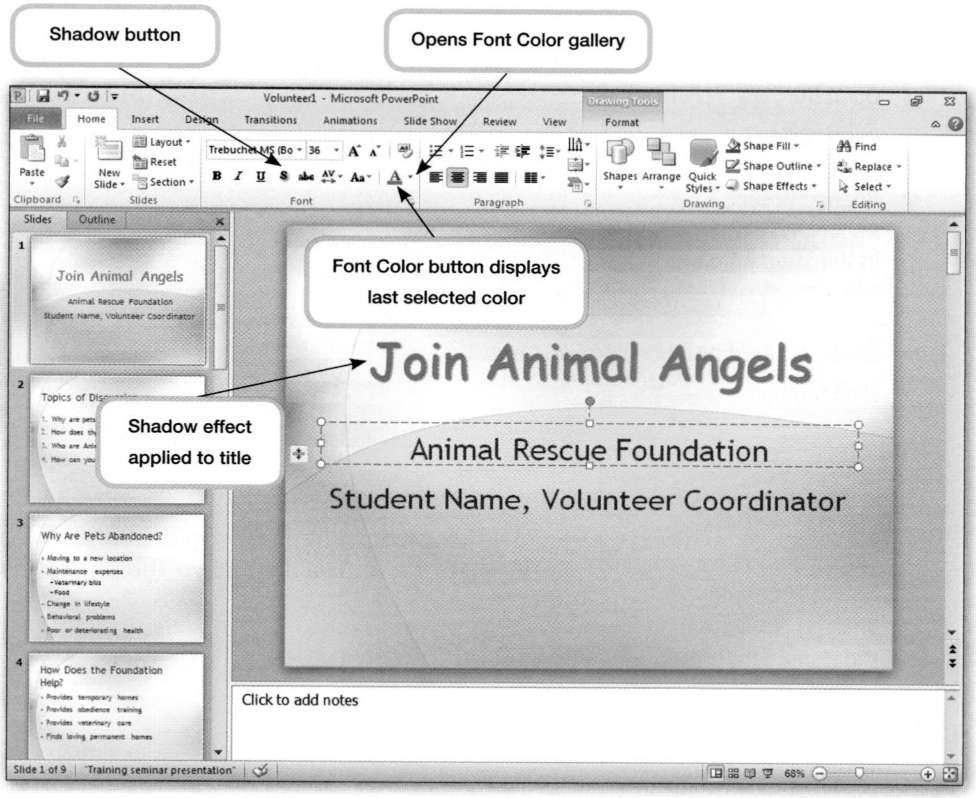

Figure 1.55

The selected color and slight shadow effect make the title much more interesting. Also notice the color in the Font Color button is the green color you just selected. This color can be quickly reapplied to other selections now simply by clicking the button.

Next you will enhance the two subtitle lines. Notice that the subtitle placeholder box does not include the second subtitle line. Although the second line was included in the placeholder when it was moved to this slide, the placeholder did not automatically increase in size to accommodate the new text. You will increase the size of the placeholder to visually include this text.

2

- Drag the bottom-middle sizing handle down to increase the size of the placeholder to include both subtitle lines.

- Select the text "Animal Rescue Foundation".

- Open the 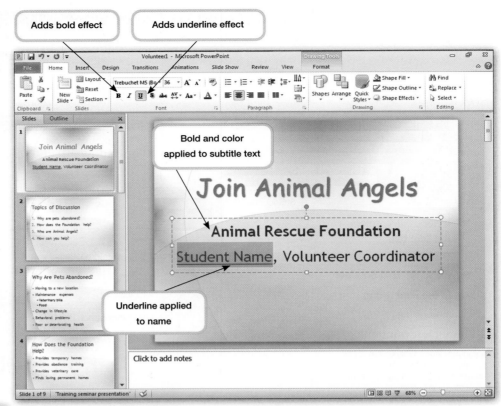 Font Color gallery.

- Choose Green, Accent 1, Darker 50% in the Theme Colors section.

- Click **B** Bold on the Mini toolbar.

Another Method

The keyboard shortcut is Ctrl + B.

- Select your name and click **U** Underline on the Home tab.

Another Method

The keyboard shortcut is Ctrl + U.

Your screen should be similar to Figure 1.56

Figure 1.56

After reviewing your changes, you decide that underlining your name doesn't have the right look. You'll italicize the entire line instead and make the font smaller.

3

- Click ⟨U⟩ Underline.

- Select the entire second line of the subtitle.

- Click ⟨I⟩ Italic.

- Click ⟨A⟩ Decrease Font Size three times.

- Click somewhere outside the placeholder.

Your screen should be similar to Figure 1.57

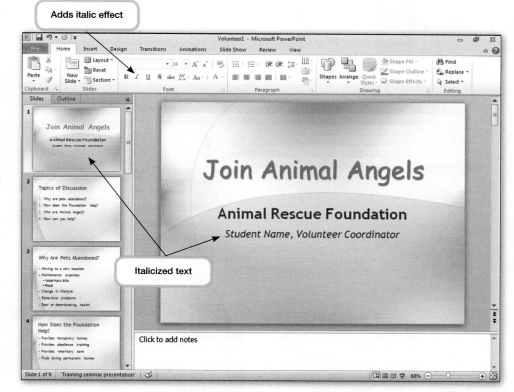

Figure 1.57

Now the title slide has much more impact.

Working with Graphics

Finally, you want to add a picture to the presentation. A picture is one of several different graphic objects that can be added to a slide.

Concept ⑤ Graphics

A **graphic** is a nontext element or object, such as a drawing or picture, that can be added to a slide. A graphic can be a simple drawing object consisting of shapes such as lines and boxes. A **drawing object** is part of your presentation document. A **picture** is an image such as a graphic illustration or a scanned photograph. Pictures are graphics that were created from another program and are inserted in a slide as **embedded objects**. An embedded object becomes part of the presentation file and can be opened and edited using the **source program**, the program in which it was created. Any changes made to the embedded object are not made to the original picture file because they are independent. Several examples of drawing objects and pictures are shown below.

Photograph

Graphic illustration

Drawing object

Add graphics to your presentation to help the audience understand concepts, to add interest, and to make your presentation stand out from others.

Graphic files can be obtained from a variety of sources. Many simple drawings called **clip art** are available in the Clip Organizer, a Microsoft Office tool that arranges and catalogs clip art and other media files stored on the computer's hard disk. The Clip Organizer's files, or clips, include art, sound, animation, and movies you can add to a presentation. Additionally, if you are connected to the Internet, Microsoft's Office.com Web site is automatically accessed for even more graphics.

Digital images created using a digital camera are one of the most common types of graphic files. You also can create graphic files using a scanner to convert any printed document, including photographs, to an electronic format. Most images that are scanned and inserted into documents are stored as Windows bitmap files (.bmp). All types of graphics, including clip art, photographs, and other types of images, can be found on the Internet. These files are commonly stored as .jpg or .pcx files. Keep in mind that any images you locate on the Internet may be protected by copyright and should only be used with permission. You also can purchase CDs containing graphics for your use.

Additional Information

When your computer is connected to a scanner, you also can scan a picture and insert it directly into a slide without saving it as a file first.

INSERTING A GRAPHIC FROM THE CLIP ORGANIZER

You want to add a graphic to the second slide. First you decide to check the Clip Art gallery to see if you can find an image that will work as an attention getter. The Insert tab includes commands that are designed to enhance a presentation by adding features such as shapes and illustrations to movies and sounds.

1

- Select slide 2.

- Open the Insert tab.

- Click Clip Art.

Having Trouble?

Your Clip Art task pane may already display graphics if this feature was previously used while the application was still running.

Your screen should be similar to Figure 1.58

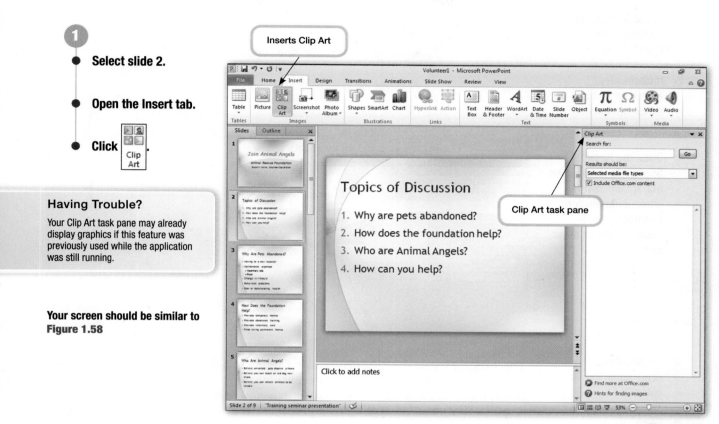

Figure 1.58

In the Clip Art task pane, you enter a word or phrase that is representative of the type of picture you want to locate. You also can specify the location to search and the type of media files, such as clip art, movies, photographs, or sound, to display in the search results. Since each of the items on this slide is a question, you decide to look for graphics of question marks.

2

- If necessary, select any existing text in the Search For text box.

- In the Search For text box, type **question**

- If necessary, select the Include Office.com content check box.

- Open the Results Should Be drop-down list, if necessary, choose Illustrations to select it, and deselect the all other options.

Having Trouble?

Click the box next to an option to select or deselect (clear the checkmark).

- Click outside the drop-down list to close it.

- Click [Go].

Having Trouble?

If your thumbnails appear in a single column, increase the width of your task pane by dragging the left edge of the pane until two columns are displayed.

Having Trouble?

Do not worry if the thumbnails displayed on your screen do not match those shown in Figure 1.59, because the online clip art is continuously changing.

Your screen should be similar to Figure 1.59

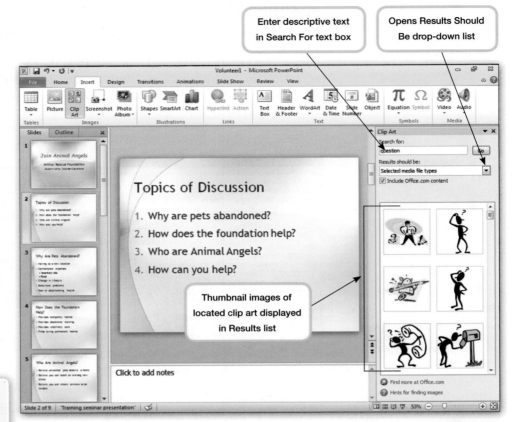

Enter descriptive text in Search For text box

Opens Results Should Be drop-down list

Thumbnail images of located clip art displayed in Results list

Figure 1.59

The program searches the Microsoft Clip Organizer on your computer and, if an Internet connection is established, searches Microsoft's Office.com Web site for clip art and graphics that match your search term. The Results list displays thumbnails of all located graphics. The pictures stored on your computer in the Microsoft Clip Art gallery appear first in the results list, followed by the Office Online clip art.

Pointing to a thumbnail displays a ScreenTip containing the **keywords**, descriptive words or phrases, associated with the graphic and other information about the picture properties. It also displays a drop-down list bar that accesses the item's shortcut menu. The shortcut menu commands are used to work with and manage the items in the Clip Organizer. Because it is sometimes difficult to see the graphic in the thumbnail, you can preview it in a larger size.

- **Scroll the Results list to view additional images.**

- **Point to any graphic and click ⊡ to open the thumbnail menu.**

- **Choose Preview/ Properties.**

Your screen should be similar to Figure 1.60

Having Trouble?

Do not worry if your preview image does not match Figure 1.60. It will only match if you selected the same graphic in the results area.

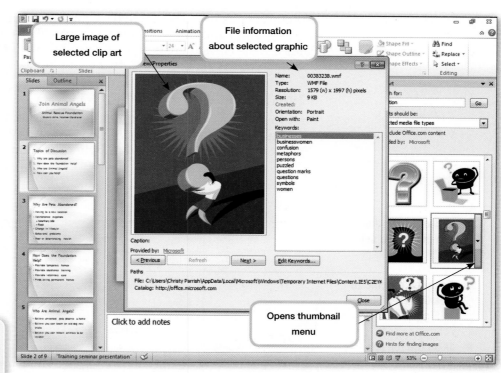

Figure 1.60

The Preview/Properties dialog box displays the selected graphic in a larger size so it is easier to see. It also displays more information about the properties associated with the graphic. Notice the search word you entered appears as one of the keywords. Now you will scroll the results list of graphics to find one you like.

④

- **Click [Close] to close the dialog box.**

- **Scroll the Results list to locate the graphic shown in Figure 1.61.**

- **Click on the graphic to insert it in the slide.**

Another Method

You also could choose Insert from the thumbnail's shortcut menu to insert the graphic.

Your screen should be similar to Figure 1.61

Having Trouble?

If this graphic is not available in the Clip Organizer, just choose a question mark graphic that you like from the results list.

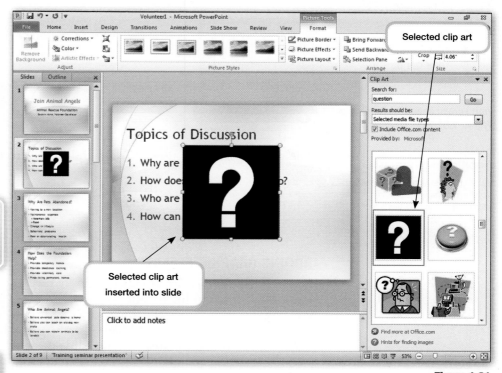

Figure 1.61

The clip art image is inserted in the center of the slide on top of the text. It is a selected object and can be sized and moved like any other selected object. The Picture Tools Format tab is automatically displayed in the Ribbon, in anticipation that you may want to modify the graphic.

SIZING AND MOVING A GRAPHIC

First you need to size and position the picture on the slide. A graphic object is sized and moved just like a placeholder. You want to decrease the graphic size slightly and move it to the bottom right of the slide.

1

- If necessary, click on the graphic to select it.

- Drag the graphic to position it as shown in Figure 1.62.

- Drag the top left corner sizing handle inward to decrease its size to that shown in Figure 1.62.

Additional Information

To maintain an object's proportions while resizing it, hold down (Shift) while dragging the sizing handle.

- Close the Clip Art task pane.

Your screen should be similar to Figure 1.62

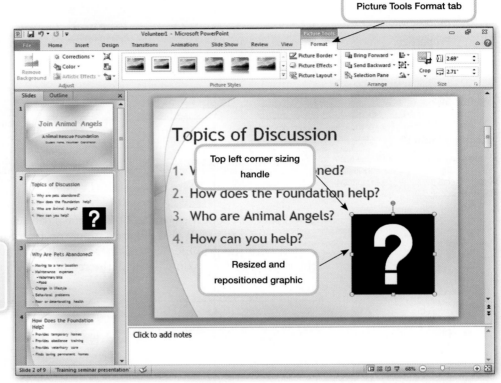

Figure 1.62

Additional Information

Be careful when increasing the size of a picture (bitmap) image, as it can lose sharpness and appear blurry if enlarged too much.

The clip art image is now smaller and placed in the correct position on the slide.

ADDING GRAPHIC EFFECTS

You can use the picture effects on the Picture Tools Format tab to customize the look of the graphic to suit your presentation. There are many effects that you can use to improve the appearance of graphics in your presentation. The first enhancement you would like to make is to change the color of the question mark so it coordinates with the slide design.

1

- With the clip art selected, click Color in the Adjust group of the Picture Tools Format tab.

- Point to the choices in the Recolor gallery to see live previews.

- Choose Light Green, Accent Color 5 Dark from the gallery (second row, fifth column).

Your screen should be similar to Figure 1.63

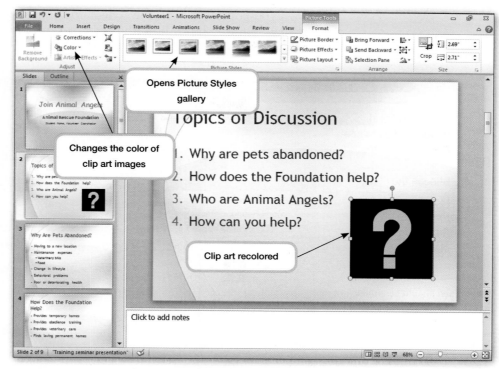

Figure 1.63

Next, you want to enhance the graphic by applying a picture style to it. **A style** is a combination of formatting options that can be applied in one easy step. In the case of **picture styles**, the combinations consist of border, shadow, and shape effects. You also can create your own picture style effects by selecting specific style elements, such as borders and shadows, individually using the Picture Border, Picture Effects, and Picture Layout commands.

2

- Click ▾ More in the Picture Styles group to open the Picture Styles gallery.

Your screen should be similar to Figure 1.64

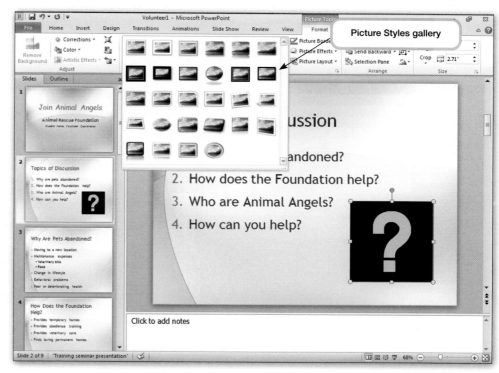

Figure 1.64

Working with Graphics   **PP1.59**

When you point to a style, the style name appears in a ScreenTip, and the Live Preview feature shows how the selected graphic will look with the selected picture style.

3

● **Point to several picture styles to see the live previews.**

● **Choose the** 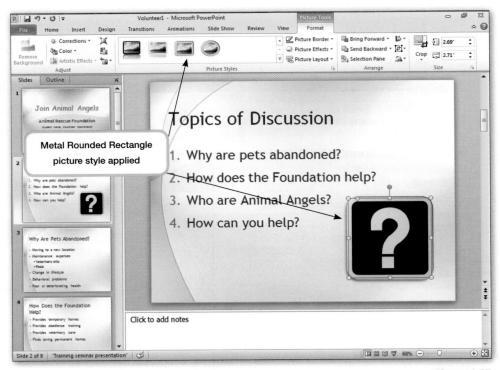 **Metal Rounded Rectangle style (bottom row, third column).**

Your screen should be similar to Figure 1.65

Figure 1.65

As you look at the picture, you decide to remove the rectangle and use the oval shape with the thin black border instead. You will then modify the picture style by changing the border color and removing the reflection.

4

● Choose the 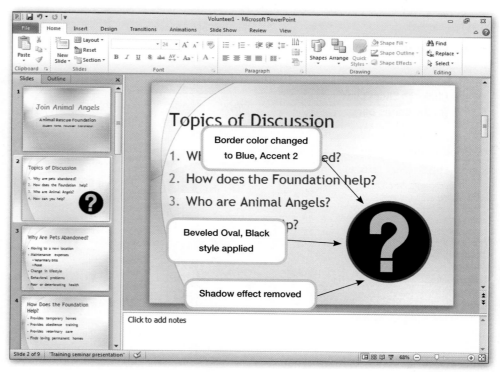 Beveled Oval, Black style in the Picture Styles gallery.

● Click Picture Border ▾ in the Picture Styles group.

● Choose Blue, Accent 2 from the Theme Colors group.

● Click Picture Effects ▾ in the Picture Styles group.

● From the Shadow group, choose No Shadow.

● Click outside the graphic to deselect the object.

Your screen should be similar to Figure 1.66

Figure 1.66

The addition of a customized graphic image gives your presentation a more polished look. Now that the slides are in the order you want and formatted, you would like to see how the presentation will look when viewed by an audience.

Rehearsing a Presentation

Rather than projecting the presentation on a large screen as you would to present it for an audience, a simple way to rehearse a presentation is to view it on your computer screen as a **slide show**. A slide show displays each slide full screen and in order. While the slide show is running during this rehearsal, you can plan what you will say while each slide is displayed.

USING SLIDE SHOW VIEW

When you view a slide show, each slide fills the screen, hiding the PowerPoint application window, so you can view the slides as your audience would. You will begin the slide show starting with the first slide.

Select slide 1 in the Slides tab.

Click Slide Show (in the status bar).

Additional Information

Using Slide Show runs the slide show beginning with the currently selected slide.

Another Method

You also can use or on the Slide Show tab or the shortcut keys F5 and Shift + F5, respectively, to start the slide show.

Your screen should be similar to Figure 1.67

First slide of the presentation displayed full screen

Join Animal Angels

Animal Rescue Foundation

Student Name, Volunteer Coordinator

Figure 1.67

The presentation title slide is displayed full screen, as it will appear when projected on a screen using computer projection equipment. The easiest way to see the next slide is to click the mouse button. You also can use the keys shown below to move to the next or previous slide.

Next Slide	Previous Slide
Spacebar	Backspace
Enter	
→	←
↓	↑
Page Down	Page Up
N (for Next)	P (for Previous)

You also can select Next, Previous, or Last Viewed from the shortcut menu. Additionally, moving the mouse pointer to the lower-left corner of the window in Slide Show displays the Slide Show toolbar. Clicking ⬅ or ➡ moves to the previous or next slide, and 🔲 opens the shortcut menu.

● Click to display the
next slide.

● Using each of the
methods described,
slowly display the
entire presentation.

● When the last slide
displays a black
window, click again
to end the slide show.

Additional Information

You can press Esc or use End Show on
the shortcut menu at any time to end
the slide show.

Your screen should be similar to
Figure 1.68

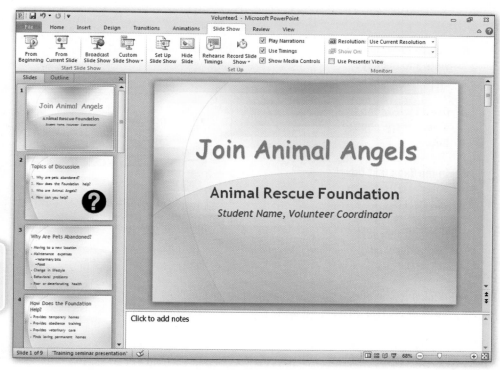

Figure 1.68

After the last slide is displayed, the program returns to the view you were last
using, in this case, Normal view.

Documenting a File

Having Trouble?

Refer to the section "Specifying
Document Properties" in the
Introduction to Microsoft Office 2010 to
review this feature.

Finally, you want to update the presentation file properties by adding your
name as the author, and a tag. The default title does not need to be changed.

- **Return to Normal view and display slide 1, if necessary.**

- **Open the File tab and, if necessary, choose Info.**

- **In the Tags text box, enter Volunteer, Recruit**

- **In the Author text box, enter your name**

- **Click anywhere outside the text box.**

Your screen should be similar to Figure 1.69

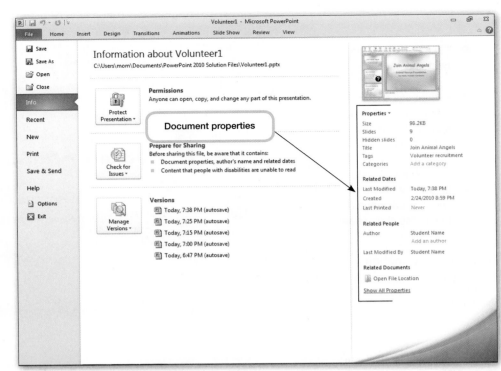

Figure 1.69

Previewing and Printing the Presentation

Although you still plan to make many changes to the presentation, you want to provide a printed copy of the presentation to the foundation director to get feedback regarding the content and layout.

PRINTING A SLIDE

Having Trouble?

Refer to the section "Printing a Document" in the Introduction to Microsoft Office 2010 to review basic printing features.

Although your presentation looks good on your screen, it may not look good when printed. Shading, patterns, and backgrounds that look good on the screen can make your printed output unreadable. Fortunately, PowerPoint displays a preview of how your printed output will appear as you specify the print settings. This allows you to make changes to the print settings before printing and reduces unnecessary paper waste.

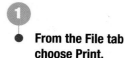

1 ● From the File tab choose Print.

Your screen should be similar to Figure 1.70

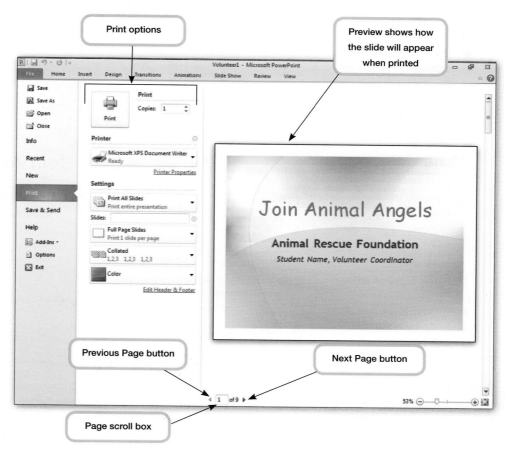

Figure 1.70

The Print window displays the print options in the left pane that are used to modify the default print settings. The preview area displays the first slide in the presentation as it will appear when printed using the current settings. It appears in color if your selected printer is a color printer; otherwise, it appears in grayscale (shades of gray). Even if you have a color printer, you can print the slides in grayscale or pure black and white. You want to print using the black and white option. The page scroll box shows the page number of the page you are currently viewing and the number of total pages. The scroll buttons on either side are used to scroll to the next and previous page.

The other change you want to make to the print settings is to only print the first slide in the presentation. To do this, you will change the settings to print the current slide only.

Additional Information

Use grayscale when your slides include patterns whose colors you want to appear in shades of gray.

2

- If you need to select a different printer, open the Printer drop-down list and select the appropriate printer.

- Click  in the Settings group.

- Choose **Pure Black and White.**

- Click  in the Settings area.

- Choose **Print Current Slide** from the submenu.

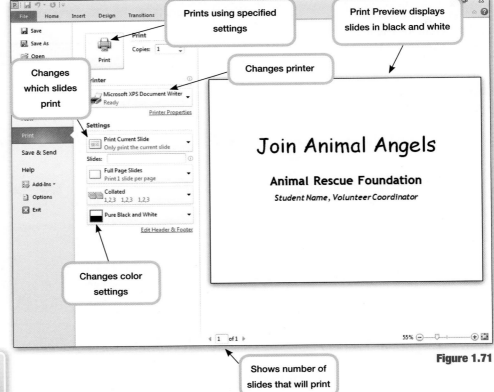

Figure 1.71

Another Method

You could also type **1** in the Slides text box to select only the title slide.

Your screen should be similar to Figure 1.71

The preview area displays how the slide will look when printed in black and white. Notice the page scroll box in the preview area now show 1 of 1, indicating that only the first slide will be printed.

Additional Information

Please consult your instructor for printing procedures that may differ from the following directions.

3

- If necessary, make sure your printer is on and ready to print.

A printing progress bar appears in the status bar, indicating that the program is sending data to the printer and the title slide should be printing.

- Click **Print.**

PRINTING HANDOUTS

You also can change the type of printed output from full page slides to any one of the output settings described in the table below. Only one type of output can be printed at a time.

Additional Information

You will learn about notes in Lab 2.

Output Type	Description
Full Page Slides	Prints one slide on a page.
Notes Pages	Prints the slide and the associated notes on a page.
Outline	Prints the slide content as it appears in Outline view.
Handouts	Prints multiple slides on a page.

To help the foundation's director get a better feel for the flow of the presentation, you decide to also print out the presentation as a handout. The handout format will allow him to see each slide as it appears onscreen.

1

● **Open the File menu and choose Print.**

● **Click** Print Current Slide / Only print the current slide **in the Settings area and choose Print All Slides.**

● **Click** Full Page Slides / Print 1 slide per page **in the Settings area and choose** 6 Slides Vertical **.**

Your screen should be similar to Figure 1.72

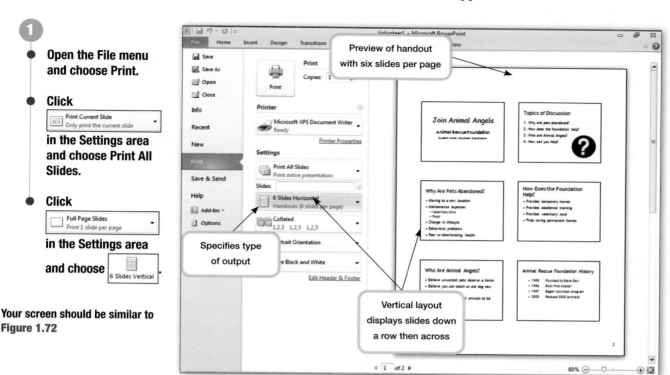

Figure 1.72

Additional Information

The Orientation setting will override the Slide Layout setting. So, even if you leave the Slide Layout setting as 6 Slides Vertical, the presentation will print horizontal to match the Orientation setting.

The preview area shows the handouts as they will print. The vertical arrangement of the slides displays the slides down a row and then across. You decide to change the orientation from the default of portrait to landscape so that the slides print across the length of the paper, to change the arrangement to horizontal, and also to increase the number of slides per page so that the entire presentation fits on one page.

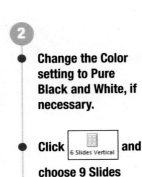

2 ● Change the Color setting to Pure Black and White, if necessary.

● Click  and choose 9 Slides Horizontal.

● Click

[Portrait Orientation ▾]

and choose Landscape Orientation.

Your screen should be similar to Figure 1.73

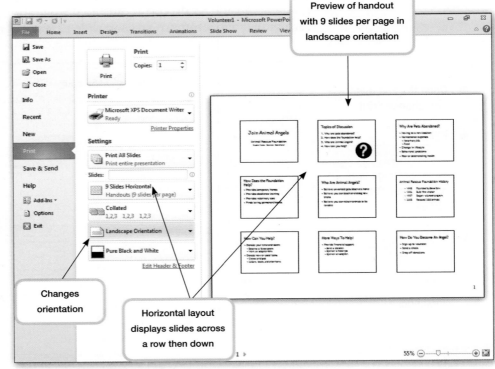

Figure 1.73

The preview area reflects your changes to the print settings. The horizontal layout displays the slides in order across a row and then down, making the presentation easier to follow.

3 ● Click [Print] Print.

Your printed output should be similar to that shown in the Case Study at the beginning of the lab.

PRINTING AN OUTLINE

The final item you want to print is an outline of the presentation. An outline will make it easier for the director to provide feedback on the overall organization of the presentation.

1

- Open the File tab and choose Print.

- Change the Color setting to Pure Black and White again, if necessary.

- Change the orientation to Portrait Orientation.

- Click and choose .

- Ensure that the correct printer is selected and ready and click [Print] .

The printed outline will be a two-page document that looks similar to the preview.

Exiting PowerPoint

Another Method

You also can exit PowerPoint using ☒ Exit in the File tab.

You have finished working on the presentation for now and will exit the PowerPoint program.

1

- Click ☒ Close in the title bar.

- If asked to save the file again, click [Save] .

FOCUS ON CAREERS

EXPLORE YOUR CAREER OPTIONS

Account Executive

Sales is an excellent entry point for a solid career in any company. Account executive is just one of many titles that a sales professional may have; field sales and sales representative are two other titles. Account executives take care of customers by educating them on the company's latest products, designing solutions using the company's product line, and closing the deal to make the sale and earn their commission. These tasks require the use of effective PowerPoint presentations that educate and motivate potential customers. The salary range of an account executive is limited only by his or her ambition; salaries range from $30,000 to more than $120,540. To learn more about this career, visit the Web site for the Bureau of Labor Statistics of the U.S. Department of Labor.

Slide (PP1.6)

A slide is an individual "page" of your presentation.

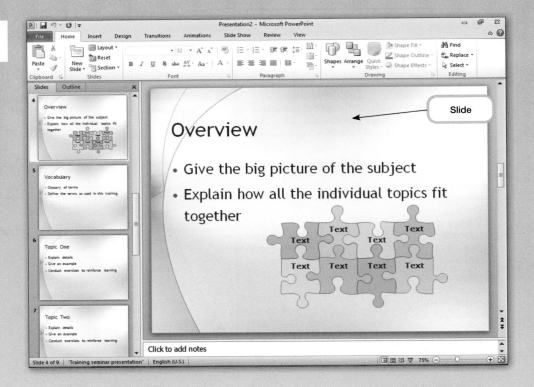

Spelling Checker (PP1.16)

The spelling checker locates most misspelled words, duplicate words, and capitalization irregularities as you create and edit a presentation, and proposes possible corrections.

AutoCorrect (PP1.18)

The AutoCorrect feature makes some basic assumptions about the text you are typing and, based on those assumptions, automatically corrects the entry.

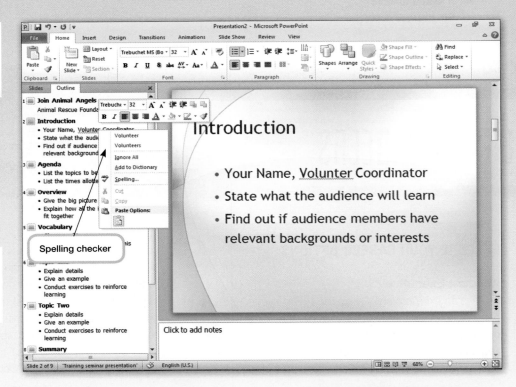

Layout (PP1.42)

A layout defines the position and format for objects and text on a slide. A layout contains placeholders for the different items such as bulleted text, titles, charts, and so on.

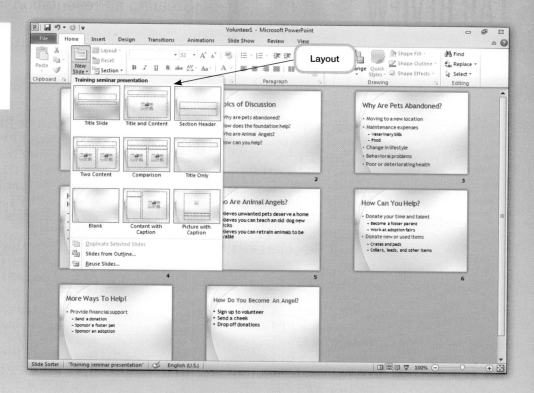

Graphic (PP1.54)

A graphic is a nontext element or object, such as a drawing or picture, that can be added to a slide.

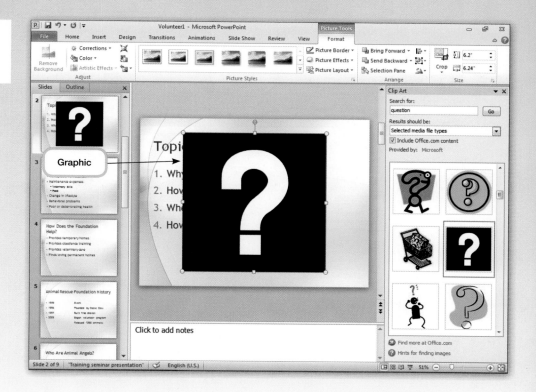

KEY TERMS

AutoCorrect PP1.18
character formatting PP1.47
clip art PP1.54
current slide PP1.9
custom dictionary PP1.16
default settings PP1.5
demote PP1.25
drawing object PP1.54
embedded object PP1.54
graphic PP1.54
keyword PP1.56
layout PP1.42
main dictionary PP1.16
Notes pane PP1.6
object PP1.6
Outline tab PP1.6
paragraph formatting PP1.47
picture PP1.54

picture style PP1.59
placeholder PP1.6
placeholder text PP1.6
promote PP1.26
sans serif font PP1.48
serif font PP1.47
sizing handles PP1.44
slide PP1.6
Slide indicator PP1.6
Slide pane PP1.6
slide show PP1.61
Slides tab PP1.6
source program PP1.54
spelling checker PP1.16
style PP1.59
text effects PP1.50
thumbnail PP1.6
view PP1.6

COMMAND SUMMARY

Command	Shortcut	Action
File tab		
Save	Ctrl + S	Saves presentation
Save As	F12	Saves presentation using new file name and/or location
Open	Ctrl + O	Opens existing presentation
Close		Closes presentation
Info		Document properties
New	Ctrl + N	Opens New Presentation dialog box
Print	Ctrl + P	Opens print settings and a preview pane
Exit		Closes PowerPoint
Quick Access Toolbar		
Save	Ctrl + S	Saves presentation
Undo	Ctrl + Z	Reverses last action
Home tab		
Clipboard group		
Paste	Ctrl + V	Pastes item from Clipboard
Cut	Ctrl + X	Cuts selection to Clipboard
Copy	Ctrl + C	Copies selection to Clipboard
Slides group		
New Slide	Ctrl + M	Inserts new slide with selected layout
Layout		Changes layout of a slide
Font group		
Trebuchet MS (He Font		Changes font type
44 Size		Changes font size

LAB REVIEW

COMMAND SUMMARY (CONTINUED)

Command	Shortcut	Action
A^		Increases font size
A˅		Decreases font size
I		Italicizes text
U		Underlines text
S		Applies a shadow effect
A ▾		Changes font color
Paragraph group		
▤ ▾ Bullets/Bullets		Formats bulleted list
▤ ▾ Numbering/Bulleted		Formats numbered lists
Editing group		
▸ Select ▾ / Select All	Ctrl + A	Selects everything in the placeholder box
Insert tab		
Illustrations group		
Clip Art		Inserts clip art
Slide Show tab		
Start Slide Show group		
From Beginning	F5	Displays presentation starting with the first slide
From Current Slide	Shift + F5	Displays presentation starting with the current slide
Review tab		
Proofing group		
ABC Spelling	F7	Spell-checks presentation

COMMAND SUMMARY (CONTINUED)

Command	Shortcut	Action
View tab		
Presentation Views group		
Normal		Switches to Normal view
Slide Sorter		Switches to Slide Sorter view
Picture Tools Format tab		
Adjust group		
9 Slides Horizontal Handouts (9 slides per page)		Modifies the color of the picture
Picture Styles group		
More		Opens Picture styles gallery to choose an overall visual style for a picture
Picture Layout		Changes layout of a drawing
Picture Border		Applies a border style to picture
Picture Effects		Applies a visual effect to picture

LAB EXERCISES

SCREEN IDENTIFICATION

1. In the following PowerPoint screen, letters identify important elements. Enter the correct term for each screen element in the space provided.

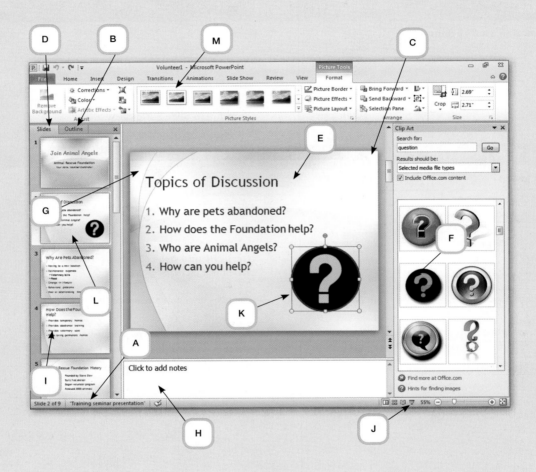

Possible answers for the screen identification are:

Clip art
Object
Picture Styles
Slide Show view
Slide pane
Slide title
Current slide

Presentation template
Outline tab
Sizing handle
Slides tab
Note pane
Thumbnail

A. _____   H. _____
B. _____   I. _____
C. _____   J. _____
E. _____   K. _____
F. _____   L. _____
G. _____   M. _____

MATCHING

Match the item on the left with the correct description on the right.

1. AutoFit _____ a. small image
2. demote _____ b. sample text that suggests the content for the slide
3. embedded object _____ c. moves the slide back to the previous slide in a presentation
4. Previous Slide button _____ d. individual page of a presentation
5. layout _____ e. displays each slide as a thumbnail
6. Notes pane _____ f. indents a bulleted point to the right
7. placeholder text _____ g. defines the position and format for objects and text that will be added to a slide
8. slide _____ h. includes space to enter notes that apply to the current slide
9. Slides tab _____ i. becomes part of the presentation file and can be opened and edited using the source program
10. thumbnail _____ j. tool that automatically resizes text to fit within the placeholder

TRUE/FALSE

Circle the correct answer to the following questions.

1. A layout contains placeholders for different items such as bulleted text, titles, and charts. **True   False**

2. PowerPoint will continue to indent to the same level when you demote a bulleted point until you cancel the indent. **True   False**

3. A slide is a set of characters with a specific design. **True   False**

4. PowerPoint identifies a word as misspelled by underlining it with a wavy blue line. **True   False**

5. PowerPoint can print multiple types of output at a time. **True   False**

6. The Previous Slide and Next Slide buttons are located at the bottom of the horizontal scroll bar. **True   False**

7. Content templates focus on the design of a presentation. **True   False**

8. Graphics are objects, such as charts, drawings, pictures, and scanned photographs, that provide visual interest or clarify data. **True   False**

9. You can rely on AutoCorrect to ensure your document is error free. **True   False**

10. After the final slide is displayed in Slide Sorter view, the program will return to the view you were last using. **True   False**

LAB EXERCISES

FILL-IN

Complete the following statements by filling in the blanks with the correct terms.

1. _____ is a set of picture files or simple drawings that comes with Office 2010.
2. The size of a _____ can be changed by dragging its sizing handles.
3. A _____ is an individual "page" of your presentation.
4. _____ define the position and format for objects and text that will be added to a slide.
5. A _____ is text or graphics that appears at the bottom of each slide.
6. When selected, a placeholder is surrounded with eight _____.
7. A _____ is a miniature of a slide.
8. _____ is a PowerPoint feature that advises you of misspelled words as you add text to a slide and proposes possible corrections.
9. A _____ is a file containing predefined settings that can be used as a pattern to create many common types of presentations.
10. An embedded object is edited using the _____ program.

MULTIPLE CHOICE

Circle the correct response to the questions below.

1. The step in the development of a presentation that focuses on determining the length of your speech, the audience, the layout of the room, and the type of audiovisual equipment available is _____.
   a. editing
   b. creating
   c. planning
   d. enhancing

2. A _____ is a file containing predefined settings that can be used as a pattern to create many common types of presentations.
   a. presentation
   b. slide
   c. template
   d. graphic

3. The _____ feature makes some basic assumptions about the text you are typing and, based on those assumptions, automatically corrects the entry.
   a. grammar checker
   b. AutoCorrect
   c. spelling checker
   d. template

4. If you want to work on all aspects of your presentation, switch to _____ view, which displays the Slide pane, Outline pane, and Notes pane.
   a. Normal
   b. Outline
   c. Slide
   d. Slide Sorter

5. _____ displays a miniature of each slide to make it easy to reorder slides, add special effects such as transitions, and set timing between slides.
   a. Slide Show view
   b. Normal view
   c. Reading view
   d. Slide Sorter view

6. If you want to provide copies of your presentation to the audience showing multiple slides on a page, you would print _____.
   a. note pages
   b. slides
   c. handouts
   d. outline area

7. A(n) _____ is an onscreen display of your presentation.
   a. slide
   b. handout
   c. outline
   d. slide show

8. A _____ is a nontext element or object, such as a drawing or picture, that can be added to a slide.
   a. slide
   b. template
   c. text box
   d. graphic

9. When the spelling checker is used, you can create a(n) _____ dictionary to hold words that you commonly use but are not included in the main dictionary.
   a. official
   b. common
   c. personal
   d. custom

10. The keyboard shortcut to view a slide show is _____.
    a. F5
    b. Alt + V
    c. F3
    d. Ctrl + V

STEP-BY-STEP

TRIPLE CROWN PRESENTATION ★

1. Logan Thomas works at Adventure Travel Tours. He is working on a presentation about lightweight hiking to be presented to a group of interested clients. Logan recently found some new information to add to the presentation. He also wants to rearrange some slides and make a few other changes to improve the appearance of the presentation. The handouts of your completed presentation will be similar to those shown here.

    a. Open the file pp01_Triple Crown. Run the slide show.

    b. Enter your name in the subtitle on slide 1.

    c. Spell-check the presentation, making the appropriate corrections.

    d. Change the layout of slide 5 to Title Only.

    e. Move slide 6 before slide 5.

    f. Insert an appropriate photograph from the Clip Art gallery on slide 4. Size and position it appropriately.

    g. Insert a new slide using the Two Content layout after slide 4.

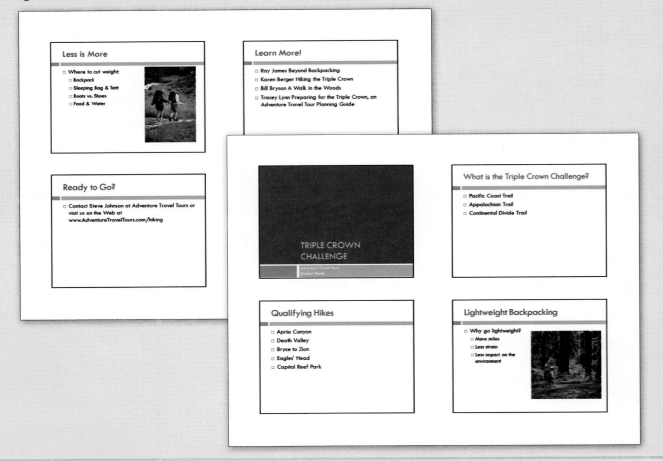

h. Enter the title **Less is More**. Insert an appropriate photograph on hiking from the Clip Art gallery in the right content placeholder. Move to slide 4 and select the second promoted bullet, "Where to cut weight:", and its subpoints. Cut this text and paste it in the left content placeholder of slide 5.

i. Change the layout of slide 7 to Title and Content layout. Add the following text in the text place-holder: **Contact Steve Johnson at Adventure Travel Tours or visit us on the Web at www. AdventureTravelTours.com/hiking.**

j. Run the slide show.

k. Save the presentation as Triple Crown Presentation. Print the slides in landscape orientation as handouts (four per page).

EMERGENCY DRIVING TECHNIQUES ★★

2. The Department of Public Safety holds monthly community outreach programs. Next month's topic is about how to handle special driving circumstances, such as driving in rain or snow. You are responsible for presenting the section on how to handle tire blowouts. You have organized the top-ics to be presented and located several clip art graphics that will complement the talk. Now you are ready to begin creating the presentation. Handouts of the completed presentation are shown here.

LAB EXERCISES

a. Open the PowerPoint presentation pp01_Handling Blowouts.

b. Run the spelling checker and correct any errors.

c. On slide 1, replace "Student Name" with your name.

   Increase the title text to 54 pts.

   Change title text color to Dark Red, Accent 1, Darker 50%.

d. On slide 5:

   Promote bullet 4.

   Demote the last bullet.

   AutoFit the content text to the placeholder

e. On slide 6, insert a clip art image on the theme of tires and position it in the lower-right corner of the slide.

f. On slide 3, change the color of the clip art to Dark Red, Accent 6, Light. Apply the Bevel Rectangle picture style to the clip art image.

g. Save the presentation as Handling Blowouts.

h. Run the slide show.

i. Print the slides as handouts (six per page, horizontal) and close the presentation.

WRITING EFFECTIVE RESUMES ★★

3. You work for the career services center of a major university and are working on a presentation to help students create effective resumes and cover letters. You are close to finishing the presentation but need to clean it up and enhance it a bit before presenting it. The handouts of your completed presentation will be similar to those shown here.

a. Open the PowerPoint presentation pp01_Resume.

b. Run the spelling checker and correct any spelling errors.

c. On slide 1: Display in normal view.

   Change title font size to 54 pt. Use the AutoFit option to fit the text into the placeholder.

   Change subtitle font size to 20 pt.

   Search the Clip Art gallery on the theme of success. Insert, size, and position an appropriate graphic.

   Apply an appropriate picture style to the selected graphic and change its color.

d. On slide 2, replace "Student Name" with your name. Use picture styles and effects to improve the appearance of the picture.

e. On slides 3 and 4, search the Clip Art gallery on the theme of success. Insert, size, and position an appropriate graphic on each slide. Apply an appropriate picture styles to the graphics and change their colors.

f. On slide 5, capitalize the first word of each bulleted item.

g. On slide 6, split the slide content into two slides. Move the first bulleted item on the new slide (7) back to slide 6 so slide 7 begins with the "Other" bulleted item. Appropriately adjust the bullet level and font size of the moved item on slide 6.

h. On slide 10, reorganize the bulleted items so "Types of cover letters" is the first item.

i. To match the slide order with the way the topics are now introduced, move slide 13 before slide 11.

j. On slide 13: Break each bulleted item into two or three bullets each as appropriate.

Capitalize the first word of each bulleted item.

Remove any commas and periods at the end of the bullets.

k. Save the presentation as Resume1.

l. Run the slide show.

m. Print the slides as handouts (nine per page, horizontal, in landscape orientation) and close the presentation.

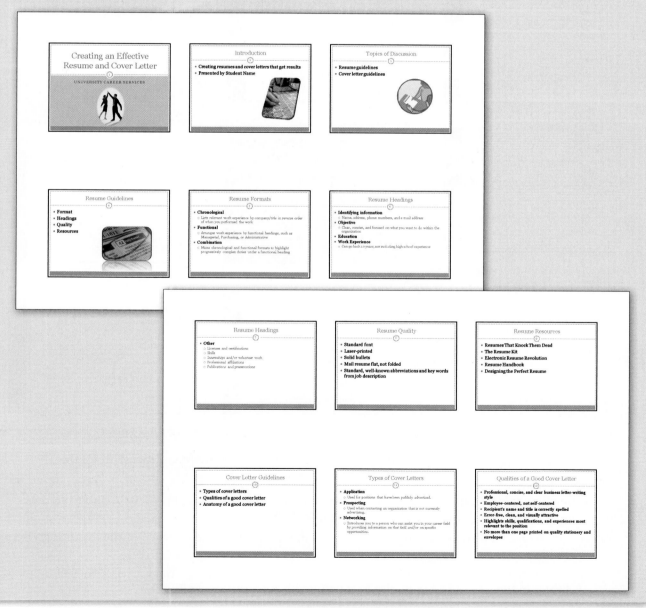

EMPLOYEE ORIENTATION ★ ★ ★

4. As the front desk manager of the Essex Inn, you want to make a presentation to your new employees about all of the amenities your hotel offers its guests as well as information on activities and dining in the area. The purpose of this presentation is to enable employees to answer the many questions that are asked by the guests about both the hotel and the town. The handouts of your completed presentation will be similar to those shown here.

a. Open pp01_Essex Inn, which uses the Opulent content template from Microsoft Online.

b. On slide 1:

Enter **Essex Inn** as the company name. Set the font to Constantia; apply Bold and Shadow. Change the font color to Ice Blue, Background 2, and size 66.

Insert, size, and position a clip art image suitable as a hotel logo in place of the "your logo here" graphic.

Insert a line after the title. Type your name on the line, and change the font size to Trebuchet MS and the font size to 20. Change the font color to White and apply italics.

c. On slide 2:

Enter **Amenities and Activities for Guests** as the title.

Change the font size of the title to 31.

Enter the sample bulleted text **What is there to do?** as the first bullet.

Enter **At the hotel or in the town?** as the second bullet.

Remove the remaining bulleted items.

d. Insert a new slide after slide 2. In this slide:

Set the layout to Title and Content.

Enter **Hotel Amenities and Activities** as the title.

Enter **Dining** as the first bullet.

Enter **Activities** as the second bullet.

Enter **Other amenities** as the third bullet.

Insert, size, and position a clip art image suitable for a hotel at the bottom center of the slide. Apply picture styles and effects.

e. Insert a new slide after slide 3. In this slide:

Set the layout to Title and Content.

Enter **Dining** as the title.

Enter **Breakfast** as the first bullet under Dining.

Enter **Eggs Benedict or custom omelet** and demote to appear as the first bullet under Breakfast.

Enter **Daily chef's special** as the second bullet under Breakfast.

Enter **Lunch** and promote to appear as the second bullet under Dining.

Enter **Custom-pack lunch for outings** and demote to appear as the first bullet under Lunch.

Enter **Build-your-own sandwich bar** as the second bullet under Lunch.

Enter **Dinner** and promote to appear as the third bullet under Dining.

Enter **Four course meal (salad, soup, entrée, dessert)** as the first bullet under Dinner.

Enter **Three nightly chef specials** as the second bullet under Dinner.

f. Insert a new slide after slide 4. In this slide:

Set the layout to Title and Content.

Enter **Activities** as the title.

Enter **Morning** as the first bullet under Activities.

Enter **Bird watching on the veranda** and demote to appear as the first bullet under Morning.

Enter **Lecture/Tour of gardens and hotel** as the second bullet under Morning.

Enter **Afternoon** and promote to appear as the second bullet under Activities.

Enter **Daily guest lecture or class** as the first bullet under Afternoon.

Enter **Historic walking tour of downtown** as the second bullet under Afternoon.

Enter **Evening** and promote to appear as the third bullet under Activities.

Enter **Champagne meet/greet** and demote to appear as the first bullet under Evening.

Enter **Live music/dancing with dinner** as the second bullet under Evening.

LAB EXERCISES

   g. Insert a new slide after slide 5. In this slide:

     Set the layout to Title and Content.

     Enter **Other Amenities** as the title.

     Enter **Special dining events** as the first bullet under Other Amenities.

     Enter **Sunday champagne brunch** and demote to appear as the first bullet under Special Dining Events.

     Enter **Saturday afternoon tea** as the second bullet under Special Dining Events.

     Enter **Extras** and promote to appear as the second bullet for Other Amenities.

     Enter **Third Tuesday cooking class** and demote to appear as the first bullet under Extras.

     Enter **Tour of haunted houses on Saturdays at nine** as the second bullet under Extras.

     Insert, size, and position a clip art image suitable for a hotel at the bottom center of the slide. Apply picture styles and effects.

   h. Delete slides 7 through 13.

   i. On the Summary slide 7.

     Enter **Hotel amenities and activities** as the first bullet under Summary.

     Enter **Dining** and demote to appear as the first bullet under Hotel amenities and activities.

     Enter **Activities** as the second bullet under Hotel amenities and activities.

     Enter **Other amenities** as the third bullet under Hotel amenities and activities.

     Enter **Always remember** and promote to appear as the second bullet under Summary.

     Enter **Our guests are our customers** and demote to appear as the first bullet under Always remember.

     Enter **Treat our guests as friends** as the second bullet under Always remember.

     Enter **Thanks for attending and put these ideas into practice** and promote to appear as the third bullet under Summary.

     Delete any remaining bullet placeholders.

   j. Save the presentation as Essex Inn Orientation.

   k. Run the slide show.

   l. Print the slides as handouts (four per page, horizontal, in landscape orientation).

WORKPLACE ISSUES ★ ★ ★

5. Tim is preparing for his lecture on "Workplace Issues" for his Introduction to Computers class. He uses PowerPoint to create presentations for each of his lectures. He has organized the topics to be presented, and located several clip art graphics that will complement the lecture. He is now ready to begin creating the presentation. Several slides of the completed presentation are shown here.

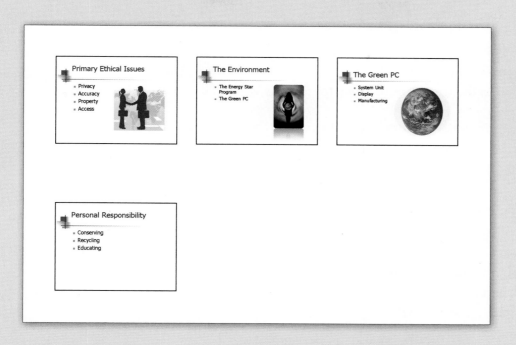

a. Open a new presentation using the Staff Training Presentation template. If you don't have access to the Internet, you can use the file pp01_Staff Training.

b. On slide 1:

Change the title to **Workplace Issues**. Change the font size to 48 and apply a bold effect.

Change the subtitle text to **Lecture 4**.

Add a line beneath the subtitle and type **Presented by Your Name**. Change the font size of this line to 24.

Insert, size, and position a clip art image suitable for the theme of an office meeting. Apply a picture style to the image.

c. On slide 2:

Enter **Topics of Discussion** as the title text.

Enter **Ergonomics** as bullet 1.

Enter **Ethics** as bullet 2.

Enter **Environment** as bullet 3.

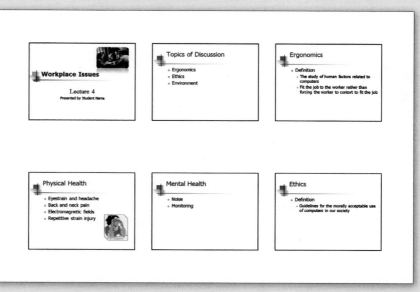

   d. On slide 3:

      Enter **Ergonomics** as the title.

      Enter **Definition** as the first bullet.

      Enter **Fit the job to the worker rather than forcing the worker to contort to fit the job** as the second bullet.

      Enter **The study of human factors related to computers** as the third bullet.

   e. Change the order of bullets 2 and 3 on slide 3.

      Demote bullets 2 and 3.

   f. On slide 4:

      Change the title to **Mental Health**.

      Include two bulleted items: **Noise** and **Monitoring**.

   g. Change the title of slide 5 to **Physical Health** and include the following bulleted items:

      Bullet 1: **Eyestrain and headache**

      Bullet 2: **Back and neck pain**

      Bullet 3: **Electromagnetic fields**

      Bullet 4: **Repetitive strain injury**

      Insert, size, and position a suitable clip art image. Use the picture formatting tools to customize the image to suit the presentation.

   h. On slide 6:

      Change the title to **Ethics**.

      Include two bullets: **Definition** and **Guidelines for the morally acceptable use of computers in our society**.

      Demote bullet 2.

   i. Change the title of slide 7 to **Primary Ethical Issues**.

      Enter **Privacy** as bullet 1.

      Enter **Accuracy** as bullet 2.

      Enter **Property** as bullet 3.

      Enter **Access** as bullet 4.

      Insert, size, and position a suitable clip art image. Use the picture formatting tools to customize the image to suit the presentation.

   j. Insert a new Two Content layout slide between slides 7 and 8. On the new slide 8:

      Enter **The Environment** as the title.

      Enter **The Energy Star Program** as the first bullet.

      Enter **The Green PC** as the second bullet.

      In the right placeholder, insert, size, and position a suitable clip art image. Use the picture formatting tools to customize the image to suit the presentation.

k. Create a duplicate of slide 8. On the new slide 9:

Enter **The Green PC** as the title.

Enter **System Unit** as the first bullet.

Enter **Display** as the second bullet.

Enter **Manufacturing** as the third bullet.

In the right placeholder, insert, size, and position an appropriate clip art image.

l. On slide 10:

Enter **Personal Responsibility** as the title.

Enter **Conserving** as the first bullet.

Enter **Recycling** as the second bullet.

Enter **Educating** as the third bullet.

m. In Slide Sorter view, move slide 5 before slide 4.

n. Change the font of the words "Lecture 4" in the subtitle on the title slide to Times New Roman and the size to 44 pt.

o. Save the presentation as Workplace Issues.

p. Run the slide show. Revised PowerPoint_2010_Brief_Solutions

q. Print the slides as handouts (six per page in landscape orientation).

ON YOUR OWN

INTERNET POLICY PRESENTATION ★

1. You are working in the information technology department at International Sales Incorporated. Your manager has asked you to give a presentation on the corporation's Internet policy to the new-hire orientation class. Create your presentation with PowerPoint, using the information in the Word file pp01_Internet Policy as a resource. Use a template of your choice. When you are done, run the spelling checker, then save your presentation as Internet Policy and print it.

TELEPHONE TRAINING COURSE ★ ★

2. You are a trainer with Super Software, Inc. You received a memo from your manager alerting you that many of the support personnel are not using proper telephone protocol or obtaining the proper information from customers who call in. Your manager has asked you to conduct a training class that covers these topics. Using the Word document pp01_Memo data file as a resource, prepare the slides for your class. When you are done, save the presentation as Phone Etiquette and print the handouts.

LAB EXERCISES

VISUAL AIDS ★★

3. You are a trainer with Super Software, Inc. Your manager has asked you to prepare a presentation on various visual aids that may be used in presentations. Using the pp01_VisualAids data file as a resource, create an onscreen presentation using an appropriate template. Add clip art that illustrates the type of visual aid. Include your name on the title slide. When you are done, save the presentation as Presentation Aids and print the handouts.

WEB DESIGN PROPOSAL ★★★

4. Your company wants to create a Web site, but it is not sure whether to design its own or hire a Web design firm to do it. You have been asked to create a presentation to management relaying the pros and cons of each approach. To gather information, search the Web for the topic "Web design," and select some key points about designing a Web page from one of the "how-to" or "tips" categories. Use these points to create the first part of your presentation, and call it something like "Creating Our Own Web Page." Then search the Web for the topic "Web designers," and select two Web design firms. Pick some key points about each firm (for example, Web sites they have designed, design elements they typically use, and/or their design philosophy). Finally, include at least one slide that lists the pros and cons of each approach. Include your name on the title slide. When your presentation is complete, save it as Web Design and print the slides as handouts.

    You will expand on this presentation in On Your Own Exercise 4 of Lab 2.

CAREERS WITH ANIMALS ★★★

5. You have been volunteering at the Animal Rescue Foundation. The director has asked you to prepare a presentation on careers with animals to present to local schools in hopes that some students will be inspired to volunteer at the foundation. Using the Word document pp01_Animal Careers data file as a resource, create the presentation. Add photos or clip art where appropriate. When you are done, save the presentation as Careers with Animals and print the handouts.

Objectives

After completing this lab, you will know how to:

1. Find and replace text.

2. Create and enhance a table.

3. Insert pictures.

4. Modify graphic objects.

5. Create and enhance shapes.

6. Create a text box.

7. Change the theme.

8. Modify slide masters.

9. Add animation, sound, and transitions.

10. Control a slide show.

11. Add speaker notes.

12. Add and hide slide footers.

13. Customize print settings.

Animal Rescue Foundation

The Animal Rescue Foundation director was very impressed with your first draft of the presentation to recruit volunteers and asked to see the presentation onscreen. While viewing it together, you explained that you plan to make many more changes to improve the appearance of the presentation. For example, you plan to use a different color theme and to include more art and other graphic features to enhance the appearance of the slides. You also explained that you will add more action to the slides using the special effects included with PowerPoint to keep the audience's attention.

The director suggested that you include more information on ways that volunteers can help. Additionally, because the organization has such an excellent adoption rate, the director wants you to include a table to illustrate the success of the adoption program.

PowerPoint 2010 gives you the design and production capabilities to create a first-class onscreen presentation. These features include artist-designed layouts and color themes that give your presentation a professional appearance. In addition, you can add your own personal touches by modifying text attributes, incorporating art or graphics, and including animation to add impact, interest, and excitement to your presentation.

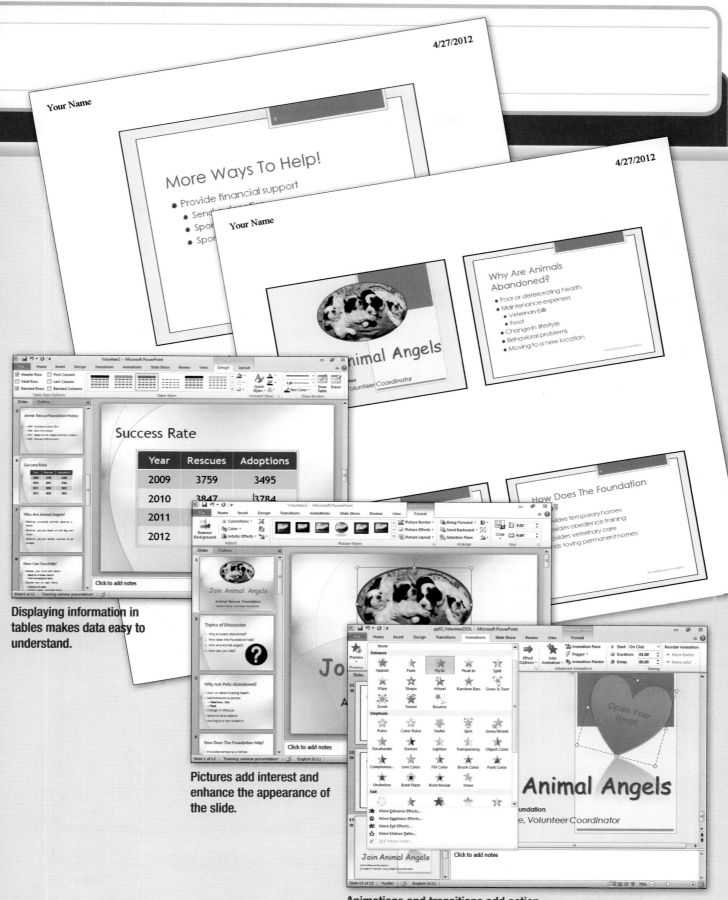

Displaying information in tables makes data easy to understand.

Pictures add interest and enhance the appearance of the slide.

Animations and transitions add action to a slide show.

The following concepts will be introduced in this lab:

1 Find and Replace To make editing easier, you can use the Find and Replace feature to find text in a presentation and replace it with other text.

2 Table A table is used to organize information into an easy-to-read format of horizontal rows and vertical columns.

3 Alignment Alignment controls the position of text entries within a space.

4 Theme A theme is a predefined set of formatting choices that can be applied to an entire document in one simple step.

5 Master A master is a special slide or page that stores information about the formatting for all slides or pages in a presentation.

6 Animations Animations are special effects that add action to text and graphics so they move around on the screen during a slide show.

Finding and Replacing Text

After meeting with the foundation director, you want to update the content to include the additional information on ways that volunteers can help the Animal Rescue Foundation.

- **Start PowerPoint 2010.**

- **Open the file pp02_Volunteer2**

- **If necessary, switch to Normal view.**

- **Replace Student Name in slide 1 with your name.**

- **Scroll the Slide pane to view the content of the revised presentation.**

Your screen should be similar to Figure 2.1

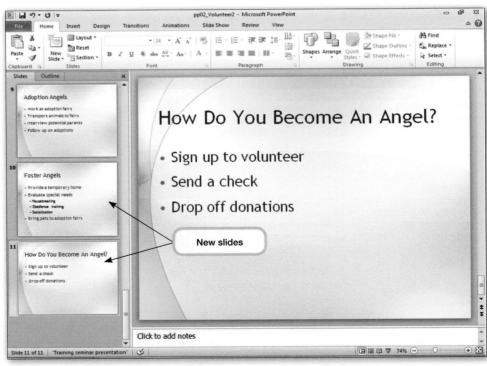

Figure 2.1

You added two new slides, 9 and 10, with more information about the Animal Angels volunteer organization, bringing the total number of slides in the presentation to 11. As you reread the content of the presentation, you decide to edit the text by finding the word "pet" and replacing it with the word "animal." To do this, you will use the Find and Replace feature.

Concept Find and Replace

To make editing easier, you can use the **Find and Replace** feature to find text in a presentation and replace it with other text. The Find feature will locate and identify any text string you specify in the presentation by highlighting it. When used along with the Replace feature, not only will the string be identified, but it will be replaced with the replacement text you specify if you choose. For example, suppose you created a lengthy document describing the type of clothing and equipment needed to set up a world-class home gym, and then you decided to change "sneakers" to "athletic shoes." Instead of deleting every occurrence of "sneakers" and typing "athletic shoes," you can use the Find and Replace feature to perform the task automatically.

The Replace feature also can be used to replace a specified font in a presentation with another. When using this feature, however, all text throughout the presentation that is in the specified font is automatically changed to the selected replacement font.

The Find and Replace feature is fast and accurate; however, use care when replacing so that you do not replace unintended matches.

FINDING TEXT

First, you will use the Find command to locate all occurrences of the word "pet" in the presentation. Because it is easier to read the text in the Slide pane, you will make that pane active before starting. If the Outline tab is active at the time you begin using Find and Replace, the located text will be highlighted in the Outline tab instead.

- **Make slide 1 active.**

- **If necessary, open the Home tab.**

- **Click** 🔍 Find **in the Editing group.**

Another Method
The keyboard shortcut is Ctrl + F.

Your screen should be similar to Figure 2.2

Figure 2.2

In the Find dialog box, you enter the text you want to locate in the Find what text box. The two options described in the following table allow you to refine the procedure that is used to conduct the search.

Option	Effect on Text
Match Case	Distinguishes between uppercase and lowercase characters. When selected, finds only those instances in which the capitalization matches the text you typed in the Find what box.
Find WholeWords Only	Distinguishes between whole and partial words. When selected, locates matches that are whole words and not part of a larger word. For example, finds "cat" only and not "catastrophe," too.

You want to find all occurrences of the complete word "pet." You will not use either option described above, because you want to locate all words regardless of case and because you want to find "pet" as well as "pets" in the presentation.

2

- Type **pet** in the Find what text box.

- Click Find Next .

- If necessary, move the dialog box so you can see the located text.

Your screen should be similar to Figure 2.3

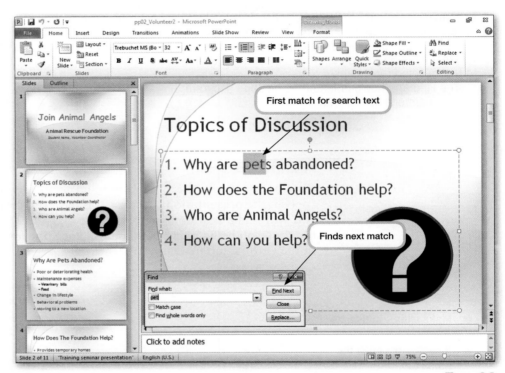

Figure 2.3

PowerPoint begins searching beginning at the cursor location for all occurrences of the text to find and locates the first occurrence of the word "pet."

3

- Continue to click Find Next to locate all occurrences of the word.

- Click OK when PowerPoint indicates the entire document has been searched.

The word "pet" is used five times in the document. Using the Find command is a convenient way to quickly navigate through a document to locate and move to specified information.

REPLACING TEXT

You want to replace selected occurrences of the word "pet" with "animal" throughout the presentation. You will use the Replace feature to specify the text to enter as the replacement text.

1

● **Click** 🔤 Replace ▾ **in the Editing group.**

Another Method

The keyboard shortcut to replace text is Ctrl + H.

Your screen should be similar to Figure 2.4

Figure 2.4

The Find dialog box changes to the Replace dialog box, and the Find text is still specified in the Find what text box. You can now enter the replacement text in the Replace with text box. The replacement text must be entered exactly as you want it to appear in your presentation.

2

- **Press** Tab **or click in the Replace with text box.**

Having Trouble?

If necessary, type **pet** in the Find what text box.

Additional Information

After entering the text to find, do not press Enter or this will choose Find Next and the search will begin.

- **Type** animal **in the Replace with text box.**

- **Click** Find Next **.**

- **If necessary, move the dialog box so you can see the located text.**

- **Click** Replace **.**

Having Trouble?

Click Find Next to move to the next occurrence if the search does not advance automatically.

Your screen should be similar to Figure 2.5

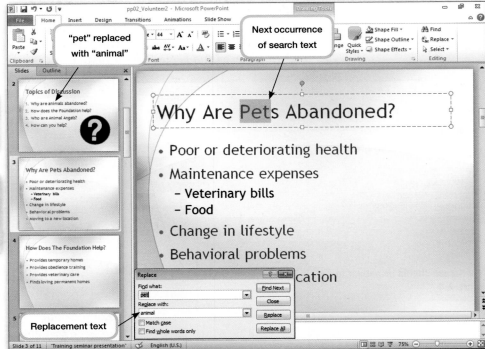

Figure 2.5

The first located Find text is replaced with the replacement text, and the next occurrence of text in the Find what box is located. You could continue finding and replacing each occurrence. You will, however, replace all the remaining occurrences at one time. As you do, the replacement is entered in lowercase even when it replaces a word that begins with an uppercase character. You will correct this when you finish replacing.

3

- Click [Replace All] to continue.

- Click [OK] in response to the finished searching dialog box.

- Click [Close] to close the Replace dialog box.

- Edit the word "animals" to "Animals" in slide 3.

- Click somewhere outside the placeholder.

- Save the presentation as Volunteer2 to you solution file location.

Your screen should be similar to Figure 2.6

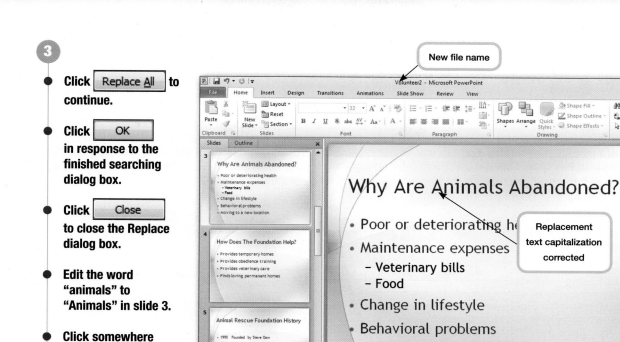

Figure 2.6

If you plan to change all occurrences, it is much faster to use [Replace All]. Exercise care when using Replace All, however, because the search text you specify might be part of another word and you may accidentally replace text you want to keep.

Creating a Simple Table

During your discussion with the director, he suggested that you add a slide containing data showing the success of the adoption program. The information in this slide will be presented using a table layout.

Concept 2 Table

A **table** is used to organize information into an easy-to-read format of horizontal rows and vertical columns. The intersection of a row and column creates a **cell** in which you can enter data or other information. Cells in a table are identified by a letter and number, called a **table reference**. Columns are identified from left to right beginning with the letter A, and rows are numbered from top to bottom beginning with the number 1. The table reference of the top-leftmost cell is A1 because it is in the first column (A) and first row (1) of the table. The third cell in column 2 is cell B3. The fourth cell in column 3 is C4.

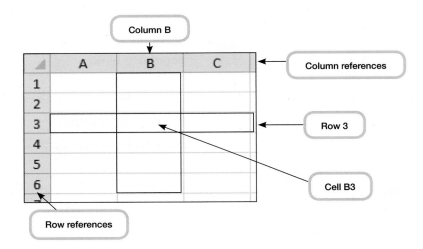

Tables are a very effective method for presenting information. The table layout organizes the information for readers and greatly reduces the number of words they have to read to interpret the data. Use tables whenever you can to make the information in your presentation easier to read.

The table you will create will display columns for the year and for the number of rescues and adoptions. The rows will display the data for the past four years. Your completed table will be similar to the one shown here.

Year	Rescues	Adoptions
2009	3759	3495
2010	3847	3784
2011	3982	3833
2012	4025	3943

CREATING A TABLE SLIDE

To include this information in the presentation, you will insert a new slide after slide 5. Because this slide will contain a table showing the adoption data, you want to use the Title and Content layout.

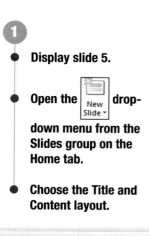

Display slide 5.

Open the 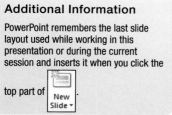 **drop-down menu from the Slides group on the Home tab.**

Choose the Title and Content layout.

Your screen should be similar to Figure 2.7

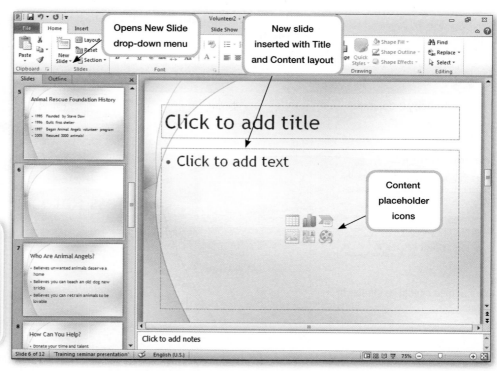

Figure 2.7

Six icons appear inside the content placeholder, each representing a different type of content that can be inserted. Clicking an icon opens the appropriate feature to add the specified type of content.

INSERTING THE TABLE

First, you will add a slide title, and then you will create the table to display the number of adoptions and rescues.

Enter the title Success Rate in the title placeholder.

Click the ▦ **Insert Table icon in the center of the slide.**

Your screen should be similar to Figure 2.8

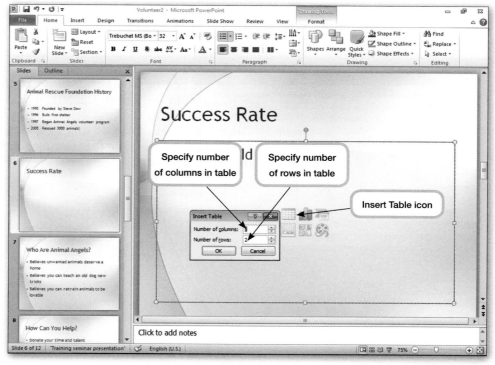

Figure 2.8

Creating a Simple Table **PP2.11**

In the Insert Table dialog box, you specify the number of rows and columns for the table.

2

● **Specify 3 columns and 5 rows.**

Having Trouble?

You can type in the number or use the scroll buttons to increase or decrease the number.

● **Click** OK .

Your screen should be similar to Figure 2.9

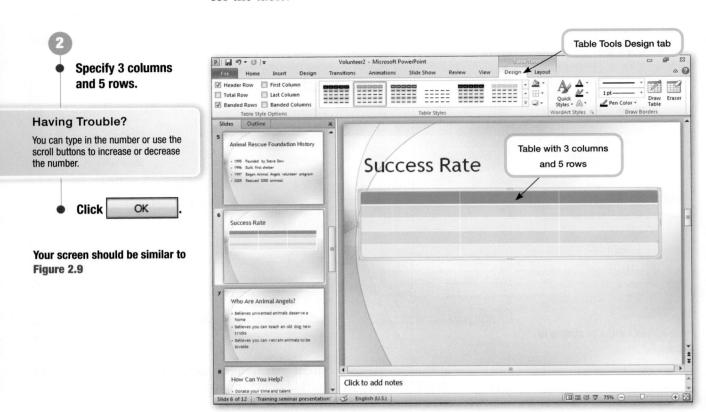

Figure 2.9

A basic table consisting of three columns and five rows is displayed as a selected object. In addition, the Table Tools Design tab opens in anticipation that you will want to modify the design of the table.

ENTERING DATA IN A TABLE

Now you can enter the information into the table. The insertion point appears in the top-left corner cell, cell A1, ready for you to enter text. To move in a table, click on the cell or use Tab to move to the next cell to the right and Shift + Tab to move to the cell to the left. If you are in the last cell of a row, pressing Tab takes you to the first cell of the next row. You also can use the ↑ and ↓ directional keys to move up or down a row. When you enter a large amount of text in a table, using Tab to move is easier than using the mouse because your hands are already on the keyboard.

1

● **Type** Year

● **Press** Tab **or click on the next cell to the right.**

Having Trouble?

Do not press Enter to move to the next cell, as this adds a new line to the current cell. If this happens, press Backspace to remove it.

Your screen should be similar to Figure 2.10

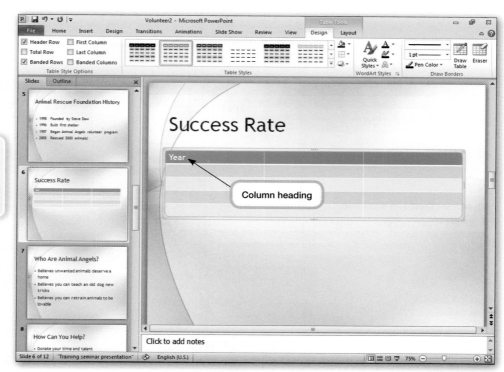

Figure 2.10

Next, you will complete the information for the table by entering the data shown below.

	Column A	Column B	Column C
Row 1	Year	Rescues	Adoptions
Row 2	2009	3759	3495
Row 3	2010	3847	3784
Row 4	2011	3982	3833
Row 5	2012	4025	3943

Add the remaining information shown above to the table.

Additional Information

You can also use the directional keys to move from cell to cell in the table.

Your screen should be similar to Figure 2.11

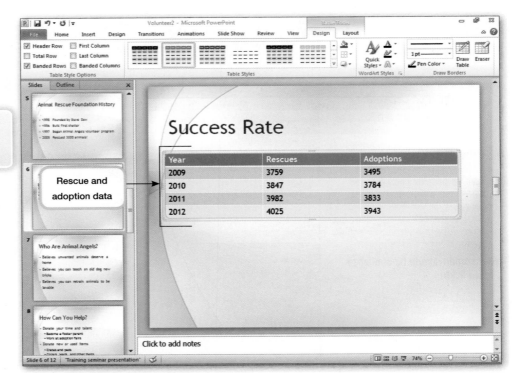

Figure 2.11

You are happy with the table but would like to increase the font size of the text to make it more readable onscreen. The size of the font in a table can be changed like any other text on a slide. However, selecting text in a table is slightly different. The following table describes how to select different areas of a table.

Area to Select	Procedure
Cell	Drag across the contents of the cell.
Row	Drag across the row or click in front of the row when the mouse pointer is a ➡.
Column	Drag down the column or click in front of the row when the mouse pointer is a ⬇.
Multiple cells, rows, or columns	Drag through the cells, rows, or columns when the mouse pointer is a ◥ or I.
	Or select the first cell, row, or column, and hold down ⇧Shift while clicking on another cell, row, or column.
Contents of next cell	Press Tab.
Contents of previous cell	Press ⇧Shift + Tab.
Entire table	Drag through all the cells or click anywhere inside the table and press Ctrl + A.

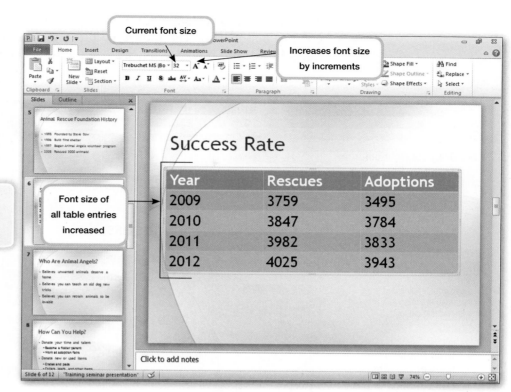

3

- Select all the text in the table.

- Open the Home tab.

- Click $A^{\blacktriangledown}$ Increase Font Size in the Font group four times.

Additional Information

Clicking $A^{\blacktriangledown}$ increases the font size by units.

Your screen should be similar to Figure 2.12

Figure 2.12

The font size has quickly been increased by four units, and at 32 points the text is much easier to read.

SIZING THE TABLE AND COLUMNS

You now want to increase the overall size of the table to better fill the space on the slide and then adjust the size of the columns to fit their contents.

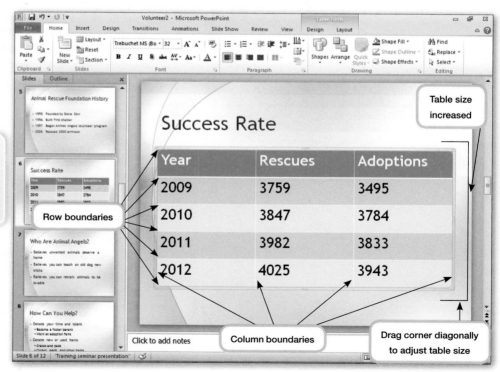

1

- Drag the lower-right corner sizing handle down to increase the table size as in Figure 2.13.

Additional Information

The mouse pointer will appear as ⬉ when you can drag the corner sizing handle and as ┼ while dragging.

Your screen should be similar to Figure 2.13

Figure 2.13

To adjust the individual column width or row height, you drag the row and column boundaries. The mouse pointer appears as a ⟷ when you can size the column and ⇳ when you can size the row. The mouse pointer appears as a ⬚ when you can move the entire table.

2

● **Drag the right column boundary line of the year column to the left to reduce the column width as in Figure 2.14.**

Additional Information

You also can double-click on the boundary line to automatically size the width to the largest cell entry.

● **Drag the boundary lines of the other two columns to the left to reduce the column widths as in Figure 2.14.**

Your screen should be similar to Figure 2.14

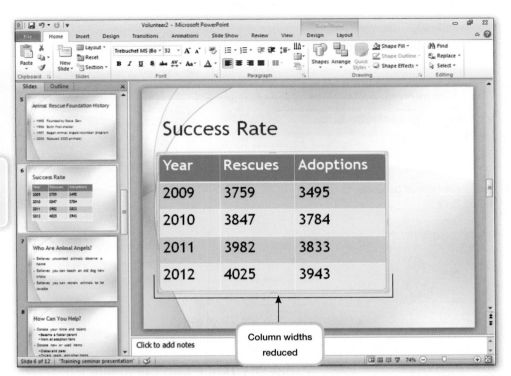

Figure 2.14

Now the columns are more appropriately sized to the data they display and the overall table size is good. You decide it would look best to align the table in the center of the slide as well. You could do this manually by moving the object to center it. A more precise method is to use the built-in alignment feature.

3

- Open the Table Tools Layout tab.

- Click 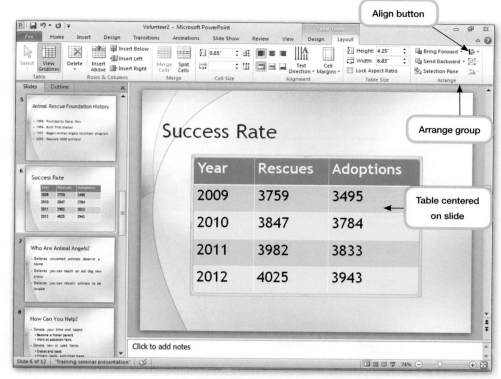 Align in the Arrange group to display the drop-down menu.

- Choose Align Center.

Your screen should be similar to Figure 2.15

Figure 2.15

ALIGNING TEXT IN CELLS

The next change you want to make is to center the text and data in the cells. To do this, you can change the alignment of the text entries.

Concept ③ Alignment

Alignment controls the position of text entries within a space. You can change the horizontal placement of an entry in a placeholder or a table cell by using one of the four horizontal alignment settings: left, center, right, and justified. You also can align text vertically in a table cell with the top, middle, or bottom of the cell space.

Horizontal Alignment	Effect on Text	Vertical Alignment	Effect on Text
Left	Aligns text against the left edge of the placeholder or cell, leaving the right edge of text, which wraps to another line, ragged.	Top	Aligns text at the top of the cell space.
Center	Centers each line of text between the left and right edges of the placeholder or cell.	Middle	Aligns text in the middle of the cell space.
Right	Aligns text against the right edge of the placeholder or cell, leaving the left edge of multiple lines ragged.	Bottom	Aligns text at the bottom of the cell space.
Justified	Aligns text evenly with both the right and left edges of the placeholder or cell.		

The commands to change horizontal alignment are on the Home tab in the Paragraph group. However, using the shortcuts shown below or the Mini toolbar is often much quicker.

Alignment	Keyboard Shortcut
Left	Ctrl + L
Center	Ctrl + E
Right	Ctrl + R
Justified	Ctrl + J

The data in the table is not centered within the cells. You want to center the cell entries both horizontally and vertically in their cell spaces.

1

- **Select the entire contents of the table.**

- **Right-click on the selection and click ☰ Center in the Alignment group.**

Another Method

You also could click ☰ Center in the Paragraph group of the Home tab.

- **Click ▤ Center Vertically in the Alignment group.**

Another Method

You can also open the ▤▾ Align Text drop-down menu in the Paragraph group and choose Middle.

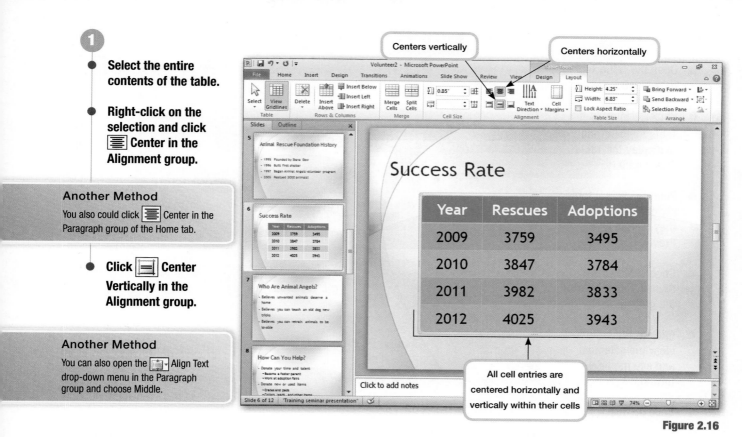

Figure 2.16

Your screen should be similar to Figure 2.16

CHANGING THE TABLE STYLE

Next, you will add a color and other formatting changes to the table. To quickly make these enhancements, you will apply a table style. Like picture styles, **table styles** are combinations of shading colors, borders, and visual effects such as shadows and reflections that can be applied in one simple step. You also can create your own table style effects by selecting specific style elements such as borders and shadows individually using the 🖌▾ Shading, ▦▾ Borders, and 🔲▾ Effects commands from the Table Styles group on the Table Tools Design tab.

1

- Open the Table Tools Design tab.

- Click ⏷ More in the Table Styles group to display the Table Styles gallery.

- Point to several table styles to see how they look in Live Preview.

- Choose Medium Style 2, Accent 2 from the gallery.

- Click in the table to clear the selection and see the new format.

- Save the file.

Your screen should be similar to Figure 2.17

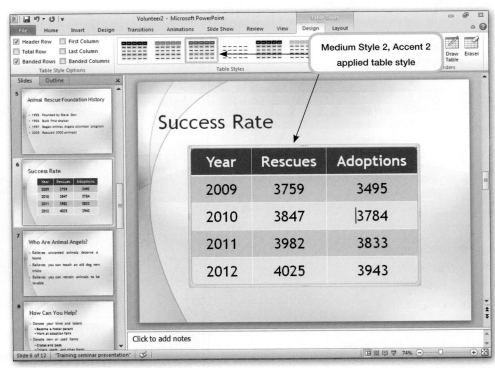

Figure 2.17

The selected table style has been applied to the table. The enhancements added to the table greatly improve its appearance, and the table now displays the information in an attractive and easy-to-read manner.

Inserting and Enhancing Pictures

Now you are ready to enhance the presentation by adding several more graphics. As you have seen, you can easily locate and add Clip Art graphics to slides. Next you want to add a picture to the presentation that you have saved as a file on your computer. You will insert the picture and then learn how to crop and enhance it using a picture style.

INSERTING A GRAPHIC FROM A FILE

You want to add the picture to the opening slide, but before you can begin, you need to reposition the placeholders to make more room for an image.

Select slide 1.

Select the title and subtitle placeholders and drag them down to position them as shown in Figure 2.18.

Having Trouble?
Click on the second placeholder while holding down Ctrl to select them both.

Your screen should be similar to Figure 2.18

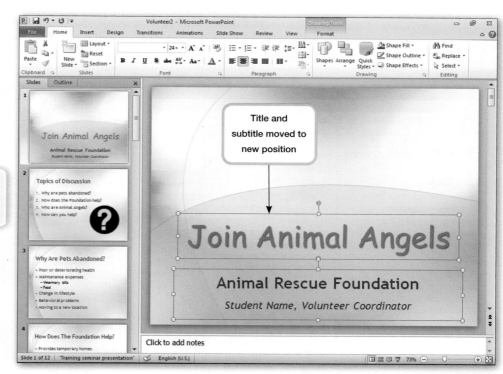

Figure 2.18

You want to see how a digital photograph of a litter of puppies you recently received from one of the foster parents would look.

Open the Insert tab.

Click [Picture] in the Images group.

Change the location to your data file location.

If necessary, click [icon] and choose Large Icons to display thumbnails.

Having Trouble?
In Windows Vista, click [Views ▼] and choose Large Icon.

Your screen should be similar to Figure 2.19

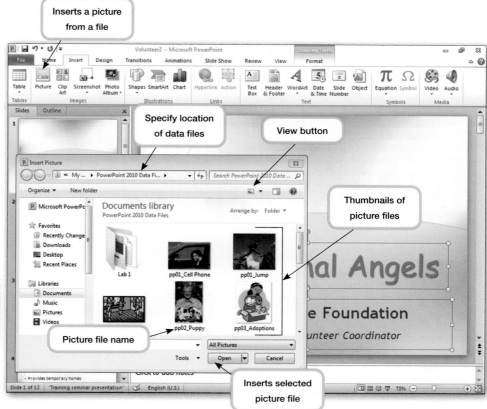

Figure 2.19

Having Trouble?

Your screen may display additional picture files or it may only display the file name.

The Insert Picture dialog box is similar to the Open and Save dialog boxes, except that the only types of files listed are those with picture file extensions. A thumbnail preview of each picture is displayed above the file name.

3

● **Select** pp02_Puppy

● **Click** [Insert ▼].

Your screen should be similar to Figure 2.20

Figure 2.20

The picture is inserted in the center of the slide on top of the text. The Picture Tools Format tab is automatically displayed in the Ribbon, in anticipation that you may want to modify the graphic.

4 Drag the bottom-right corner sizing handle inward to decrease its size to that shown in Figure 2.21.

Additional Information

To maintain an object's proportions while resizing it, hold down (Shift) while dragging the sizing handle.

Your screen should be similar to Figure 2.21

Figure 2.21

Although this is better, you decide it is not the right shape for the space. You decide that you can draw more attention to the dogs by cropping the picture on the slide.

CROPPING A GRAPHIC

Trimming or removing part of a picture is called **cropping**. Cropping removes the vertical or horizontal edges of a picture to help focus attention on a particular area. You will remove the upper part of the picture by cropping it to show the puppies only. This will make the picture smaller and rectangular shaped.

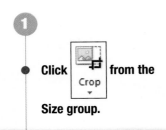

● **Click**  **from the Size group.**

● **Point to the upper-left corner of the photo, and when the mouse pointer changes to a ⌐, drag down to just above the puppies.**

● **Click**  **from the Size group to turn off this feature.**

Your screen should be similar to Figure 2.22

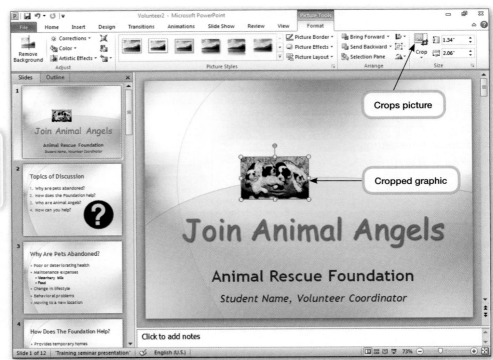

Figure 2.22

The upper part of the picture has been removed, leaving the puppies as the focus of attention. Next you want to increase the graphic's size and position it in the space above the title.

- Size the picture as in Figure 2.23 (approximately 3 by 4.5 inches).

Additional Information

The Shape Height and Shape Width buttons in the Size group display the current shape's size as you drag.

- Open the ⊟▾ Align drop-down menu in the Arrange group of the Picture Tools Format tab and choose Align Center.

- If necessary, position the graphic vertically on the slide as shown in Figure 2.23.

Your screen should be similar to Figure 2.23

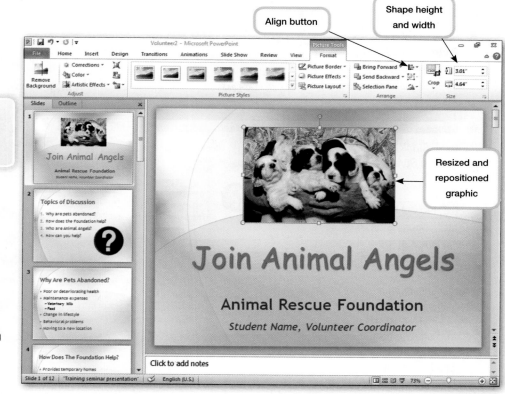

Figure 2.23

ENHANCING A PICTURE

You decide to enhance the graphic on the title slide to match the picture effects that you applied to the question mark clip art image on slide 2. Repeating the same picture effects here will add consistency to the presentation. First you will select a picture style.

1

- Click ⏷ **More** in the Picture Styles group to display all the options in the Picture Styles gallery.

- Choose 🔘 **Beveled Oval, Black** from the Picture Styles group.

- Click 🖋 **Picture Border ⏷** and choose **Blue, Accent 2** in the Theme Colors section of the gallery.

- Click ⬭ **Picture Effects ⏷** and choose **No Shadow** from the Shadow group.

Your screen should be similar to Figure 2.24

Figure 2.24

The addition of the picture of the puppies makes the title slide much more interesting and effective.

Inserting and Enhancing Shapes

At the end of the presentation, you want to add a concluding slide. This slide needs to be powerful, because it is your last chance to convince your audience to join Animal Angels.

ADDING A SHAPE

Additional Information

Most shapes also can be inserted from the Clip Organizer as well.

To create the concluding slide, you will duplicate slide 1 and then replace the picture with a graphic of a heart that you will create. To quickly add a shape, you will use one of the ready-made shapes supplied with PowerPoint. These shapes include rectangles and circles, lines, a variety of basic shapes, block arrows, flowchart symbols, stars and banners, action buttons, and callouts.

- Duplicate slide 1.

- Move slide 2 to the end of the presentation.

- Select the picture and press [Delete].

- Click in the Drawing group of the Home tab.

Having Trouble?

If a small gallery of shapes is displayed in the Drawing group instead of ![Shapes], click ▼ to open the Shapes gallery.

Another Method

You also can access the Shapes gallery using ![Shapes] on the Insert tab.

Your screen should be similar to Figure 2.25

Additional Information

The selected shape will be added to the Recently Used Shapes section of the Shapes gallery.

Figure 2.25

Next, you need to select the shape you want from the Shapes gallery and then indicate where you want the shape inserted on the slide. When inserting a shape, the mouse pointer appears as ╋ when pointing to the slide. Then, to insert the shape, click on the slide and drag to increase the size.

- Click ♡ Heart in the Basic Shapes section.

- Click above the title on the slide and drag to insert and enlarge the heart.

Another Method

To maintain the height and width proportions of the shape, hold down [Shift] while you drag.

- Size and position the heart as in Figure 2.26.

Additional Information

A shape can be sized and moved just like any other object.

Your screen should be similar to Figure 2.26

Figure 2.26

The heart shape is inserted and the Drawing Tools Format tab is available.

ENHANCING A SHAPE

Next, you will enhance the heart graphic's appearance by selecting a shape style and adding a reflection. Just like the other styles in PowerPoint 2010, **shape styles** consist of combinations of fill colors, outline colors, and effects.

1

- **Open the Drawing Tools Format tab.**

- **Click ⏷ More in the Shape Styles group to open the Shape Styles gallery.**

- **Choose Intense Effect—Green, Accent 1 from the Shape Styles gallery.**

- **Click** **Shape Effects ▾ and choose Half Reflection, 4 pt offset from the Reflection gallery.**

Additional Information

The offset controls the amount of space between the object and the reflection.

Your screen should be similar to Figure 2.27

Figure 2.27

The addition of style and reflection effects greatly improves the appearance of the heart.

ADDING TEXT TO A SHAPE

Next, you will add text to the heart object. Text can be added to all shapes and becomes part of the shape; when the shape is moved, the text moves with it.

1

- **Right-click on the heart to open the shortcut menu, and choose Edit Text.**

- **Type Open Your Heart**

Having Trouble?

If the inserted text does not fit into the heart shape, increase the size of the heart.

Your screen should be similar to Figure 2.28

Figure 2.28

Next, you want to improve the appearance of the text using character effects.

2

- Select the text in the heart.

- Click **B** Bold and **I** Italic on the Mini toolbar.

- Increase the font size to 24 points.

- Open the **A** ▾ Font Color gallery and choose Blue, Accent 2 in the Theme Colors section.

- Click outside the heart to deselect the shape.

Your screen should be similar to Figure 2.29

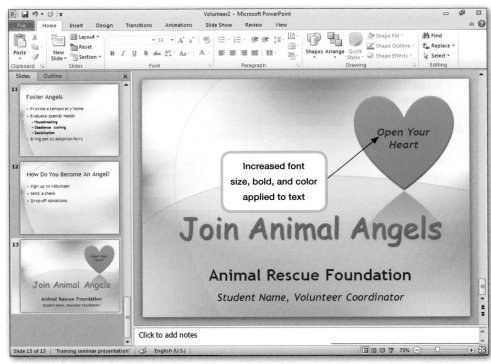

Figure 2.29

ROTATING THE OBJECT

Finally, you want to change the angle of the heart. You can rotate an object 90 degrees left or right, flip it vertically or horizontally, or specify an exact degree of rotation. You will change the angle of the heart to the right using the ⬤ **rotate handle** for the selected object, which allows you to rotate the object to any degree in any direction.

1

- Select the heart graphic.

- Drag the rotate handle to the right slightly.

Additional Information

The mouse pointer appears as 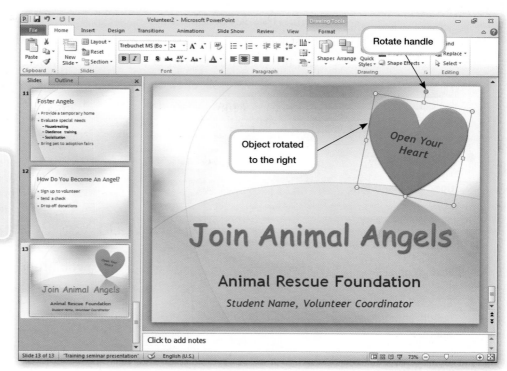 when positioned on the rotate handle, and Live Preview shows how the object will look as you rotate it.

Your screen should be similar to Figure 2.30

Figure 2.30

The graphic is a nice addition to the final slide of the presentation.

Working with Text Boxes

On slide 12, you want to add the foundation's contact information. To make it stand out on the slide, you will put it into a text box. A **text box** is a container for text or graphics. The text box can be moved, resized, and enhanced in other ways to make it stand out from the other text on the slide.

CREATING A TEXT BOX

First you create the text box, and then you add the content. When inserting a text box, the mouse pointer appears as ⬚ when pointing to the slide. Then, to create the text box, click on the slide and drag to increase the size.

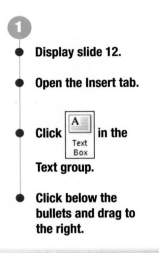

- Display slide 12.

- Open the Insert tab.

- Click [A Text Box] in the Text group.

- Click below the bullets and drag to the right.

Additional Information

The mouse pointer appears as ✛ when dragging to create the text box.

Your screen should be similar to Figure 2.31

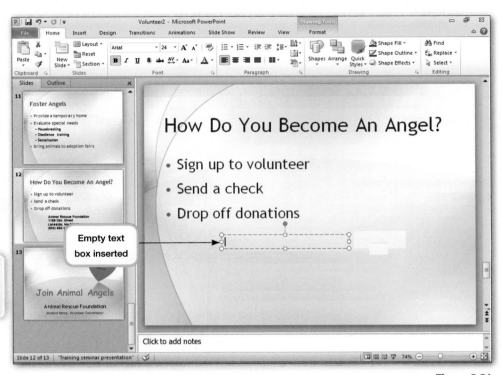

Figure 2.31

The text box is created and is a selected object. It is surrounded with a dashed border indicating you can enter, delete, select, and format the text inside the box.

ADDING TEXT TO A TEXT BOX

The text box displays a cursor, indicating that it is waiting for you to enter the text. As you type the text in the text box, it will increase in length automatically as needed to display the entire entry.

1

● **Type the organization's name and address shown below in the text box. Press** Enter **to start a new line.**

Animal Rescue Foundation

1166 Oak Street

Lakeside, NH 03112

(603) 555-1313

● **Select all the text and increase the font size to 24 points and bold.**

● **If necessary, increase the width of the text box to display the name of the foundation on a single line.**

Your screen should be similar to Figure 2.32

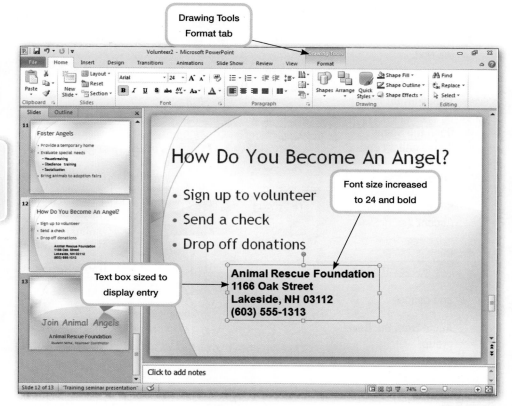

Figure 2.32

The text box is now more prominent and the content is easier to read.

ENHANCING THE TEXT BOX

Like any other object, the text box can be sized and moved anywhere on the slide. It also can be enhanced by adding styles and effects. You want to change the color and add a bevel effect around the box to define the space.

1

- If necessary, deselect the text.

- Open the Drawing Tools Format tab.

- Open the Shape Styles gallery and choose **Abc** Subtle Effect, Blue Accent 2.

- Click **Shape Effects** and choose Angle from the Bevel group.

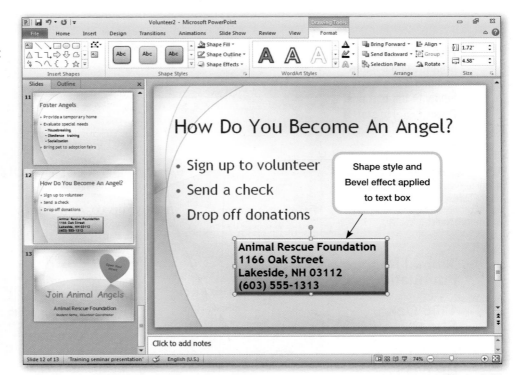

Figure 2.33

Your screen should be similar to Figure 2.33

Next, you will position the text within the text box and the box on the slide. You want to expand the margin on either side of the text to focus the attention on the text and not the box. By default, PowerPoint uses the AutoFit feature on text boxes, which automatically sizes the text box to fit around the text. You'll want to turn off the AutoFit feature so that you control the position of the text.

2

- Right-click within the text of the text box and choose Format Text Effects.

- Select Do Not AutoFit.

- Change the left and right internal margins to .3.

- Choose Middle Centered in the Vertical Alignment drop-down box.

- Close the Format Text Effects dialog box.

- Adjust the size of the text box to display the information as in Figure 2.34.

- Move the text box to the position shown in Figure 2.34.

- Deselect the text box.

- Save the presentation.

Your screen should be similar to Figure 2.34

NOTE If you are ending your session now exit PowerPoint 2010. When you begin again, open this file.

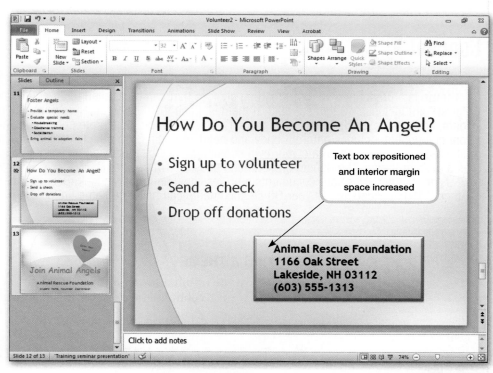

Figure 2.34

The information in the text box now stands out from the other information on the slide.

Changing the Presentation Design

When you first started this presentation, you used a PowerPoint template that included sample text as well as color and design elements. Now you are satisfied with the presentation's basic content and organization, but you would like to change its design style and appearance by applying a different document theme.

Concept 4 — Theme

A **theme** is a predefined set of formatting choices that can be applied to an entire document in one simple step. PowerPoint includes 40 named, built-in themes. Each theme includes three subsets of components: colors, fonts, and effects. Each theme consists of 12 colors that are applied to specific elements in a document. Each font component includes different body and heading fonts. Each effects component includes different line and fill effects. You also can create your own custom themes by modifying an existing document theme and saving it as a custom theme. The default presentation uses the Office Theme.

Using themes gives your documents a professional and modern look. Because themes are shared across Office 2010 applications, all your Office documents can have the same uniform look.

APPLYING A THEME

A theme can be applied to the entire presentation or to selected slides. In this case, you want to change the design for the entire presentation.

1

- Display slide 1.

- Open the Design tab.

- Click ⩒ More in the Themes group to open the Themes gallery.

- Point to Aa Office Theme.

Your screen should be similar to Figure 2.35

Figure 2.35

The Themes gallery displays samples of the document themes. The This Presentation area displays a preview of the theme that is currently used in the presentation. This is the theme associated with the presentation template you used to start the presentation. The Built-In area displays examples of the themes that are available in PowerPoint. The Live Preview shows how the presentation would look if the Office Theme were used. As you can see, the slide colors, background designs, font styles, and overall layout of the slide are affected by the theme.

You will preview several other themes, and then use the Austin theme for the presentation.

2

● Preview several other themes.

● Choose the Austin theme.

Your screen should be similar to Figure 2.36

Figure 2.36

Additional Information

To apply a theme to selected slides, preselect the slides to apply the themes to in the Slide pane, and use the Apply to Selected Slides option from the theme's shortcut menu.

The Austin theme has been applied to all slides in the presentation. When a new theme is applied, the text styles, graphics, and colors that are included in the design replace the previous design settings. Consequently, the layout may need to be adjusted. For example, the photo on slide 1 will need to be repositioned and sized.

However, if you had made individual changes to a slide, such as changing the font of the title, these changes are not updated to the new theme design. In this case, the title font is still the Comic Sans MS that you selected; however, it has a smaller point size.

③

- Use the Slides tab to select each slide and check the layout.

- Make the adjustments shown in the table below to the indicated slides.

- Switch to Slide Sorter view to see how all your changes look.

- Reduce the zoom to display all the slides in the window.

Your screen should be similar to Figure 2.37

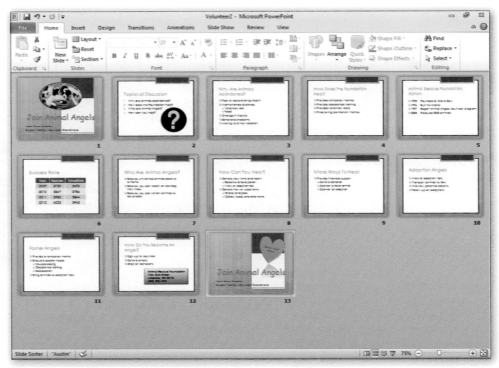

Figure 2.37

Slide	Adjustment
1	Increase the size of the graphic slightly. Realign the graphic to the center of the slide.
2	If needed, adjust the position of the text content placeholder so the bullets align with the title text. If needed, adjust the size of the graphic and reposition it slightly.
5	Select both content placeholders and move them slightly to the right to align the bullets with the title text.
6	Appropriately adjust the size and position of the table.
7	Reduce the width of the content placeholder so that more than one word wraps to a second line.
12	Adjust the position of the text box as needed.
13	If necessary, rotate, move, and resize the heart to fit the upper-right area of the slide.

CHANGING THE THEME COLORS

To make the presentation livelier, you decide to try changing the colors associated with the selected theme. Although each theme has an associated set of colors, you can change the colors by applying the colors from another theme to the selected theme.

1

- Display slide 1 in Normal view.

- Open the Design tab.

- Click Colors ▾ in the Themes group.

Your screen should be similar to Figure 2.38

Figure 2.38

Additional Information

The colors in the 🔲 Colors ▾ button reflect the current theme colors.

The colors used in each of the themes are displayed in the Built-In drop-down list. Each theme's colors consist of eight coordinated colors that are applied to different slide elements. The Austin theme colors are selected because they are the set of colors associated with the Austin theme. You want to see how the colors used in the Oriel theme would look.

2

- Preview several other color themes.

- Select the Oriel theme colors.

Your screen should be similar to Figure 2.39

Figure 2.39

The slides are all converted to the colors used in the Oriel theme. You like the slightly softer colors associated with the Oriel theme. Using predefined theme colors gives your presentation a professional and consistent look.

CHANGING THE BACKGROUND STYLE

Although you like the color theme of the presentation now, you think it is a bit too dark. The quickest way to brighten up the look of a presentation is to change the background style. **Background styles** are a set of theme colors and textures that you can apply to the back of your slides.

The PowerPoint Background Styles gallery contains four background colors that can be combined with the three theme backgrounds, giving you twelve different background style options. In addition to the preselected background colors, you can also apply a picture, clip art, or watermark as a background style. When you apply one of these elements or use one of the built-in styles, you can make your presentation truly unique.

1

- **Click**  **in the Background group of the Design tab.**

- **Choose Style 2.**

Your screen should be similar to Figure 2.40

Figure 2.40

Background Style 2 has been applied to all slides in the presentation. Whenever you change the background style or theme colors of a presentation, you should go back through the presentation and adjust font and graphic colors as necessary. For example, the picture border on slide 1 needs to be changed to make it stand out more from the background. Also you want to change the title text color on the opening and closing slides from orange to a deep red.

2

- Select the picture on slide 1 and change the border color to the Red, Accent 3 theme color (top row, seventh column).

- Click  Picture Border ▾ from the Picture Styles group.

- Select Weight and then choose 2¼ pt.

- Change the color of the title font on slides 1 and 13 to the Red, Accent 3 Theme color.

- Make slide 1 active.

- Save the presentation.

Your screen should be similar to Figure 2.41

Figure 2.41

Working with Master Slides

While viewing the slides, you think the slide appearance could be further improved by changing the bullet design on all slides. Although you can change each slide individually, you can make the change much faster to all the slides by changing the slide master.

Concept 5 Master

A **master** is part of a template that stores information about the formatting for the three key components of a presentation—slides, speaker notes, and handouts. Each component has a master associated with it. The masters are described below.

Slide master	Defines the format and layout of text and objects on a slide, text and object placeholder sizes, text styles, backgrounds, color themes, effects, and animation.
Handout master	Defines the format and placement of the slide image, text, headers, footers, and other elements that will appear on every handout.
Notes master	Defines the format and placement of the slide image, note text, headers, footers, and other elements that will appear on all speaker notes.

Any changes you make to a master affect all slides, handouts, or notes associated with that master. Each theme comes with its own slide master. When you apply a new theme to a presentation, all slides and masters are updated to those of the new theme. Using the master to modify or add elements to a presentation ensures consistency and saves time.

You can create slides that differ from the slide master by changing the format and placement of elements in the individual slide rather than on the slide master. For example, when you changed the font settings of the title on the title slide, the slide master was not affected. Only the individual slide changed, making it unique. If you have created a unique slide, the elements you changed on that slide retain their uniqueness, even if you later make changes to the slide master. That is the reason that the title font did not change when you changed the theme.

MODIFYING THE SLIDE MASTER

You will change the title text font color and the bullet style in the slide master so that all slides in the presentation will be changed.

1

- Open the View tab.

- Click [Slide Master] in the

Master Views group.

Another Method

You also can hold down [Shift] and click [■] Normal View in the status bar to display Slide Master view.

Your screen should be similar to Figure 2.42

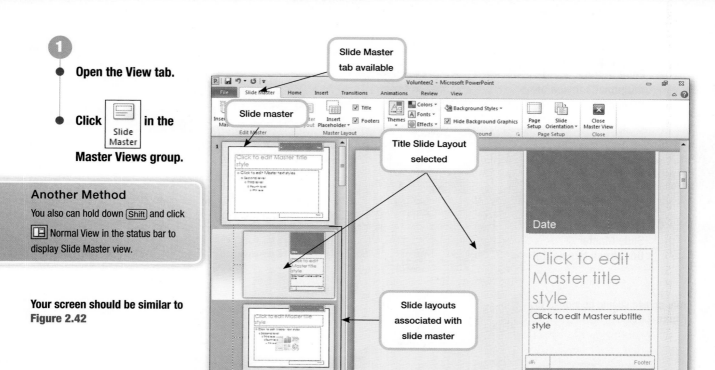

Figure 2.42

Additional Information

Every presentation contains at least one slide master. Each slide master contains one or more built-in or custom layouts.

The view has changed to Slide Master view, and a new tab, Slide Master, is displayed. Slide Master view consists of two panes: the slide thumbnail pane on the left containing slide thumbnails for the slide master and for each of the layouts associated with the slide master and the Slide pane on the right displaying the selected slide. In the slide thumbnail pane, the slide master is the larger slide image, and the associated layouts are positioned below the slide master. The slide master and all supporting layouts appear in the current theme, Austin, with the Oriel theme colors. Each slide layout displays a different layout arrangement. The thumbnail for the Title Slide Layout is selected, and the Slide pane displays the slide.

If you modify the slide master, all layouts beneath the slide master are also changed. If you modify a slide layout, although you are essentially also modifying the slide master, the changes effect only that layout under the slide master. You want to change the slide master so that your changes effect all the associated layouts.

● **Point to the thumbnails to see the ScreenTip.**

Additional Information

The ScreenTip identifies the selected master or layout and the slides where it is used in the presentation.

● **Click on the Austin Slide Master thumbnail to select it.**

Your screen should be similar to Figure 2.43

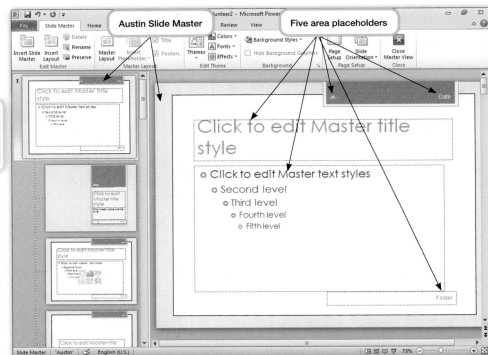

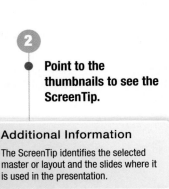

Figure 2.43

The Austin Slide Master consists of five area placeholders that control the appearance of all slides: title, content, date, slide number, and footer. The title and content areas display sample text to show you how changes you make in these areas will appear. You make changes to the slide master in the same way that you change any other slide. First you will change the font color for the title text throughout the presentation to match the dark red you applied to slides 1 and 13.

③

● **Click on the title area placeholder border to select it.**

Having Trouble?

Do not select an individual item within the content area or the changes will be applied to that item only.

● **Open the Home tab.**

● **Click** 🅰 ▾ **to apply the selected color (Red, Accent 3 Theme color).**

Your screen should be similar to Figure 2.44

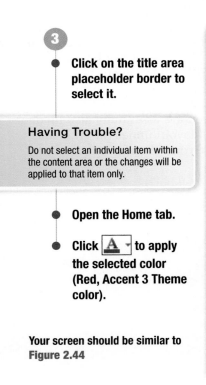

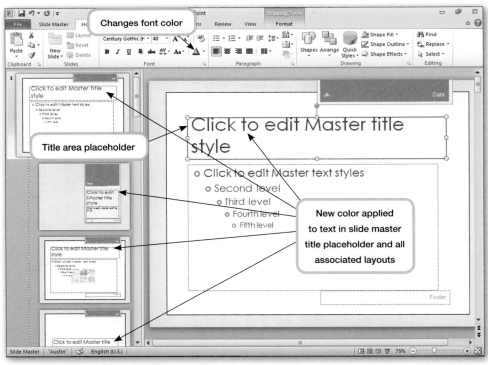

Figure 2.44

Next, you will modify the content area placeholder and change the current round bullet style to a picture bullet style.

4

- Click on the content area placeholder border to select it.

- Open the [icon] Bullets drop-down menu.

- Choose Bullets and Numbering.

- Click [Picture...].

Your screen should be similar to Figure 2.45

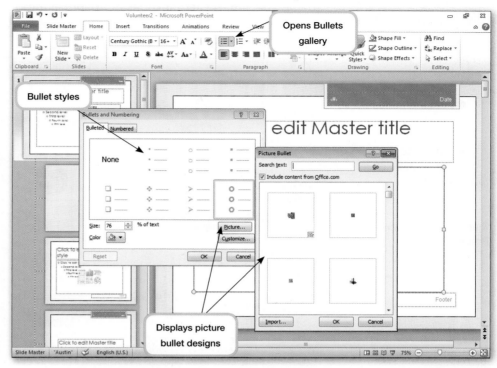

Figure 2.45

From the Picture Bullet dialog box, you select the bullet design you want to use from the bullet styles listed. You will use a round bullet design in a color that coordinates with the theme colors.

5

- Scroll the gallery and choose [●] bullets, network blitz (first column of the seventh row).

Having Trouble?

If this bullet style is not available, select another of your choice.

- Click [OK].

Your screen should be similar to Figure 2.46

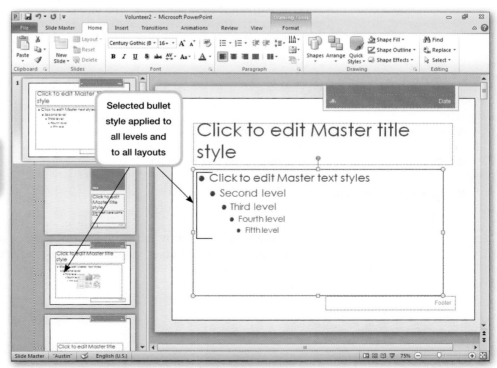

Figure 2.46

Working with Master Slides   **PP2.45**

The selected bullet style has been applied to all levels of items in the content area and to all layouts under the slide master that have bulleted items.

Now you want to see how the changes you have made to the slide master have affected the actual slides in the presentation.

- Click 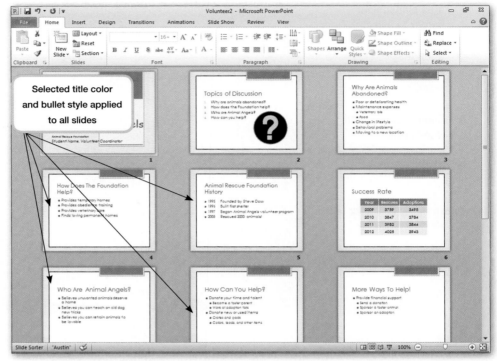 Slide Sorter view.

- Increase the magnification to 100%.

Your screen should be similar to Figure 2.47

Figure 2.47

You can now see that the change you made to the bullet style in the slide master is reflected in all slides in the presentation. Using the slide master allows you to quickly make global changes to your presentation.

You will run the slide show next to see how the changes you have made look full screen.

- Run the slide show beginning with slide 1.

- Click on each slide to advance through the presentation.

- Save the presentation.

Now that you are happy with the look of the presentation, you want to incorporate animation effects to change the way the text appears on the slides.

You are pleased with the changes you have made to the presentation so far. However, you have several places in mind where using animation will make the presentation more interesting.

Concept 6 Animations

Animations are special effects that add action to text and graphics so they move around on the screen during a slide show. Animations provide additional emphasis for items or show the information on a slide in phases. There are two basic types of animations: object animations and transitions.

    Object animations are used to display each bullet point, text, paragraph, or graphic independently of the other text or objects on the slide. You set up the way you want each element to appear (to fly in from the left, for instance) and whether you want the other elements already on the slide to dim or shimmer when a new element is added. For example, because your audience is used to reading from left to right, you could select animations that fly text in from the left. Then, when you want to emphasize a point, bring a bullet point in from the right. That change grabs the audience's attention.

    Transitions control the way that the display changes as you move from one slide to the next during a presentation. You can select from many different transition choices. You may choose Dissolve for your title slide to give it an added flair. After that, you could use Wipe Right for all the slides until the next to the last, and then use Dissolve again to end the show. As with any special effect, use slide transitions carefully.

When you present a slide show, the content of your presentation should take center stage. You want the animation effects to help emphasize the main points in your presentation—not draw the audience's attention to the special effects.

ADDING TRANSITION EFFECTS

First, you want to add a transition effect to the slides. Although you can add transitions in Normal view, you will use Slide Sorter view so you can more easily preview the action on the slides.

1

- Switch to Slide Sorter view, if necessary.

- Select slide 1.

- Open the Transitions tab.

- Click ⊽ More in the Transition to This Slide group to open the Transitions gallery.

Your screen should be similar to Figure 2.48

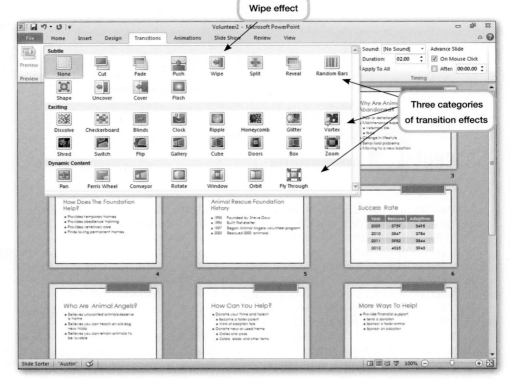

Figure 2.48

There are three transition categories, Subtle, Exciting and Dynamic Content, with each containing variations on the category effect. You want to use a simple transition effect that will display as each slide appears. As you choose a transition effect next, watch the live preview of the effect on the selected slide.

2

- **Click** 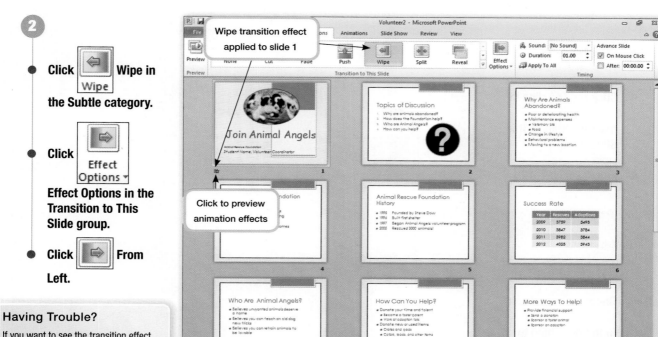 **Wipe** in the **Subtle** category.

- **Click** **Effect Options** in the **Transition to This Slide** group.

- **Click** **From Left.**

Having Trouble?

If you want to see the transition effect again, click ☒ below the slide in Slide Sorter view.

Another Method

You can also see the transition effect that is applied to a slide by selecting the slide and clicking **Preview** in the Preview group of the Transitions tab.

Your screen should be similar to Figure 2.49

Additional Information

You also can select transition effects from the Transitions gallery by scrolling the list in the Transition to This Slide group.

Figure 2.49

The selected slide displays the Wipe Left transition effect. This effect displays the next slide's content by wiping over the previous slide from the right with the new slide content. You want to use the same effect on slide 13. For the final slide, you want to use the default Wipe direction, which is from the right. You also want to try a similar effect on the other slides using the Push transition effect.

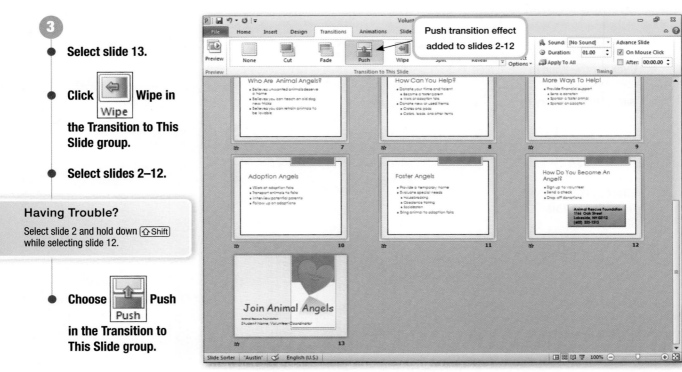

3

- Select slide 13.

- Click  Wipe in the Transition to This Slide group.

- Select slides 2–12.

Having Trouble?

Select slide 2 and hold down ⇧Shift while selecting slide 12.

- Choose Push in the Transition to This Slide group.

Your screen should be similar to Figure 2.50

Figure 2.50

The transition animation effects associated with the selected slides were individually previewed beginning with slide 2, and each slide now displays a transition icon.

4

- Switch to Normal view.

- Save the presentation.

Notice an animation icon appears below each slide number in the Slides tab.

ANIMATING AN OBJECT

Next, you want to add an animation effect to the heart shape on the final slide. There are four different types of animation effects, described below. Animation effects can be used by themselves or in combination with other effects.

Type	Effect
Entrance	Makes an object appear on the slide using the selected effect.
Exit	Makes an object leave the slide using the selected effect.
Emphasis	Makes an object more noticeable by applying special effects to the object such as changing the text size and colors or adding bold or underlines.
Motion Path	Makes an object move in a selected pattern such as up, down, or in a circle.

1

- Display slide 13 in Normal view.

- Select the heart shape.

- Open the Animations tab.

- Point to several effects in the Animation group to see the Live Preview.

- Choose 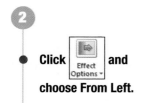.

Your screen should be similar to Figure 2.51

Figure 2.51

As you add animated items to a slide, each item is numbered. The number determines the order in which they display. A nonprinting numbered tag appears on the slide near each animated item that correlates to the effects in the list. This number does not appear during a slide show.

Next, you want to change the Fly In effect to come in from the left and to run slower.

2

- Click Effect Options and choose From Left.

- In the Duration box in the Timing group, increase the duration to 1.00.

- Click Preview in the Preview group to preview the new animation settings.

Your screen should be similar to Figure 2.52

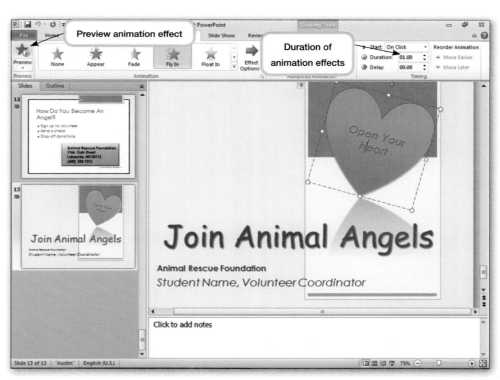

Figure 2.52

You like the way the animation effect livens up the final slide of the presentation, so you decide to apply the same effect to the text box on slide 12. Since you plan to use the same animation settings for both slides, the easiest way to duplicate an effect is to use the Animation Painter.

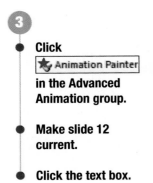

● Click 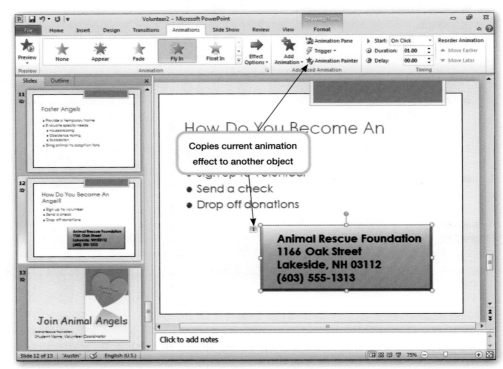Animation Painter in the Advanced Animation group.

● Make slide 12 current.

● Click the text box.

Your screen should be similar to Figure 2.53

Figure 2.53

The Fly In animation effect is applied to the text box and previewed for you.

ADDING SOUND EFFECTS

Now that you have added animations to your presentation, you decide to give the animation on slide 13 extra emphasis by adding sound to the animation effect. To add the more advanced animation effects, you need to display the Animation pane.

Select the heart on slide 13.

Click
Animation Pane in the Advanced Animation group.

Click ► Play **in the Animation pane.**

Your screen should be similar to Figure 2.54

Figure 2.54

Additional Information

You will learn more about using the Animation pane in later labs.

This pane shows information about each animation effect on a slide. This includes the type of effect, the order of multiple effects in relation to one another, the name of the object affected, and the duration of the effect. It also is used to manage the animations and to add advanced effects to existing animations. You will use it to add a sound to the Fly In effect.

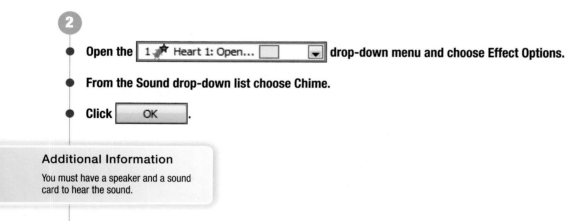

Open the 1 ✱ Heart 1: Open... ▼ **drop-down menu and choose Effect Options.**

From the Sound drop-down list choose Chime.

Click OK .

Additional Information

You must have a speaker and a sound card to hear the sound.

Run the slide show beginning with the current slide.

Click on the slide to start the animation.

Press Esc **to end the slide show.**

The slide transition effect is followed by the heart fly-in animation and the sound effect being played as it will when the slide show is run. You had to click the mouse button to start the heart animation, because this is the default setting to start an animation.

ANIMATING A SLIDE MASTER

The next effect you want to add to the slides is an animation effect that will display each bullet or numbered item progressively on a slide. When the animation is applied to a slide, the slide initially shows only the title. The bulleted text appears as the presentation proceeds. You want to add this effect to all the slides that have bulleted items (slides 2–5 and 7–12). However, you do not want slide 5, which contains the foundation's history, to display with an animation because you want the history to appear all at the same time.

To apply the animation to the bulleted items, you could add the effect to each slide individually. However, when there are many slides, it is faster to add the effect to the slide master so all slides based on the selected slide layout display the effect. You will move to slide 2, the first slide in the presentation to use bullets, and apply the animation effects to the associated slide layout under the slide master.

1

- Make slide 2 current.

- Change to Slide Master view.

- Point to the slide layout thumbnail to see the slide layout name and confirm that the correct slides will be affected (Title and Content Layout: used by slide(s) 2–4, 6–9, 12).

Having Trouble?
If this is not your selected slide master, change the selection to this master.

- Select the content placeholder.

- Open the Animations tab.

- Scroll the Animation gallery to see the second row of effects.

- Click .

- Click  and choose From Right.

Your screen should be similar to Figure 2.55

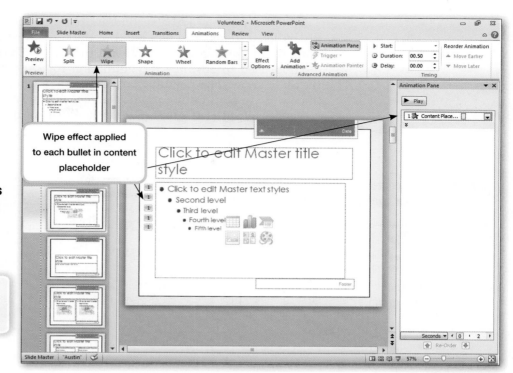

Figure 2.55

Animation icons appear next to each bulleted item in the content placeholder, and the Animation pane displays the information about the animation. The preview demonstrated how this effect will appear on the slide. Although the slide master preview does not show it, each bullet will appear individually on the slide. You can confirm this because a number tab appears next to each bullet in the content area indicating that the effect will be applied to each line.

You also want to add a second animation effect to give more emphasis to the bulleted items. You will add the Darken animation effect and change the Start timing setting associated with the effect. The Start settings control the method used to advance the animation for each bullet item while you run the slide show. The default Start setting, On Click, means you need to click the mouse to start each animation effect. You want the Darken effect to begin automatically after the first animation effect is finished.

2

- Select the content placeholder again.

- Click ★ Add Animation ▾ in the Advanced Animation group.

- Choose ★ Darken Darken from the Emphasis category.

- Click Start: ▾ in the Timing group and choose After Previous.

- Click ► Play to view the effect.

Your screen should be similar to Figure 2.56

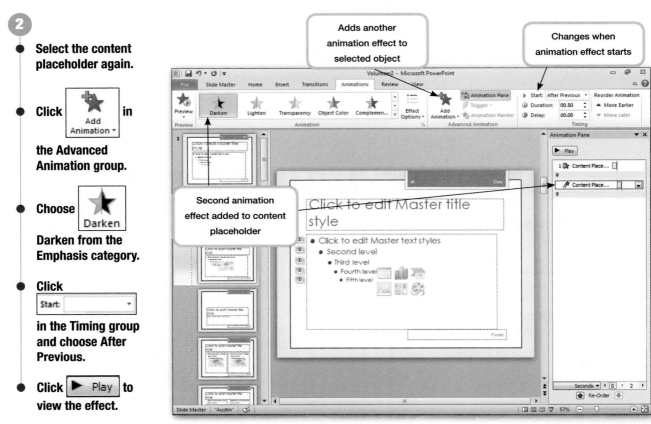

Figure 2.56

The preview showed that the Darken effect correctly started after the Wipe effect ended. You are concerned, however, that the timing for the Wipe effect is too fast and the Darken emphasis is too subtle. You will lengthen the duration for the Wipe effect and change the Darken emphasis to another.

3

- Click on
  1 ⭐ Content Place... ☐
  in the Animation pane
  to select it.

- Increase the Duration
  setting in the Timing
  group to 3.00.

- Click on
  ⭐ Content Place...
  in the Animation pane
  to select it.

- Choose **Bold Reveal**
  from the Animation
  gallery.

- Click ▶ Play .

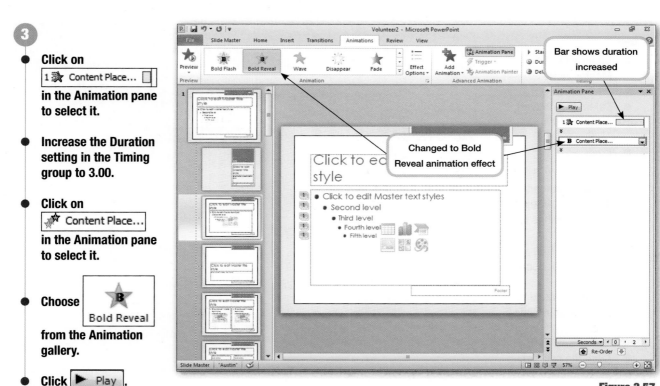

Figure 2.57

Your screen should be similar to Figure 2.57

Additional Information

The bar in each effect in the Animation pane indicates the length of the duration.

The changes in the animation effects are shown in the Animation pane and have been applied to slides 2–4, 6–9, and 12. To check how the animation effects actually appear in a slide, you will return to Normal view and preview the animations.

4

- **Change to Normal view and preview the animation on slide 2.**

The preview demonstrates how the Wipe effect and then the Bold Reveal emphasis appears one-by-one on each bullet. Since you like the way the animation looks, you want to apply it to all the other bulleted slides except 5.

5

- Change to Slide Master view.

- Select the content placeholder.

- Click 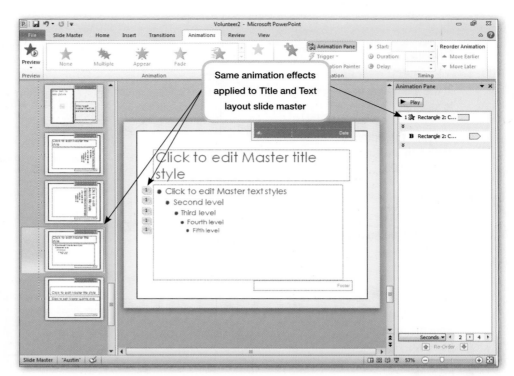 Animation Painter in the Advanced Animation group of the Animations tab.

- Select the Title and Text Layout: used by slide(s) 10–11 slide master (second to last layout in Slide pane).

- Click the content placeholder.

Figure 2.58

Your screen should be similar to Figure 2.58

The same animation effects that are on the Title and Content Layout (slides 2–4, 6–9, and 12) have been quickly copied to the Title and Text Layout (slides 10–11). If a new slide were inserted using one of these layouts, it would have the same animation effects. However, if the layout for a slide containing animations were changed to another layout, it would then have the animation effects (if any) associated with that layout.

Now slides 1 and 5 are the only slides that are not animated. You will change back to Normal view and check the animation effects in several slides.

6

- Return to Normal view.

- Preview the animation on slides 10 and 11.

- Move to slide 5 and verify that there are no animations associated with it.

- Play the animation on slide 6.

You noticed on slide 11 that the animation effects were applied individually to first-level bullets, and any sub-bullets were included with the first-level bullets. This seems appropriate. The animation effect on slide 6 was applied to the table as a whole. This is because the slide was created using the Title and Content layout and the table is considered a single bulleted item.

REMOVING ANIMATION EFFECTS

You want to remove the animation from slide 6. However, because the animation is associated with the slide master, removing it would remove it from all slides using that layout. Instead, you will change the slide layout to another layout that does not have an animation associated with it. Then you will add some other animation effects to this slide and apply these same effects to slide 5.

1

- Change the slide layout of slide 6 to the Title Only layout.

- Center the table in the slide space.

- Select the title placeholder and apply the Fly In from Left animation.

- Change the Start setting to With Previous.

- Select the table, click **Add Animation ▼** and choose the Random Bars animation.

- Copy the title placeholder animation to the title placeholder of slide 5.

- Copy the table animation from slide 6 to both content placeholders on slide 5.

- Preview the animations on slide 5.

Your screen should be similar to Figure 2.59

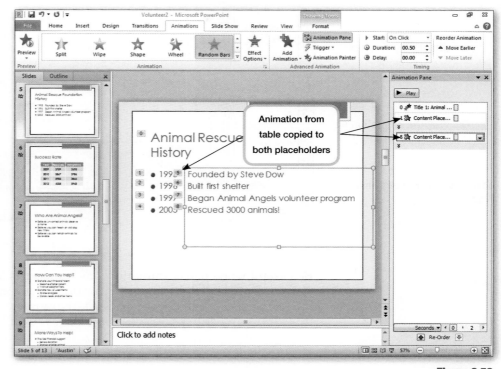

Figure 2.59

You like the title animation; however, you decide to remove the animations associated with the two content placeholders.

2

● **Select both content placeholders.**

Having Trouble?

Hold down ⇧Shift while clicking on each placeholder to select them both.

● **Choose** 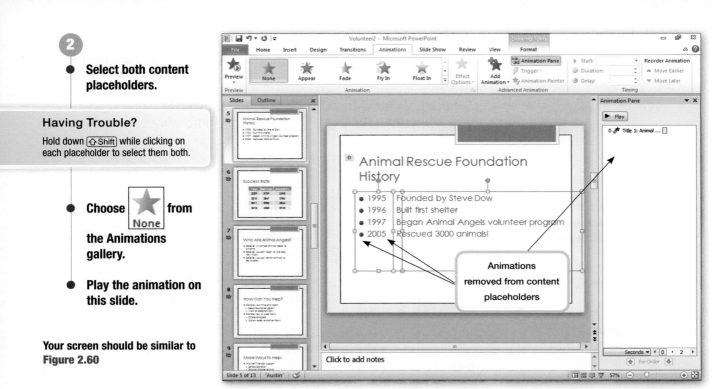 **from the Animations gallery.**

● **Play the animation on this slide.**

Your screen should be similar to Figure 2.60

Figure 2.60

Be careful when using animations, as sometimes too many animation effects distract from the slide content. You think your animation changes will add interest without making the presentation appear too lively. To see how the transitions and animations work together, you will run the slide show next.

3

● **Close the Animation pane.**

● **Save the presentation.**

As you run the slide show to see the animation effects, you will also practice preparing for the presentation. As much as you would like to control a presentation completely, the presence of an audience usually causes the presentation to change course. PowerPoint has several ways to control a slide show during the presentation.

NAVIGATING IN A SLIDE SHOW

Running the slide show and practicing how to control the slide show help you to have a smooth presentation. For example, if someone has a question about a previous slide, you can go backward and redisplay it. You will try out some of the features you can use while running the slide show.

1

- **Start the slide show from the beginning.**
- **Click to advance to slide 2.**
- **Click 4 times to display the four bullets.**

Your screen should be similar to Figure 2.61

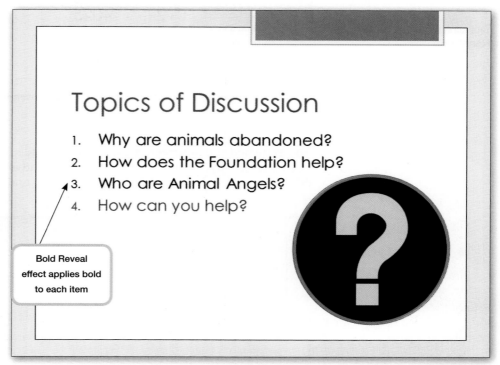

Figure 2.61

Another Method

You can also use the mouse wheel to move forward or backward through a presentation.

The first slide appeared using the Wipe From Left transition effect associated with the slide. The second slide appeared using the Push transition effect. Each bulleted item on slide 2 appeared when you clicked using the Wipe animation effect, and the Bold Reveal animation effect started automatically as soon as the last bullet appeared.

When an animation is applied to the content area of a slide, the content items are displayed only when you click or use any of the procedures to advance to the next slide. This is because the default setting to start an animation is On Click. This allows the presenter to focus the audience's attention and to control the pace of the presentation. The Bold Reveal associated with slide 2 started automatically because you changed the Start setting to After Previous.

Continue to click or press Spacebar **until the title of slide 8, "How Can You Help?", appears.**

Press Backspace **(5 times).**

Additional Information

You can return to the first slide in the presentation by holding down both mouse buttons for two seconds.

Your screen should be similar to Figure 2.62

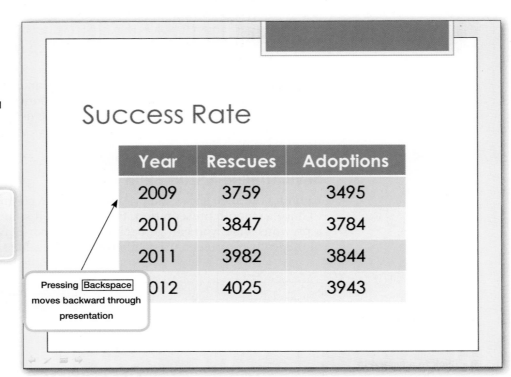

Success Rate

Year	Rescues	Adoptions
2009	3759	3495
2010	3847	3784
2011	3982	3844
2012	4025	3943

Pressing Backspace moves backward through presentation

Figure 2.62

You returned the onscreen presentation to slide 6, but now, because the audience has already viewed slide 7, you want to advance to slide 8. To go to a specific slide number, you type the slide number and press Enter.

Type 8 **and press** Enter**.**

Another Method

You also can choose Go to Slide from the shortcut menu and select a slide to display.

Click two times to display the bulleted items.

Click again to display slide 9.

Your screen should be similar to Figure 2.63

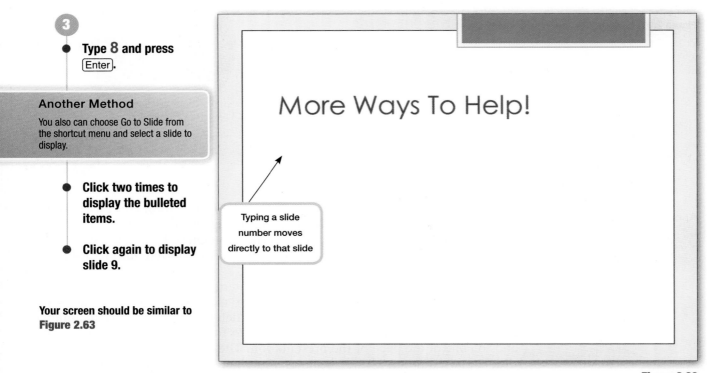

More Ways To Help!

Typing a slide number moves directly to that slide

Figure 2.63

Slide 9, More Ways To Help!, is displayed.

Sometimes a question from an audience member can interrupt the flow of the presentation. If this happens to you, you can black out the screen to focus attention on your response.

● **Press b or B.**

The screen goes to black while you address the topic. When you are ready to resume the presentation, you can bring the slide back.

● **Click, or press b.**

● **Click to display the bulleted items on slide 9.**

ADDING FREEHAND ANNOTATIONS

During your presentation, you may want to point to an important word, underline an important point, or draw checkmarks next to items that you have covered. To do this, you can use the mouse pointer during the presentation. When you move the mouse, the mouse pointer appears and the Slide Show toolbar is displayed in the lower-left corner of the screen. The mouse pointer in its current shape can be used to point to items on the slide. You also can use it to draw on the screen by changing the mouse pointer to a ballpoint pen, felt-tip pen, or highlighter, which activates the associated freehand annotation feature.

● **Move the mouse on your desktop to display the mouse pointer and the Slide Show toolbar.**

● **Click** [pen icon] **in the Slide Show toolbar to display the Pointer Options menu.**

Another Method
You also can select Pointer Options from the shortcut menu.

Your screen should be similar to Figure 2.64

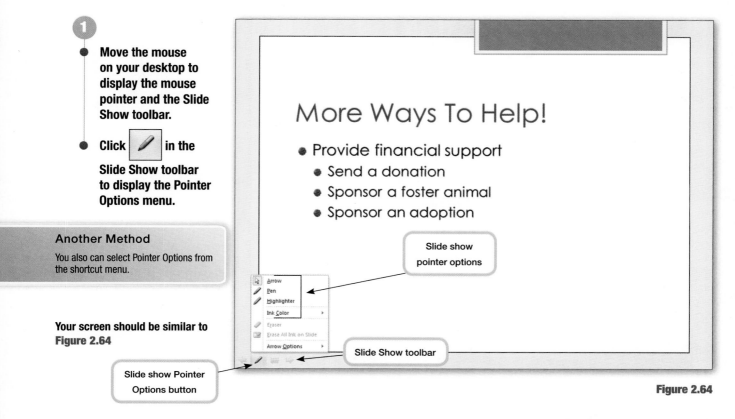

Figure 2.64

The mouse pointer and arrow options are described in the following table.

Pointer Options	Effect
Arrow	Displays the mouse pointer as an arrow.
Pen	Changes the mouse pointer to a diamond shape and turns on ballpoint pen annotation.
Highlighter	Changes the mouse pointer to a bar shape and turns on highlighter.
Ink Color	Displays a color palette to select a color for the annotation tool.
Eraser	Erases selected annotations.
Erase All Ink on Slide	Removes all annotations from the slide.
Arrow Options	**(These options apply only if Arrow is selected.)**
Automatic	Hides the mouse pointer if it is not moved for 15 seconds. It reappears when you move the mouse. This is the default setting.
Visible	Displays the mouse pointer as an arrow and does not hide it.
Hidden	Hides the mouse pointer until another pointer option is selected.

You will try out several of the freehand annotation features to see how they work. To draw, you select the pen style and then drag the pen pointer in the direction you want to draw.

● Choose Pen.

Another Method

You also can use Ctrl + P to display the Pen.

● Move the dot pointer to near the word "Send" and then drag the dot pointer until a circle is drawn around the word "Send".

● Select Ink Color from the Pointer Options menu and choose Light Blue from the Standard Colors bar.

Additional Information

The Automatic ink color setting determines the default color to use for annotations based upon the slide theme colors.

● Draw three lines under the word "Help!".

● Choose Highlighter from the Pointer Options menu and highlight the word "donation".

Additional Information

The mouse pointer changes shape depending upon the selected annotation tool.

Your screen should be similar to Figure 2.65

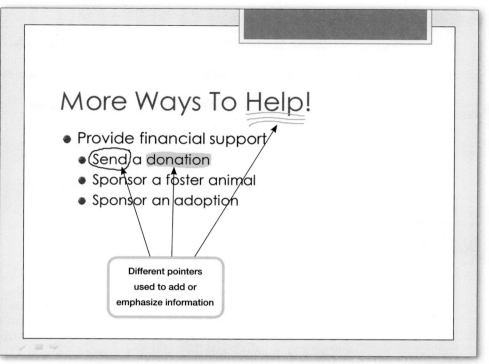

Figure 2.65

The freehand annotation feature allows you to point out and emphasize important information on a slide during the presentation.

3

● **Practice using the freehand annotator to draw any shapes you want on the slide.**

● **To erase the annotations, choose Erase All Ink on Slide from the Pointer Options menu.**

Another Method

The keyboard shortcut to erase annotations is E.

● **To turn off freehand annotation, choose Arrow from the Pointer Options menu.**

Another Method

You also can use [Ctrl] + A to display the arrow.

The freehand annotation feature allows you to point out and emphasize important information on a slide during the presentation.
Another feature that you can use to emphasize information on a slide is to change the mouse pointer to a laser pointer.

4

● **Click to display the four bulleted items on slide 10.**

● **Press [Ctrl] and hold down the left mouse button to turn the mouse pointer into a laser light.**

Additional Information

You can control the color of the laser light by clicking Set Up Slideshow on the Slide Show tab. You can then click the Laser pointer color drop-down list to choose a different color.

● **Use the laser pointer to point to the first bulleted item on the slide.**

Your screen should be similar to Figure 2.66

Figure 2.66

The laser pointer is much brighter than the regular mouse pointer; however, it is not as convenient because you have to hold [Ctrl] while using the feature.

If you do not erase annotations before ending the presentation, you are prompted to keep or discard the annotations when you end the slide show. If you keep the annotations, they are saved to the slides and will appear as part of the slide during a presentation.

When making your presentation, there are some critical points you want to be sure to discuss. To help you remember the important points, you can add notes to a slide and then print the **notes pages**. These pages display the notes below a small version of the slide they accompany. You can create notes pages for some or all of the slides in a presentation. You decide to add speaker notes on slide 9 to remind you to suggest foster care donations.

1

- Press [Esc] to end the slide show.

- Display slide 9 in Normal view.

- Increase the size of the Notes pane to that shown in Figure 2.67.

Having Trouble?

Adjust the size of the notes pane by dragging the pane splitter bar.

- Click in the Notes pane and type the following:

Suggested foster animal donations per month

Cat: $10

Dog: $15/small $20/medium $25/large

Having Trouble?

Press [Tab ⇥] to separate the dollar amounts.

Your screen should be similar to Figure 2.67

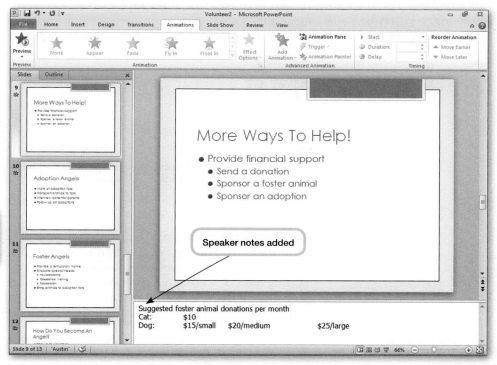

Figure 2.67

You will preview the notes page to check its appearance before it is printed.

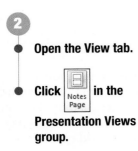

Open the View tab.

Click **in the Presentation Views group.**

Your screen should be similar to Figure 2.68

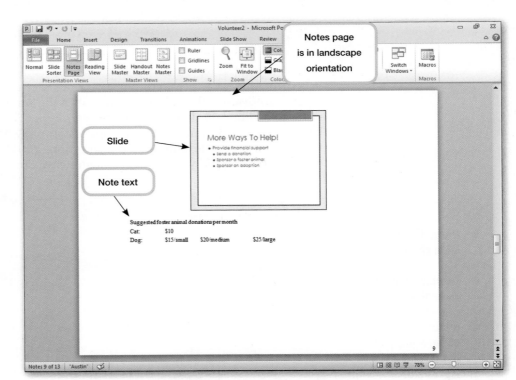

Figure 2.68

The notes pages display the note you added below the slide that the note accompanies. The notes page is in landscape orientation because the orientation for handouts was set to landscape (end of Lab 1). The page orientation setting affects both handouts and notes pages and is saved with the file.

To make the speaker notes easier to read in a dimly lit room while you are making the presentation, you will increase the font size of the note text.

Click on the note text to select the placeholder.

Select the note text.

Use the Mini toolbar to increase the font size to 20.

Click outside the note text border.

Your screen should be similar to Figure 2.69

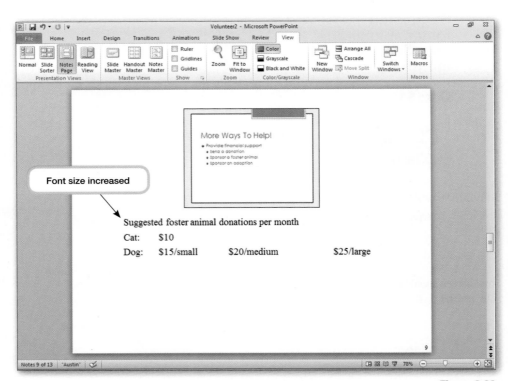

Figure 2.69

Adding Headers and Footers

Currently, the only information that appears in the footer of the notes page is the page number. You want to include additional information in the header and footer of the notes and handouts. The header and footer typically display information inside the margin space at the top and bottom of each printed page. Additionally, slides also may include header and footer information.

ADDING A HEADER TO A NOTES PAGE

You want to include the date and your name in the header of the notes pages.

1

● Open the Insert tab.

● Click 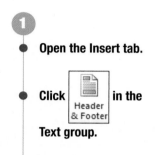 in the Text group.

● If necessary, open the Notes and Handouts tab.

Your screen should be similar to Figure 2.70

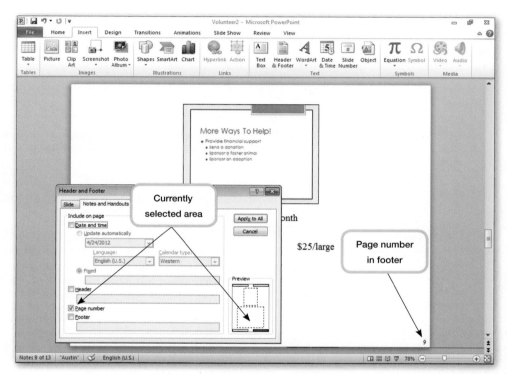

Figure 2.70

On notes and handouts, you can include header text and a page number. The Preview box identifies the four areas where this information will appear and identifies the currently selected areas, in this case page number, in bold.

2

- **Choose Date and Time to turn on this option and, if necessary, choose Update Automatically.**

- **Choose Header and enter your name in the Header text box.**

- **Click** Apply to All **.**

Your screen should be similar to Figure 2.71

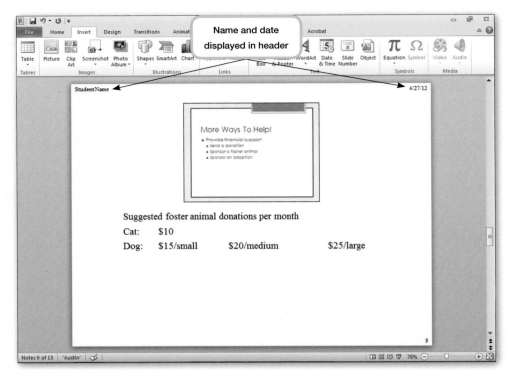

Figure 2.71

The information is displayed in the header as specified.

ADDING SLIDE FOOTER TEXT

You also would like to include the name of the foundation and slide number in a footer on the slides. The slide master controls the placement and display of the footer information but does not control the information that appears in those areas.

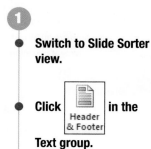

1

● Switch to Slide Sorter view.

● Click in the Text group.

● If necessary, open the Slide tab.

Your screen should be similar to Figure 2.72

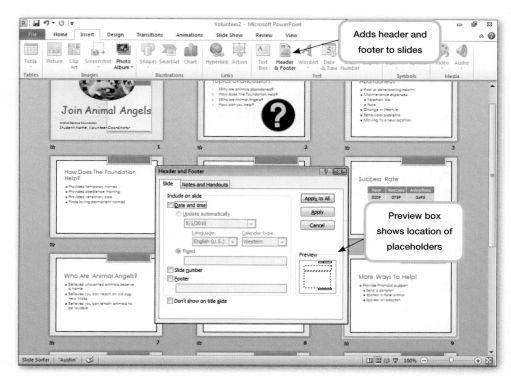

Figure 2.72

Slides can display the date and time, slide number, or footer text. The Preview box shows the location of the placeholders for each of these elements on the selected slide. When specified, this information can be displayed on all slides or selected slides only. You also can turn off the display of this information in title slides only. You would like to add the foundation name in the footer and the slide number to all slides, except the title slides.

2

- Choose the Slide Number option.

- Choose the Footer option.

- Type **Animal Rescue Foundation** in the Footer text box.

- Choose the Don't Show on Title Slide option.

- Click Apply to All.

Additional Information

The Apply command button applies the settings to the current slide or selected slides only.

- Double-click slide 3.

- Save the presentation.

Your screen should be similar to Figure 2.73

Additional Information

You can also delete the footer and slide number placeholders from individual slides to remove this information.

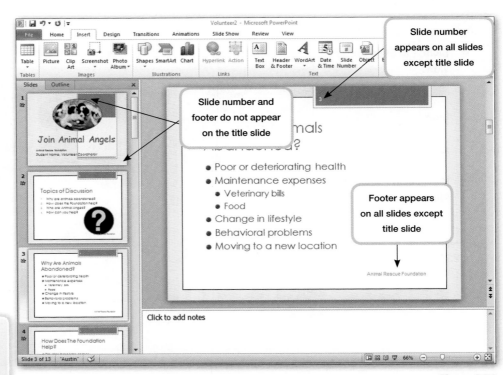

Figure 2.73

The text you entered is displayed in the Footer area placeholder, and the slide number appears in the blue bar. No footer information is displayed on the first or last slides in the presentation because they use the Title Slide layout.

Customizing Print Settings

You have created both slides and a notes page for the presentation. Now you want to print the notes page and some of the slides. Customizing the print settings by selecting specific slides to print and scaling the size of the slides to fill the page are a few of the ways to make your printed output look more professional.

PRINTING NOTES PAGES

First you will print the notes page for the slide on which you entered note text.

<table>
<tr><td>

1

● Make slide 9 current.

● Open the File tab and choose Print.

● If necessary, select the printer.

● Choose Print Current Slide as the slide to print.

● Choose Notes Pages as the layout.

● Change the orientation to Portrait Orientation.

● If necessary, change the color setting to Grayscale.

Your screen should be similar to Figure 2.74

</td><td>

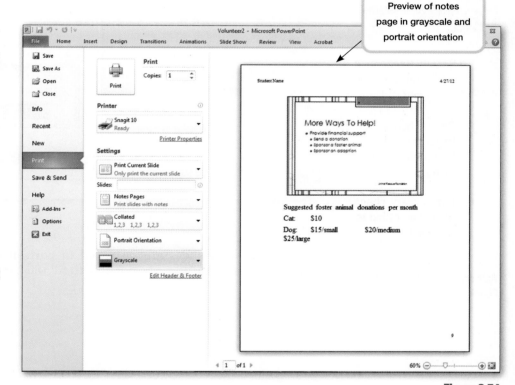

Figure 2.74

</td></tr>
</table>

The notes page is displayed in grayscale and in portrait orientation, as it will appear when printed.

2

● Click  .

Additional Information

To print multiple Notes pages, enter the slide number of each slide (separated by commas) you want to print in the Slides text box.

Customizing Print Settings **PP2.73**

PRINTING SELECTED SLIDES

Next you will print a few selected slides to be used as handouts. You will change the orientation to portrait and scale the slides to fit the paper size.

1

- **Open the File tab and choose Print.**

- **In the Slides text box, type 1,6,12,13**

Additional Information

The print setting automatically changes to Custom Range.

- **Specify Handouts 4 Slides Horizontal as the layout.**

- **Choose Scale to Fit Paper from the Layout drop-down menu.**

- **If necessary, change the color setting to Grayscale.**

Your screen should be similar to Figure 2.75

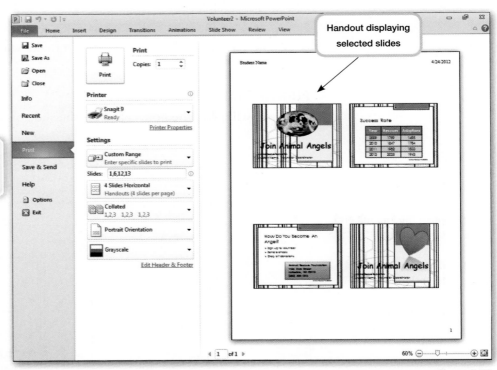

Figure 2.75

The four selected slides are displayed in portrait orientation, and the slide images were sized as large as possible to fill the page.

2

● Print the handout.

● Open the File tab and if necessary, choose Info.

● In the Properties pane, enter your name in the Author text box.

● In the Tags text box, enter Volunteer, Recruit

● Save the completed presentation.

● Exit PowerPoint.

The view you are in when you save the file is the view that will be displayed when the file is opened.

FOCUS ON CAREERS

EXPLORE YOUR CAREER OPTIONS

Communications Specialist

Are you interested in technology? Could you explain technology in words and pictures? Communications specialists, also known as public relations specialists, assist sales and marketing management with communications media and advertising materials that represent the company's products and services to customers. In high-tech industries, you will take information from scientists and engineers and use PowerPoint to transform the data into eye-catching presentations that communicate effectively. You also may create brochures, develop Web sites, create videos, and write speeches. If you thrive in a fast-paced and high-energy environment and work well under the pressure of deadlines, then this job may be for you. Typically a bachelor's degree in journalism, advertising, or communications is desirable. Typical salaries range from $38,400 to $98,000, depending on the industry. To learn more about this career, visit the Web site for the Bureau of Labor Statistics of the U.S. Department of Labor.

Find and Replace (PP2.5)

To make editing easier, you can use the Find and Replace feature to find text in a presentation and replace it with other text as directed.

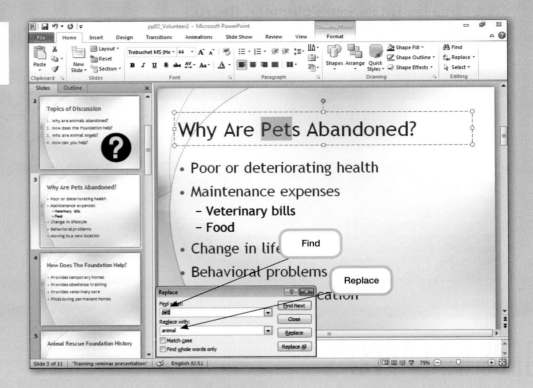

Table (PP2.10)

A table is used to organize information into an easy-to-read format of horizontal rows and vertical columns.

Alignment (PP2.18)

Alignment controls how text entries are positioned within a space.

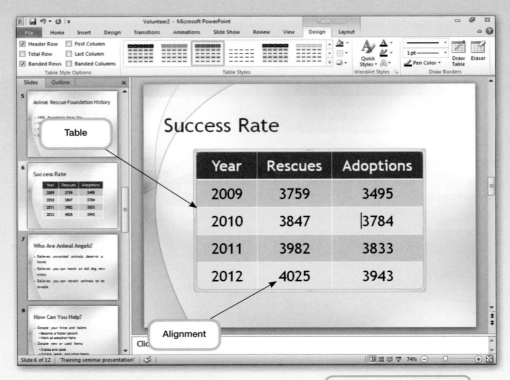

Theme (PP2.36)

A theme is a predefined set of formatting choices that can be applied to an entire document in one simple step.

Master (PP2.42)

A master is a special slide or page that stores information about the formatting for all slides in a presentation.

Animations (PP2.47)

Animations are special effects that add action to text and graphics so they move around on the screen during a slide show.

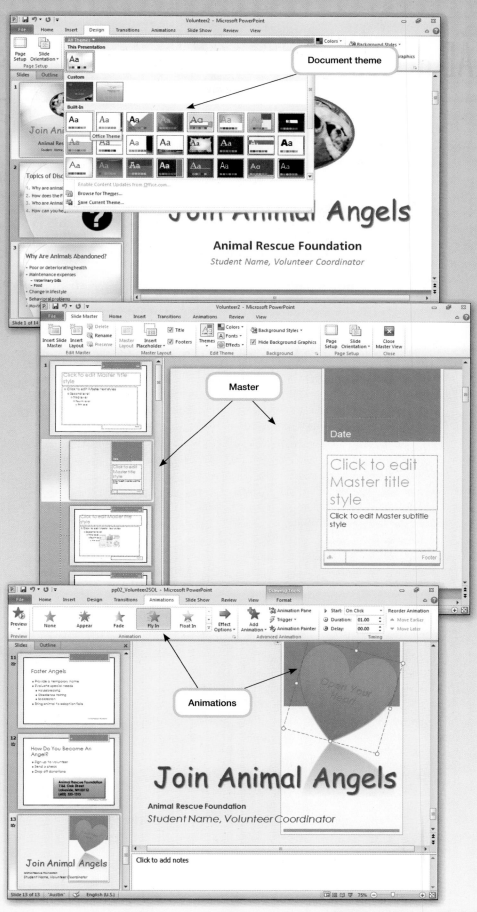

KEY TERMS

alignment PP2.18
animation PP2.47
background styles PP2.40
cell PP2.10
cropping PP2.23
Find and Replace PP2.5
master PP2.42
notes pages PP2.67
object animations PP2.47

rotate handle PP2.30
shape styles PP2.28
table PP2.10
table reference PP2.10
table styles PP2.19
text box PP2.31
theme PP2.36
transition PP2.47

COMMAND SUMMARY

Command	Shortcut	Action
Home tab		
Paragraph group		
Align Left	Ctrl + F	Aligns text to the left
Align Center	Ctrl + E	Centers text
Align Right	Ctrl + R	Aligns text to the right
Justify	Ctrl + F	Aligns text to both the left and right margins
Align Text		Sets vertical alignment of text
Drawing group		
Shapes		Inserts a shape
Editing group		
Find	Ctrl + F	Finds specified text
Replace	Ctrl + H	Replaces located text with replacement text
Insert tab		
Images group		
Picture		Inserts picture from a file
Illustrations group		
Shapes		Inserts a shape
Text group		
Text Box		Inserts text box or adds text to selected shape
Header & Footer		Inserts a header and footer
Design tab		
Themes group		
More		Opens gallery of document themes

COMMAND SUMMARY (CONTINUED)

Command	Shortcut	Action
■ Colors ▾		Changes the color for the current theme
Transitions tab		
Preview group		
Preview		Displays the transition effect
Transition to This Slide group		
Effect Options ▾		Opens a gallery of effect options
▼		Opens gallery of transition effects
Animations tab		
Preview group		
Preview		Displays the transition effect
Animation group		
Effect Options ▾		Opens a gallery of effect options
▼		Opens a gallery of animation effects
Advanced Animation group		
Preview ▾		Adds animation effect to selected object
⬚ Animation Pane		Opens the Animation pane
⭐ Animation Painter		Copies animation effect to another object
Timing group		
Start: ▾		Sets the trigger for the animation
⏱ Duration: 00.50 ⬍		Controls the amount of time for the animation to complete
View tab		
Presentation Views group		
Notes Page		Displays current slide in Notes view to edit the speaker notes
Slide Master		Opens Slide Master view to change the design and layout of the master slides

COMMAND SUMMARY (CONTINUED)

Command	Shortcut	Action
Drawing Tools Format tab		
Shapes Styles group		
More		Opens the Shape Styles gallery to select a visual style to apply to a shape
Shape Effects ▾		Applies a visual effect to a shape
Arrange group		
		Rotates or flips the selected object
Picture Tools Format tab		
Adjust group		
Color ▾		Recolors picture
Picture Styles		
More		Opens Picture Styles gallery to select an overall visual style for picture
Picture Effects ▾		Applies a visual effect to picture
Arrange group		
Align		Aligns edges of multiple selected objects
Size group		
Crop		Crops off unwanted section of a picture
Table Tools Design tab		
Table Styles group		
More		Opens the Table Styles gallery to choose a visual style for a table
Shading		Colors background behind selected text or paragraph
Border		Applies a border style
Effects		Applies a visual effect to the table such as shadows and reflections
Table Tools Layout group		
Alignment group		
Center		Centers the text within a cell
Center Vertically		Centers the text vertically within a cell
Arrangement group		
Align		Aligns edges of multiple selected objects

LAB EXERCISES

MATCHING

Match the item on the left with the correct description on the right.

1. rotate handle   _____ a. consists of 12 colors that are applied to specific elements in a document
2. color theme   _____ b. organizes information into an easy-to-read format of horizontal rows and vertical columns
3. table   _____ c. allows you to spin an object to any degree in any direction
4. object animation   _____ d. controls the way the display changes as you move from one slide to the next
5. animation   _____ e. predefined set of formatting choices that can be applied to an entire document
6. theme   _____ f. the intersection of a row and column
7. transition   _____ g. motion, such as clip art that flies in from the left
8. Animation Painter   _____ h. special effects that add action to text and graphics
9. master   _____ i. quickly copies an animation effect and applies it to a different object
10. cell   _____ j. slide that stores information about the formatting for all slides or pages in a presentation

TRUE/FALSE

Circle the correct answer to the following questions.

1. A master is a special slide or page on which the formatting for all slides or pages in your presentation is defined.	**True**	**False**
2. You can print 12 slides per page using notes pages.	**True**	**False**
3. Columns in a table are identified by letters.	**True**	**False**
4. When you create a footer, it is automatically applied to every slide in the presentation.	**True**	**False**
5. Masters are professionally created slide designs that can be applied to your presentation.	**True**	**False**
6. A theme can be applied to selected slides in a presentation.	**True**	**False**
7. Find and Replace makes it difficult to locate specific words or phrases.	**True**	**False**
8. Tables contain rows and columns.	**True**	**False**
9. Alignment controls the position of text entries in a placeholder.	**True**	**False**
10. When adding text to a text box in PowerPoint, the text box will lengthen automatically to display the entire entity.	**True**	**False**

FILL-IN

Complete the following statements by filling in the blanks with the correct terms.

1. _____ provides access to a combination of different formatting options such as edges, gradients, line styles, shadows, and three-dimensional effects.

2. Cells in a table are identified by a letter and number, called a _____.

3. Object _____ are used to display each bullet point, text, paragraph, or graphic independently of the other text or objects on the slide.

4. A _____ is a container for text or graphics.

5. The _____ slide is a special slide that stores information about the formatting for all slides or pages in a presentation.

6. _____ add action to text and graphics so they move on the screen.

7. _____ controls the position of text entries within a space.

8. The _____ tool allows you to change the shape of a graphic.

9. A _____ is part of a template that stores information about the formatting for the three key components of a presentation—slides, speaker notes, and handouts.

10. You can align text _____ in a table cell with the top, middle, or bottom of the cell space.

LAB EXERCISES

MULTIPLE CHOICE

Circle the letter of the correct response to the questions below.

1. A(n) _____ is a predefined set of formatting choices that can be applied to an entire document in one simple step.
   a. theme
   b. animation
   c. slide layout
   d. master

2. Each _____ theme consists of eight coordinated colors that are applied to different slide elements.
   a. color
   b. document
   c. master
   d. slide layout

3. _____ control the way that the display changes as you move from one slide to the next during a presentation.
   a. Graphics
   b. Transitions
   c. Animations
   d. Slide masters

4. If you want to display information in columns and rows, you would create a _____.
   a. slide layout
   b. shape
   c. table
   d. text box

5. You can change the horizontal placement of an entry in a placeholder or a table cell by using one of the four horizontal alignment settings: left, center, right, and _____.
   a. located
   b. marginalized
   c. highlighted
   d. justified

6. To substitute one word for another in a presentation, you would use the _____ feature.
   a. Find and Replace
   b. Duplicate
   c. Copy
   d. Locate and Move

7. If you wanted to add a company logo on each slide in your presentation, you would place it on the _____.
   a. master
   b. notes page
   c. handout
   d. outline slide

8. To help you remember the important points during a presentation, you can add comments to slides and print _____.
   a. notes pages
   b. handouts
   c. slide handouts
   d. preview handouts

9. The _____ defines the format and placement of the slide image, note text, headers, footers, and other elements that will appear on all speaker notes.
   a. handouts master
   b. title master
   c. slide master
   d. notes master

10. _____ add action to text and graphics so they move around on the screen.
   a. Animations
   b. Slides
   c. Transitions
   d. Masters

STEP-BY-STEP

ENHANCING A STAFF TRAINING PRESENTATION ★

1. You are working on the staff training presentation for the Sleepy Time Inn. You have already created the introductory portion of the presentation and need to reorganize the topics and make the presentation more visually appealing. Three slides from your modified presentation will be similar to those shown here.

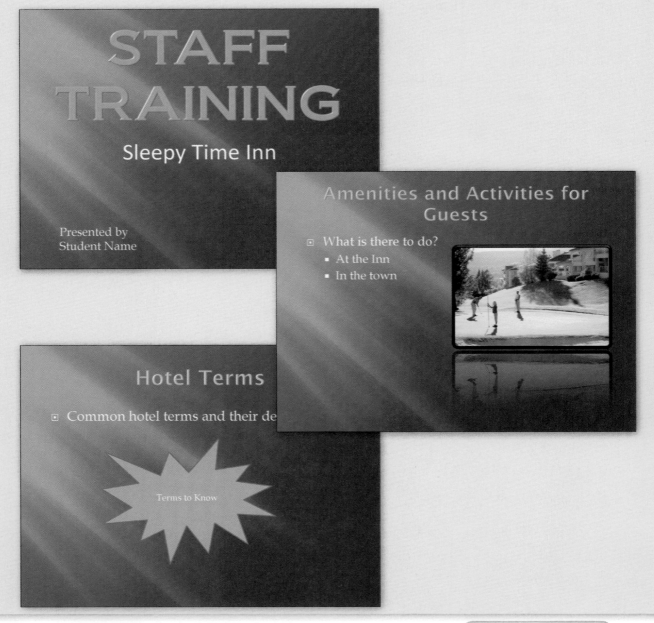

a. Open the file pp02_Sleepy Time Staff Training.

b. Run the slide show to see the progress so far.

c. Spell-check the presentation, making the appropriate corrections.

d. Find and replace any occurrence of "city" with the word **town**.

e. In slide 1:

> Insert a text box below the subtitle.
>
> Type **Presented by Your Name**.
>
> Set the font size to 24 and position the text box appropriately on the slide.
>
> Add the following speaker note: **Be sure to introduce yourself and play the name game**.

f. In slide 4:

> Add a shape of your choice to emphasize the text on the inserted shape.
>
> Enter and format the text **Terms to Know**.
>
> Position and size the shape appropriately. Add an animation effect of your choice to the shape.

g. In slide 5:

> Set the Picture Style to Reflected Bevel, Black.
>
> Set the Picture Effect to Half Reflection, 4 pt offset.

h. Move slide 4 after slide 12.

i. Change the design of the slides to one of your choice from the Themes gallery. Check all slides and make any needed adjustments.

j. Duplicate slide 1 and move it to the end of the presentation. Delete the speaker note from slide 15.

k. Add a transition effect of your choice to all slides. Add an animation effect and sound to the first slide.

l. Add your name to the File properties. Save the file as Sleepy Time Training.

m. Print slides 1, 4, 12, and 15 as handouts (four slides horizontal in portrait orientation).

EMERGENCY DRIVING TECHNIQUES ★

2. To complete this problem, you must have completed Step-by-Step Exercise 2 in Lab 1. You have completed the first draft of the presentation on tire blowouts, but you still have some information to add. Additionally, you want to make the presentation look better using many of the presentation features. Several slides of the modified presentation are shown here.

a. Open the presentation Handling Blowouts, which was saved at the end of Step-by-Step Exercise 2 in Lab 1. If necessary, switch to Normal view.

b. In Slide Master view, make the following adjustments to the Title Slide Layout:

Delete the page number placeholder.

Change the font of the title and subtitle to Tahoma or a similar font. Add a shadow.

Decrease the title text to 54 pts.

Change title text color to Dark Red, Accent 1, Darker 50%.

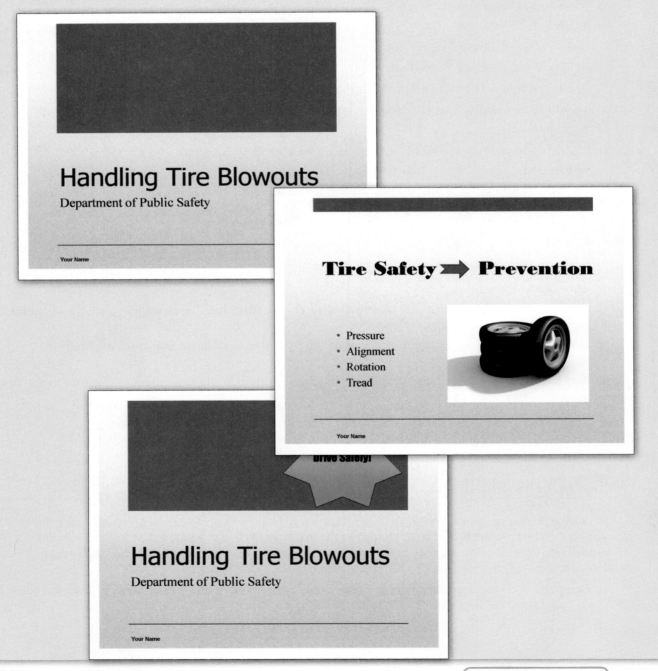

c. On slide 6, replace the = in the title with a right-facing block arrow AutoShape. Add a Fly In from the Left animation to the AutoShape. Modify slide title text as necessary to fit on one line.

d. Select slide 1. On the Home tab, click Reset in the slides group to see the changes you made to the Title Slide Layout in slide master view.

e. Duplicate the title slide and move it to the end of the presentation. Add a drawing object to this slide that includes the text **Drive Safely!**. Modify the shape style.

e. Select an animation scheme of your choice to add transition effects to all the slides. Run the slide show.

f. Add the following note to slide 7 in a point size of 18:

   Underinflation is the leading cause of tire failure.

   Maximum inflation pressure on tire is not recommended pressure.

g. Add the following note to slide 10 in a point size of 18:

   Penny test–tread should come to top of the head of Lincoln.

h. Add file documentation and save the completed presentation as Blowouts2.

i. Print the notes page for slide 7. Print slides 1, 6, and 11 as handouts with three slides per page.

ENHANCING THE ASU PRESENTATION ★ ★

3. Bonnie is the Assistant Director of New Admissions at Arizona State University. Part of her job is to make presentations at community colleges and local high schools about the university. She has already created the introductory portion of the presentation and needs to reorganize the topics and make the presentation more visually appealing. Several slides of the modified presentation are shown here.

a. Open the file pp02_ASU Presentation.

b. Run the slide show to see what Bonnie has done so far.

c. Spell-check the presentation, making the appropriate corrections.

d. Move slide 5 before slide 4.

e. Use the Find and Replace feature to locate all occurrences of "Arizona State University" and replace them with "ASU" on all slides except the first and second slides.

f. Enter your name as the subtitle in slide 1. Insert the picture pp02_PalmWalk on the title slide. Size the picture and position the placeholders on the slide appropriately.

g. Demote all the bulleted items on slides 8 and 9 except the first item.

h. Change the document theme to one of your choice. Change the color theme to a color of your choice. If necessary, reposition graphics and change font sizes.

i. Modify the text color of the all titles in the presentation using the slide master.

j. Duplicate slide 1 and move the duplicate to the end of the presentation. Replace your name with **Apply Now!**.

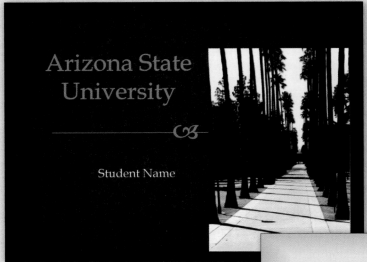

k. Bonnie would like to add some picture of the building at the end of presentation. Switch to Slide Sorter view and select slides 12, 13, and 14. Apply the Two Content layout. Insert the picture pp02_Student Services in slide 12, the picture pp02_Library in slide 13, and the picture pp02_Fine Arts in slide 14. (Hint: Use the Insert/Picture command to insert the picture and then drag the inserted picture into the clip art placeholder.)

l. Add a custom animation and sound to the picture on the title slide.

m. Apply random transitions to all slides in the presentation.

n. Apply the Fly In From Right build effect to all slides with bullet items.

o. Run the slide show.

p. Add file documentation and save the presentation as ASU Presentation1. Print slides 1, 2, and 12–15 as handouts (six per page).

4. To complete this problem, you must have completed Step-by-Step Exercise 1 in Lab 1. Logan's work on the Triple Crown Presentation was well received by his supervisor. She would like to see some additional information included in the presentation, including a table of upcoming qualifying hikes. Four slides from your updated presentation will be similar to those shown here.

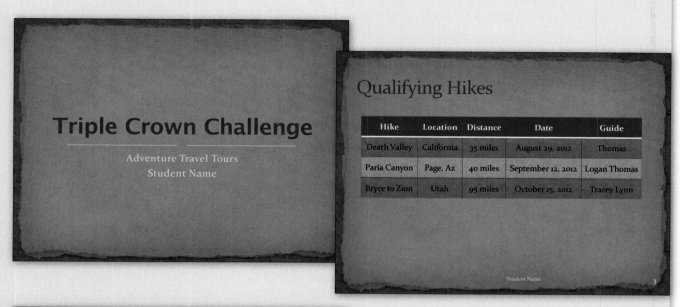

a. Open the file Triple Crown Presentation.

b. Change the document theme to one of your choice. Change the color theme to a color of your choice. If necessary, reposition graphics and change font sizes.

c. Using the slide master, change the text color of the titles and subtitles. Change the bullet styles.

d. Use the Find and Replace command to replace any occurrence of "Paria Canyon" with **Emerald Pools**.

e. Replace slide 3 with a new Title and Content slide. In this slide:

Enter the title **Qualifying Hikes**.

Create a table with five columns and four rows.

Enter the following information in the table:

Hike	Location	Distance	Date	Guide
Death Valley	California	35 miles	August 29, 2012	Logan Thomas
Paria Canyon	Page, AZ	40 miles	September 12, 2012	Logan Thomas
Bryce to Zion	Utah	95 miles	October 15, 2012	Tracey Lynn

Adjust the column and row size as needed.

Center the cell entries both horizontally and vertically in their cell spaces.

Change the table style to one of your choice.

Position the table appropriately.

f. Add a footer that does not display the date and time but does display your name and the slide number on all slides except the title slide.

g. Add the Float In animation to the graphics on slides 4 and 5. Add an animation effect of your choice to all slides that include bullets. Add a transition effect of your choice to all slides.

h. Duplicate slide 1 and place the copy at the end of the presentation. In this slide:

Change the title to **Adventure is Waiting!**.

Add the slide footer. (Hint: Use Copy and Paste to copy your name and the slide number to the final slide.)

Add a shape of your choice to the final slide with the text: **Call us Today!**.

i. Add the following information to the file properties:

Author: **Your Name**

Title: **Triple Crown Presentation**

j. Save the file as Triple Crown Presentation2.

k. Print slides 1, 3, 5, and 8 as a handout with four slides, horizontal, on one page.

COMPLETING THE WORKPLACE ISSUES PRESENTATION ★ ★ ★

 5. To complete this problem, you must have completed Step-by-Step Exercise 5 in Lab 1. Tim has completed the first draft of the presentation for his class lecture on workplace issues, but he still has some information he wants to add to the presentation. Additionally, he wants to make the presentation look better using many of the PowerPoint design and slide show presentation features. Several slides of the modified presentation are shown here.

LAB EXERCISES

a. Open the presentation Workplace Issues, which was saved at the end of Step-by-Step Exercise 5 in Lab 1. If necessary, switch to Normal view.

b. Change the design template to Waveform. Change the color scheme to a color of your choice. Modify fonts as appropriate.

c. Change to Slide Sorter view and check the slide layouts. Make the following adjustments:

> Title Slide Layout (in Slide Master view):
>
> > Delete the date area and number area placeholders.
> >
> > Change the text color of the subtitle to a color of your choice and bold it.
>
> Slide master:
>
> > Change the bullet style to a picture style of your choice.
> >
> > Reduce the size of the object area placeholder and center it on the slide.
>
> Slide 1:
>
> > Change the font of the title to Verdana or a similar font. Apply the shadow effect.

d. Check the slide layouts again in Slide Sorter view and fix the placement and size of the placeholders as needed.

e. Apply the Two Content layout to slide 2. Insert the clip art pp02_Arrows into the slide. Modify the AutoShape color to coordinate with the colors in your color scheme. Add a custom animation and sound to the clip art.

f. Change the angle of the clip art in slide 4.

g. Duplicate the title slide and move it to the end of the presentation. Delete the graphic and add a drawing object to this slide that includes the text **End of Class**. Format the object and text appropriately.

h. Add transition effects to all the slides. Run the slide show.

i. Add the following notes to slide 3 in a point size of 18:

> **Computers used to be more expensive—focus was to make people adjust to fit computers**
>
> **Now, people are more expensive—focus is on ergonomics**
>
> **Objective—design computers and use them to increase productivity and avoid health risks**
>
> **Physical as well as mental risks**

j. Add a bullet format to the notes on slide 3.

k. Add file documentation and save the completed presentation as Workplace Issues2.

l. Print the notes page for slide 3. Print slides 1, 2, 6, and 11 as handouts with four slides per page.

ON YOUR OWN

CLUTTER CONTROL ★

1. You work for a business that designs and builds custom closet solutions. You have been asked to prepare a presentation for new clients that will help them prepare for the construction phase. Clients need to organize and categorize their items before the crews arrive on-site; your presentation will serve as an organization guide. Research ideas on reducing clutter on the Web. Add transitions, animations, and a document theme that will catch the viewer's attention. Include your name and the current date in a slide footer. When you are done, save the presentation as Custom Closets, and print the presentation as handouts, nine per page.

PROMOTING A TRIP ★ ★

2. Your travel club is planning a trip next summer. You want to visit Rome and Venice, and you want to prepare a presentation on cost and key tourist attractions to help convince your club to add those cities to the itinerary. Research these two cities on the Web to determine flight costs, train costs between cities, hotel costs, and key tourist attractions. Start a new presentation and add appropriate text content. Include a table. Add transitions, graphics, animations, and a document theme that will catch the viewer's attention. Include your name and the current date in the slide footer. When you are done, save the presentation as Travel Italy and print the handouts.

ENHANCING THE CAREERS WITH ANIMALS PRESENTATION ★ ★ ★

3. To add interest to the Careers with Animals presentation that you created in Lab 1, On Your Own Exercise 5, select a document theme and color theme of your choice. Add clip art, animation, sound, and transitions that will hold your audience's interest. Add speaker notes with a header that displays your name. Include your name and the current date in a slide footer. When you are done, add appropriate documentation to the file, save the presentation as Careers with Animals2, print the presentation as handouts, and print the notes pages for only the slides containing notes.

ENHANCING THE INTERNET POLICY PRESENTATION ★ ★ ★

4. After completing the Internet Policy presentation you created in Lab 1, On Your Own Exercise 1, you decide it could use a bit more sprucing up. You want to add some information about personal computing security. Do some research on the Web to find some helpful tips on protecting personal privacy and safeguarding your computer. Enter this information in one or two slides. Add some animated clip art pictures and transitions to help liven up the presentation. Make these and any other changes that you think would enhance the presentation. Add a table and format it appropriately. Include speaker notes for at least one slide. Add appropriate documentation to the file. When you are done, save it as Internet Policy2; print the presentation as handouts, nine per page; and print the notes pages (with a header displaying your name and the current date) for only the slides containing notes.

LAB EXERCISES

ENHANCING THE WEB DESIGN PRESENTATION ★ ★ ★

5. After completing the Web Design presentation in Lab 1, On Your Own Exercise 4, you decide it needs a bit more sprucing up. First of all, it would be more impressive as an onscreen presentation with a custom design. Also, the pros and cons information would look better as a table, and a few animated clip art pictures, nonstandard bullets, builds, and transitions wouldn't hurt. Make these and any other changes that you think would enhance the presentation. Include speaker notes for at least one slide. Include your name and the current date in a slide footer. When you are done, add appropriate documentation to the file and save it as Web Design2. Print the presentation as handouts and print the notes pages for only the slides containing notes.

Working Together 1: Copying, Embedding, and Linking between Applications

CASE STUDY

Animal Rescue Foundation

The director of the Animal Rescue Foundation has reviewed the PowerPoint presentation you created and has asked you to include an adoption success rate chart that was created using Excel. Additionally, the director has provided a list of dates for the upcoming volunteer orientation meetings that he feels would be good content for another slide.

Frequently you will find that you want to include information that was created using a word processing, spreadsheet, or database application in your slide show. As you will see, you can easily share information between applications, saving you both time and effort by eliminating the need to re-create information that is available in another application. You will learn how to share information between applications while you create the new slides. The new slides containing information from Word and Excel are shown here.

NOTE The Working Together section assumes that you already know how to use Microsoft Word and Excel 2010 and that you have completed PowerPoint Lab 2.

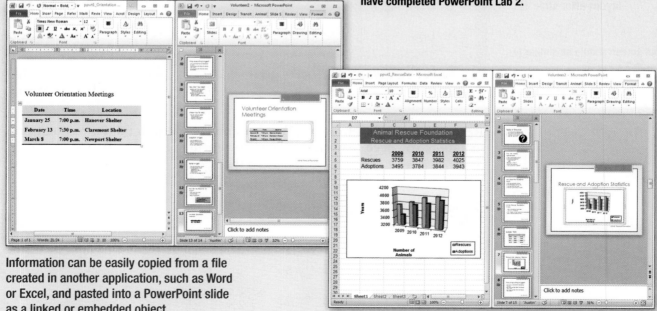

Information can be easily copied from a file created in another application, such as Word or Excel, and pasted into a PowerPoint slide as a linked or embedded object.

Copying between Applications

The orientation meeting information was already prepared in a document using Word 2010. As you have learned, all the Microsoft Office system applications have a common user interface, such as similar Ribbons and commands. In addition to these obvious features, the applications have been designed to work together, making it easy to share and exchange information between applications.

Rather than retype the list of orientation meeting dates provided by the director, you will copy the list from the Word document into the presentation. You also can use the same commands and procedures to copy information from PowerPoint or other Office applications into Word.

COPYING FROM WORD TO A POWERPOINT SLIDE

First, you need to modify the PowerPoint presentation to include a new slide for the orientation meeting dates.

1

- **Start PowerPoint 2010.**

- **Open the presentation Volunteer2 (saved at the end of Lab 2).**

Having Trouble?

If this file is not available, open ppwt1_Volunteer2. Be sure to change Student Name on the first slide to your name

- **Insert a new slide using the Title Only layout after slide 12.**

Your screen should be similar to Figure 1

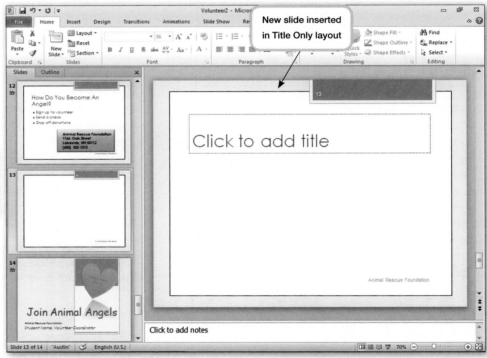

Figure 1

To copy information from the Word document file into the PowerPoint presentation, you need to open the Word document.

2

- **Start Word 2010.**

- **Open the document** ppwt1_Orientation Meetings

- **If necessary, maximize the window, hide the rulers, and set the magnification to 100%.**

Having Trouble?
Click ⬚ View Ruler at the top of the vertical scroll bar to view/hide the ruler.

Your screen should be similar to Figure 2

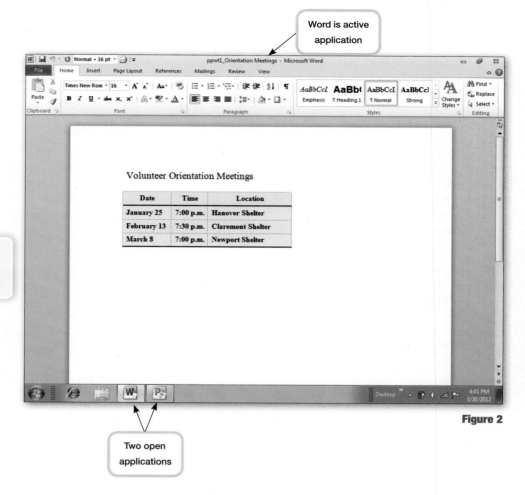

Word is active application

Two open applications

Figure 2

There are now two open applications, Word and PowerPoint. PowerPoint is open in a window behind the Word application window. Both application buttons are displayed in the taskbar. There are also two open files, ppwt1_Orientation Meetings in Word and Volunteer2 in PowerPoint. Word is the active application, and ppwt1_Orientation Meetings is the active file. To make it easier to work with two applications, you will display the windows next to each other to view both on the screen at the same time.

3

- Right-click on a blank area of the taskbar to open the shortcut menu.

- Choose Show Windows Side by Side.

- If necessary, click in the Word window to make it the active window.

Another Method

With Microsoft Windows 7, you also can use the Snap feature to quickly tile your windows. Simply drag the Word application window all the way to the left side of the screen and the PowerPoint window all the way to the right. The windows will automatically resize so that they each take up half the screen.

Your screen should be similar to Figure 3

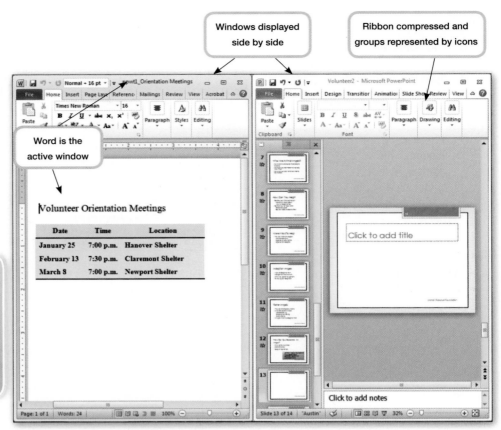

Windows displayed side by side

Ribbon compressed and groups represented by icons

Word is the active window

Figure 3

The active window is the window that displays the cursor and does not have a dimmed title bar. It is the window in which you can work. Because the windows are side by side and there is less horizontal space in each window, the Ribbon groups are compressed. To access commands in these groups, simply click on the group button and the commands appear in a drop-down list.

First, you will copy the title from the Word document into the title place-holder of the slide. While using the Word and PowerPoint applications, you have learned how to use cut, copy, and paste to move or copy information within the same document. You can also perform these same operations between documents in the same application and between documents in different applications. The information is pasted in a format that the application can edit, if possible.

④

- Select the title "Volunteer Orientation Meetings."

- Click 📋 ▾ **Copy** on the Home tab in Word.

- Click on the PowerPoint window to make it the active window.

- Right-click in the title placeholder in the Slide pane in PowerPoint.

- Choose 📋 **Keep Text Only** in the Paste Options area of the shortcut menu to apply the slide formatting to the title.

Another Method

You also could use drag and drop to copy the text to the slide.

- Click on the slide to deselect the placeholder.

Your screen should be similar to Figure 4

Additional Information

You could also click 📋 **Reset** Reset in the Slides group of the Home tab to quickly convert all the text on the slide to match the presentation's theme.

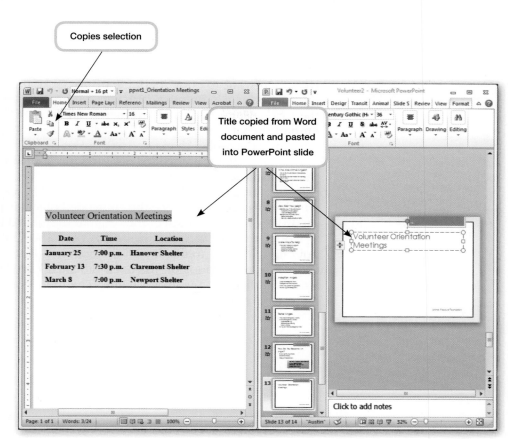

Figure 4

The title has been copied into the slide and can be edited and manipulated within PowerPoint. Because you used the Keep Text Only paste option, the formats associated with the slide master were applied to the copied text.

Next, you want to copy the table of orientation dates and place it below the title in the slide. Because you know that you are going to want to change the formatting of the table to match the look of your presentation, you will **embed** the table in the slide. Embedding the object will give you the freedom to modify the table's shape and appearance.

An object that is embedded is stored in the file in which it is inserted, called the **destination file**, and becomes part of that file. The embedded object can then be edited using features from the source program, the program in which it was created. Since the embedded object is part of the destination file, modifying it does not affect the original file, called the **source file**.

Notice that because the window is tiled, the Ribbon is smaller and there is not enough space to display all the commands. Depending on how small the Ribbon is, the groups on the open tab shrink horizontally and show a single icon that displays the group name. The most commonly used commands or features are left open. Clicking the icon opens the group and displays the commands.

1

● **Make the Word window active.**

● **Click within the table and open the Layout tab.**

● **Click** 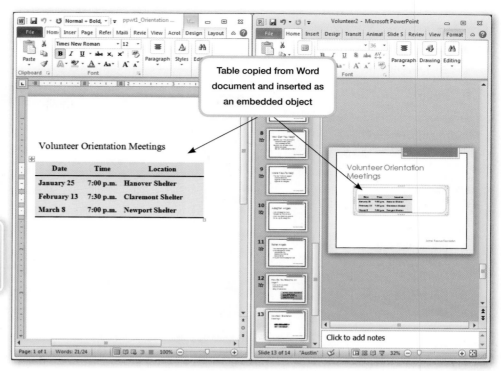 **Select ▾ in the Table group and choose Select Table.**

Another Method

You can also click the ⊕ Table Selection Handle or drag to select the entire table.

● **Open the Home tab and click** 📋 **▾ Copy.**

● **Click on the PowerPoint window.**

● **Open the** **Paste** **drop-down menu and choose** **Embed.**

Having Trouble?

See "Copying and Moving Selections," in the Introduction to Microsoft Office for more information on the Paste Options feature.

Your screen should be similar to Figure 5

Figure 5

The table, including the table formatting, is copied into the slide as an embedded object that can be manipulated. The object container is larger than the table it holds.

EDITING AN EMBEDDED OBJECT

As you look at the table, you decide to change the size and appearance of the table. To do this, you will edit the embedded object using the source program.

Choose Undo Show Side by Side from the taskbar shortcut menu.

Additional Information
If you use Windows 7, you can click on the title bar of the PowerPoint window and simply drag it to the top of the screen to maximize it.

- **If necessary, maximize the PowerPoint window.**

- **Double-click the table.**

Your screen should be similar to Figure 6

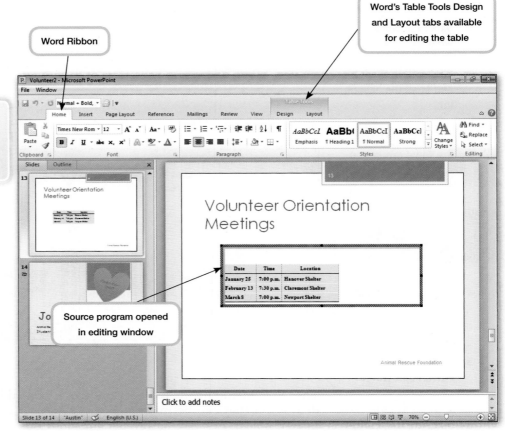

Word Ribbon

Word's Table Tools Design and Layout tabs available for editing the table

Source program opened in editing window

Figure 6

Additional Information
You must have the source program on your system to be able to open and edit an embedded object.

Additional Information
If you want to see gridlines in your table, open the Layout tab and click .

The source program, in this case Word 2010, is opened. The Word Ribbon replaces the PowerPoint Ribbon. The embedded object is displayed in an editing window. If your table does not display gridlines, this is because this feature is not on in your application. First, you will increase the size of the embedded object so that you can increase the size of the table within it.

2 ● Drag the bottom-center sizing handle down to increase the object's size as in Figure 7.

Your screen should be similar to Figure 7

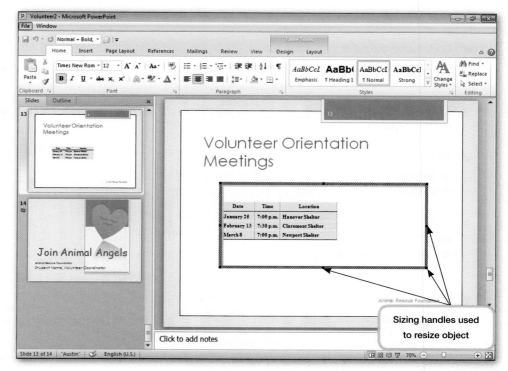

Figure 7

Now that the embedded object's container is larger, you can resize and reposition the table within the container.

3

- Click inside the table and open the Layout tab.

- Click 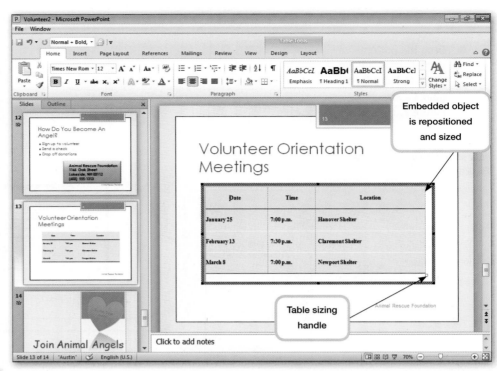 **Properties** in the Tables group.

- Click **Positioning...** in the Properties dialog box.

- In the Vertical area, open the Position drop-down menu and choose Top.

- Click **OK** and then click **OK**.

Having Trouble?

If the entire table is not visible, click in the table and press [Shift] + [Tab] until the first column is visible. You can also use the scroll wheel to adjust it vertically.

- Drag the bottom-right corner sizing handle of the table to increase the size of the table in the object's container.

Having Trouble?

If you can't see the table's bottom-right corner sizing handle, try clicking in the table and scrolling up and down until it appears.

Having Trouble?

If the table gets too large to fit in the container, click ↻ ▾ Undo to reset it and try again.

Your screen should be similar to Figure 8

Figure 8

Next, you will use the Word commands to edit the object. You want to apply a different table design style, change the appearance of the text in the table.

4

- Open the Design tab.

- Click ⬇ More in the Table Styles group.

- Choose ▦ Light List, Accent 1 from the Table Styles gallery (third column, eighth row).

- Drag to select the table and open the Layout tab.

- In the Alignment group, choose ≣ Align Center Left.

- With the table still selected, open the Home tab and click A⁺ Grow Font once to increase the font size to 14.

- Drag to select the first row of table headings and click A⁺ Grow Font two more times to increase the font size of the three headings to 18.

- Click anywhere outside the object twice to close the source program and deselect the object.

Your screen should be similar to Figure 9

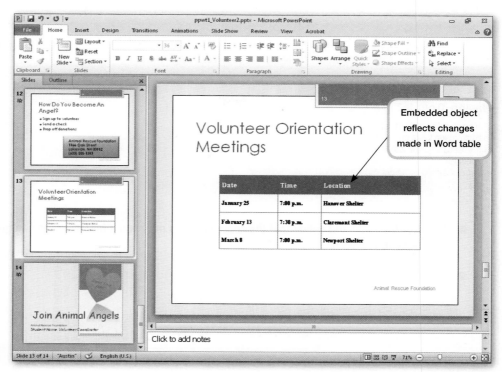

Figure 9

The embedded object in the PowerPoint slide is updated to reflect the changes you made in the Word table.

4

● Click **W** in the taskbar to switch to the Word application.

● Deselect the table and notice that the source file has not been affected by the changes you made to the embedded object.

● Exit Word.

Linking between Applications

Next, you want to copy the chart of the rescue and adoption data into the presentation. You will insert the chart object into the slide as a **linked object**, which is another way to insert information created in one application into a document created by another application. With a linked object, the actual data is stored in the source file (the document in which it was created). A graphic representation or picture of the data is displayed in the destination file (the document in which the object is inserted). A connection between the information in the destination file and the source file is established by creating a link. The link contains references to the location of the source file and the selection within the document that is linked to the destination file.

When changes are made in the source file that affect the linked object, the changes are automatically reflected in the destination file when it is opened. This connection is called a **live link**. When you create linked objects, the date and time on your machine should be accurate. This is because the program refers to the date of the source file to determine whether updates are needed when you open the destination file.

LINKING AN EXCEL CHART TO A POWERPOINT PRESENTATION

The chart of the rescue and adoption data will be inserted into another new slide following slide 6.

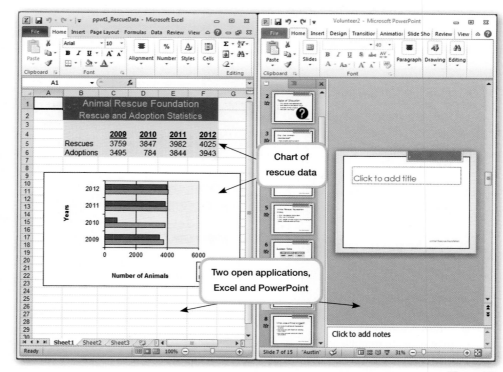

1

- Insert a new slide following slide 6 using the Title Only layout.

- Start Excel 2010 and open the workbook ppwt1_RescueData from your data files.

- Display the application windows side by side.

Your screen should be similar to Figure 10

Figure 10

The worksheet contains the rescue and adoption data for the past four years as well as a bar chart of the data. Again, you have two open applications, PowerPoint and Excel. Next you will copy the second title line from the worksheet into the slide title placeholder.

2

- Click on cell B2 to select it.

- Click [icon] Copy in the Home tab.

- Make the PowerPoint window active.

- Right-click the title placeholder in the slide and choose [A] Keep Text Only from the Paste Options area of the shortcut menu.

- Press [Backspace] five times to remove the extra blank lines below the title and the extra space at the end of the title.

- Click on the slide to deselect the placeholder.

Your screen should be similar to Figure 11

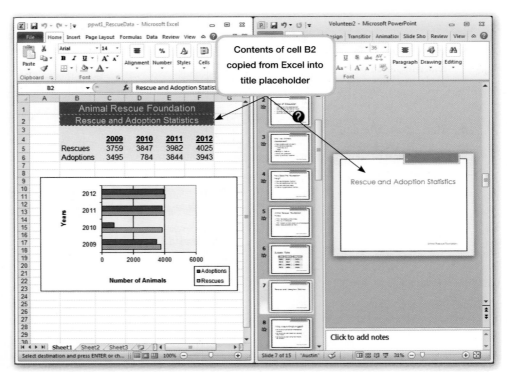

Figure 11

Now you are ready to copy the chart. By making the chart a linked object, it will be updated automatically if the source file is edited.

3

● Make the Excel window active.

● Press Esc to deselect B2 and the click on the chart object in the worksheet to select it.

Having Trouble?

Click on the chart to select it when the ScreenTip displays "Chart Area."

● Click ▾ Copy.

● Click on the slide.

● Open the [Paste] drop-down menu and choose Paste Special.

Your screen should be similar to Figure 12

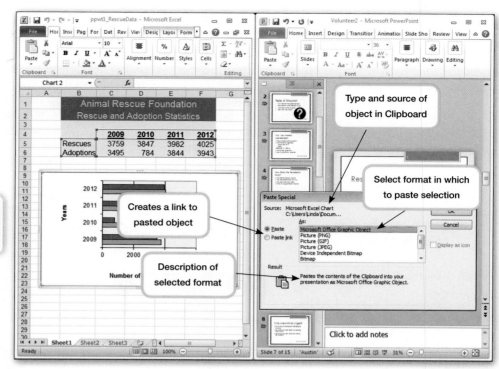

Figure 12

The Paste Special dialog box displays the type of object contained in the Clipboard and its location in the Source area. From the As list box, you select the type of format in which you want the object pasted into the destination file. The Result area describes the effect of your selections. In this case, you want to insert the chart as a linked object to Microsoft Excel.

4

● Choose Paste link.

● Click [OK].

● Appropriately size and center the linked object on the slide.

Your screen should be similar to Figure 13

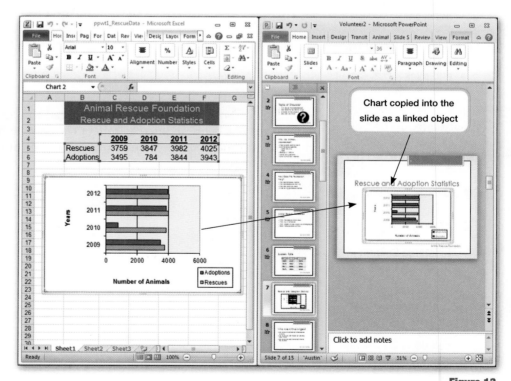

Figure 13

The chart object was inserted as a picture, and a link was created to the chart in the source file.

UPDATING A LINKED OBJECT

While looking at the chart in the slide, you decide to change the chart type from a bar chart to a column chart. You believe that a column chart will show the trends more clearly. You also notice the adoption data for 2010 looks very low. After checking the original information, you see that the wrong value was entered in the worksheet and that it should be 3784.

To make these changes, you need to switch back to the Excel application. Double-clicking on a linked object quickly switches to the open source file. If the source file is not open, it opens the file for you. If the application is not started, it both starts the application and opens the source file.

1

- **Double-click the chart object in the slide.**

Another Method

You can also right-click the edge of the object and select Linked Worksheet Object/Edit.

- **Make the Excel window active.**

- **Maximize the Rescue Data workbook within Excel.**

- **Click on the chart object to select it, if necessary.**

- **Open the Design tab and click** Change Chart Type.

Another Method

You could also right-click one of the columns and choose Change Series Chart Type.

- **Choose Column.**

- **Choose** 3-D **Clustered Column (first row, fourth item)**

- **Click** OK.

- **Change the value in cell D6 to 3784 and press Enter.**

Your screen should be similar to Figure 14

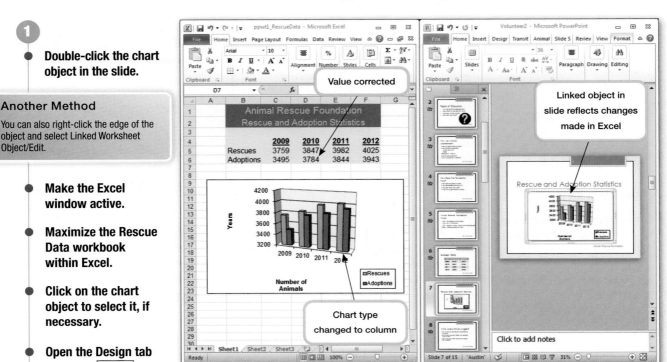

Figure 14

The chart in both applications has changed to a column chart, and the chart data series has been updated to reflect the change in data. This is because any changes you make in the chart in Excel will be automatically reflected in the linked chart in the slide.

2

- Undo the side-by-side window display.

- Save the revised Excel workbook.

- Exit Excel.

- If necessary, maximize the PowerPoint window.

Linking documents is a very handy feature, particularly in documents whose information is updated frequently. If you include a linked object in a document, make sure the source file name and location do not change. Otherwise the link will not operate correctly.

Printing Selected Slides

Next, you will print the two new slides.

1

- Open the File tab and choose Print.

- If necessary, select the printer.

- Enter 7,14 in the Slides text box to specify the slides to print.

- Specify Handouts (2 slides) as the type of output.

- Change the color setting to Grayscale.

- If necessary, click the Edit Header & Footer link and change the header to display your name.

- Print the page.

- Save the PowerPoint presentation as Volunteer3 Linked and exit PowerPoint.

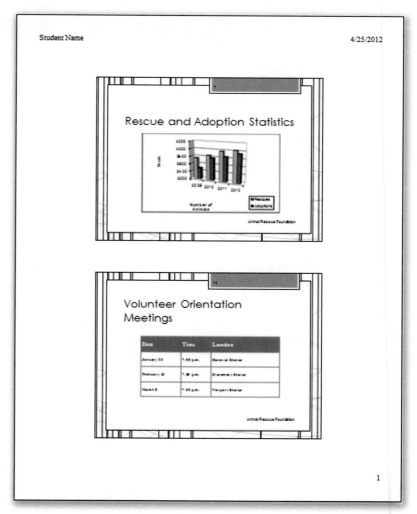

Figure 15

Your screen should be similar to Figure 15

Your printed output will be similar to that shown here.

KEY TERMS

destination file PPWT1.6
embed PPWT1.6
linked object PPWT1.12

live link PPWT1.12
source file PPWT1.6

COMMAND SUMMARY

Command	Shortcut	Action
Home tab		
Clipboard group		
Paste / Embed		Embeds an object from another application
Paste /Paste Special/Paste Link		Inserts an object as a linked object
Paste	Paste	Inserts the copied text or object
A	Keep Text Only	Keeps the format associated with the destination format.
Slides group		
Reset	Reset	Converts all the slides content to match the presentation's theme.

STEP-BY-STEP

EMBEDDING A TABLE OF MASSAGE PRICES ★

1. At the Hollywood Spa and Fitness Center, you have been working on a presentation on massage therapy. Now that the presentation is almost complete, you just need to add some information to the presentation about prices. Your manager has already given you this information in a Word document. You will copy and embed this information into a new slide. The completed slide is shown below.

   a. Start Word and open the file ppwt1_MassagePrices.

   b. Start PowerPoint and open the Massage Therapy2 presentation.

   c. Add a new slide after slide 9 using the Title Only layout.

   d. Copy the title from the Word document into the slide title placeholder. Use the Keep Text Only option.

   e. Copy the table into the slide as an embedded object. Exit Word.

   f. Size and position the object on the slide appropriately.

   g. Edit the table to change the font color to an appropriate font color.

   h. Change the fill color of the table to match the slide design.

   i. If necessary, change the footer to display your name.

   j. Save the presentation as Massage Therapy.

   k. Print the new slide.

Massage Price List

Swedish Massage	$65 per hour
Reflexology	$65 per hour
Shiatsu and Acupressure	$75 per hour
Sports Massage Therapy	Make appointment for evaluation

Student Name

LAB EXERCISES

CONTINUING EXERCISES

EMBEDDING A TABLE OF BLOWOUT INDICATORS ★ ★

2. To complete this problem, you must have completed Step-by-Step Exercise 2 in Lab 2. The Blowouts section for the Department of Safety presentation is almost complete. You just need to add some information to the presentation about the indicators of a flat tire. This information is already in a Word document as a table. You will copy and embed it into a new slide. The completed slide is shown below.

   a. Start Word and open the ppwt1_BlowoutSigns file.

   b. Start PowerPoint and open the Blowouts2 presentation. If this file is not available, you can use ppwt1_Blowouts2.

   c. Add a new slide after slide 3 using the Title Only layout.

   d. Copy the title from the Word document into the slide title placeholder.

   e. Copy the table into the slide as an embedded object. Exit Word.

   f. Size and position the object on the slide appropriately.

   g. Change the design of the table to suit your presentation.

   h. Change the fonts and font sizes of the table headings.

   i. If necessary, change the footer to display your name.

   j. Save the presentation as Blowouts3.

   k. Print the new slide.

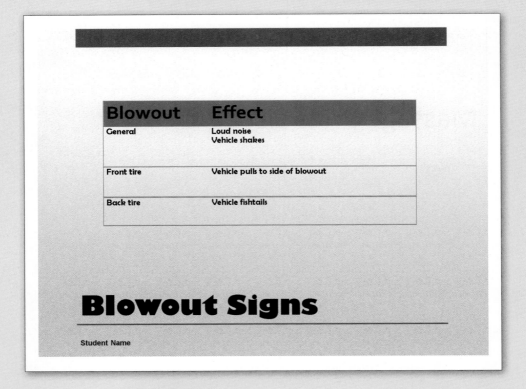

3. To complete this problem, you must have completed Step-by-Step Exercise 4 in Lab 2. Logan has found some interesting data on the increase in Americans hiking and wants to include this information in his lecture presentation. The completed slide is shown below.

   a. Start PowerPoint and open the Triple Crown Presentation2 file. If this file is not available, you can use ppwt1_Triple Crown Presentation2. Save the presentation as Triple Crown Presentation3.

   b. Start Excel and open the ppwt1_Forest Use worksheet. Save the worksheet as Forest Use Linked.

   c. Add a new slide after slide 6 using the Title Only layout.

   d. Copy the worksheet cell A1 and paste it in the title placeholder using the Keep Text Only.

   e. Change the look of the presentation by apply the Hardcover theme and the Austin color theme.

   f. Copy the worksheet range A2 through B6 as a linked object into slide 7. Size and position it appropriately.

   g. Format the linked data so that it blends appropriately with the presentation.

   h. Add an appropriate Shape Outline to the linked object's container in the slide.

   i. You notice that the percentage for hiking seems low. After checking the original source, you see you entered the value incorrectly. In Excel, change the value in cell B5 to 42%.

   j. Copy the text in cell A8 and paste it into the Notes for slide 7.

   k. Exit Excel.

   l. If necessary, change the footer to display your name.

   m. Save the changes to the presentation as Triple Crown Presentation3.

   n. Print the new slide.

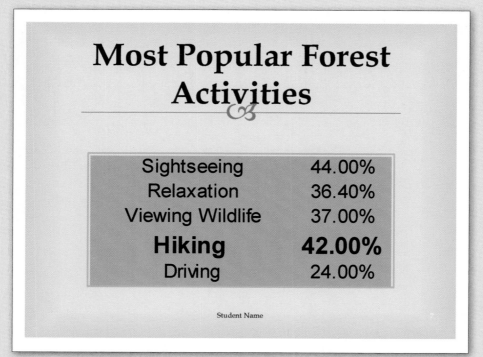

Objectives

After completing this lab, you will know how to:

1 Create a presentation from multiple sources.

2 Create, enhance, and animate SmartArt graphics.

3 Create and modify an organization chart.

4 Create and modify a chart.

5 Create and modify a WordArt object.

6 Add animated graphics.

7 Organize slides into sections.

8 Deliver presentations using timings and rehearsal features.

9 Create custom shows with hyperlinks.

Animal Rescue Foundation

The volunteer recruitment presentation you created for the Animal Rescue Foundation was a huge success. Now the agency director has asked you to create a new presentation to use during new volunteer orientation programs. To create the orientation presentation, you will modify and expand the recruitment presentation.

As you create the orientation presentation, you will use several specialized PowerPoint 2010 tools to create

an organization chart of the foundation's management structure, chart numeric data, and illustrate processes. You will further enhance the presentation using special text effects and animated graphics. Finally, you will use several features that will make it easier to deliver the presentation. These features include rehearsing timings, inserting sections, creating custom shows, and inserting hyperlinks.

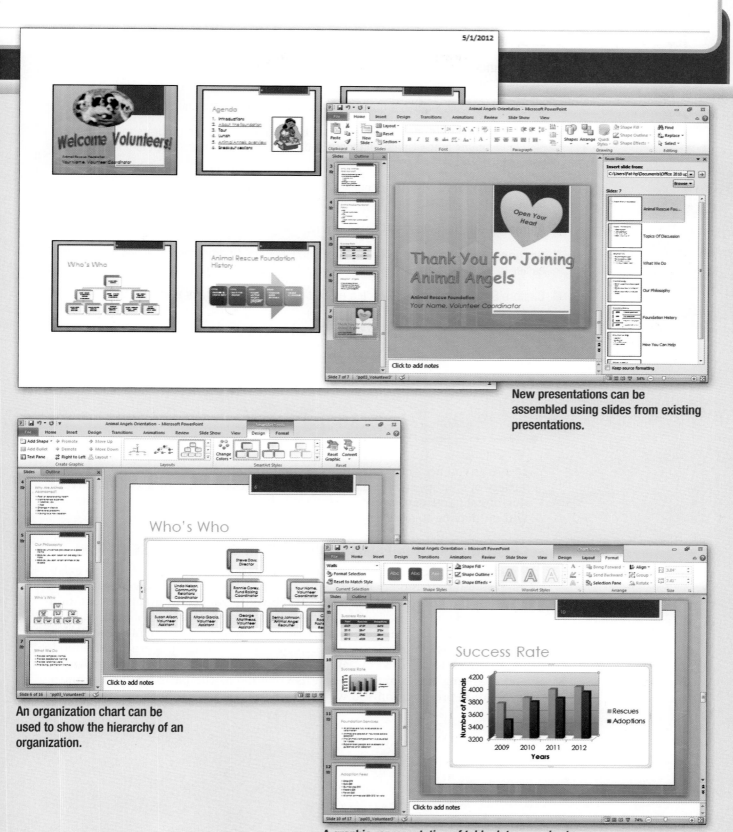

New presentations can be assembled using slides from existing presentations.

An organization chart can be used to show the hierarchy of an organization.

A graphic representation of table data as a chart makes data easier to understand.

The following concepts will be introduced in this lab:

1 SmartArt A SmartArt graphic is used to create a visual representation of textual information.

2 Organization Chart An organization chart graphically represents the structure of an organization.

3 Chart A chart, also called a graph, is a visual representation of numeric data.

4 Collect and Paste Collecting and pasting is the capability of the program to store multiple copied items in the Office Clipboard and then paste one or more of them into another document.

5 WordArt WordArt is used to enhance your documents by changing the shape of text and adding special effects such as 3-D and shadows.

6 Animated GIF An animated GIF file is a type of graphic file that has motion.

7 Sections Sections are used to organize and label logical groupings of slides to make it easier to locate specific slides and to navigate through a lengthy presentation.

8 Custom Show A custom show is a presentation that runs within a presentation.

Creating a Presentation from Multiple Sources

Often, as you are developing a presentation, you will have information from a variety of sources such as slides from other presentations or text from a Word document. You can easily incorporate this information into a presentation without having to create it again.

CREATING A NEW PRESENTATION FROM AN EXISTING PRESENTATION

To make the task of creating the new presentation easier, you will use an existing presentation, modify it to fit your needs, and save it as a new presentation. Much of the information included in the volunteer recruitment presentation you created will be used again in the volunteer orientation presentation.

You have already started to work on revising the recruitment presentation to fit the needs of the orientation presentation by adding new graphics, removing many slides whose content does not pertain to the orientation program, and changing the theme. You will use this file as the basis for the volunteer orientation presentation you will create next.

1

- **Start Microsoft PowerPoint 2010.**

- **Open the File tab and choose New.**

- **Choose New from existing.**

Your screen should be similar to Figure 3.1

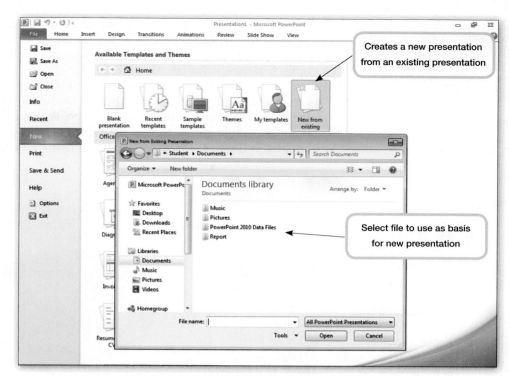

Figure 3.1

From the New from Existing Presentation dialog box, you select the file to be used to create the new presentation.

2

- **Select the location that contains your data files.**

- **Double-click on pp03_Volunteer3.**

- **If necessary, click Enable Editing.**

Your screen should be similar to Figure 3.2

Figure 3.2

The eight slides from the pp03_Volunteer3 presentation are inserted into a new unnamed presentation. As you can see, several slides and animation effects were removed, the title slide graphic was changed, and the Austin theme was applied. Notice however, that the Austin theme name was changed to reflect the file name of the presentation on which the new presentation was based.

You will continue to revise the presentation by changing the title of the opening and ending slides. You also will delete a slide that does not contain information relevant to the orientation. Then, before you make any additional changes, you will save the presentation using a new file name.

3

- Modify the title of slide 1 to display **Welcome** on the first line and **Animal Angels** on the second line.

- Replace Student Name with your name in the subtitle.

- Modify the title of slide 8 to have **Thank You for Joining** on the first line and **Animal Angels** on the second line.

- Replace Student Name with your name in the subtitle.

- Delete slide 7.

- Save the revised presentation as Animal Angels Orientation to your solution file location.

Your screen should be similar to Figure 3.3

Figure 3.3

The new presentation now consists of seven slides. By modifying an existing presentation and saving it as a new presentation, you have saved a lot of time in the creation of your new presentation.

INSERTING SLIDES FROM ANOTHER PRESENTATION

Next, you want to add slides to the presentation containing information about the philosophy of the foundation and what it does. To save time, you will copy and insert slides containing this material from another presentation into the new presentation.

1

● Open the  **New Slide ▾** drop-down list in the Slides group on the Home tab.

● **Choose Reuse Slides.**

Your screen should be similar to Figure 3.4

Having Trouble?

If your slide does not fill the available space, click ⊞ Fit slide to current window in the right end of the status bar.

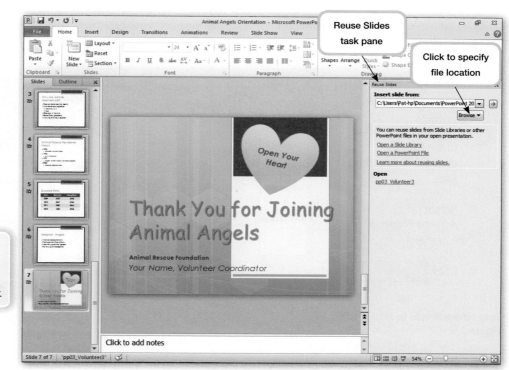

Figure 3.4

The Reuse Slides task pane provides access to presentations stored in the Slide Library or to presentations stored on your computer. The **Slide Library** is a location on an Office SharePoint Server 2010 that stores and maintains updates to presentation files centrally for use by others in an organization. You will insert a slide from the foundation's fund-raising presentation.

2

- On the Reuse Slides task pane, click [Browse ▼] and choose Browse File.

- Change the location to the location containing your data files.

- Select pp03_ Animal Rescue Fund Raising.

- Click [Open ▼]

Your screen should be similar to Figure 3.5

Figure 3.5

Additional Information

The Reuse Slides feature only displays slides from PowerPoint 2010 presentations. If you want to use this feature to view slides from a previous version of PowerPoint, first convert the file to a PowerPoint 2010 presentation format by opening and saving it using PowerPoint 2010.

Thumbnails of the slides from the Animal Rescue fund raising presentation are displayed in the Reuse Slides task pane. You will insert the "What We Do" and "Our Philosophy" slides into the orientation presentation after slide 2.

3

- Select slide 2 in the Animal Angels Orientation presentation.

- Click the "What We Do" and "Our Philosophy" thumbnails in the Reuse Slides task pane.

- Close the Reuse Slides task pane.

Your screen should be similar to Figure 3.6

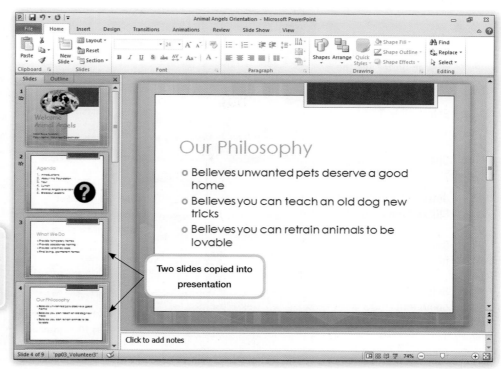

Figure 3.6

The selected slides from the pp03_Animal Rescue Fund Raising presentation file were copied and inserted after the current slide in the Animal Angels Orientation presentation. Additionally, the theme used in the current presentation was applied to the inserted slides.

Now you would like to add more information about the foundation and about the Animal Angels volunteer group.

INSERTING SLIDES FROM A WORD OUTLINE

You have already started developing the content for the new orientation presentation by creating an outline in Word. Instead of retyping this information, you will insert slides containing the Word text for the presentation by importing the outline. For best results, the document you want to import should be formatted using heading styles so PowerPoint can easily convert the file content to slides. PowerPoint uses the heading levels to determine the slide title and levels for the slide body text. If heading levels are not available, PowerPoint determines these features from the paragraph indentations.

When you created the outline in Word, you used Outline view, which automatically applied heading styles to the text. Now all you have to do is import the outline into PowerPoint. You will insert the new content at the end of the presentation and then move the slides to the appropriate location in the presentation.

- **Switch to Slide Sorter view to better see the sequence of topics.**

- **Select slide 9.**

- **Open the** **drop-down list and choose Slides from Outline.**

- **Change to your data file location.**

- **Select the Word document** pp03_ Orientation Outline.

- **Click** Insert ▾.

- **Reduce the zoom to 75%.**

Your screen should be similar to Figure 3.7

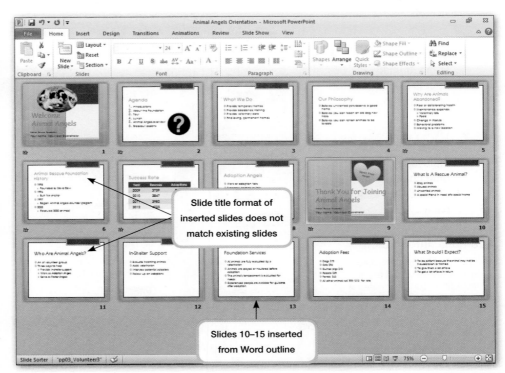

Figure 3.7

The outline text is imported into the presentation and inserted as six separate slides at the end of the presentation. Each level 1 heading in the outline is used as the slide title. Text formatted as a level 2 heading is a main body text point, a level 3 heading is a second-level body text point, and so on. The inserted slides correctly use the Title and Text slide layout.

Notice, however, that the format of the slide titles of the inserted slides is not the same as the format of the titles used in the original slides. This is because the format of the text in the inserted slides is based on the heading styles used in the outline document, not on those specified in the slide layout. You will fix this by resetting the format of the inserted slides to the default. Then you will apply the Push transition to any slides that are missing transition effects and rearrange the slide order.

2

- Select slides 10 through 15 and click `Reset` in the Slides group.

- Add slides 3 and 4 to the selected group of slides.

- Open the Transitions tab and click `Push`.

- Rearrange the slides so they are in this order:

  1 **Welcome Animal Angels**

  2 **Agenda**

  3 **What Is a Rescue Animal?**

  4 **Why Are Animals Abandoned?**

  5 **Our Philosophy**

  6 **What We Do**

  7 **Animal Rescue Foundation History**

  8 **Success Rate**

  9 **Foundation Services**

  10 **Adoption Fees**

  11 **Who Are Animal Angels?**

  12 **In-Shelter Support**

  13 **Adoption Angels**

  14 **What Should I Expect?**

  15 **Thank You for Joining Animal Angels**

- Save the changes you have made to the presentation.

- Run the slide show from the beginning.

Your screen should be similar to Figure 3.8

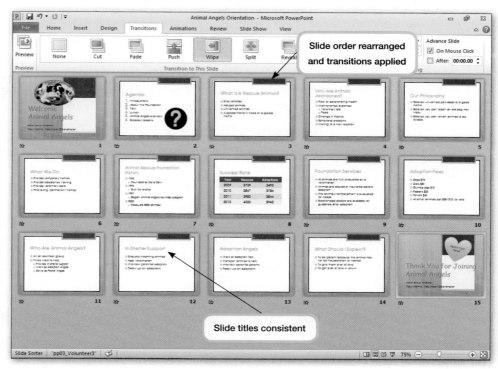

Figure 3.8

Now that the new slides are in the correct order and the majority of the content for the presentation is complete, you are ready to add some more enhancements to the presentation.

Creating a SmartArt Graphic

The director liked the inclusion of the history of the foundation in the presentation but would like you to make that slide look more interesting. You decide to create a diagram of this information using a SmartArt graphic.

Concept 1 SmartArt

A **SmartArt** graphic is used to create a visual representation of textual information. The SmartArt graphics feature consists of predesigned diagrams whose purpose is to illustrate different concepts. There are eight types of SmartArt graphics you can use. The type of SmartArt graphic you choose depends on the purpose of the diagram and the type of concept you want to illustrate. The table below describes the SmartArt graphic types and uses.

Type	Use
List	Shows nonsequential information
Process	Shows steps in a process or timeline
Cycle	Shows a process that has a continuous cycle
Hierarchy	Creates an organization chart or decision tree that shows hierarchical-based relationships
Relationship	Illustrates connections
Matrix	Shows areas of overlap between and among elements
Pyramid	Shows proportional relationships
Picture	Shows a picture to convey a message

When selecting a SmartArt graphic layout, you need to consider the amount of text to include in the diagram and the number of shapes you will need. In general, it is best to keep the number of shapes and the amount of text to key points. Larger amounts of text can distract from the visual appeal of the graphic and make it harder to convey the message.

You can insert a SmartArt graphic and replace placeholder text with your text or you can convert bulleted text to a SmartArt graphic. Animation can be applied to a SmartArt graphic, too.

CONVERTING TEXT TO A SMARTART GRAPHIC

You decide to convert the bulleted list to a SmartArt graphic to better highlight that information and emphasize the major events in the history of the Animal Rescue Foundation.

1

● Display slide 7 in Normal view.

● Select all of the bulleted text.

● Click [icon] Convert to SmartArt Graphic in the Paragraph group of the Home tab.

Additional Information

The shortcut menu gallery of graphic shapes displays only those shapes that PowerPoint determined work best with bulleted lists.

● Choose More SmartArt graphics.

Your screen should be similar to Figure 3.9

Additional Information

Additional SmartArt graphic layouts are available from the Office.com web site.

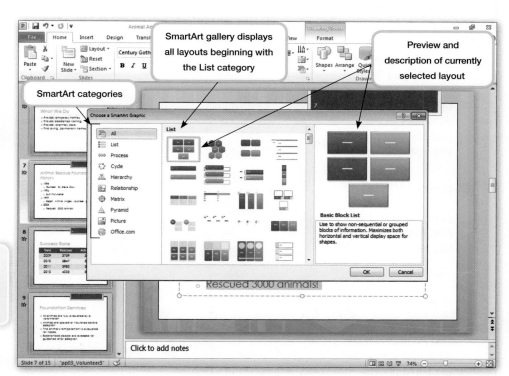

Figure 3.9

The complete gallery of SmartArt graphic layouts is displayed. As you select each type, the dialog box displays an enlarged color preview of the layout and a brief description of its use. Because the history slide content shows a timeline of events, you will use a layout in the Process category.

- **Choose Process from the category list.**

- **Click on several different Process graphics and read the descriptions.**

- **Choose**

- **Accent Process (first row, fourth column) and click** `OK`.

- **If necessary, click** the arrows.

Text Pane on the left edge of the SmartArt graphic object to open the Text pane.

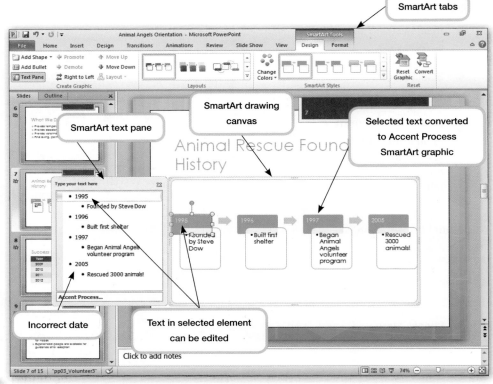

Figure 3.10

Your screen should be similar to Figure 3.10

The selected text in the slide was converted to the Accent Process SmartArt shape consisting of four shape boxes. The dates that were the first-level bullet items were entered in the upper series of boxes and the second-level bullet items were placed in the corresponding subordinate boxes. A drawing canvas surrounds the entire graphic and keeps all pieces of the graphic together as a unit. Additionally, the SmartArt Tools tabs are automatically displayed to help you add shapes, modify the layout, and enhance the graphic.

EDITING CONTENT USING THE TEXT PANE

You notice the last date, 2005, is incorrect and should be 2000. To enter or edit text in a SmartArt shape, you can type or copy the information directly in the shapes. Alternatively, you can add and edit text using the Text pane. Each bullet in the Text pane represents one of the shapes in the graphic. The currently selected box shape is surrounded with a solid border line. The corresponding item in the Text pane is highlighted and contains the cursor, indicating it can be edited.

1

- Click on the 2005 bullet in the Text pane.

- Edit the date to **2000**.

- Click ⬚ Close (top-right of Text pane) to close the Text pane.

Your screen should be similar to Figure 3.11

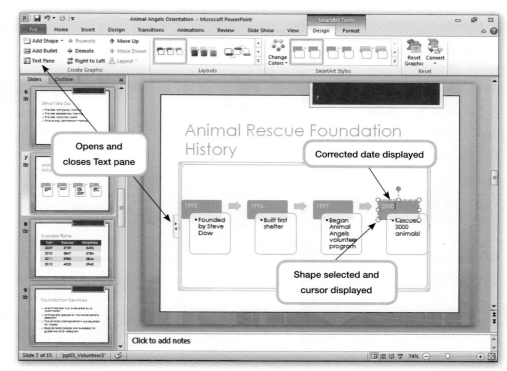

Figure 3.11

The edited text appears in the selected graphic shape. Notice now that the Text pane is closed, the shape is surrounded with a dashed border line, and the cursor is displayed inside the shape. When a shape within the SmartArt graphic is selected, it can be surrounded with either a solid or a dashed line. The dashed line indicates the content of the shape can be edited and always displays the cursor. A solid line indicates the entire shape is selected and can be modified; however, because the cursor is not displayed, the text cannot be edited. As soon as you begin to type, however, the border line changes to dashed.

INSERTING A SMARTART SHAPE

Next, you want to include another important event in the history slide. To do this, you will add a new shape to the SmartArt graphic and then enter the content.

To add a shape, you first select an existing shape that is located closest to where you want to add the new shape. Then you add the new shape relative to the location of the selected shape. In this case, you want to add a shape after the 2000 shape. Depending upon the layout of the SmartArt graphic, you can add a shape after, before, above, or below. As you add and delete shapes, the graphic will automatically resize to fit the drawing canvas.

Additional Information

In the Text pane, adding a shape is accomplished by selecting the bullet that represents the shape closest to where you want the new shape inserted and pressing Enter.

1

- If necessary, select the shape containing the date 2000.

- Open the SmartArt Tools Design tab.

- Click

  📋 Add Shape ▾

  in the Create Graphic group.

Additional Information

Inserting the shape after the selected shape is the default option.

- Type the year **2010**

- Select the shape below the 2010 year and type the text **Raised $1,000,000!**

Your screen should be similar to Figure 3.12

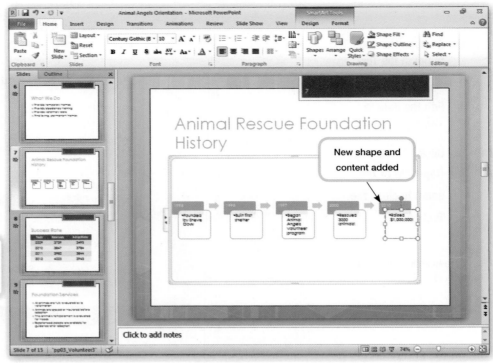

Figure 3.12

With the addition of the new shape, the SmartArt graphic automatically resized to fit within the drawing canvas. Consequently, the size of the text within the graphic is much smaller.

CHANGING THE SMARTART LAYOUT

Although you like the change to a SmartArt graphic from the bulleted list, you decide to try another layout. You would like to find a layout that may better visually represent the information with larger text.

1

- **Click [More] More in the Layouts group.**
- **Point to several layouts in the Process category to see the Live Preview.**
- **Choose Continuous Block Process.**

Your screen should be similar to Figure 3.13

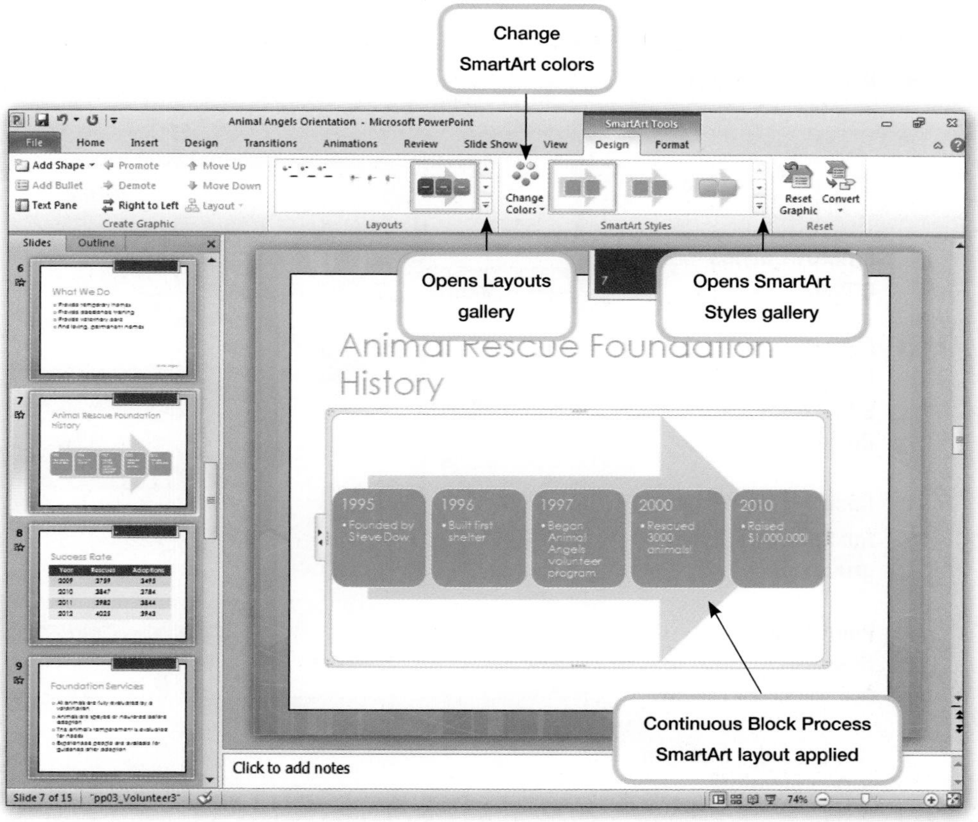

Figure 3.13

The Continuous Block Process SmartArt layout has been applied. The new graphic design with the arrow in the background well suits the content and the text is larger, making the content easier to read.

CHANGING THE SMARTART COLOR AND STYLE

Additional Information

Although the document theme determines the available colors, you can also choose colors from the Standard colors bar or create custom colors.

When a SmartArt graphic is first created, the graphic colors that are used are determined by the default color in the document theme.To make the graphic more interesting, you want to enhance its appearance. You could select each element and select a different color and format each individually, but this would take quite a bit of time. Instead, you can use one of the predesigned SmartArt Styles. A SmartArt style is a combination of different formatting options such as edges, gradients, line styles, shadows, and three-dimensional effects that can be quickly applied to the entire graphic in one easy step. You also can choose different color combinations. As you point to the design choices, Live Preview shows how the graphic will look.

You can try different combinations of colors and styles until you find the one that suits your presentation.

1

- **With the SmartArt graphic selected, click**  **in the SmartArt Styles group.**

- **Choose Colorful Range–Accent Colors 5 to 6 from the Colorful category.**

- **Click** ⬇ **More from the SmartArt Styles group.**

- **Point to several SmartArt designs to see the Live Preview.**

- **Choose Inset from the 3-D category.**

- **Change the text to bold.**

- **Click outside the graphic to deselect it.**

Your screen should be similar to Figure 3.14

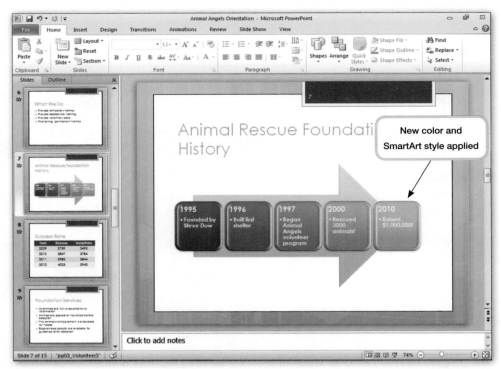

Figure 3.14

The selected SmartArt colors and style features were quickly applied to all the shapes in the graphic. You think the changes to the history slide greatly improve its appearance and readability.

ANIMATING A SMARTART GRAPHIC

Finally, you will animate the SmartArt graphic. The entire graphic can be animated or the individual parts can be animated to show the information in phases.

Additional Information

If, after making many formatting changes to a SmartArt graphic, you want to return to the original graphic design, use .

1

● **Click on the SmartArt graphic to select it.**

● **Open the Animations tab.**

● **Click ▼ More in the Animation group.**

Your screen should be similar to Figure 3.15

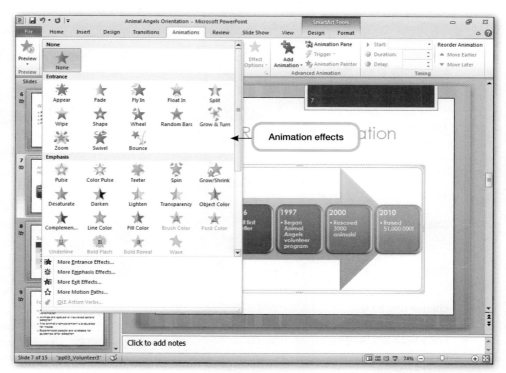

Animation effects

Figure 3.15

The Animation gallery displays animations that are available for the layout of your SmartArt graphic. Those animations that are not available are dimmed. You will choose an animation effect and then specify how you want the effect applied to the SmartArt graphic. The animation effect options are different for SmartArt graphics than for other graphic objects because the animation plays in the order that the shapes appear. This order begins with the first item listed in the text pane and moves down. As you point to the different animations, a Live Preview demonstrates the effect.

2

- **Point to several animations to see the Live Preview.**

Having Trouble?

If Live Preview is not displayed, choose AutoPreview from the Preview drop-down list.

- **Choose Fade.**

- **Click Effect Options ▾ and choose One by One.**

- **From the Start drop-down list, choose After Previous.**

- **Increase the Duration to 01:00.**

- **Click Preview ▾ to test the animation.**

- **Save the presentation.**

Your screen should be similar to Figure 3.16

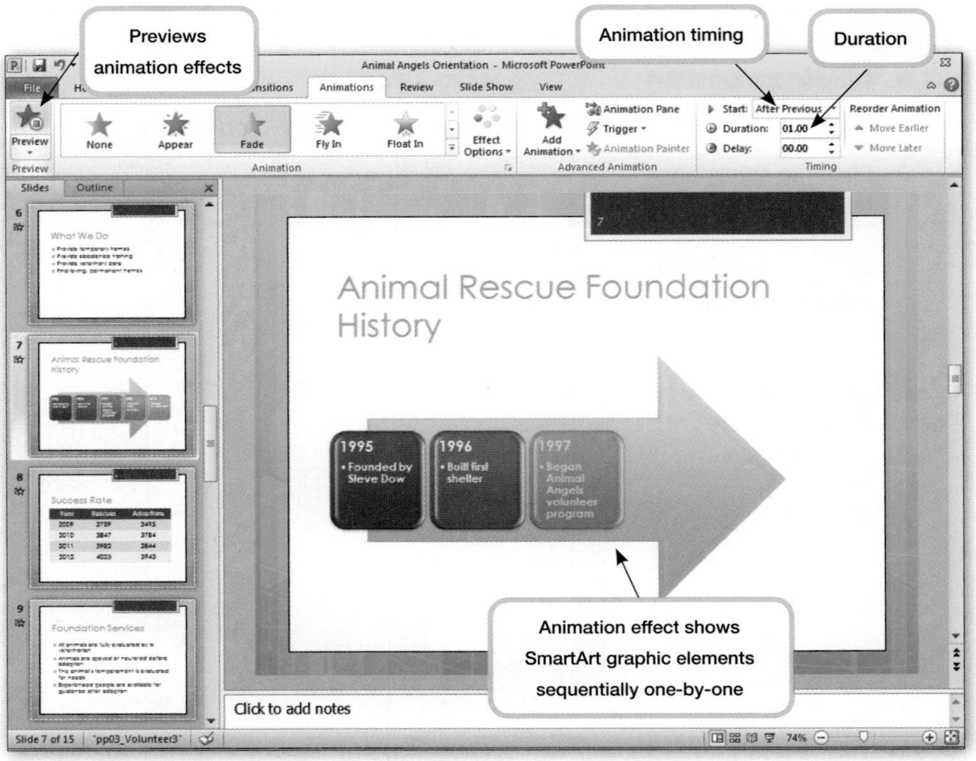

Figure 3.16

The underlying graphic, in this case the arrow, appeared first using a Fade effect. Then each box appeared in sequence also using the same effect.

Creating an Organization Chart

Next, you want to add information to the presentation about the organizational structure of the Animal Rescue Foundation. To do this, you will include an organization chart SmartArt graphic in the presentation.

Concept ② Organization Chart

An **organization chart** graphically represents the structure of an organization. Traditionally, it includes names and job titles, but also can include any items that have a **hierarchical relationship**. A **hierarchy** shows ranking, such as reporting structures within a department in a business.

You can choose from several different styles of organization charts depending on how you would like to display the hierarchy and how much room you have on your slide. A basic organization chart is shown below. All organization charts consist of different levels that represent the hierarchy. A level is all the shapes at the same hierarchical position regardless of the shapes each reports to. The topmost shape in the organization chart is at level 1. All shapes that report directly to it are at level 2. Those shapes reporting to a level 2 shape are at level 3, and so forth. An organization chart can have up to 50 levels.

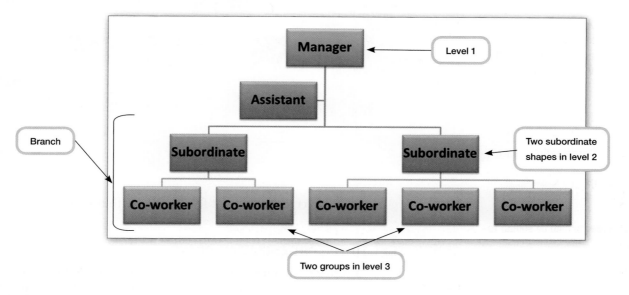

The **manager shape** is the top-level shape of a group. Subordinate shapes report to the manager shape. **Coworker shapes** are shapes that have the same manager. Co-workers form a group. A group consists of all the shapes reporting to the same manager, excluding assistant shapes. **Assistant shapes** represent administrative or managerial assistants to a manager. A **branch** is a shape and all the shapes that report to it.

You will add a new slide following slide 5 to display the organization chart. To create the chart, you will use a SmartArt graphic. Organization chart diagrams are in the Hierarchy SmartArt category.

1

- Insert a new Title and Content slide after slide 5.

- Click the  Insert SmartArt Graphic icon in the content placeholder.

- Choose Hierarchy as the category.

- Choose several of the organization chart layouts and read the description.

- Choose Organization Chart.

- Click OK

Your screen should be similar to Figure 3.17

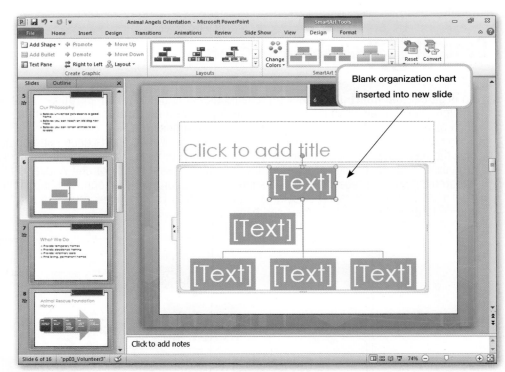

Figure 3.17

A blank organization chart, consisting of five shapes with text placeholders, is displayed.

ADDING TEXT TO THE ORGANIZATION CHART

Next you need to replace the placeholder text with the information you want to appear in the organization chart. You will use the Text pane to enter the name of the director of the Animal Rescue Foundation in the top-level shape. Each bullet in the Text pane represents one of the shapes in the graphic.

1

- Display the Text pane.

- Click in the bullet and type **Steve Dow, Director**

- Click on the next bullet in the Text pane and type **Linda Nelson, Community Relations Coordinator**

Your screen should be similar to Figure 3.18

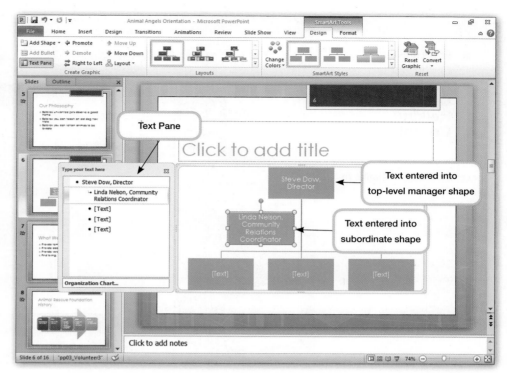

Figure 3.18

The text for the director appears in the top-level manager shape and the text for the community relations coordinator appears in the subordinate shape below it.

The next position you want to add is also at the subordinate level in the organization. Since there are no other shapes at this level, you will need to add a shape at the same level. In the Text pane, this is accomplished simply by pressing (Enter) to complete the current entry and to create a new shape at the same level.

● **Press** Enter.

● **Type** Ronnie Carey, Fund Raising Coordinator

Your screen should be similar to Figure 3.19

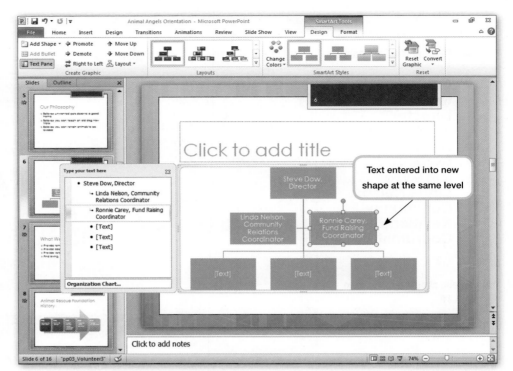

Figure 3.19

Each time you press Enter, a new shape is added at the same level. Notice that the font size of the text decreases in all the shapes to the size needed to display the largest entry in the shapes. You have two more names and positions to add. You will enter the text for the last positions directly in the shape, remove the last empty shape, and enter a title for the slide.

3

- Close the Text pane.

- Click on the placeholder in the next empty shape to activate it.

- Type **Your Name, Volunteer Coordinator**

- Click on the placeholder of the next empty shape to activate it.

- Type **Carlos Rodriguez, Foster Angel Recruiter**

- Select the next empty shape (not the text within the shape) and press [Delete] to eliminate the shape.

- Type **Who's Who** as the slide title.

Your screen should be similar to Figure 3.20

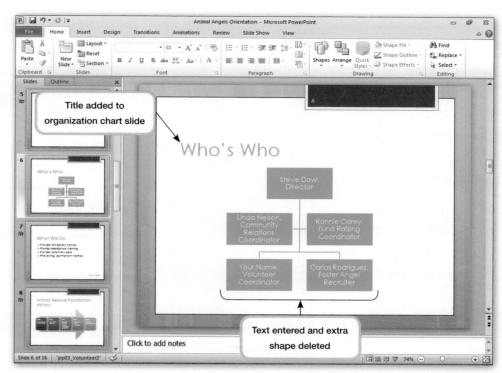

Figure 3.20

The new positions have been added and the extra shape deleted. Although the layout of the organization chart is close to what you need, it still does not reflect the hierarchy within the organization.

CHANGING THE ORGANIZATION CHART LAYOUT

You will change the layout to better illustrate the foundation's staffing.

1

- Select the
Organization Chart
object.

- Open the SmartArt
Tools Design tab.

- Click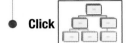

Hierarchy in the
Layouts gallery.

Your screen should be similar to
Figure 3.21

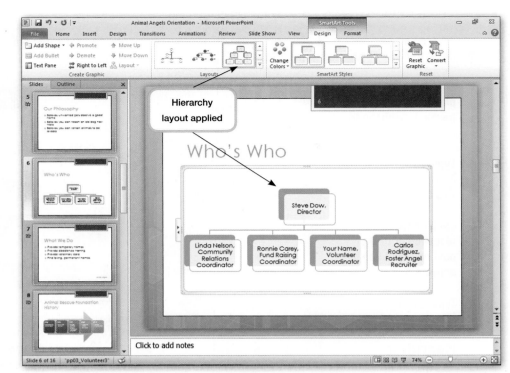

Figure 3.21

This new layout better reflects the organization structure. You, Ronnie, and
Linda report directly to the director. However, Carlos Rodriguez works in your
department and reports directly to you. You will change the layout to reflect
this.

2

- Select the shape for
Carlos Rodriguez.

- Click ➡ Demote
in the Create Graphic
group.

Your screen should be similar to
Figure 3.22

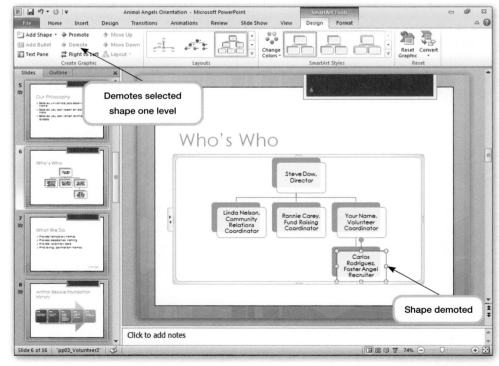

Figure 3.22

The organization chart now correctly identifies the relationships of the people in the organization. Now, you realize you have forgotten to include the name of the Animal Angel recruiter in the organization. This person also reports to the Volunteer Coordinator.

ADDING SHAPES TO THE ORGANIZATION CHART

You will need to add an additional shape to accommodate the missing position. To add a shape, you first select an existing shape that is located closest to where you want to add the new shape. Then you add the new shape relative to the location of the selected shape. In this case, you want to add a shape at the same level as the Carlos Rodriguez shape.

1

- **If necessary, select the shape for Carlos Rodriguez.**

- **Open the** Add Shape **drop-down list in the Create Graphic group of the SmartArt Tools Design tab.**

- **Choose Add Shape Before.**

- **Type Serina Johnson, Animal Angel Recruiter**

Your screen should be similar to Figure 3.23

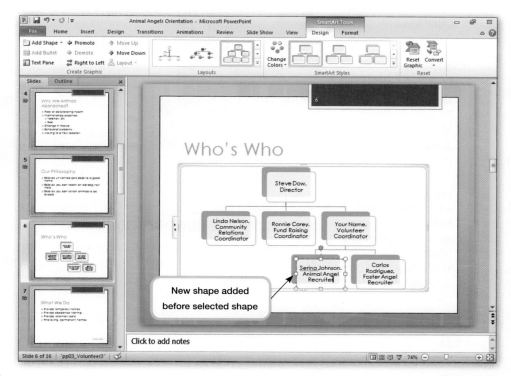

Figure 3.23

The new shape takes the same position as the selected shape, but before it. You also decide to add to the chart the names of the volunteer assistants who work for the coordinators.

- Select the shape with Linda Nelson's name.

- From the **Add Shape ▾** drop-down list, choose Add Shape Below .

- Click **Add Shape ▾** and choose Add Shape After to add a second shape at the same level.

- Enter **Susan Allison, Volunteer Assistant** and **Maria Garcia, Volunteer Assistant** into the shapes.

- In a similar manner, add a shape below Ronnie Carey's shape and enter **George Matthews, Volunteer Assistant**

Your screen should be similar to Figure 3.24

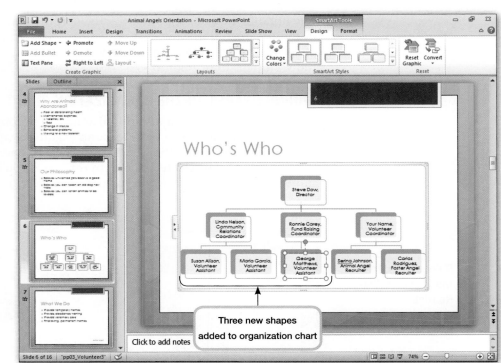

Figure 3.24

ENHANCING THE ORGANIZATION CHART

To make the organization chart more interesting, you will enhance its appearance using a SmartArt Style. You will change both the colors and the design characteristics.

1

- With the organization chart selected,

  click 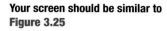 in the

  SmartArt Styles group.

- **Choose Colorful Range-Accent Colors 5 to 6 from the Colorful category.**

- **Click** ⊽ **More in the SmartArt Styles group.**

- **Choose Inset from the 3-D category.**

Your screen should be similar to Figure 3.25

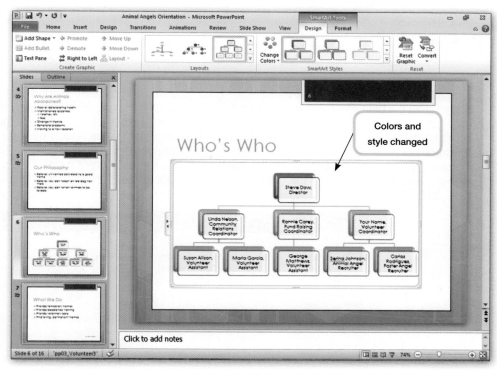

Figure 3.25

The changes to the organization chart are complete. You can click on the chart to further modify the chart at any time.

2

- **Save the presentation.**

- **To see how all the changes you have made to the presentation look, run the presentation beginning with slide 1.**

Additional Information

Press F5 to quickly start the presentation from the beginning.

Creating a Chart Slide

The next change you want to make is to show the adoption success rate data in slide 9 as a chart rather than a table.

Concept ③ Chart

A **chart**, also called a **graph**, is a visual representation of numeric data. Presenting data as a chart provides more impact than the data alone and makes it easier to see trends and comparisons. PowerPoint 2010 uses the Excel 2010 chart tools to create and modify charts. Charts that you create are embedded in the PowerPoint document and the chart data is stored in an Excel worksheet that is incorporated in the PowerPoint file. If Excel is not installed on the computer, then Microsoft Graph is used, although advanced data-charting features are not available.

Each type of chart represents the data differently and has a different purpose. It is important to select the type of chart that will provide the right emphasis to support your presentations. The basic chart types are described below.

Type of Chart	Description
Column	Similar to a bar chart, except categories are organized horizontally and values vertically. Shows data changes over time or comparison among items.
Line	Shows changes in data over time, emphasizing time and rate of change rather than the amount of change.
Pie	Shows the relationship of each value in a data series to the series as a whole. Each slice of the pie represents a single value in a data series.
Bar	Displays categories vertically and values horizontally, placing more emphasis on comparisons and less on time. Stacked bar charts show the relationship of individual items to a whole by stacking bars on top of one another.
Area	Shows the relative importance of a value over time by emphasizing the area under the curve created by each data series.

Most charts are made up of several basic parts, as identified in the figure and described below.

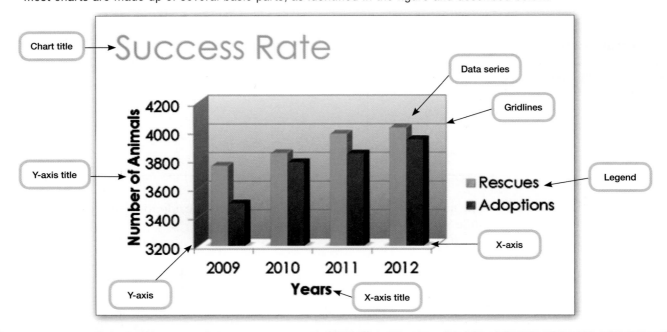

Part	Description
X axis	The bottom boundary of the chart, also called the category axis, is used to label the data being charted; the label may be, for example, a point in time or a category.
Y axis	The left boundary of the chart, also called the value axis, is a numbered scale whose numbers are determined by the data used in the chart. Each line or bar in a chart represents a data value. In pie charts, there are no axes. Instead, the data being charted is displayed as slices in a circle or pie.
Data Series	Each group of related data that is plotted in a chart.
Legend	A box containing a brief description identifying the patterns or colors assigned to the data series in a chart.
Titles	Descriptive text used to explain the contents of the chart.

You will create the chart in a new slide following the slide containing the table of data on success rates.

1

- **Insert a new slide using the Title and Content slide layout after slide 9.**

- **Click the**  **Insert Chart icon in the content placeholder.**

Another Method

You also can click  Chart on the Insert tab to add a chart object to a slide.

Your screen should be similar to Figure 3.26

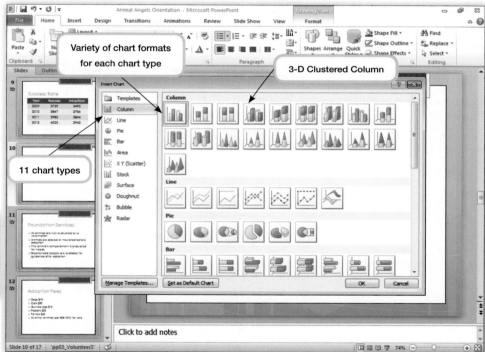

Figure 3.26

From the Insert Chart dialog box, you select the type of chart you want to create.

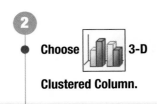

2

● Choose  3-D Clustered Column.

Additional Information

When you point to the chart icon, a ScreenTip displays the chart name.

● Click **OK** .

● If necessary, right click the taskbar menu and choose **Show windows side by side** to display the Excel 2010 window next to the PowerPoint 2010 window.

Having Trouble?

Right-click on a blank area of the taskbar to display the taskbar menu.

Your screen should be similar to Figure 3.27

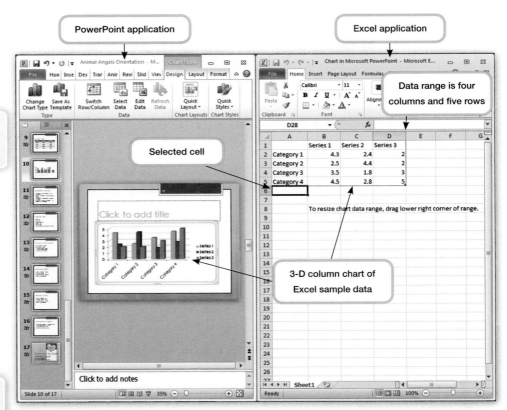

Figure 3.27

The Excel 2010 application opens and displays in a separate window. The Excel worksheet contains sample data and the PowerPoint slide displays a 3-D column chart of the sample data. A worksheet is similar to a table in that it consists of intersecting rows and columns that create cells for holding data. Each row is labeled with a number and each column is labeled with a letter. The cell that is surrounded by the border is the selected cell and is the cell you can work in.

In addition to displaying sample data, the worksheet also contains place-holders for the row labels, which are used as the legend in the chart, and for the column labels, which are used as X-axis labels.

SPECIFYING THE CHART DATA

You need to replace the sample data in the worksheet with the success rate data in the table. Rather than retype the data that is in the table, you will copy it into the Excel worksheet. You also will copy the slide title from the table slide to the chart slide.

Before you begin, however, you need to change the Excel chart data range, identified by the blue border line, from four columns and five rows to match the PowerPoint success rate data of three columns and five rows. You will do this by deleting the last column containing data (D) in the Excel worksheet.

1 ● Right-click on the column heading and choose Delete from the shortcut menu.

● Display slide 9.

Your screen should be similar to Figure 3.28

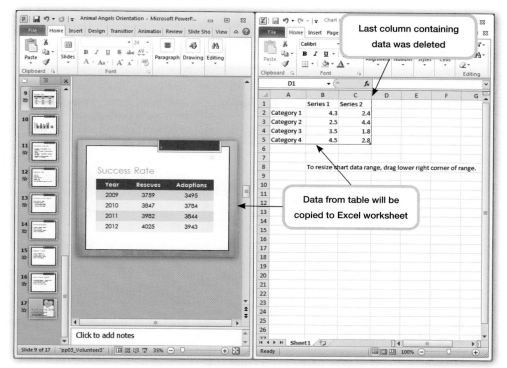

Figure 3.28

Now the chart data range matches the size of the PowerPoint table data so when you copy from PowerPoint and paste into Excel, the correct number of columns will display.

You will copy the data from the table into the Excel worksheet and the title text from slide 9 into the chart slide. You could copy and paste the selections one after the other, or you can use the Office Clipboard to collect multiple items and paste them as needed.

Concept **Collect and Paste**

Collecting and pasting is the capability of the program to store multiple copied items in the **Office Clipboard** and then paste one or more of them into another document. For example, you could copy a chart from Excel and a paragraph from Word, then switch to PowerPoint and copy the two stored items into a slide in one easy step. This saves you from having to switch back and forth between documents and applications multiple times.

The Office Clipboard and the system Clipboard are similar, but separate, features. The major difference is that the Office Clipboard can hold up to 24 items, whereas the system Clipboard holds only a single item. The last item you copy to the Office Clipboard is always copied to the system Clipboard. When you use the Office Clipboard, you can select from the stored items to paste in any order.

The Office Clipboard is available in all Office 2010 applications and is accessed through the Clipboard task pane. Once the Clipboard task pane is opened, it is available for use in any program, including non-Office programs. In some programs where the Cut, Copy, and Paste commands are not available, or in non-Office programs, the Clipboard task pane is not visible, but it is still operational. You can copy from any program that provides copy and cut capabilities, but you can only paste items stored in the Office Clipboard into Office programs. You can always paste the last-copied item that is stored in the system Clipboard into any programs that support copy and paste.

First you will copy the slide title text from slide 9 to the Office Clipboard.

2

- **Open the PowerPoint Home tab.**

- **Click [⬚] in the Clipboard group to open the Office Clipboard task pane.**

- **If necessary, click [✗ Clear All] to empty the Office Clipboard contents.**

- **Make the Clipboard task pane narrower so your slide will be larger.**

- **Triple-click on the title text of slide 9 to select it.**

- **Click [📋].**

Your screen should be similar to Figure 3.29

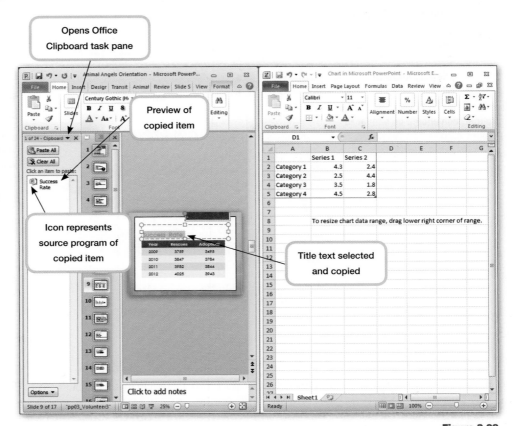

Figure 3.29

The Clipboard task pane displays a PowerPoint icon identifying PowerPoint as the application source of the copied item and a preview of the copied selection. Next, you will copy the contents of the table into the Clipboard. As items are copied, they are added sequentially to the Clipboard task pane with the last-copied item at the top of the list.

3

- Click in the table in slide 9 to select the object.

- Select all table cells.

- Click 📄 .

Your screen should be similar to Figure 3.30

Additional Information

The Office Clipboard is automatically activated if you copy or cut two different items consecutively in the same program; if you copy one item, paste the item, and then copy another item in the same program; or if you copy one item twice in succession.

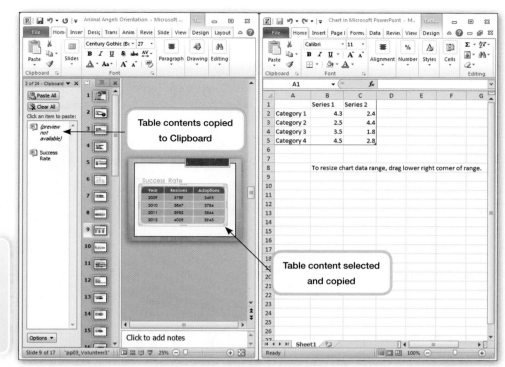

Figure 3.30

The Clipboard task pane now contains two PowerPoint document icons, one for each copied item. A preview for the copied table is not available. Next, you will paste the title into slide 10.

4

- Display slide 10.

- Click in the slide title placeholder.

- Click on the "Success Rate" item in the Clipboard task pane.

Your screen should be similar to Figure 3.31

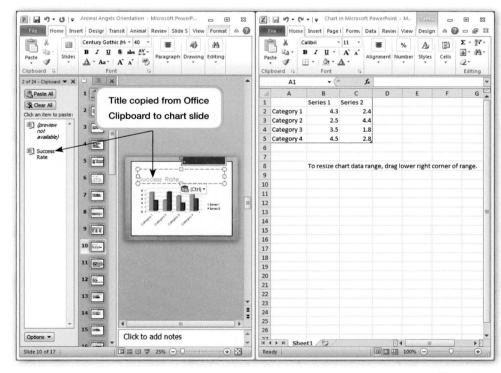

Figure 3.31

The contents of the first-copied item are pasted from the Office Clipboard into the title of the slide.

Now you are ready to replace the sample data in Excel with the data from the table. When you copy from the Clipboard, the sample data will be replaced and first inserted with the table formatting. You will clear the formatting for Excel.

5

- **Click in cell A1 of the Excel worksheet.**

- **In Excel, open the Clipboard.**

- **Click on the table data item in the Clipboard.**

- **Click** (Ctrl) ▾ **Paste Options and then click** **Match Destination Formatting.**

Your screen should be similar to Figure 3.32

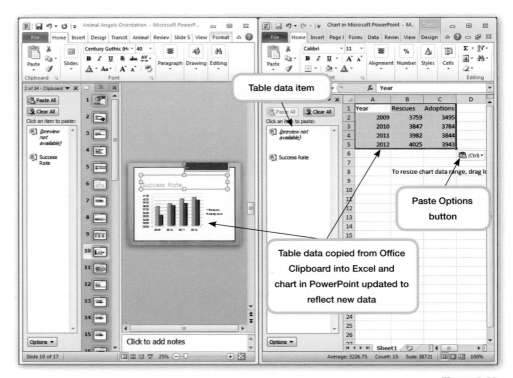

Figure 3.32

The worksheet displays the data and the chart in the slide represents the new worksheet data.

6

- Click ![Clear All] to clear the contents of the Office Clipboard.

- Close the Excel Clipboard task pane and exit Excel.

- Close the PowerPoint Clipboard task pane.

- If necessary, maximize the PowerPoint window and adjust the width of the Slides tab.

Your screen should be similar to Figure 3.33

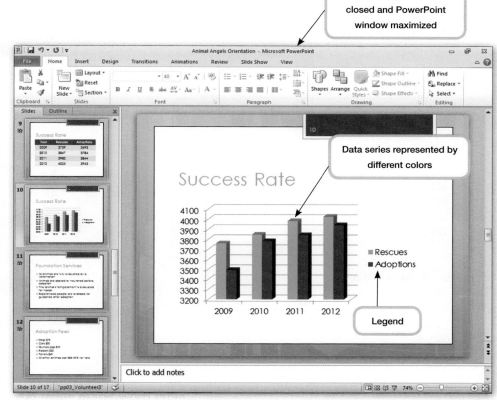

Figure 3.33

Excel is closed and the PowerPoint application is active and maximized in the window. The column chart is a visual representation of the data in slide 9. Each data series has a unique color or pattern assigned to it to identify the different series. The legend identifies the color or pattern associated with each data series.

ADDING AXIS TITLES

Next you want to add labels along the axes to clarify the information in the chart. The Chart Tools Layout tab is used to add features to a chart, including titles, legends, and gridlines, that make it easier to understand the data in the chart. You will add titles along the two axis lines.

1

- If necessary, click on the the chart object to select it.

- Open the Chart Tools Layout tab.

- Click in the Axis Titles ▾ Labels group.

- Select Primary Vertical Access Title and choose Rotated Title.

Your screen should be similar to Figure 3.34

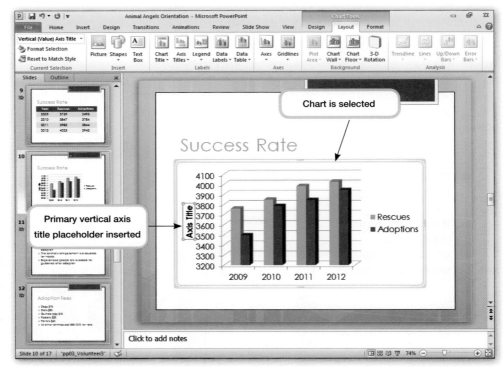

Figure 3.34

An Axis Title placeholder appears along the vertical axis with the text rotated. The chart also has been resized to accommodate the title. You will enter the title text and then add another title along the horizontal axis.

2

- Type **Number of Animals** in the Primary Vertical Axis text box.

- Click .

- Select Primary Horizontal Access Title and choose Title Below Axis.

- Type **Years** in the Primary Horizontal Axis text box.

Your screen should be similar to Figure 3.35

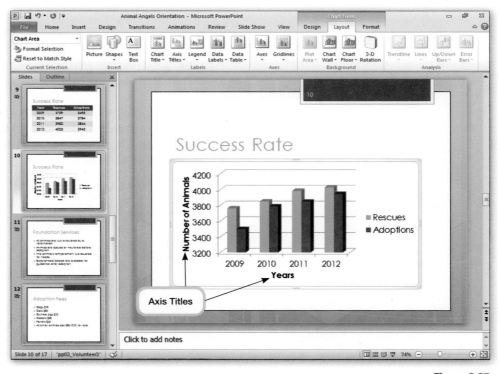

Figure 3.35

The labels you entered appear along the appropriate axes and the chart has been resized to allow space for the new titles.

CHANGING THE CHART STYLE

Next, you want to make the data series more distinctive and add color to the chart background to separate it from the slide background. To do this, you will change the chart style and apply color to the walls of the chart.

1

- If necessary, select the chart object.

- Open the Chart Tools Design tab.

- Click ⊽ More in the Chart Styles group.

- Choose Style 18 (third row, second column).

- Open the Chart Tools Format tab.

- Click on the back wall of the chart to select both the back and side walls.

Another Method

You can also choose Walls from the Chart Elements drop-down menu.

- Choose Subtle Effect– Olive Green, Accent 4 (fourth row, fifth column) from the Shape Styles gallery.

- Save the presentation.

Your screen should be similar to Figure 3.36

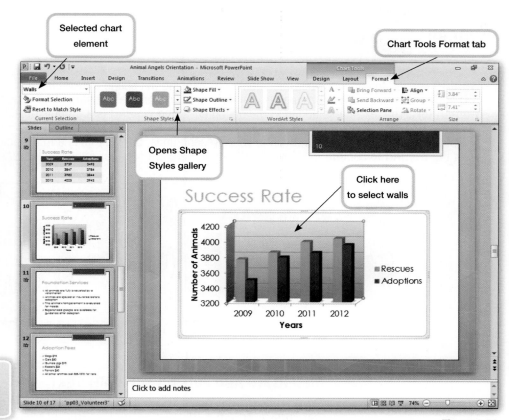

Figure 3.36

The chart is now more attractive and the labels make it easy to interpret.

The next change you want to make is to change the title on slide 1 to make it more interesting. To make the title unique and more distinctive, you will enter it using the WordArt feature.

Concept 5 WordArt

WordArt is used to enhance your documents by changing the shape of text and adding special effects such as 3-D and shadows. You can also align text in different ways or use adjustment handles to rotate, flip, and skew WordArt text. The text that is added to the document using WordArt is a graphic object that can be edited, sized, or moved to any location in the document.

Use WordArt to add a special touch to your presentations, but limit its use to a single element on a slide. You want the WordArt to capture the viewer's attention. Here are some examples of WordArt.

INSERTING AND EDITING WORDART TEXT

You will create a WordArt object for the slide title to appear next to the graphic on slide 1. It will replace the title text that is currently on the slide.

1

- Display slide 1.

- Delete the Title text and Title placeholder.

- Click in the Text group of the Insert tab.

Your screen should be similar to Figure 3.37

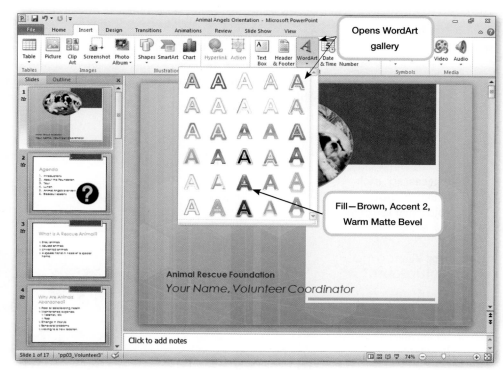

Figure 3.37

The first step is to select one of the 30 styles or designs of WordArt from the WordArt gallery. These styles are just a starting point. As you will see, you can alter the appearance of the style by selecting a different color, shape, and special effect.

2

- Choose Fill–Brown, Accent 2, Warm Matte Bevel (fifth row, third column).

Your screen should be similar to Figure 3.38

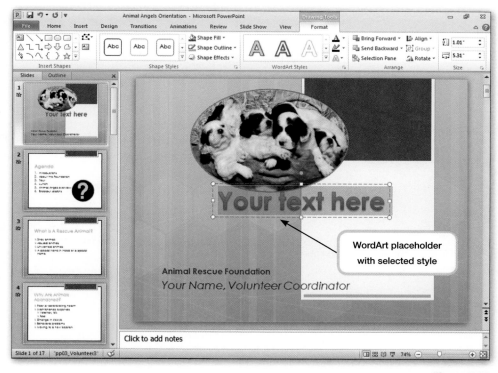

Figure 3.38

Having Trouble?

When a WordArt object is surrounded with a solid border, click on the text to change the border to a dashed border and display the cursor so you can enter or edit the text.

When the WordArt object first appears, it is selected and has a dashed border. The placeholder text is automatically highlighted ready for you to replace it with your text. A WordArt object also can be surrounded with a solid border indicating that the entire object is selected and you cannot edit text or format individual items within the object. Any changes you make will affect the entire object.

3

- If necessary, click in the WordArt object and select the placeholder text.

- Type Welcome Volunteers!

- Move the WordArt object to position it on the slide as shown in Figure 3.39.

Having Trouble?

Drag the selected WordArt object to move it just like any other object.

Your screen should be similar to Figure 3.39

Figure 3.39

Additional Information

You can easily edit the WordArt text at any point by selecting the object.

Now the text you entered is displayed in the selected WordArt style on the slide. Whenever a WordArt object is selected, the Drawing Tools Format tab is available for use with the shape.

ENHANCING A WORDART OBJECT

Now you want to change the appearance of the WordArt object to make it more interesting. You will change the color, bevel effect, shape, and size of the object using the Drawing Tools Format tab.

1

- If necessary, select the WordArt object.

- Click Text Fill in the WordArt Styles group and choose the Orange, Accent 6, Darker 50% (bottom row, last column) Theme color.

- Click [A ▾] Text Effects in the WordArt Styles group, select Bevel and choose

  [Angle icon] Angle (second row, first column).

- Click [A ▾] Text Effects in the WordArt Styles group and select Transform.

Your screen should be similar to Figure 3.40

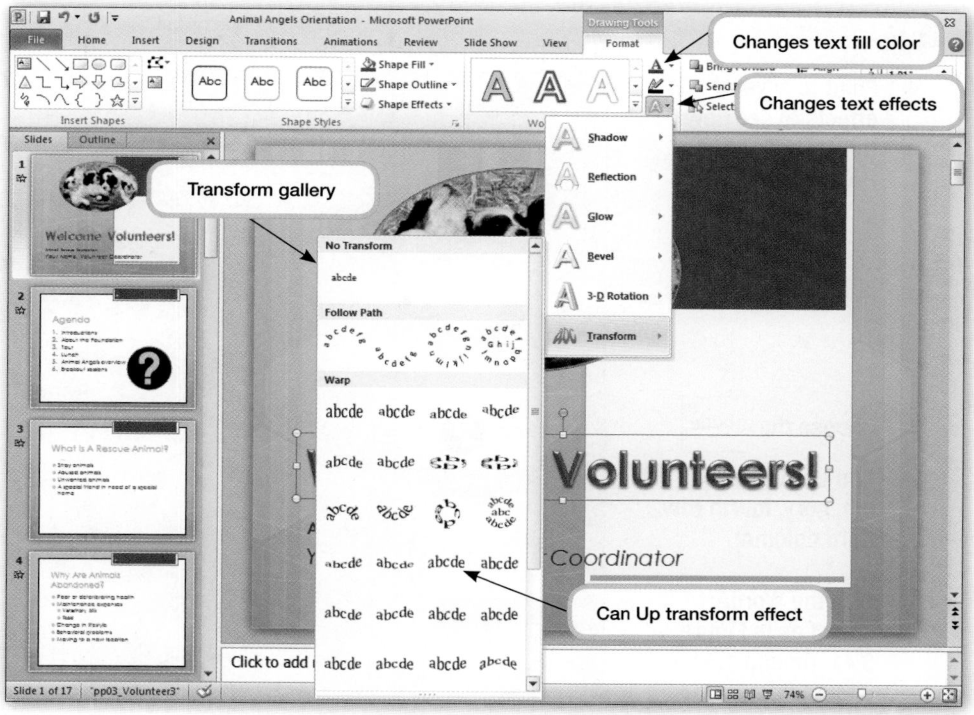

Figure 3.40

A variety of transform effects are available that will change the warp or path of the text of your WordArt object. You will preview several and then select an effect.

2

- **Point to several effects to see how they look in Live Preview.**

Additional Information

Use the scrollbar to see all of the effects in this gallery.

- **Choose the** $\boxed{abcde}$ **Can Up (Warp category, fourth row, third column).**

- **Size the WordArt object as in Figure 3.41 (height 1.5" × width 9")**

- **Drag the** 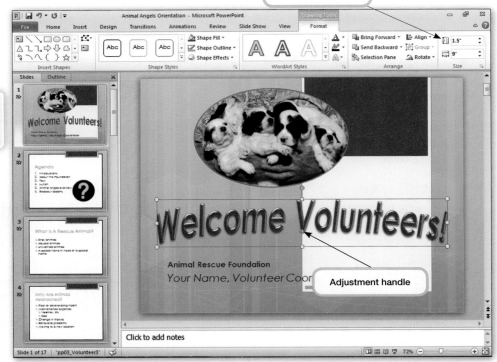 **adjustment handle upward to increase the curve of the text.**

Additional Information

The mouse pointer appears as when positioned on the adjustment handle and Live Preview shows how the object will look as you adjust it.

- **Save the presentation.**

Your screen should be similar to Figure 3.41

Figure 3.41

Using WordArt has made the presentation title much more dramatic.

Next, you want to enhance the Agenda slide by adding an animated graphic from an animated GIF file.

Concept Animated GIF

An **animated GIF** file is a type of graphic file that has motion. It consists of a series of GIF (Graphic Interchange Format) images that are displayed in rapid succession to produce an animated effect. They are commonly used on Web pages and can be used in PowerPoint presentations, too. You can find animated GIF files by searching for videos in the Clip Art task pane.

Because of the way animated GIF files are created, be very careful about resizing to make them larger. The image will be blurred or distorted if you increase the size of the image too much. You cannot modify an animated graphic image using the features in PowerPoint. If you want to make changes to the graphic, such as changing the fill color or border, you need to use software that can edit animated GIF files.

FINDING AND INSERTING ANIMATED GRAPHICS

You want to add several animated graphics that will capture the attention of viewers and add humor to your presentation. You will insert them first and then resize and position them. To make space for the new graphic on slide 2, you will first move the question mark graphic to slide 4.

1

- On slide 2, select the question mark graphic.

- Click ✂ Cut.

- Display slide 4.

- Click 📋 Paste.

- Resize and position the graphic as in Figure 3.42.

Your screen should be similar to Figure 3.42

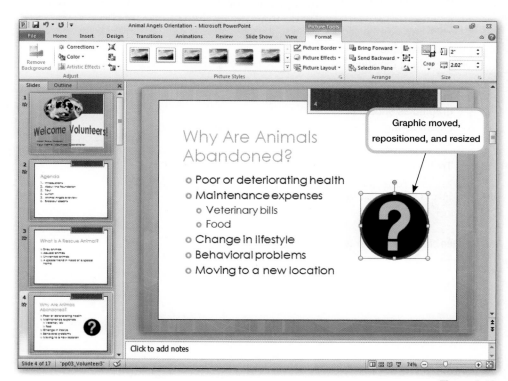

Figure 3.42

Now you will add an animated graphic to slide 2. Like other graphics, you can locate animated graphics using the Videos media type category of the Clip Art gallery. To see the animation, you need to open it in the Preview/Properties window.

2

- Display slide 2.

- Click  from the Images group on the Insert tab.

- Enter **cat** as the search term, choose Videos as the media type, and click [Go].

- Choose Preview/ Properties from the first thumbnail's shortcut menu.

- Click [Ne*x*t >] and preview the animations until you preview the graphic shown in Figure 3.43.

- Click [Close] and insert the graphic in the slide.

- Size and position the graphic as shown in Figure 3.43.

Having Trouble?

If this graphic is not available, insert pp03_Adoptions from your data file location.

Your screen should be similar to Figure 3.43

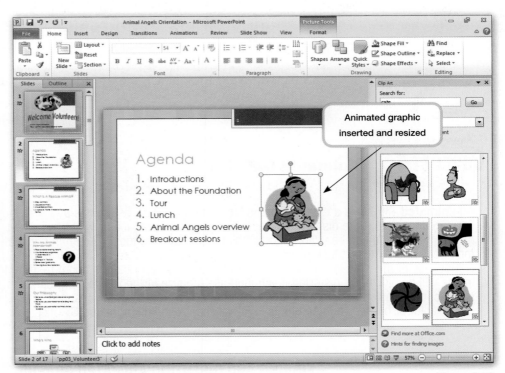

Figure 3.43

You probably noticed that the animated graphic images are quite small when inserted into the slide. This limits how much you can increase their size with acceptable results. Next, on slide 3 you will insert an animated graphic of a turtle that one of the volunteers came across and you saved on your computer.

3

- Close the ClipArt task pane.

- Display slide 3.

- Click **Picture** from the Images group on the Insert tab.

- Specify your data file location and select pp03_Turtle.

- Click **Insert**.

- Size and position the graphic as shown in Figure 3.44.

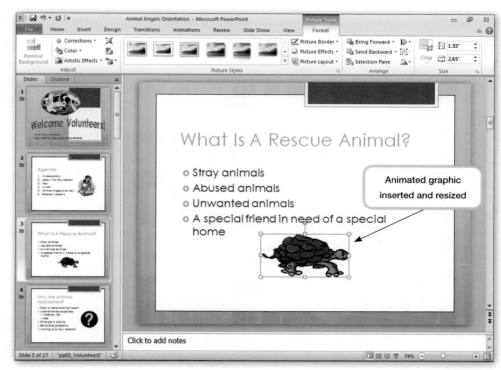

Figure 3.44

Additional Information

Be careful when increasing the size of an animated GIF object as the image can become pixilated and can look very blurred or distorted when made too large.

Your screen should be similar to Figure 3.44

The turtle animated graphic is displayed; however, you have not yet seen it animated.

MODIFYING AND VIEWING ANIMATED GRAPHICS

Once animated graphics are inserted in a slide, you can view the animation by displaying the slide in Slide Show view. You also can modify the graphic using some of the features in the Picture Tools Format tab. Be careful when applying formats to an animated graphic, as it may stop the animation effect. If this happens, you may be able to undo your format changes to restore the animation. If this does not restore the animation effect, you would need to reinsert the graphic and try again. Next you will add several enhancements to the graphics then display the slides in Slide Show view to see their animation.

- **Select the graphic on slide 2.**

- **Open the Picture Styles gallery on the Picture Tools Format tab and choose Compound Frame, Black.**

- **Change the color of the picture border to Orange, Accent 6, Darker 50%.**

Your screen should be similar to Figure 3.45

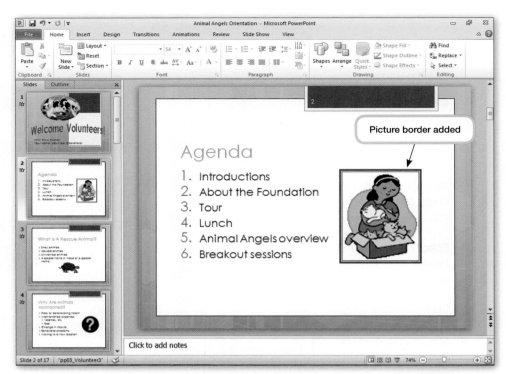

Figure 3.45

Next you want to enhance the turtle graphic by flipping the graphic and adding a shadow effect. You also decide to duplicate the turtle twice so that multiple images will have more impact.

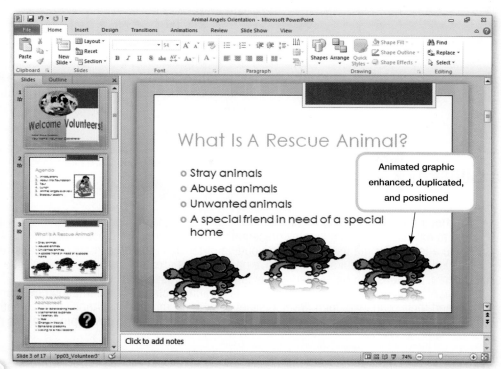

Figure 3.46

2

- Select the turtle graphic on slide 3.

- Click ◢▾ **Rotate** in the Arrange group of the Picture Tools Format tab and choose Flip Horizontal.

- Click ◓ Picture Effects ▾, select Reflection and choose Tight Reflection, touching.

- Press Ctrl + D twice to duplicate the turtle two times.

Additional Information

Using the keyboard shortcut Ctrl + D is a quick way to replicate a slide object on the current slide.

- Position the second and third turtles as shown in Figure 3.46.

Your screen should be similar to Figure 3.46

Next, you will view the slides in Slide Show view to see the animation effects.

3

- Display slides 2 and 3 in Slide Show view.

- Press Esc to stop the slide show.

- Save the presentation.

The animation effects on both slides look good. You particularly like the turtle animation because it runs continuously while the slide is displayed whereas the animation on slide 2 only runs the animation once.

Organizing Slides into Sections

After reviewing the orientation slide show, you realize that portions of the content can be used for different situations. You decide to add sections to divide the content.

Concept 7 Sections

Sections are used to organize and label logical groupings of slides to make it easier to locate specific slides and to navigate through a lengthy presentation. By structuring a presentation in this way, the sections are similar to a table of contents, providing an outline of topics in the presentation. For this reason, sections should be labeled with meaningful and descriptive names. Once created, sections can easily be revised, rearranged, and deleted. Sections can be applied at any time during presentation development.

An effective way to use sections is at the beginning stage of presentation development to identify major topics and their sequence, then develop slides to support those ideas. Additionally, creating sections makes it easy to assign specific sections to other colleagues to work on during development of the presentation.

CREATING AND RENAMING SECTIONS

You will create several sections to identify different parts of the presentation. To add sections, you can use the Section command in the Slides group of the Home tab. Using this method adds a section above the current slide. Alternatively, you can right-click between the slides where you want the section to appear and choose Add Section from the context menu. The first section will identify information about the Foundation in general.

- In Normal view, select slide 4 in the Slides pane.

- Click Section ▾ in the Slides group and choose Add Section.

- Click Section ▾ in the Slides group and choose Rename Section.

- Enter the section name **Foundation** and click Rename.

Your screen should be similar to Figure 3.47

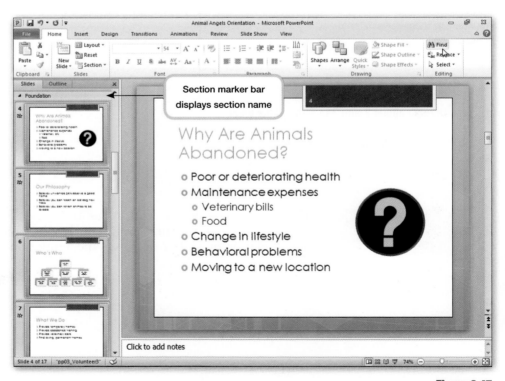

Figure 3.47

WWW.MHHE.COM/OLEARY

PowerPoint 2010

A yellow section marker bar containing the section name is displayed above slide 4 and identifies the beginning of the section. All following screens are highlighted in yellow to show that they are part of that section.

You will add the next section while viewing the presentation in Slide Sorter view. This makes it much easier to see the slide content while deciding where to divide the presentation into sections. The next section will identify slides about the Animal Angels volunteer group.

2

- Switch to Slide Sorter view.

- Right-click between slides 12 and 13 and choose Add Section.

- Right-click on the Untitled Section marker and choose Rename Section.

- Rename the section **Animal Angels**

Your screen should be similar to Figure 3.48

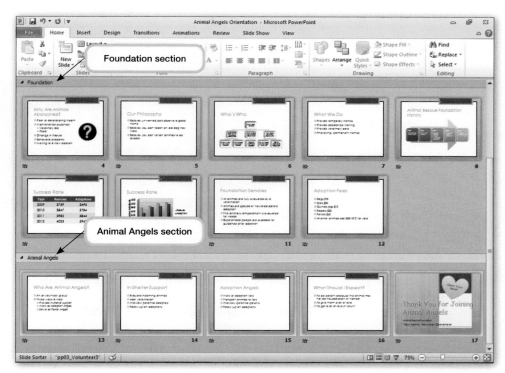

Figure 3.48

The Foundation section consists of slides 4 through 12 and the Animal Angels section consists of slides 13 through 17. Additionally, at the beginning of the presentation, a Default Section was automatically inserted that contains slides 1 through 3. You will add two more sections to identify specific areas of the presentation.

- Add a section before slide 9 and name it **Our Success**

- Add another section between slides 15 and 16 and name it **Closing**

- Change the name of the first Default Section at the beginning of the presentation to **Introduction**

- Reduce the zoom to 20%.

Your screen should be similar to Figure 3.49

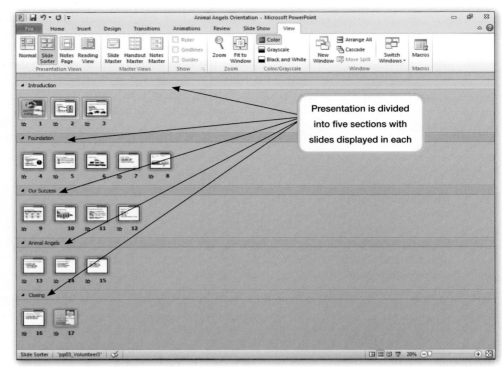

Presentation is divided into five sections with slides displayed in each

Figure 3.49

The presentation is divided into five sections.

MOVING AND REMOVING SECTIONS

After examining the slide sequence in Slide Sorter view, you decide that you want to reorganize the order of several slides, change the sequence of the sections, and then remove a section.

1

- Increase the zoom to 70%.

- Select slide 4, Why Are Animals Abandoned? and drag it to after slide 2, Agenda.

- Move slide 16 to follow slide 15 in the Animal Angels section.

- Right-click the Our Success section marker and choose Move Section Up so the section appears before the Foundation section.

- Right-click the Our Success section marker and choose Move Section Down to return to the original sequence.

- Right-click the Our Success section and choose Remove Section.

Your screen should be similar to Figure 3.50

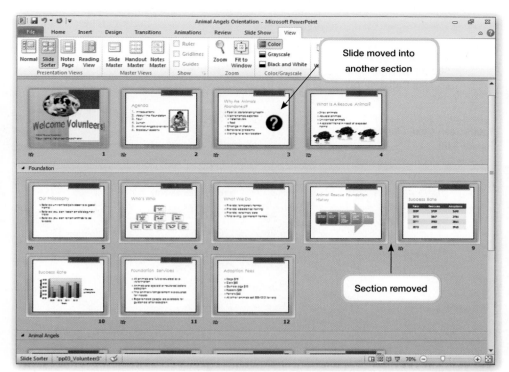

Figure 3.50

Removing a section removes the section marker bar and combines the slides that were in that section with the previous section.

As a final check you will examine the section order by collapsing the sections to display only the section titles.

Right-click on any section marker and choose Collapse All.

Your screen should be similar to Figure 3.51

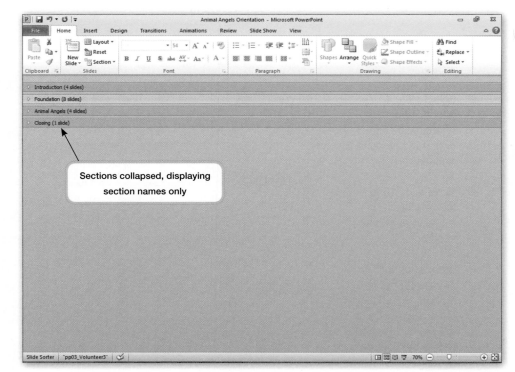

Figure 3.51

Only the section names are displayed, followed by the number of slides in each section.

Collapsing sections is helpful when developing the major topics of a presentation or for reorganizing sections. Sections also can be rearranged and removed while collapsed. Since the Closing section consists of only a single slide, you decide to remove it.

3

Right-click the Closing section marker bar and choose Remove Section.

Right-click any section marker bar and choose Expand All.

Save the presentation.

Your screen should be similar to Figure 3.52

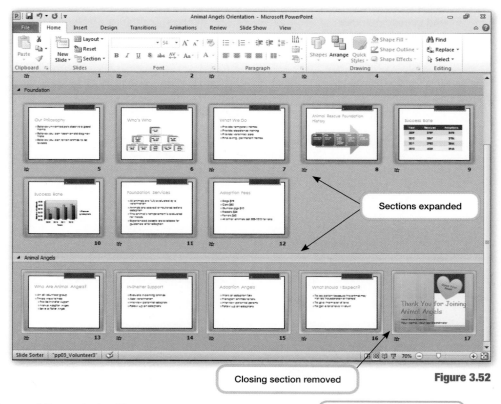

Figure 3.52

The Closing section was removed and the presentation now consists of three sections. The Introduction section has 4 slides, the Foundation section has 8 slides, and the Animal Angels section has 5 slides.

Delivering Presentations

Typically, presentations are delivered by connecting a computer to a projector to display the slides on a large screen. Before delivering a presentation, it is important to rehearse it so that you are well prepared and at ease with both the equipment and the materials. It is best to rehearse in a setting as close as possible to the real situation with a small audience who will give you honest feedback. Since most presentations are allotted a set amount of time, as part of the rehearsal, you also may want to keep track of the time spent on each slide and the total time of the presentation.

REHEARSING TIMING

To help with this aspect of the presentation, PowerPoint includes a **rehearse timings** feature that records the length of time spent on each slide and the total presentation time while you are rehearsing. If the presentation runs either too long or too short, you can quickly see which slides you are spending too much or too little time on and adjust the presentation accordingly.

Additional Information

If your computer has a microphone, you could even record your narration using 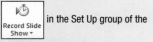 in the Set Up group of the Slide Show tab.

1

● Open the Slide Show tab.

● Click 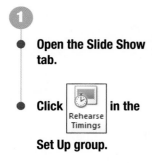 in the Set Up group.

Your screen should be similar to Figure 3.53

Figure 3.53

The Recording toolbar appears and starts a clock to time your delivery. The ⇨ button advances to the next step in the show and the ⏸ button will pause the timing. You also can return to the previous slide to repeat the rehearsal and apply new timings to the slide using the ↩ button on the toolbar.

Normally you would talk from notes you had prepared for your presentation. For this exercise, think about what you would say for each slide. The toolbar will record the time for each slide. When you reach the end of the presentation, a message box displays the total time for the presentation.

2

- Advance through the slide show as you would during the actual presentation.

- When finished, click ⬚Yes⬚ to keep the slide timings.

Your screen should be similar to Figure 3.54

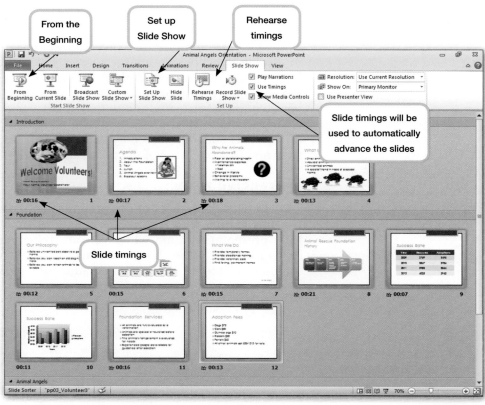

Figure 3.54

Additional Information

You also can set slide timings manually for each slide by selecting After under Advance Slide in the Timing group of the Transitions tab and entering the number of seconds you want the slide to display before advancing to the next slide.

Slide Sorter view is displayed and the timings for each slide appear below each slide. Now that you can see the individual timings, you can easily see where you are spending too little or too much time. Once slide timings are set, you can decide whether to use the timings to automatically advance the slides or to run the show manually. The default setting uses the timings if present. Clearing the ☑ Use Timings check box in the Setup group turns this feature on and off.

HIDING SLIDES AND SHOWING HIDDEN SLIDES

As you reconsider the presentation, you think it may be running a little long and decide not to show the Success Rate table slide unless someone asks about the specific rescue rates. To do this, you will **hide slide** 9.

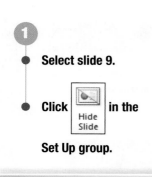

1

● Select slide 9.

● Click in the Set Up group.

Another Method

You could also choose **Hide Slide** from the slide's shortcut menu.

Your screen should be similar to Figure 3.55

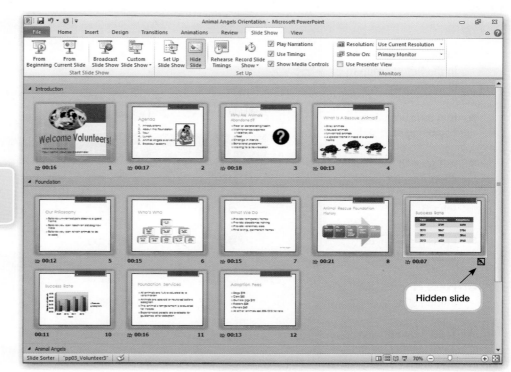

Figure 3.55

Notice that the slide number for slide 9 is surrounded by a box with a slash drawn through it, which indicates that the slide is hidden. Next, you will turn off the use of slide timings and run the slide show manually to see how hidden slides work. You will begin the show at the slide before the hidden slide.

- **Click** ☑ Use Timings in the Setup group to clear the checkmark.

- **Run the slide show beginning with slide 8.**

- **Advance to the next slide, which should be Success Rate (chart).**

- **Press** Page Up **to display slide 8 again.**

- **Press** H **to see the hidden slide 9.**

- **Type** 1 **and press** Enter **to display the title slide.**

- **Type** 9 **and press** Enter **to display slide 9.**

Another Method

You also can use Go to Slide on the shortcut menu to display a hidden slide.

Your screen should be similar to Figure 3.56

Success Rate

Year	Rescues	Adoptions
2009	3759	3495
2010	3847	3784
2011	3982	3844
2012	4025	3943

Slide 9 displayed in slide show

Figure 3.56

USING TIMINGS

Once the slide show includes preset timings for each slide, you can use the timings to advance the slides automatically for you during the presentation. The hidden slide will not be displayed.

1

- **Press** Esc **to end the slide show.**

- **Click** ☑ Use Timings **to turn this feature back on.**

Another Method

You also can turn this feature on or off

using in the Set Up group

and choosing Use timings, if present in the Advance slides category of the Set Up Show dialog box..

- **Click** **from the Start Slide Show group and watch the slide show advance automatically.**

- **Press** Esc **to end the slide show.**

Using this feature is ideal for creating a presentation that is self-running, such as in a **kiosk** (a stand-alone device that provides information and services on a computer screen), or if you are very sure of your timings. Generally, when presenting a slide show personally, it is just as easy to advance the slides manually; this allows you to pace the show to the audience. You also could use a combination of these methods to advance most slides manually but automate sections where you need rapid changes.

Creating Custom Shows

After rehearsing the presentation, you have decided to divide the presentation into two parts for sessions in the morning and afternoon. To do this, you will create two custom shows based on the Foundation and Animal Angels sections you have already prepared.

Concept **Custom Show**

A **custom show** is a presentation that runs within a presentation. For example, you may have one presentation that you need to give to two different groups. The overview slides are the same for both groups, but there are a few slides that are specific to each group. Rather than create two separate presentations, you can include all the slides in your main presentation and then group the specific slides into two custom shows that run after the overview slides. While you are running the slide show, you can jump to the specific custom show that you created for that audience.

DEFINING AND EDITING CUSTOM SHOWS

The morning session will cover the materials about the foundation and the afternoon session will cover the materials about the Animal Angels volunteer group. You will create two custom shows that will display only those slides for each session.

You will create the custom show for the afternoon session first.

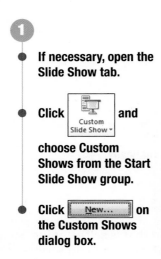

- If necessary, open the Slide Show tab.

- Click **Custom Slide Show** and choose Custom Shows from the Start Slide Show group.

- Click **New...** on the Custom Shows dialog box.

Your screen should be similar to Figure 3.57

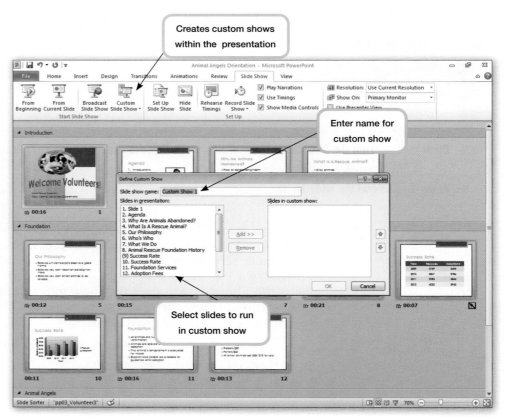

Figure 3.57

In the Define Custom Show dialog box, you name the custom show and select the slides that will run within the show. All the slides in a custom show also must be in the main presentation.

2

- In the Slide show name text box, type **Animal Angels**

- In the Slides in presentation list box, select slides 13 through 17.

Having Trouble?

Click slide 13 and then hold Shift when you click slide 17 to select all slides in this range.

- Click [Add >>].

Your screen should be similar to Figure 3.58

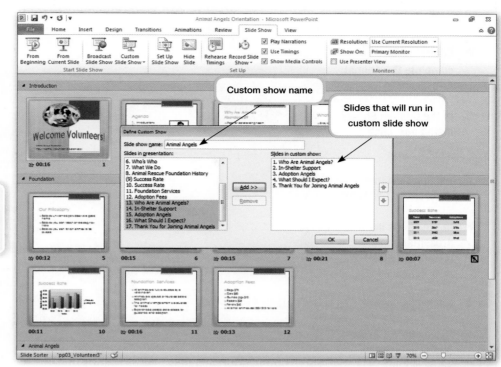

Figure 3.58

The selected slides are listed in the Slides in custom show area.

Next you want to create the custom slide show for the morning session about the Foundation in general. When the custom show ends, you want the Agenda slide to display again, so you are ready to begin the afternoon session. To do this, you will include the Agenda slide as the last slide in the custom show. After adding the slides for the custom show, you will change the slide order so that the Agenda slide will be last. This will enable you to link directly to the second custom show without closing the first one.

To change the order of the slides in the custom show, select a slide in the Slides in custom show list box and then click [↑] to move the slide up in the list or [↓] to move the slide down.

3

- Click [OK] to complete the Animal Angels show.

- In the Custom Shows dialog box, click [New...].

- Name the custom show Foundation.

- In the Slides in presentation list box, select slides 2 through 12.

- Click [Add >>].

- Select slide 1 in the Slides in custom show list box.

- Click [⬇] 10 times to move it to the bottom of the list.

Your screen should be similar to Figure 3.59

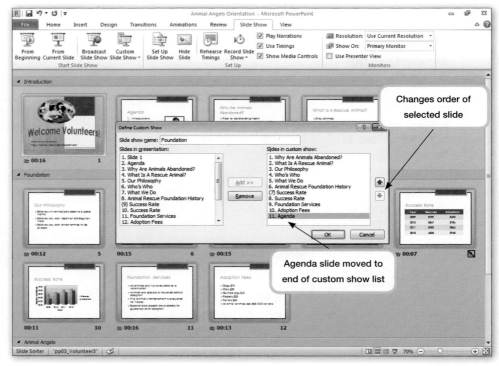

Figure 3.59

Changing the slide order in a custom show does not change the order of the slides in the main presentation. Now you will test how the Foundation custom show runs.

4

- Click [OK].

- Click [Show] to run the Foundation custom show.

- View the slides and press [Esc] to end the custom show when the Agenda slide is displayed.

The Foundation custom show displays the slides in the order they were listed in the custom show list. The timings associated with the slides also are used.

ADDING HYPERLINKS TO RUN A CUSTOM SHOW

Next, you need to create a method to start the custom shows from the Animal Angels Orientation presentation. To do this, you will add hyperlinks from the bulleted item on the Agenda slide to its corresponding custom show.

A **hyperlink** is a connection to a location in the current document, another document, or a Web site. It provides a quick way to move to or jump to other slides, custom shows, presentations, objects, e-mail addresses, or Web pages. You can jump to sites on your own system or network as well as to sites on the Internet and the Web. The user jumps to the referenced location by clicking on the hyperlink. You can assign the hyperlink to text or to any object, including pictures, tables, clip art, and graphs.

You will add a hyperlink from the About the Foundation topic in the Agenda slide to the Foundation custom show.

1

● Display slide 2 in Normal view.

● Select the second bulleted item.

● Click  from the Links group of the Insert tab.

Your screen should be similar to Figure 3.60

Figure 3.60

Your next step is to specify the location of the document to link to and the specific slide or custom show in the document.

2

● Choose Place in This Document from the Link to list.

● Choose Foundation under Custom Shows.

Having Trouble?

Use the vertical scroll bar to display the Foundation Custom Show name.

● Click OK .

● Click outside the selection on the Agenda slide to clear the highlight.

Your screen should be similar to Figure 3.61

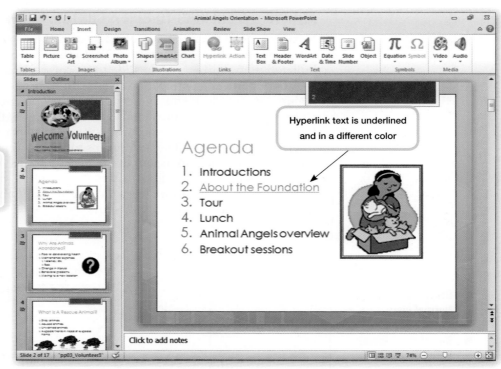

Figure 3.61

The hyperlink text appears underlined and in a different font color. The color of the hyperlink text is determined by the theme colors of the presentation. Next, you need to add the hyperlink to the Animal Angels custom show.

3

● Create another hyperlink from Agenda item 5 to the Animal Angels custom show.

The fifth bulleted agenda item is now a hyperlink to the custom slide show.

USING HYPERLINKS

Now you want to try out one of the hyperlinks to see how they work. To activate the hyperlinks, you need to run the slide show. Then, clicking on the hyperlink while the slide show runs will run the associated custom show.

● **Run the slide show from the beginning.**

Having Trouble?
Pressing F5 starts the slide show at slide 1.

● **Click on the Animal Angels overview hyperlink when slide 2 is displayed.**

Additional Information
During a slide show, the mouse pointer shape changes to a 🖑 when pointing to a hyperlink.

● **Press Esc to end the show when the last slide is displayed.**

● **Add appropriate file documentation.**

● **Save the presentation.**

● **Print a handout with six slides horizontal per page showing slides 1, 2, 4, 6, 8, and 10 in landscape orientation and scaled to fit the paper.**

FOCUS ON CAREERS

EXPLORE YOUR CAREER OPTIONS

Training Specialist

In today's job market, learning new skills is the only way to keep current with ever-changing technology. A training specialist in a corporate environment is responsible for teaching employees how to do their jobs, which usually involves computer training. Training specialists use PowerPoint to create materials for their lectures, can automate presentations, and can publish them to the Web or provide them on a CD to send to employees at remote locations. The position of training specialist usually requires a college degree. Typical salaries range from $30,120 to $85,860 depending on experience and skill. To learn more about this career, visit the Web site for the Bureau of Labor Statistics of the U.S. Department of Labor.

SmartArt (PP3.12)

A SmartArt graphic is used to create a visual representation of textual information.

Organization Chart (PP3.21)

An organization chart graphically represents the structure of an organization.

Chart (PP3.30)

A chart, also called a graph, is a visual representation of numeric data.

Collect and Paste (PP3.33)

Collecting and pasting is the capability of the program to store multiple copied items in the Office Clipboard and then paste one or more of them into another document.

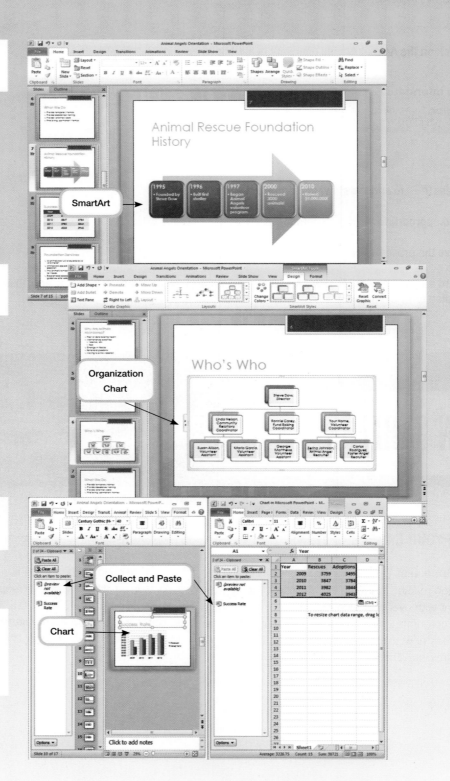

WordArt (PP3.40)

WordArt is used to enhance your presentation by changing the shape of text and adding special effects such as 3-D and shadows.

Animated GIF (PP3.45)

An animated GIF file is a type of graphic file that has motion.

Sections (PP3.50)

Sections are used to organize and label logical groupings of slides to make it easier to locate specific slides and to navigate through a lengthy presentation.

Custom Show (PP3.59)

A custom show is a presentation that runs within a presentation.

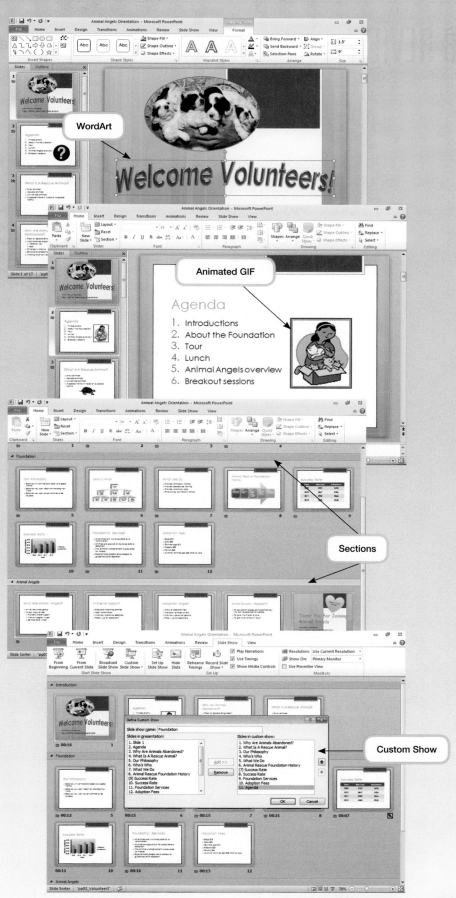

KEY TERMS

animated GIF   PP3.45
assistant shape   PP3.21
branch   PP3.21
chart   PP3.30
collecting and pasting   PP3.33
coworker shape   PP3.21
custom show   PP3.59
graph   PP3.30
hierarchical relationship   PP3.21
hierarchy   PP3.21

hyperlink   PP3.63
kiosk   PP3.59
manager shape   PP3.21
Office Clipboard   PP3.33
organization chart   PP3.21
rehearse timings   PP3.55
sections   PP3.50
Slide Library   PP3.7
SmartArt   PP3.12
WordArt   PP3.40

COMMAND SUMMARY

Command	Shortcut	Action
File tab		
New/New from existing		Inserts an existing presentation as a new unnamed presentation
Home tab		
Clipboard group		
☐ Dialog box launcher		Turns on Office Clipboard
Slides group		
New Slide ▾ /Slides from Outline		Inserts new slides using a Word outline
New Slide ▾ /Reuse Slides		Inserts new slides from another presentation
🔲 Section ▾ /Add Section		Inserts an untitled section that can be renamed
Paragraph group		
🔲 ▾		Converts selected text to a SmartArt graphic
Insert tab		
Illustrations group		
SmartArt		Inserts a SmartArt graphic
Chart		Inserts a chart
Links group		
Hyperlink	Ctrl + K	Creates a link to a slide, custom show, other file, or Web page

COMMAND SUMMARY (CONTINUED)

Command	Shortcut	Action
Text group		
WordArt		Inserts a WordArt graphic object
Slide Show tab		
Start Slide Show group		
From Beginning		Starts the slide show from the first slide of the presentation
Custom Slide Show		Creates or plays a custom slide show
Set Up group		
Set Up Slide Show		Specifies advanced options for a slide show
Hide Slide		Marks a slide so it will be hidden during a presentation
Rehearse Timings		Practices timing or pace of a presentation
Use Timings		Turns timing on and off
Chart Tools Design tab		
Chart Styles group		
More		Opens the Chart Styles gallery to choose alternative chart styles including chart color and appearance

COMMAND SUMMARY (CONTINUED)

Command	Shortcut	Action
Chart Tools Layout tab		
Labels group		
Axis Titles ▾		Adds labels to the vertical and horizontal axes
Chart Tools Format tab		
Shape Styles group		
▾ More		Opens the Shape Style gallery to choose a visual style for the shape or line
Drawing Tools Format tab		
WordArt Styles group		
▾ More		Opens the WordArt Style gallery to choose a visual style for the WordArt text
A ▾ Text Effects		Provides options for special text effects such as bevel, reflection, and more
SmartArt Tools Design tab		
Create Graphic group		
Add Shape ▾		Adds a shape to SmartArt graphic
⇨ Demote		Demotes selected element of SmartArt graphic
Layouts group		
▾ More		Opens the Layouts gallery to choose the layout for the SmartArt shape
SmartArt Styles group		
Change Colors ▾		Changes the color variation of a SmartArt graphic
▾ More		Opens the SmartArt Styles gallery to choose an overall visual style for the SmartArt graphic

LAB EXERCISES

MATCHING

Match the item on the left with the correct description on the right.

1. column chart   ____ a. Used to emphasize text through decorative effects or changing its shape

2. organization chart   ____ b. Provide logical groupings of slides that organize them for easy navigation

3. custom show   ____ c. Used to show a progression of sequential steps in a task or workflow

4. Office Clipboard   ____ d. Graphically represents the structure of an organization

5. hierarchy   ____ e. Shows data changes over time or comparisons among items

6. process   ____ f. Provides a quick way to jump to other slides, custom shows, presentations, objects, e-mail addresses, or Web pages

7. sections   ____ g. Presentation that runs within a presentation

8. WordArt   ____ h. Shows ranking such as reporting structures within a department in a business

9. GIF   ____ i. Used to store multiple copied items so they can be copied into other locations or documents

10. hyperlink   ____ j. Animated graphic file type

MULTIPLE CHOICE

Circle the letter of the correct answer to the following questions.

1. A _____ is a presentation that runs within a presentation.
   a. build
   b. custom show
   c. related show
   d. transition

2. If you need to create a chart that shows the relationship of each value in the data series to the series as a whole, you would select the _____ chart.
   a. bar
   b. column
   c. line
   d. pie

3. An animated _____ file is a type of graphic file that has motion.
   a. AVI
   b. GIF
   c. MOV
   d. MPEG

4. _____ is used to store multiple copied items and then paste one or more of the items into another location or document.
   a. Office Clipboard
   b. System Clipboard
   c. System Collector
   d. Office Collector

5. Hyperlinks provide a quick way to _____ other slides, custom shows, presentations, objects, e-mail addresses, or Web pages.
   a. align
   b. copy from
   c. jump to
   d. paste to

6. To discard formatting changes made to a SmartArt graphic, use the _____ command.
   a. Invert Graphic
   b. Replace Styles
   c. Remove Borders
   d. Reset Graphic

7. A(n) _____ chart can include any items that have a hierarchical relationship.
   a. area
   b. bar
   c. organization
   d. pie

8. One method for organizing the slides in a presentation is to add _____.
   a. Sections
   b. Outlines
   c. Shapes
   d. SmartArt

9. The _____ is the top-level shape of a group.
   a. branch
   b. co-worker shape
   c. manager shape
   d. subordinate shape

10. When applying animation, the _____ command controls the sequence for how SmartArt graphics appear on the slide.
    a. Appear
    b. Effect Options
    c. Preview
    d. Reveal Items

LAB EXERCISES

TRUE/FALSE

Circle the correct answer to the following questions.

1.	Slides can be created using a Word outline.	True	False
2.	Sections can be applied at any time during presentation development.	True	False
3.	An animated GIF is a map of a group, which usually includes people, but can include any items that have a hierarchical relationship.	True	False
4.	When reusing slides from another presentation, slides can be inserted and their formatting will change to match the current presentation.	True	False
5.	A bar chart shows the relative importance of a value over time by emphasizing the area under the curve created by each data series.	True	False
6.	In a pie chart, each slice of the pie represents a single value in a data series.	True	False
7.	After using the Rehearse Timings feature, the time spent on each slide is displayed below the slide in Slide Sorter view.	True	False
8.	Once effects are applied to a SmartArt graphic, they can be removed using the Convert feature.	True	False
9.	The Y axis is also known as the category axis.	True	False
10.	A custom show is a presentation that runs within a presentation.	True	False

FILL-IN

Complete the following statements by filling in the blanks with the correct terms.

1. The _____ command is used to avoid displaying a slide during a slide show.

2. A(n) _____ is a visual representation of numeric data that is used to help an audience grasp the impact of the data.

3. When rearranging slides or adding sections, use the _____ to see more slides at one time.

4. A(n) _____ chart emphasizes the area under the curve.

5. In an organization chart, a(n) _____ is a shape and all the shapes that report to it.

6. The _____ feature is used to emphasize text through decorative effects and text shapes.

7. The _____ contains a brief description identifying the patterns or colors assigned to the data series in a chart.

8. All organization charts consist of different levels that represent the _____.

9. When a(n) _____ GIF file is inserted into a PowerPoint slide, it does not display action until you run the presentation.

10. The _____ feature can be used to record the time spent on each slide as you practice your presentation.

STEP-BY-STEP

POOL SAFETY PRESENTATION ★

1. As an employee at Backyard Oasis, you have been asked to prepare a pool safety presentation for parents who are considering a home pool or who already have a home pool. Most of the presentation is complete, but you want to add some enhancements to emphasize text by using WordArt and SmartArt. Several slides of your completed presentation will be similar to those shown here.

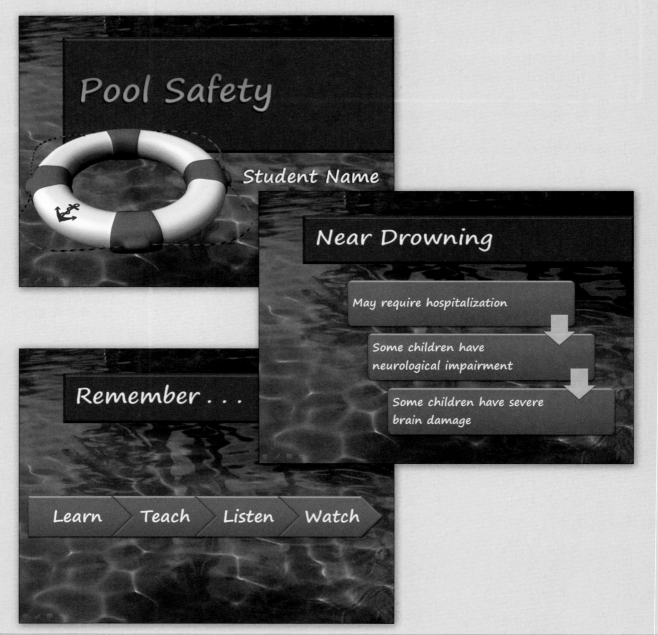

a. Open the PowerPoint file pp03_Pool Safety.

b. On the title slide, add your name. Apply a Wave 2 Transform effect to the title.

c. On slides 3 and 4, select the bulleted text and convert it to a Staggered Process SmartArt graphic from the Process category. Make these changes:

- Font: Segoe Print to match the other text used in the presentation, 20 points.
- Color Fill: Accent 2.
- Style: Intense Effect.

d. On slide 9, resize the bulleted list to fit on the right beside the picture of lightning.

e. On slide 11, convert the bulleted text to a Closed Chevron Process from the Process category SmartArt graphic. Change the font, color, and style to match slides 3 and 4. Increase the size of the SmartArt graphic to emphasize the shapes more.

f. On slide 12, create WordArt with the text **Enjoy!** using the Segoe Print font. Size and position the shape to fit over the picture on the bottom right. Apply an appropriate color and text effects.

g. Insert one section between slides 2 and 3 named **The Importance** and another section between slides 3 and 4 named **Pool Safety Rules**.

h. Change the default section name to **Introduction**.

i. Save your completed presentation as Pool Safety2. Print the presentation as handouts with six slides per page.

FITNESS PRESENTATION ★ ★

2. Annette Ramirez is the new Lifestyle Fitness Club manager. She would like to use a presentation on exercise currently in use by the club to discuss the benefits of an exercise plan. She has asked you to modify the current presentation to include some information on fitness trends. Several slides of your completed presentation will be similar to those shown on the next page.

a. Start PowerPoint and open the file pp03_LF Exercise.

b. Change the slide design to one of your choice. Check all slides and adjust the text and graphics as needed throughout.

c. On slide 1:

- Change the title to **Achieving Fitness**
- Apply a WordArt style and customize the effects. Reposition the title and subtitle as needed.

d. Change the layout of slides 3, 4, and 10 to Title and Content. Resize the content placeholders so the text does not extend above the picture.

e. On slide 9, change Circuit Training to **Advanced Step** in three cells.

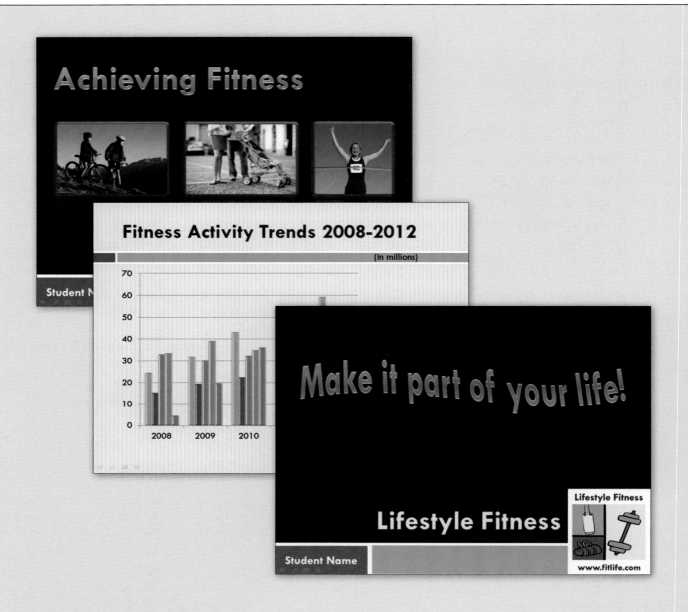

f. Insert a new Title and Content slide after slide 10. On this slide:

● Add the title **Fitness Activity Trends 2008–2012**

● Insert a text box for **(in millions)** and position it below the title.

- Insert a Clustered Column chart using the data below:

	2008	2009	2010	2011	2012
Free Weights	24.5	31.7	43.2	53.8	59.3
Resistance Machines	15.3	19.4	22.5	28.4	35.6
Running/Jogging	32.9	30.1	32.3	34.2	35.1
Stationary Cycling	33.4	39.1	34.8	33.8	32.3
Treadmill	4.4	19.7	36.1	42.1	45.2

- Change the color and appearance of the chart by selecting a chart style of your choice.

g. Move slide 11 after slide 7 so Fitness Activity Trends follows Improve Lifestyle. Hide slide 11, Exercise Makes Life More Fun!

h. On slide 9, search for an animated graphic for exercise and insert it. Resize the graphic as needed.

i. On the last slide, delete the text box and the subtitle placeholder. Create WordArt in a shape of your choice and add the text **Make it part of your life!** Set a WordArt style and Transform style of your choice. Size and position the WordArt appropriately.

j. Insert the logo pp03_LF Logo into slides 1 and 12. Position and resize the logo as needed.

k. Insert a text box with your name on slides 1 and 12.

l. Run the presentation and make any changes necessary for consistency in how slide content is positioned. Save the presentation as LF_Fitness Program Benefits. Print the presentation as handouts in landscape orientation with six slides per page.

EMPLOYEE MOTIVATION PRESENTATION ★ ★

3. Chirag Shah works in the personnel department of a manufacturing company. Chirag has recently been studying the ways that employee morale can affect production levels and employee job satisfaction. Chirag has been asked to hold a meeting with department managers to suggest methods that can be used to improve employee morale. He has started a PowerPoint presentation to accompany his talk but still needs to make several changes and enhancements to the presentation. Several slides of your completed presentation will be similar to those shown on the next page.

LAB EXERCISES

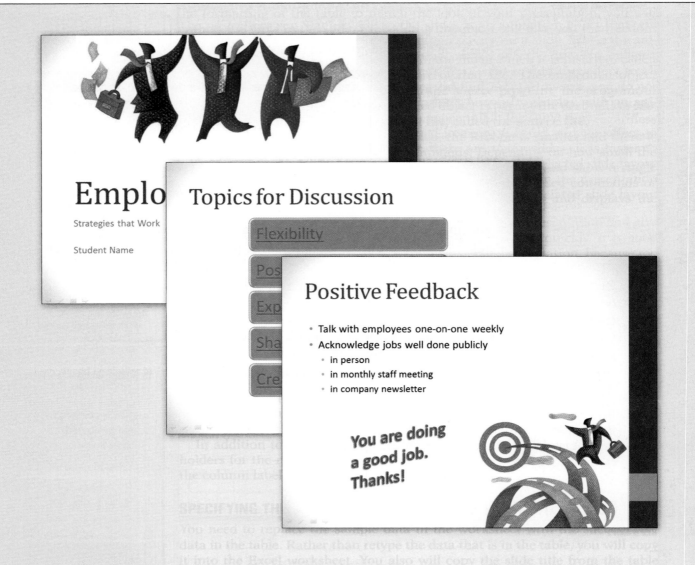

a. Open the presentation pp03_Motivation Strategies. Replace the Student Name placeholder with your name.

b. After slide 2, insert a new Title and Content slide with the title **Topics for Discussion**. Insert a Vertical Bullet List from the SmartArt graphics List category. Use the text pane to delete the indented items and type five level 1 items:

Flexibility

Positive feedback

Expert input

Sharing the wealth

Creating a team

c. Resize the SmartArt graphic so the shapes better fit the words without reducing the size of the text. Move the SmartArt to the center of the slide and apply the Intense Effect style.

d. Change the design layout on slide 4 to Two Content. Insert the graphic picture pp03_Teamwork into the right placeholder and move the image to the bottom right of the slide.

e. Reuse slides from pp03_EmployeeMorale. Insert the slides into the presentation as follows:
- "Vision Statement" after slide 2.
- "Available Options" after slide 5.
- "Recommendation" after slide 10.

f. Demote the last three bullets on slide 7.

g. Create WordArt using a style of your choice with the text **You are doing a good job. Thanks!** to slide 7. Size and position the shape appropriately on the slide.

h. On slide 11, search for an animated graphic for teamwork and insert it. Resize the graphic as needed.

i. Change the theme of the presentation to one of your choice with a white background because of the images being used that have white backgrounds. Adjust the text and images on the slides as needed.

j. On slide 4, select each shape in the SmartArt graphic and add the following hyperlinks:
- From Flexibility to slide 5.
- From Positive feedback to slide 7.
- From Expert input to slide 8.
- From Sharing the wealth to slide 9.
- From Creating a team to slide 10.

k. Run the presentation to review the slides and test the hyperlinks. Press **4** and press (Enter) to return to the topic slide after viewing individual slides. Make any changes necessary.

l. Save the presentation as Motivation Incentives. Print the presentation as handouts, six slides per page.

LAB EXERCISES

OUR CITY—STRONG AND GROWING ★★

4. You work as an intern in the mayor's office of your community. The mayor, Michael Augustine, will soon present his annual progress report at the November Town Hall Meeting. The presentation is partially completed, and you have been asked to help enhance it. You will reuse some of the slides from another presentation you are working on and add a pie chart and an organization chart. Then you will divide the presentation into sections. As you design the slides, you want to add several black accents for a modern appearance. Several slides of your completed presentation will be similar to those shown here.

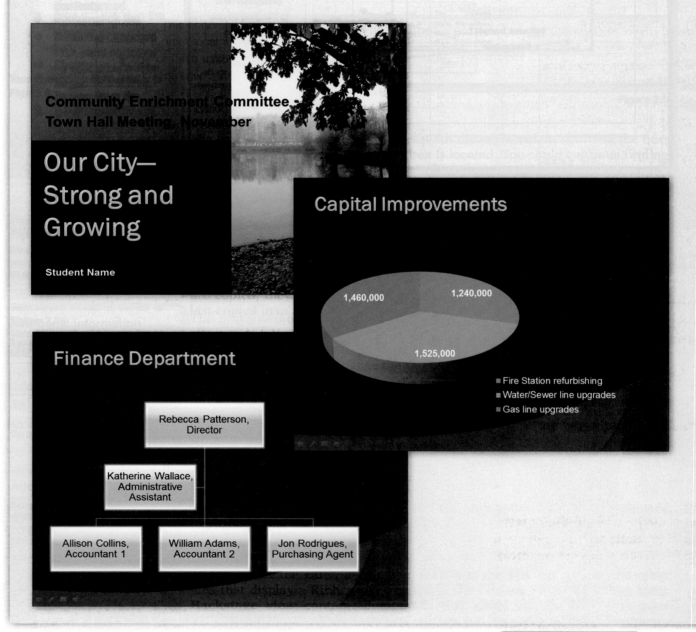

a. Open the pp03_Strong City presentation. Enter your name on the first slide in place of Student Name. Copy your name and paste it on the last slide.

b. On the title slide, to emphasize the presentation title, draw a black rectangle, then size it to fit on the left of the slide and send it behind the title text.

c. On slide 2,
- Move the title to the bottom of the slide.
- Insert the picture pp03_Autumn Road and position it near the top of the slide on the left.
- Resize the title placeholder so the text fits on one line and reduce the vertical size (approximate height 0.8" 3 width 9.5").
- Change the title placeholder fill color to black and bring it forward. Position it at the bottom of the picture extending to the right edge of the slide.

d. On slide 3, insert the picture pp03_Community. Select the title text, apply the Wave 1 Transform effect in the WordArt Styles group. Move the text below the picture and resize the WordArt object slightly so the text fits better below the picture.

e. Reuse all five slides from pp03_Budget Regulations and insert them in order after slide 8.

f. Change the title of slide 9 to **Manage Our Budget Responsibly** and change the subtitle to **Assure Appropriate Spending**

g. After slide 11, insert a new Title and Content slide with the title **Finance Department**, then create an organization chart showing the people in this department:

Rebecca Patterson, Director (level 1)

Katherine Wallace, Administrative Assistant (level 2)

Allison Collins, Accountant 1 (level 3)

William Adams, Accountant 2 (level 3)

Jon Rodrigues, Purchasing Agent (level 3)

h. In the organization chart, stretch the director shape so Rebecca Patterson fits on one line.

i. Change the color of the organization chart to Colored Outline – Accent 1. Apply the Polished SmartArt style.

j. After slide 7, insert a Title and Content slide with the title **Additional Proposed Projects**, then create a 3-D Pie chart with these items:

Fire Station refurbishing	1,240,000
Water/Sewer line upgrades	1,525,000
Gas line upgrades	1,460,000

k. Change the slide title to **Capital Improvements**. If a chart title appears, delete it.

l. Show the costs on the pie slices by choosing Data Labels, then Inside End.

m. Resize the legend to avoid word wrapping and move the legend to the lower right of the chart area.

n. Insert a section titled **The Future** between slides 3 and 4. Insert another section titled **Manage Budget** between slides 9 and 10. Change the default section name to **Introduction**.

o. Save the presentation as Strong and Growing. Print the presentation as handouts with nine slides per page, scaled to fit paper, and in landscape orientation.

LAB EXERCISES

5. You work in the student health services of a local university. You have been asked to create a presentation that will help students stay healthy during flu season. You have already started to compile the information you will present, but you still need to make several changes to the presentation. Your final presentation will include a chart on infection rates and a graphic that describes the life cycle of the virus. Several slides of your completed presentation will be similar to those shown here.

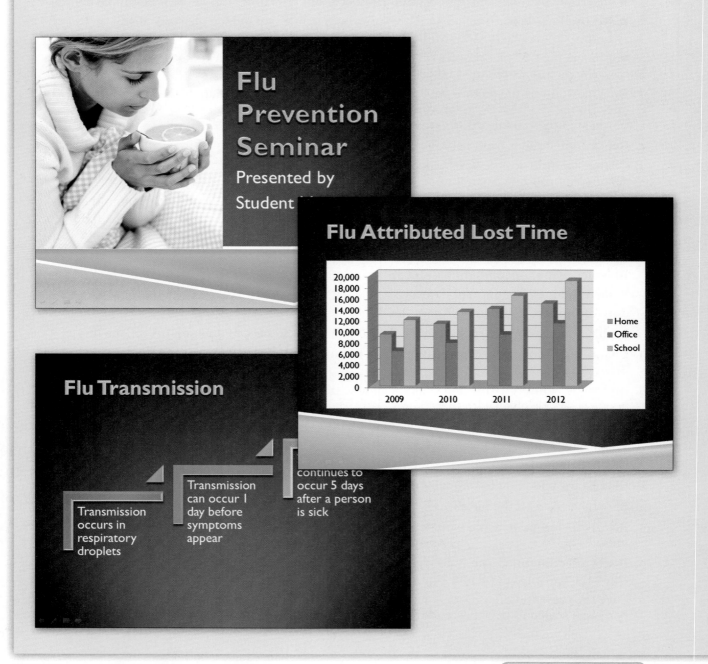

a. Open the file pp03_Flu Prevention.

b. Replace the student name with your name in the subtitle on slide 1.

c. Reuse slides from pp03_Flu Prevention Techniques. Insert all the slides, except slide 1, into the presentation after slide 3.

d. Before the last slide, insert the outline pp03_Flu Symptoms. Reset the newly inserted slides using the Title and Content layout to fix the slide format.

e. Insert a new slide using the Title and Content slide layout after slide 5 with the title **Flu Attributed Lost Time**, then create a 3-D Clustered Column chart using the data in the following table:

	Home	Office	School
2009	9,314	6,309	11,913
2010	11,211	7,833	13,418
2011	13,981	9,323	16,391
2012	15,002	11,354	19,010

f. Change the color and appearance of the chart by selecting a chart style and shape style of your choice.

g. Add WordArt on the last slide with the text **Flu Prevention Starts with You!** Select a WordArt style and text effects of your choice. Size and position the WordArt appropriately. Apply an animation effect to make the WordArt appear on click.

h. On slide 10, Flu Transmission, convert the bulleted text to a Step Up Process SmartArt graphic. Change the colors and design of the SmartArt graphic by selecting a SmartArt style of your choice.

i. Insert the following humorous images, then resize and position them appropriately:

Slide 3   pp03_Sick

Slide 5   pp03_At Home (animated GIF that moves once)

Slide 7   pp03_Sneeze

Slide 8   pp03_Hands

Slide 12   pp03_Vaccine

j. Add a shadow effect to the images on slides 7 and 8.

k. On slide 11, insert an animated GIF that you find using the Clip Art task pane. Try using words such as headache, illness, or healthcare.

l. Add a section after slide 3 named **Protect Yourself** and a section after slide 9 named **Flu Basics**; change the default section name to **Introduction**

m. Create a custom slide show named **What to Do if You Get Sick** using slides 4, 5, 7, 8, and 9. Create a second custom show named **Flu Basics** using slides 10 through 13.

n. On slide 2, insert hyperlinks so each of the agenda items links to the appropriate slide.

LAB EXERCISES

o. Apply one transition to all slides, then change the transition on two or three slides to better emphasize the slide content.

p. Run the presentation and also check the custom shows. Make any necessary changes.

q. Save the presentation as Flu_Prevention_Seminar. Print slides 1, 2, 5, 6, 10, and 14 with six slides per page. Rehearse the timing of the presentation.

ON YOUR OWN

FAMILY REUNION PRESENTATION ★

1. Your family is holding a reunion in Las Vegas this year. They have heard about your new computer skills, and one of your aunts has requested that you put on a presentation about your family following the welcome dinner. Create a presentation that includes an organization chart of your family tree, photos you have scanned, family anecdotes, and graphics. Format the slides attractively. Save your presentation as Family Reunion and print handouts with six slides per page.

YOUR HOME GYM ★ ★

2. As a sales associate for the Sports Connection, you have been asked to prepare a presentation featuring comparisons of some top-selling products to be used for customers who need an overview of equipment that is available for home use. This equipment would include such devices as treadmills, weight benches, stair climbers, and other resistance equipment. Using the skills you have learned so far, create a presentation that includes descriptions of the particular types of product with a comparison (either as a list or table) of features for two or three models for one of the products. Include a chart showing equipment pricing arranged from lowest to highest cost. Use photographs and other graphic features to add interest to the presentation. Save your presentation as Your Home Gym and print handouts with six slides per page.

CANADA BY RAIL ★ ★ ★

3. Another trip being considered by Getaway Travel Club members is a train tour of Canada. You need to research the available tours, their destinations, and duration. Find out costs including air fare to get to and from the train from your home location. Show the comparison of several trips using tables and charts to make it easier to understand. Include SmartArt to show the process of travel between destinations. Include pictures to illustrate the scenery on the trip and feature one or two of the exclusive hotels where you will stay for selected nights during the trip. Provide source information for images obtained on the Web. Include a topic slide early in the presentation with hyperlinks to your various topics. Save your updated presentation as Travel Canada. Print handouts with six slides per page.

TIME MANAGEMENT ★ ★ ★

4. You have been asked to talk about time management for one of the student organizations at your college. You want to prepare a presentation that is meaningful, but also colorful and entertaining. Use animated GIFs and illustrated images to add humor. Apply special effects with WordArt styles and text effects. Include a chart showing the typical distribution of a college student's activities during a 24-hour period. Create a process diagram to show key steps to better schedule time and manage activities. Include your name as a subtitle on the first slide. Divide the presentation into sections. Save your presentation as Time Management. Print handouts with six slides per page.

AVOIDING CYBER THEFT ★ ★ ★

5. Your computer survey class requires you to do a research project on cyber theft. Research this topic on the Web to learn about a variety of activities that are illegal and potentially very damaging to businesses and individuals. Identify what can be done to reduce vulnerability and protect both businesses and individuals from these threats. Create a PowerPoint presentation that includes definitions, examples, and suggested defense strategies. Reference the sources of any copyrighted images or quotes that you use. Use SmartArt graphics to show several important relationships. Insert sections based on your topics. Include your name and the current date as a footer on all the slides. Save your presentation as Cyber Theft. Print handouts with six slides per page.

Creating a Self-Running Presentation

Objectives

After completing this lab, you will know how to:

1. Modify a design theme with customized colors and background.

2. Customize graphics, change stacking order, group/ungroup/regroup, and align.

3. Insert a screenshot.

4. Create and enhance a complex table.

5. Set up a presentation for a kiosk with audio and self-running transitions.

6. Make a presentation self-running with hyperlinks and action buttons.

7. Save a presentation as a design template.

Animal Rescue Foundation

The director of the Animal Rescue Foundation has asked you to create a presentation promoting the organization that will run on a kiosk in the local shopping mall. This self-running presentation needs to capture the attention of passers-by in a very busy area. You will add several theme and graphic enhancements to the presentation along with music that will play throughout the entire presentation. At the end, the presentation will loop back to the first slide and continue playing.

The Animal Rescue Foundation main

shelter has a computer in the lobby that they want to use to show this same presentation. Rather than have the presentation run continuously, you will modify the presentation so viewers can use the mouse to control navigation through the presentation. To make it easier for viewers to navigate, you will add action to several objects that lets viewers move to specific slides and include navigation buttons that go forward and backward through the slides. Several slides from the completed self-running presentation are shown on the facing page.

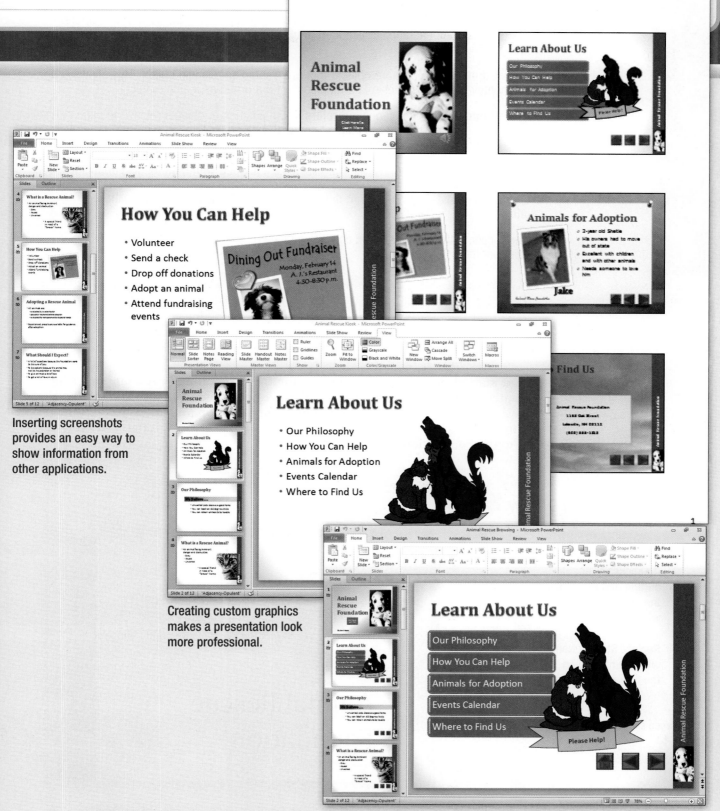

Inserting screenshots provides an easy way to show information from other applications.

Creating custom graphics makes a presentation look more professional.

Providing navigation features puts the viewer in control of the presentation.

The following concepts will be introduced in this lab:

1 Stacking Order Stacking order is the order in which objects are inserted in the different layers of a slide. As each object is added to the slide, it is added to the top, creating a new layer.

2 Group A group is two or more objects that are treated as a single object. This allows you to easily move, resize, flip, or rotate all pieces of the group as a single unit.

3 Object Alignment Object alignment refers to the position of objects relative to each other or to the slide. Objects are aligned horizontally by their left, center, or right edges; objects are aligned vertically by their top, middle, or bottom edges.

4 Audio and Video Files Almost all PCs today are equipped with multimedia capabilities, which means they can play the most commonly used audio and video files. An audio file is a type of file that plays sounds or music, and a video file plays a motion picture with sound.

5 Action Action is the capability of an object to perform a task when you click on or pass the mouse over the object.

Modifying the Design Theme

You started developing the content for the promotional presentation using content from several presentations you created earlier. You also added several new slides of animals that are available for adoption and added new formatting and graphics to enhance the presentation. Before continuing, you showed it to the Foundation director for his input.

Open the file pp04_ Animal Rescue Promotion.

If necessary, enable editing and maximize the application window.

Replace Student Name with your name on the title slide.

Your screen should be similar to Figure 4.1

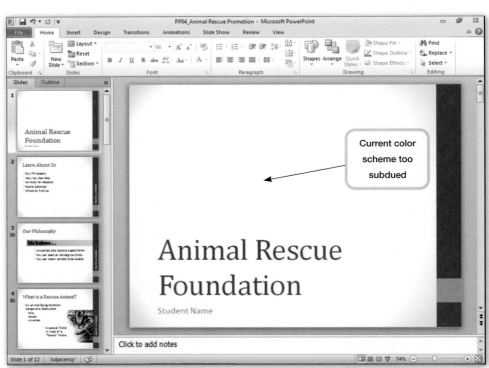

Figure 4.1

The new presentation currently consists of 12 slides and uses the Adjacency theme. Although the director thinks the content is good, he suggests that you change the color scheme to bright colors that would be better suited to creating an eye-catching kiosk-style presentation. Additionally, he wants you to change the title and closing slides to a more eye-catching design.

CUSTOMIZING A THEME

Although you like the Adjacency design theme, you want to change the colors to a different theme's colors and then customize the colors to better suit the presentation.

1

● Open the Design tab.

● Click ▣ Colors ▾ and choose the Opulent color theme.

● Click ▣ Colors ▾ and choose Create New Theme Colors.

Your screen should be similar to Figure 4.2

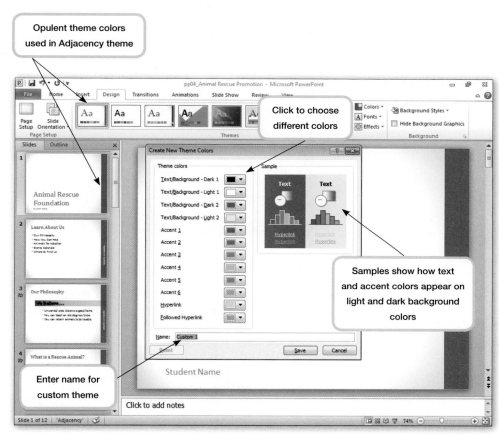

Figure 4.2

Each color theme has light and dark variations of text and background colors, six accent colors, and two hyperlink colors. The sample in the dialog box identifies how the 12 Opulent theme colors are applied to different elements of the slide on a light or dark slide background. For example, Accent 1 is used each time you draw a shape; several accent colors are used when you create a chart or SmartArt. You will change the color for the background and title text.

2

- Click  Text/Background—Dark 2 and choose Pink, Background 2, Darker 25%.

- Replace the default name with **Adjacency-Opulent** in the Name text box.

- Click **Save**.

- Display the slides in Slide Sorter view.

Your screen should be similar to Figure 4.3

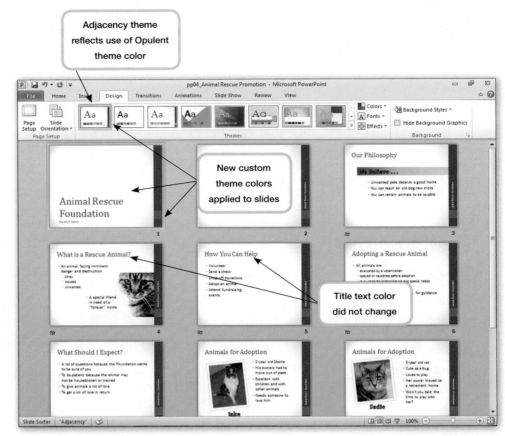

Figure 4.3

Notice that the colors displayed in the Adjacency theme icon in the Themes gallery have been updated to the new custom theme colors. The color of the bar along the right side of the slide appropriately changed to the new background color for all slides. However, the color of the title text only changed on the title slide. You will save the changes you made to the Adjacency theme as a new custom theme. Then you will use the new custom theme to update all the slides in the presentation.

3

- Open the Themes gallery and choose **Save Current Theme.**

- In the Save Current Theme dialog box, enter **Adjacency-Opulent** as the file name.

- Click  Save .

- Click **Aa**

  Adjacency-Opulent in the Themes gallery.

- Save the presentation as *Animal Rescue Kiosk.*

- Click Colors ▾ .

Your screen should be similar to Figure 4.4

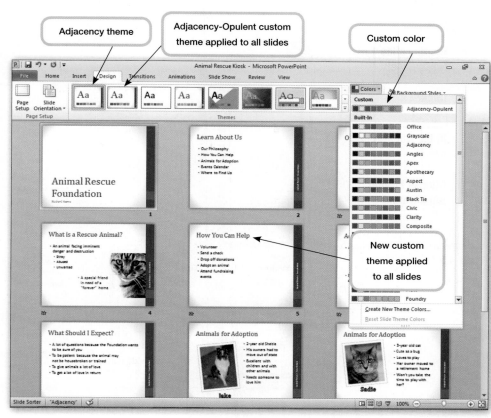

Figure 4.4

All the slide titles are updated to the new theme colors. The Adjacency-Opulent custom theme now appears in the Themes gallery and can be quickly applied to another document just like the built-in themes. Additionally, the custom colors you saved appear in the Custom category of available theme colors list. This makes it easy to reapply the custom color settings in the future to another theme.

Additional Information

You can specify how to apply a theme color by choosing the appropriate option from the theme color shortcut menu.

CREATING A CUSTOM BACKGROUND

As you look at the slides you decide you want to make several changes to add interest. First you will add a gradient color to the title slide background so it stands out from other slides. A **gradient** is a gradual progression of colors and shades, usually from one color to another or from one shade to another of the same color. Currently the slide background is white that radiates out to a faint gradient of gray in the four corners of the slide.

1

- **Display slide 1 in Normal view.**

- **Click** Background Styles ▾ **in the Background group.**

- **Choose Format Background.**

Your screen should be similar to Figure 4.5

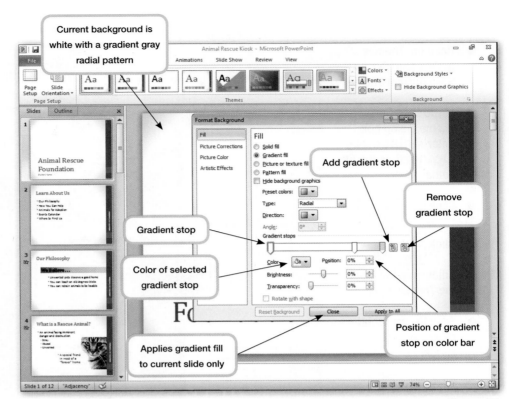

Figure 4.5

You can select a predefined gradient pattern using the Preset colors gallery, or customize the type of fill using the Type, Direction, and Angle options. You can further customize the gradient pattern by adjusting the settings on the Gradient stops bar, hand-picking the gradient colors. The default background color setting for the slide is a gradient fill that ranges from white to light gray with 0% brightness and 0% transparency. The type setting is a radial pattern that starts from the center of the slide.

First, you will change the gradient colors to a gold, white, and pink combination using the Gradient stops bar. Then you will change the pattern of the gradient. As you make your changes, Live Preview will instantly show you how they look.

2

● Move the dialog box to the bottom of the window.

● If necessary, click Stop 1 (the first stop) on the Gradient stops bar.

● Click  and change the color to Gold, Accent 4.

● Select the middle Gradient stop and change the color to White, Background 1.

● Drag the middle gradient stop to position 55%.

● Select the third Gradient stop and change the color to Pink, Accent 1, Darker 25%.

● From the Type drop-down menu, choose Linear.

● From the Direction drop-down menu, choose Linear Diagonal—Top Left to Bottom Right.

Your screen should be similar to Figure 4.6

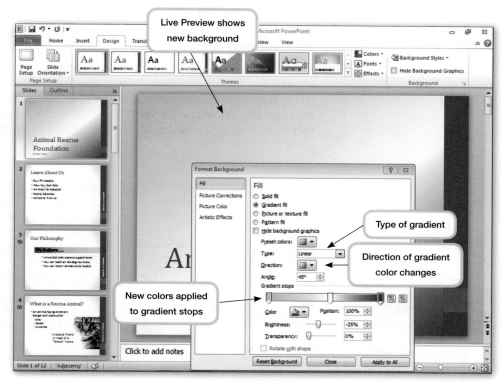

Figure 4.6

The blending of the colors is shown on the color bar behind the Gradient stops and Live Preview shows the colors as you change them on your current slide. You want to apply these colors to the title slide only. Closing the dialog box applies the background changes to the current slide only.

3

● Click [Close].

Additional Information

Clicking [Apply to All] on the Format Background dialog box applies the selected background to all the slides in the presentation. To remove a background effect, choose [Reset Background].

The gradient style background on the title slide makes it more distinctive.

ADDING GRAPHICS AND TEXT EFFECTS ON A SLIDE MASTER

The next change you want to make is to add a picture to the title slide and to repeat that picture in each slide in the presentation. You also want to change the title text on all the slides to a WordArt design and remove the date and slide number placeholders. As you know, the most efficient way to make repeating elements appear on slides is to use the slide master to make those changes.

1

- Open the View tab and click Slide Master.

- Select the Adjacency-Opulent slide master.

- Select the title text placeholder and open the Drawing Tools Format tab.

- Click ▼ in the WordArt Styles group and choose the WordArt style of Fill—Purple, Accent 2, Warm Matte Bevel (fifth row, third column).

- Change the title text fill color to Pink, Accent 5, Darker 50% (bottom row, fifth column).

- Delete the date placeholder and the slide number placeholder.

- Increase the font size of the footer to 20 points.

Your screen should be similar to Figure 4.7

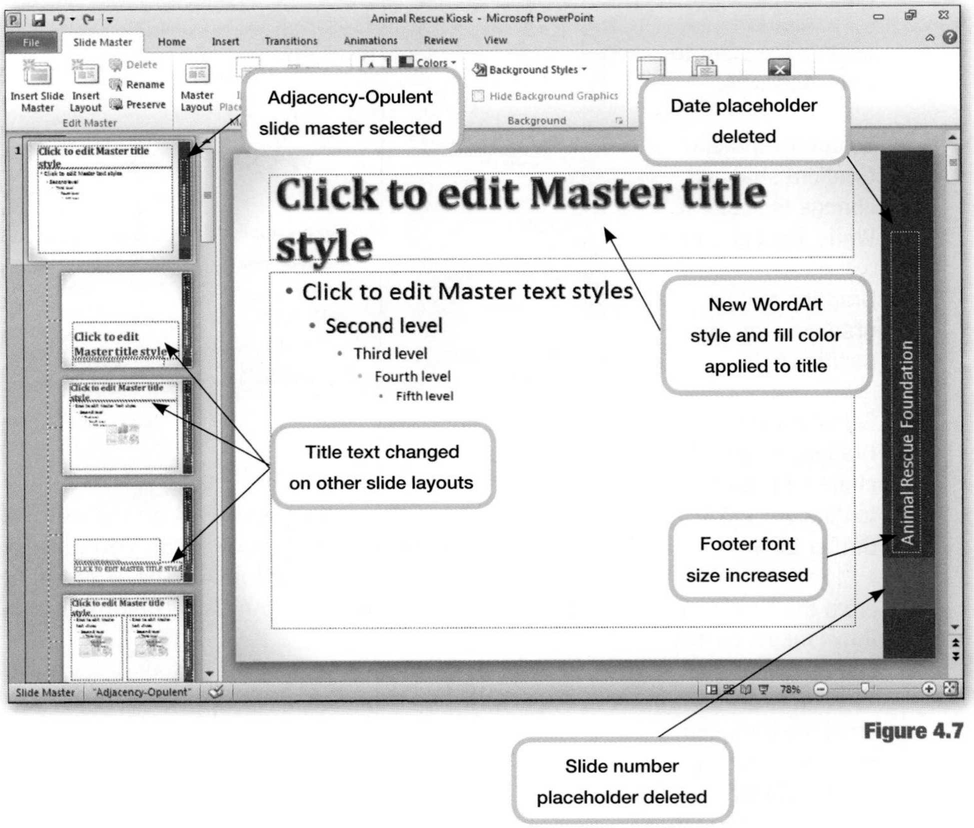

Figure 4.7

Notice that the formatting changes you made to the title text are displayed in all the other slide layouts. The footer changes are not reflected. Even though the footer changes are not displayed in the other layouts in Slide Master view, all the changes you made to the slide master layout affect all other layouts in the presentation as you will see when you switch back to Normal view.

Next you will modify the Title Slide Layout by inserting a picture and changing the placement of the title text placeholder.

2

- Choose the Title Slide Layout (second layout).

- Insert the picture pp04-Dalmation from your data file location and size and position it as in Figure 4.8.

- Resize the title placeholder and position it on the left of the slide as shown in Figure 4.8.

- Select the subtitle placeholder and change the text to black and bold.

- Left align the title and the subtitle placeholders.

Your screen should be similar to Figure 4.8

Figure 4.8

To help continue a common graphic element throughout the presentation, you will position a miniature version of the dog picture on the Title and Content and Title Only slide layouts. All slides using these layouts will show the picture.

Additional Information

At any time when you are working with placeholders on **slide master layouts**, you can check how that change affects your slide by clicking [icon] Slide Show to view the slide at full-screen size. Click (Esc) to return to Slide Master view.

3

- Copy the dog picture.

- Select the Title and Content slide layout and paste the dog picture.

- Reduce the picture size to fit on the lower right of the slide as shown in Figure 4.9.

- Copy the small picture and insert it in the same location on the Title Only Layout.

Your screen should be similar to Figure 4.9

Figure 4.9

Notice the small copied picture is automatically inserted in the same location and size in the destination layout as it was in the source layout.

4

- Display Slide Sorter view and reduce the zoom to 90% to see all the slides.

Your screen should be similar to Figure 4.10

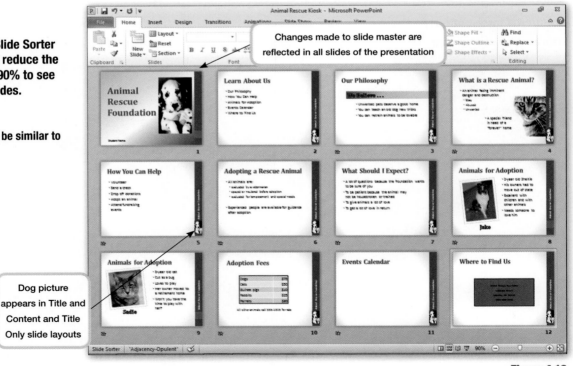

Figure 4.10

You can now see the changes you made to the title and footer of the slide master appear in all slides in the presentation. The dog picture appears in only those slides using the Title and Content and the Title Only slide layouts.

APPLYING A THEME TO SELECTED SLIDES

Next you want to change the theme for the two slides that feature pictures of animals that are available for adoption. Themes can be applied to selected slides as well as to an entire presentation. When combining two themes, however, be sure they coordinate well together.

1

- Select slides 8 and 9.

- Open the Design tab.

- Right-click on the Pushpin theme and choose Apply to Selected Slides from the shortcut menu.

Your screen should be similar to Figure 4.11

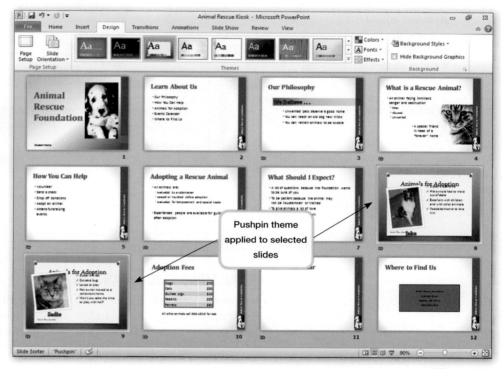

Figure 4.11

This Pushpin theme adds an interesting treatment to these slides that feature animal pictures. However, the current colors do not coordinate with your presentation. Because you saved your color changes as a custom color theme, you can easily apply them to these slides.

2

- If necessary, select slides 8 and 9 and open the Design tab.

- Click ▣ Colors ▾ and choose the Adjacency-Opulent theme color.

- Switch to Normal view and adjust the size and position of the objects on slides 8 and 9 as needed.

Your screen should be similar to Figure 4.12

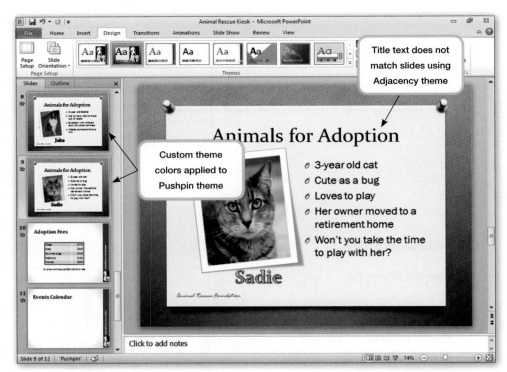

Figure 4.12

Now these two slides have a different appearance but they coordinate with the overall look of the presentation.

REVISING MULTIPLE SLIDE MASTERS

As you can see by looking at the slides with the Pushpin theme, the slide title text does not match the text used in the main presentation using the Adjacency theme where text effects were applied. You will again use the slide master to fix the titles of the two slides using the Pushpin theme.

1

● Select slide 8 and display Slide Master view.

● Scroll the slide thumbnail pane up to see the Adjacency-Opulent slide master at the top of the pane.

● Scroll back down to display the last Adjacency-Opulent slide layout at the top of the pane.

Your screen should be similar to Figure 4.13

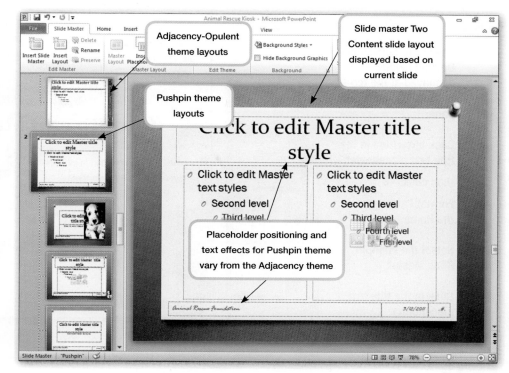

Figure 4.13

Because the presentation includes two design themes, the slide thumbnail pane displays layouts for both the Adjacency-Opulent and Pushpin themes. The currently selected slide layout is the Two Content Layout, used by the current slide in the presentation.

Notice the graphics inserted in the two layouts of the Adjacency-Opulent theme also display on the same layouts in the Pushpin theme. Generally when making changes to the master slide layouts, the changes are independent between themes. You could delete these graphics, but because they do not affect the Pushpin Two Content Layout you are using in the presentation, you will leave them.

You will use Format Painter to copy the WordArt design from the Adjacency-Opulent title to the title in the Pushpin slide master.

2

- Select the Adjacency-Opulent layout displayed at the top of the slide thumbnail pane.

- Click anywhere in the title text placeholder, then click Format Painter on the Home tab.

- Select the Pushpin Slide Master.

- Click in the title text placeholder.

Your screen should be similar to Figure 4.14

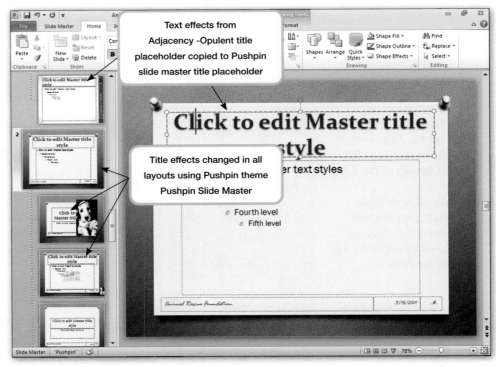

Text effects from Adjacency-Opulent title placeholder copied to Pushpin slide master title placeholder

Title effects changed in all layouts using Pushpin theme Pushpin Slide Master

Figure 4.14

The WordArt text effects used for titles in the Adjacency-Opulent theme are now applied to all the titles in the Pushpin theme.

3

- Display Normal view.

Your screen should be similar to Figure 4.15

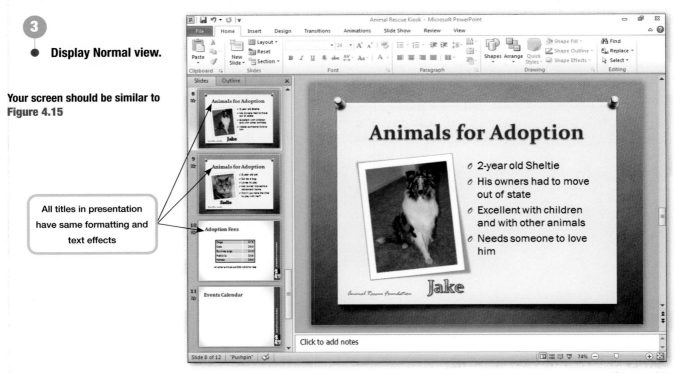

All titles in presentation have same formatting and text effects

Figure 4.15

The changes you made to the Pushpin Slide Master are displayed in both slides using this theme. The titles in all slides are now consistent.

ADDING A PICTURE BACKGROUND

Finally, you decide to use a different slide background for the last slide in the presentation. You will use a picture of a sunrise.

1

- Display slide 12 in Normal view.

- Right-click anywhere on the slide background and choose Format Background.

- Choose Picture or texture fill.

- Click **File...**.

- Change to the location of your data files and select pp04_Sunrise.

- Click **Insert**.

Your screen should be similar to Figure 4.16

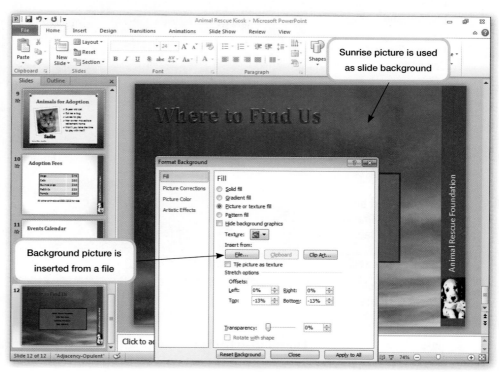

Figure 4.16

The sunrise picture has been applied to the slide background. However, you feel it is a little too dark.

2

- If necessary, move the dialog box to better see the slide background.

- Choose Picture Corrections.

- Change the Brightness to +20% and the Contrast to −10%.

- Click [Close].

- Select the text box and open the Drawing Tools Format tab.

- Click [Shape Fill ▾] and choose Gold, Accent 4, Lighter 60%.

- Click [Shape Effects ▾], select Glow, and choose Orange, 18 pt glow, Accent color 6.

- Remove the shape outline and increase the font size of the text to 20 points.

- Deselect the text box.

- Save the presentation.

Your screen should be similar to Figure 4.17

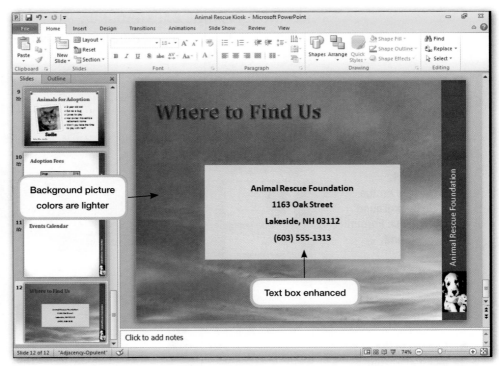

Figure 4.17

The sunrise background is lighter and the enhancements you made to the text box greatly improve the appearance of the slide.

Customizing Graphics

The next change you want to make is to add a graphic of a cat and a dog to slide 2. You were unable to find a graphic of a cat and dog together that you liked, so you decide to create a custom graphic from two separate graphics. You will do this by opening and modifying the graphics individually, then grouping them into one object.

CONVERTING GRAPHICS TO DRAWING OBJECTS

First you will insert the graphic of a cat. To make complex graphics easier to work with, you will hide the display of the pane that contains the Slides and Outline tabs and increase the magnification of the Slide pane. In Normal view the slide is sized by default to fit within the Slide pane and is about 75 percent of full (100 percent) size. In PowerPoint, you can increase the onscreen display size up to four times the normal display (400 percent) or reduce the size to 33 percent.

1

- Display slide 2 in Normal view.

- Insert the graphic file pp04_Cat from your data file location.

- Drag the splitter bar between pane containing the Slides tab and the Slide pane to the left edge of the window to hide the Slides and Outline tab pane.

- Increase the zoom to 100%.

Your screen should be similar to Figure 4.18

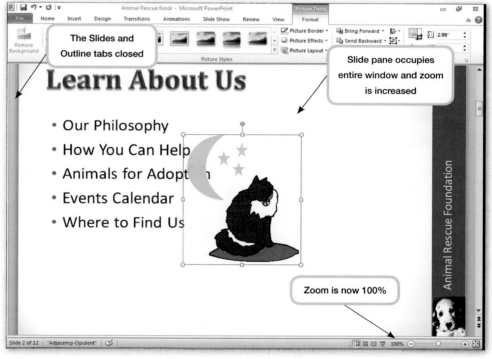

Figure 4.18

The slide pane occupies the entire document window and because the zoom is increased to 100 percent the entire slide is now too large to fully display in the window. The graphic is much larger, and you will be able to more easily select different parts of it as you make changes.

You want to modify the graphic first by changing the color of the pillow below the cat. You can customize graphics by adding and deleting pieces of the graphic, changing the fill and line colors, and otherwise editing the graphic using features on the Drawing Tools Format tab. However, because this is an imported graphic (it was not originally created within PowerPoint using the Drawing features), it first needs to be converted to a drawing object that can be modified using features on the Drawing Tools Format tab.

Right-click on the graphic and choose Edit Picture.

Click [Yes] **to convert the graphic to a Microsoft Office drawing object.**

Click on the red pillow to select it.

Your screen should be similar to Figure 4.19

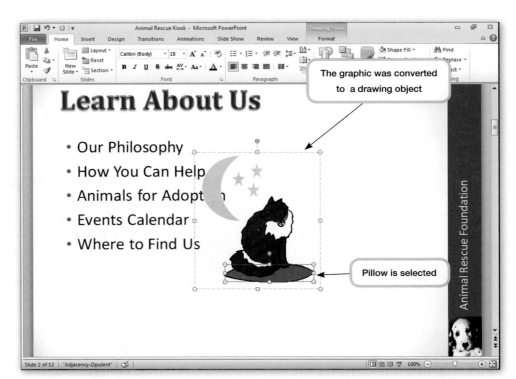

Figure 4.19

Once a graphic has been converted to a drawing object, the individual parts can be selected and edited just as you would an individual drawing object that you created using commands in the Drawing Tools Format tab.

FORMATTING AND DELETING GRAPHIC ELEMENTS

You will change the fill color of the pillow and the collar to coordinate better with the theme colors. Then you will delete the moon and stars.

1

- Open the Drawing Tools Format tab.

- Click  Shape Fill ▾ and select any color from the Themes Color gallery.

- Select the cat's collar and change the color to the same color as the pillow.

- Click the moon to select the shape.

- Press Delete.

- In the same manner, select and delete the three stars.

Figure 4.20

Additional Information

Select multiple objects by holding down Ctrl while clicking on each object.

Your screen should be similar to Figure 4.20

Additional Information

The graphic was made by starting with a black outline of the entire image filled with black, and then overlaying colored shapes to construct the cat. Because of this construction, certain areas of the graphic cannot be deleted.

The color of the pillow and collar objects within the graphic object has changed to the color you specified and the moon and stars have been deleted.

CHANGING THE STACKING ORDER

Now you are ready to add a graphic of a dog to the slide.

Insert the graphic pp04_Dog from your data file location.

Your screen should be similar to Figure 4.21

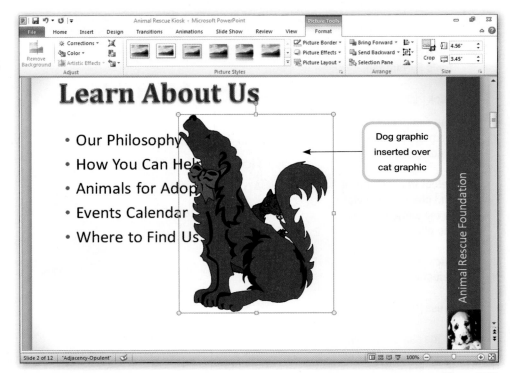

Figure 4.21

The dog graphic appears in the center of the slide over the cat graphic. This is because as each new object is added to a slide, it is added to a separate drawing layer that stacks on top of the previous layer.

Concept 1   Stacking Order

Stacking order is the order in which objects are inserted into different layers of a slide. As each object is added to the slide, it is added in a new layer at the top of the stack. Adding objects to separate layers allows each object to be positioned precisely on the slide, including in front of or behind other objects. As objects are added to a slide, they may overlap. You can rearrange the order of stacked objects on a slide by moving objects up and down one layer at a time or by moving an object to the top or bottom of the stack using Arrange commands on the Home tab, the Picture Tools Format tab, or the Drawing Tools Format tab.

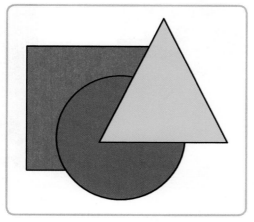

Triangle is on top of stack

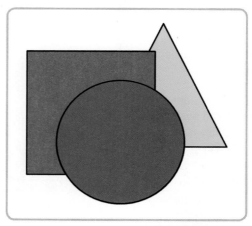

Triangle is sent to the back

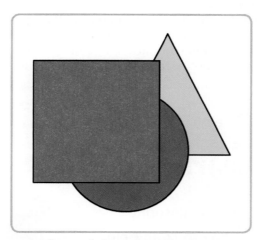

Square is brought to the front

Sometimes it is easy to lose an object behind another. If this happens, you can press [Tab] to cycle forward or [Shift] + [Tab] to cycle backward through the stacked objects until the one you want is selected. You also can display the Selection pane to help select individual objects and elements within a graphic and to rearrange the stacking order of the objects. The Selection pane is accessed from the Arrange group in both the Picture Tools Format tab and the Drawing Tools Format tab. It is also an option in the ⌖ Select ▾ menu in the Home tab or using the keyboard shortcut [Alt] + [F10].

Now you want to reposition, resize, and rearrange the order of the graphics to improve their layout on the slide. To change the order of these two objects, you will send the dog graphic to the back of the stack.

2

● Reduce the size of the dog graphic as in Figure 4.22.

● Drag the dog graphic to the right side of the cat graphic as in Figure 4.22.

● Click in the Arrange group of the Picture Tools Format tab.

● If necessary, adjust the size and position the graphics as in Figure 4.22.

Your screen should be similar to Figure 4.22

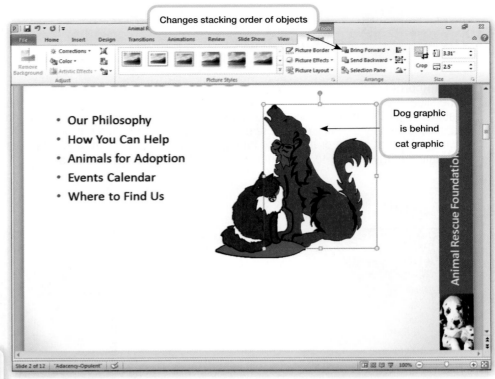

Figure 4.22

The dog graphic is now smaller and behind the cat graphic.

Now you want to change the color of the dog to a darker brown using commands from the Adjust group on the Picture Tools Format tab. Color changes with this command modify all the colors in an image based on overall tones of grayscale, sepia, or dark and light variations of accent colors. Therefore the graphic does not need to be converted to a drawing object first.

3

● With the dog selected, click Color ▾.

● Choose Orange, Accent color 3 Dark (row 2, column 4).

Your screen should be similar to Figure 4.23

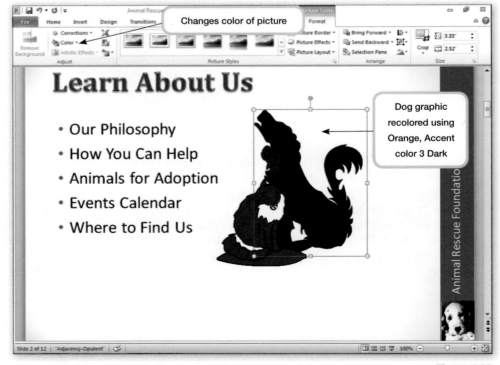

Figure 4.23

You think the brown color works well for the dog, but not for the bow color. So you decide to reset the graphic's color back to the original variations and then adjust the brightness and contrast of the graphic. Brightness refers to the overall lightness or darkness of an image. Contrast refers to the difference between the lightest and darkest colors used.

4

- Click 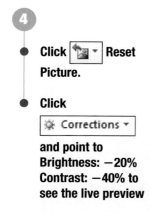 Reset Picture.

- Click **⚙ Corrections ▾** and point to Brightness: −20% Contrast: −40% to see the live preview

Your screen should be similar to Figure 4.24

Figure 4.24

On the Corrections gallery, the thumbnails show changes in brightness ranging from lowest on the left to highest on the right. Changes in contrast range from lowest on the top to highest on the bottom.

You like the darker brown color of the dog and now the bow color is more noticeable.

5

- Choose Brightness: −20% Contrast: −40%.

- On the Status bar, click Fit slide to current window.

GROUPING OBJECTS

Now you want to combine the two graphics into one by grouping them, and then you will size and position them appropriately on the slide.

Concept ② Group

A **group** is two of more objects that are treated as a single object. This allows you to easily move, resize, flip, or rotate all pieces of the group as a single unit. Features or attributes such as line or fill color associated with all objects in the group also can be changed at one time.

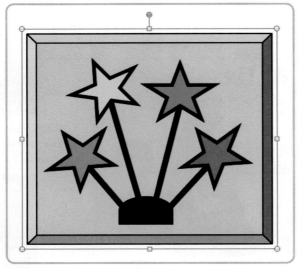

Grouped

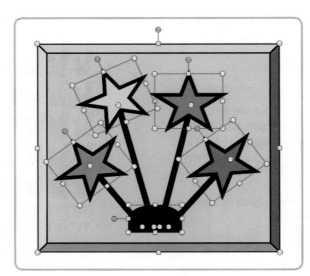

Ungrouped

When objects are grouped, the individual elements making up the object can still be selected and modified independently. Sometimes, however, you may want to **ungroup** the objects in a group to make it easier to make extensive changes or to remove an object from a group. Then, you can easily regroup the objects if desired after making modifications.

You will combine the two graphics into one by grouping them and then you will resize and position them on the slide.

- Select both graphics.

- Click 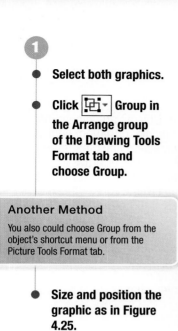 Group in the Arrange group of the Drawing Tools Format tab and choose Group.

Another Method

You also could choose Group from the object's shortcut menu or from the Picture Tools Format tab.

- Size and position the graphic as in Figure 4.25.

Additional Information

Hold down (Shift) while you resize with a corner sizing handle to assure that the object changes size while keeping the same proportions.

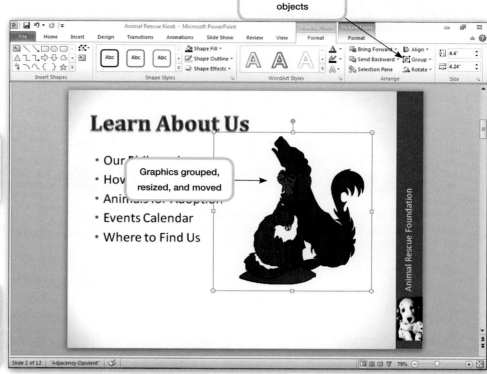

Figure 4.25

Your screen should be similar to Figure 4.25

Because the two graphic objects are grouped, they size and move as a single object. Be careful when moving grouped objects to select the object on the border when dragging. If you click inside the grouped object and then drag, then individual parts of the image may move depending on the type of image or how it is grouped.

MODIFYING GROUPED OBJECTS

As you look at the grouped graphic, you decide it would look better if the bottoms of the two graphics were evenly aligned. Although you can position objects on your slides visually by dragging to the approximate location, you can use tools in PowerPoint to more precisely align and position objects.

Concept ③ Object Alignment

Object alignment refers to the position of objects relative to each other or to the slide. Objects are aligned horizontally by their left, center, or right edges; objects are aligned vertically by their top, middle, or bottom edges.

Objects can be aligned in several ways. You can align objects to a grid, a set of intersecting lines that form small squares on the slide. The grid is not displayed by default, but whenever you move, resize, or draw an object, the object's corners automatically "snap" to the grid. You can display the grid to help align objects more accurately. You can also snap an object to other shapes so that new objects align themselves with the preexisting shapes. The grid lines run through the vertical and horizontal edges of other shapes, and the new shape aligns with the closest intersection of that grid.

Another way to align an object is to use a guide. A guide is a line, either vertical or horizontal, that you position on the slide. When an object is close to the guide, the object's center or corner (whichever is closer) snaps to the guide.

A third way to align objects is to other objects. For example, you can align the centers or the left edges of two objects. Using this method allows you to precisely align the edges or tops of selected shapes. At least two objects must be selected to align them.

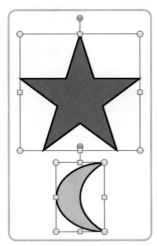

Center aligned

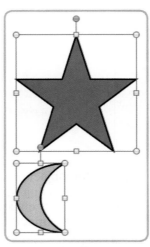

Left aligned

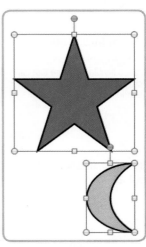

Right aligned

Middle aligned

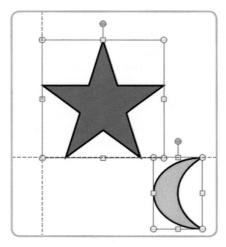

Aligned to guides

Objects can also be aligned relative to the slide as a whole, such as to the top or side of a slide. Objects can further be arranged or distributed so that they are an equal distance from each other vertically, horizontally, or in relation to the entire slide. You must have at least three objects selected to distribute them.

Even though an object is part of a grouped object, it can still be selected and modified individually. The tabs and features that are available depend on the type of object that is selected within the group.

You will display the slide gridlines and then evenly position the bottoms of the two graphics.

1

- Open the View tab and choose Gridlines.

- Select both graphics inside the grouped object.

Your screen should be similar to Figure 4.26

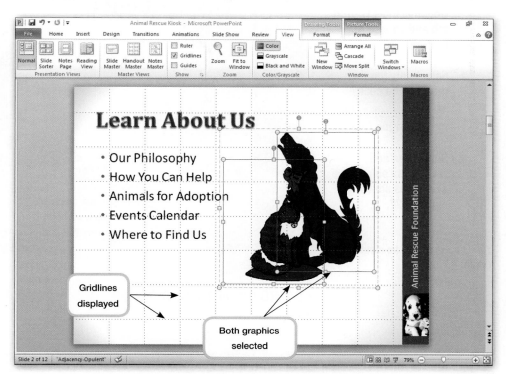

Figure 4.26

All slides in the presentation display a grid consisting of evenly spaced horizontal and vertical dotted lines. The borders of the two selected graphics are solid lines, indicating the entire graphic object is selected. The border of the grouped object is dashed, indicating objects inside it are selected. When selecting objects within a grouped object be careful to select the correct object or element as the changes you make will apply to the selected objects only. Now you can easily align the bottom of the graphics.

With both the cat and dog selected, click 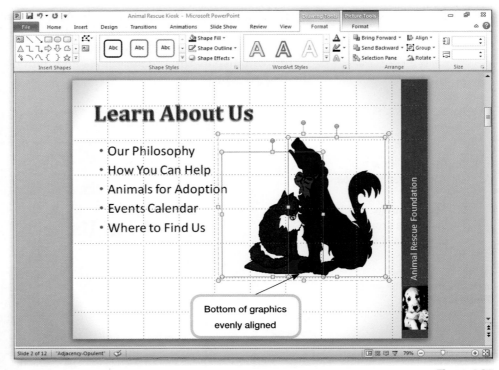 **Align in the Arrange group of the Drawing Tools Format tab and choose Align Bottom.**

Select only the dog graphic and click Bring Forward ▾ **to move it to the front.**

Reposition and realign the objects as needed as shown in Figure 4.27.

Your screen should be similar to Figure 4.27

Figure 4.27

ADDING OBJECTS TO A GROUP

To add more impact to the graphic, below the grouped graphic, you decide to add a banner.

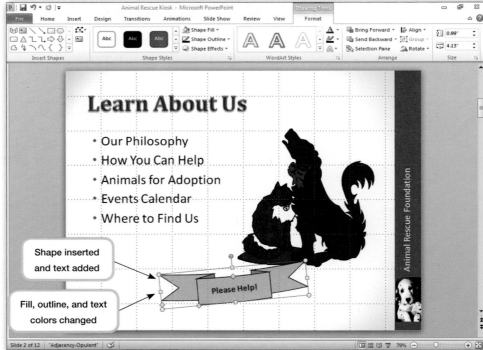

Create a Curved Down Ribbon banner shape below the graphic as shown in Figure 4.28.

Change the fill color to Gold, Accent 4.

Apply a 1 point black outline.

Edit the banner to include the text Please Help!

Change the font color to Plum—Text 2, Darker 25% and apply bold.

Click outside the shape to turn off text editing.

Size, position, and rotate the banner as shown in Figure 4.28.

Your screen should be similar to Figure 4.28

Figure 4.28

Next you want to center the banner below the grouped dog and cat. You will align the centers of the two objects and then group them into one object.

WWW.MHHE.COM/OLEARY

PowerPoint 2010

2

- Move the banner below the grouped dog and cat.

- Send the banner to the back of the stack.

- Select the banner and the grouped dog and cat.

- Click ▐▤ Align ▾ and choose Align Center.

Having Trouble?

Make sure Align Selected Objects is selected. If Align to Slide is selected, using Align Center will align the object with the center of the slide.

- Group the two objects together.

- Position the grouped object as in Figure 4.29.

- Click on the slide to deselect the grouped object.

- On the View tab, deselect Gridlines.

- Drag the splitter bar along the left edge of the window to show and widen the pane containing the Slides tab.

- Save the presentation.

Your screen should be similar to Figure 4.29

Figure 4.29

The addition of the custom graphic has made this slide much more interesting.

The next addition you want to make to the presentation is to add information about an upcoming fundraising event. You recently created a flyer about this event and you want to show part of the flyer on slide 5. You will add this information using the **Screenshot** feature to take a picture of what is displayed on the screen in any application for use in PowerPoint. This feature is useful for capturing information displayed on Web pages or from documents where it would be difficult to preserve all the formatting. You can capture from any open document as long as it has not been minimized.

You will open the Word application and the flyer document file and insert a Screenshot of the entire Word application window in the PowerPoint slide.

1

- Open the Word file pp04_Fundraiser from your data file location.

- Maximize the Word application window.

- If necessary, adjust the zoom so you can see most of the document (the dog picture and all text above).

Your screen should be similar to Figure 4.30

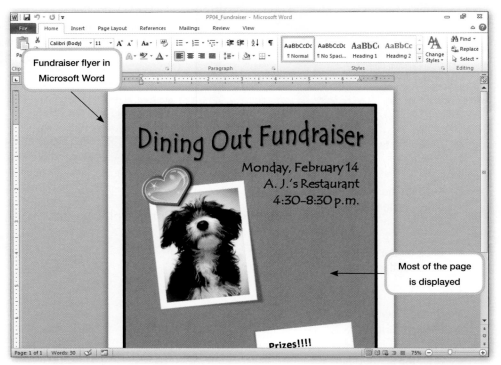

Figure 4.30

Next you need to switch to the PowerPoint application window and select the window containing the information you want to display in slide 5.

2

- Switch to the PowerPoint application window and display slide 5.

- Click  in the Images group of the Insert tab.

- Click the thumbnail of the pp04_Fundraiser document displayed in the Available Windows gallery.

Additional Information

A ScreenTip displaying the program name and document title appears when you point to the thumbnail.

Your screen should be similar to Figure 4.31

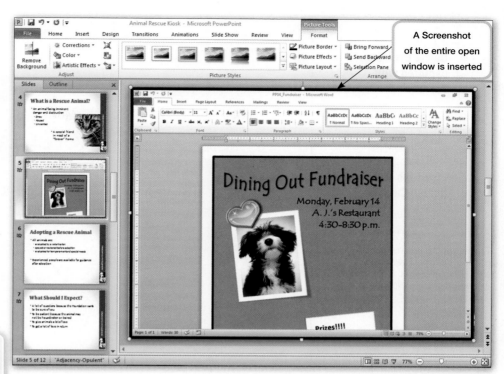

Figure 4.31

A screenshot image of the entire Word window is captured and displayed in the slide. It can be sized and moved like any other picture object. The picture of the entire application window is effective when capturing a Web page or another application where showing the entire window is important. However, for the current slide you want to show only some of the content of the flyer. At this point you could crop the screenshot image to show only the information you want; however, using the **Screen Clipping** feature provides a more efficient way to get just the image you need initially.

When using Screen Clipping, the PowerPoint window is automatically minimized and the window you viewed immediately before using this feature is displayed and available for clipping. This window will appear opaque or grayed out. As you specify the area of the window to capture, the selection will be clear.

3
- Delete the image captured with Screenshot.
- Click  in the Insert tab and choose Screen Clipping.

Additional Information

The window that was viewed immediately before PowerPoint is automatically displayed as the window to specify the screen clipping.

Your screen should be similar to Figure 4.32

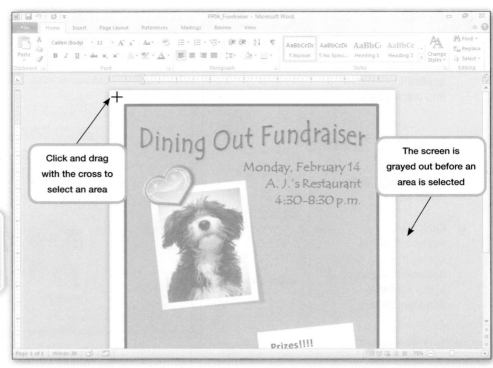

Figure 4.32

The PowerPoint window was minimized and the Word application window displayed. The window appears opaque and the mouse pointer has changed to a cross, indicating it can be used to specify the area of the window to include in the screenshot image. The selection area will show in color.

4

- Position the cross at the top left corner of the black border in the flyer.
- Press and hold the left mouse button then drag across and down to just below the picture of the dog to specify the area to capture (see Figure 4.33).
- Release the mouse button and the image of the selected area appears on the slide.

Your screen should be similar to Figure 4.33

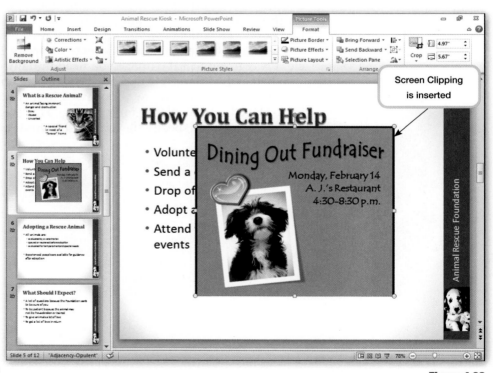

Figure 4.33

Having Trouble?

If your selection is not as you want it, then delete that capture and simply try again until you are satisfied with the results.

The image created by Screen Clipping can be edited as any other picture. You will apply a picture style then resize and position the image.

5

- Apply the Rotated, White Picture Style.

- Size and position this image on the right side of the slide as in Figure 4.34.

- Click outside the graphic to clear the selection.

- Close the Word document.

Your screen should be similar to Figure 4.34

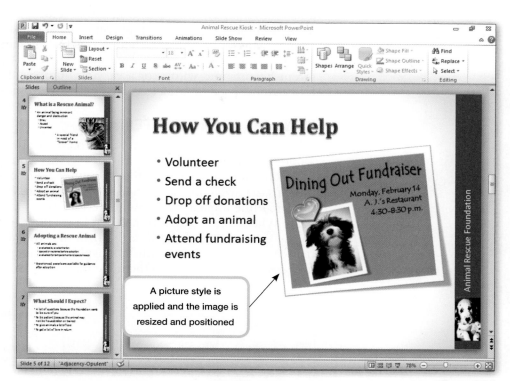

Figure 4.34

Creating a Complex Table

Next you need to add a calendar of events in a table format to the presentation. The table will display the type, date, and location of the event. Your completed table will be similar to that shown below.

What	When	Where
	Saturday, February 18	Pets4U South
Adoption Fairs	Saturday, March 10	Pets4U North
	Sunday, April 15	South Park Mall
Puppy Class	Monday, April 9	Grover Elementary
Obedience Class	Tuesday, April 10	Oak View High

PowerPoint includes several different methods that you can use to create tables. One method is to choose the Insert Table icon from a slide layout that contains content placeholders as you did to create a simple table in Lab 2.

Another method uses on the Insert tab to specify the number of rows and columns needed by dragging across a table grid. This method also creates a simple table of even rows and columns. The last method you can use to create a table is Draw Table. Although this feature can be used to create any type of table, it is most useful for creating complex tables that contain cells of different heights and widths or a varying number of columns per row. Drawing tools can be used on tables created with any of these methods.

USING THE DRAW TABLE FEATURE

You will use the Draw Table feature to create the table of events. Using Draw Table to create a table is similar to the way you would use a pen to draw a table on paper. First you define the outer table boundary by dragging diagonally to the size you want. Then you drag to create the column and row lines. A dotted line appears to show the boundary or lines you are creating as you drag. When creating row or column lines, drag from the beginning boundary to the end to extend the line the distance you want. When creating a table using this feature, it is helpful to display the ruler so you can more accurately judge spacing as you draw the table lines.

1

- Display slide 11, Events Calendar in Normal view.

- Choose Ruler in the Show group of the View tab to display the ruler.

- Click  in the Tables group of the Insert tab and choose Draw Table.

Your screen should be similar to Figure 4.35

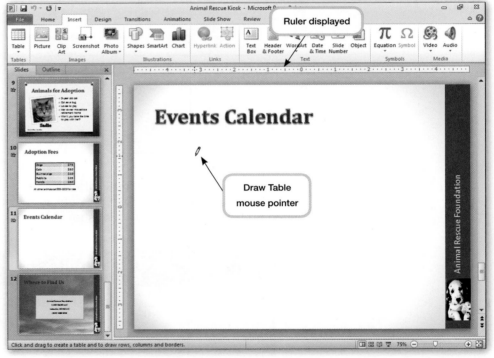

Figure 4.35

The mouse pointer changes to a pen when positioned on the slide. This indicates the Draw Table feature is on. Now you will create the table boundary and then divide the table into columns and rows. As you do, refer to Figure 4.36 for guidance.

2

- Drag downward and to the right to create an outer table boundary of approximately 3.5 inches by 7.5 inches.

- Click 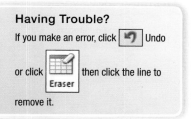 in the Draw Borders group of the Table Tools Design tab to reactivate the pen.

- Add two vertical column lines at positions 2.5 and 5.5 on the ruler.

- Draw five horizontal lines to create the rows as shown in Figure 4.36. (Lines 2 and 3 begin at the end of the first column.)

Having Trouble?

If you make an error, click ↶ Undo

or click [Eraser] then click the line to remove it.

Your screen should be similar to Figure 4.36

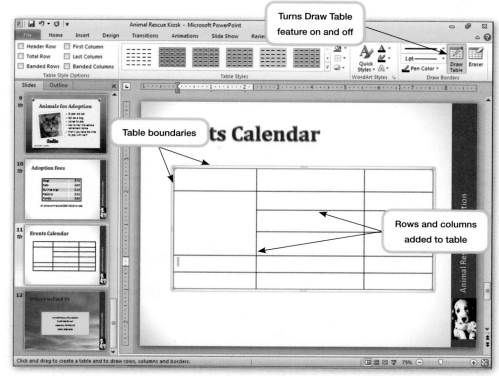

Figure 4.36

Do not be concerned if your table is not exactly like that in Figure 4.36. You will adjust the table lines shortly.

Now you are ready to enter the information into the table.

3

● Press [Esc] to turn off the Draw Table feature.

Another Method

Typing in any cell will also turn off Draw Table.

● Enter the data shown below in the specified table cells.

Additional Information

You can copy and paste similar table entries then edit them to save time.

	Col A	Col B	Col C
Row 1	What	When	Where
Row 2	Adoption Fairs	Saturday, February 18	Pets4U South
Row 3		Saturday, March 10	Pets4U North
Row 4		Sunday, April 15	South Park Mall
Row 5	Puppy Class	Monday, April 9	Grover Elementary
Row 6	Obedience Class	Tuesday, April 10	Oak View High

Your screen should be similar to Figure 4.37

Figure 4.37

ENHANCING THE TABLE

Next you want to adjust the font size of the text, size the columns and rows appropriately, and add other enhancements to the table. As you continue to modify the table, the contents of many cells can be selected and changed at the

same time by dragging or using on the Table Tools Layout tab.

First you will increase the size of the text, then you will adjust the column widths so the cell contents display on a single line. You also will adjust the heights of the rows so they are all the same and center the text in several cells.

Having Trouble?

See Lab 2 to review selecting areas in a table and sizing columns and rows.

①

- **Select the entire table.**

- **Increase the font size to 20 points.**

Having Trouble?

Clicking increases the font size by units.

- **Adjust the column widths as needed until all text appears on a single line.**

Having Trouble?

Drag the column boundary lines to adjust the width.

- **Select the table.**

- **Click** ⊞ **Distribute Rows in the Cell Size group of the Table Tools Layout tab.**

- **Click** ▤ **Center Vertically in the Alignment group to center all text vertically in the rows.**

- **Select row 1, increase the font size to 24 points, and center the column headings horizontally.**

Your screen should be similar to Figure 4.38

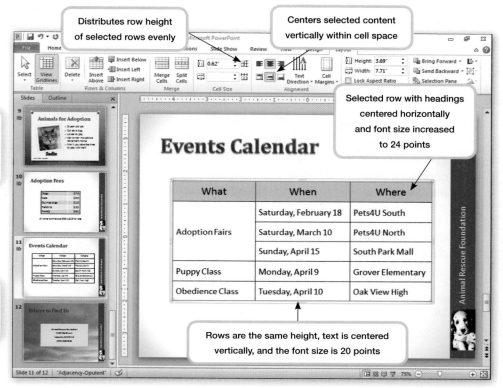

Figure 4.38

The row sizes are now all the same and the text is centered vertically within the cell space. Notice that "Adoption Fairs" is vertically centered in the larger cell space.

Next you will add some color and effects to the table.

2

- Open the Table Tools Design tab.

- From the Table Style Options group, choose Header Row and Banded Columns.

- Apply a Table Style of your choice.

- Select row 1.

- Click 🔲 ▾ Effects, select Cell Bevel, and choose Circle.

- Click 🪣 ▾ Shading and choose a darker color and, if necessary, change the font color to white.

- Click in the table to clear the selection.

Your screen should be similar to Figure 4.39

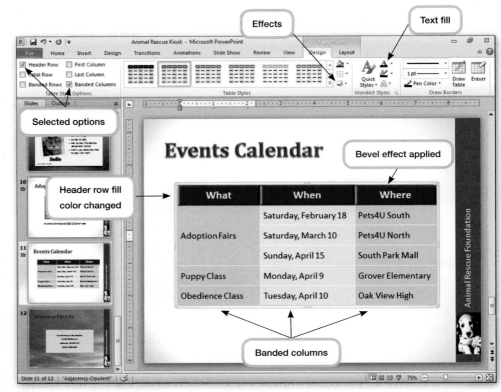

Figure 4.39

The final enhancement is to make the table border wider and a different color.

3

- **Select the entire table.**

- **Open the**

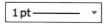

  Border Width drop-down list in the Draw Borders group and choose 6 pt.

- **Open the**

  drop-down list and choose any color.

- **Click ▦ ▾ Borders and choose Outside Borders.**

Having Trouble?

You can also use the Pen tool to add, change, and remove borders.

- **Position the table as in Figure 4.40.**

- **Click outside the table to deselect it.**

- **Turn off the display of the ruler.**

- **Save the presentation.**

Your screen should be similar to Figure 4.40

Ruler display off

Events Calendar

What	When	Where
Adoption Fairs	Saturday, February 18	Pets4U South
	Saturday, March 10	Pets4U North
	Sunday, April 15	South Park Mall
Puppy Class	Monday, April 9	Grover Elementary
Obedience Class	Tuesday, April 10	Oak View High

Border enhanced

Figure 4.40

The table displays the information in an attractive and easy-to-read manner. Now that you have completed adding content to the presentation and have enhanced its appearance, you are ready to prepare it to be self-running on a kiosk.

Setting Up a Presentation for a Kiosk

Additional Information

When recording a voice narration, you need a sound card and a microphone on your computer. Open the Slide Show tab and choose Record Slide Show. The slide show runs while you speak into the microphone. Once the slide show is complete, you can choose to save the timings along with the narration.

A presentation that is designed to run unattended on a **kiosk** has several special requirements. Because there is no one available while the slide show is running to clarify content and answer questions, you could record a narration to accompany the presentation. However, you feel the presentation content is both clear and complete and you decide to simply include background music to attract attention and to make the presentation more enjoyable as it runs. Next, you need to add slide transitions and to specify how long to display a slide before advancing to the next slide. Finally, you need to set up the presentation to be self-running.

ADDING SOUND

The first change you want to make is to add some background music to the presentation as it is playing on the kiosk. There are several ways to add sound to a presentation. As you have learned, one method is to add sound effects to animations. Another is to record a narration for your presentation; this, however, will override any other sounds you have previously inserted. A third is to play music from an audio file that runs continuously throughout the presentation. You can also incorporate video clips into a presentation.

Concept  4 Audio and Video Files

Almost all PCs today are equipped with multimedia capabilities, which means they can play the most commonly used audio and video files. An **audio file** is a type of file that plays sounds or music, and a **video file** plays a motion picture with sound. This table lists some of the most common audio and video file types.

Audio Files	File Extension
Windows Audio file (Wave Form)	.wav
MIDI (Musical Instrument Digital Interface)	.mid or .midi
MP3 (MPEG Audio Layer 3)	.mp3
Windows Media Audio file	.wma
Video Files	
Windows Video file (Audio Video Interleave)	.avi
Windows Media Video file	.wmv
MPEG Video (Moving Picture Expert Group)	.mpeg
QuickTime Movie file (requires Apple QuickTime player)	.mov

WAV files are typically used for sounds, while MIDI files are typically used for music. AVI and WMV files work well in PowerPoint. Both MPEG and MOV files may require special software depending on how your computer is configured.

The capability of computers to handle video and the quality of video are constantly improving. When you are presenting with your own equipment, you can test everything to be sure all files are running correctly. However, when you plan to run a presentation on other computers, choose file types that are most commonly used. If you cannot control the computer on which your presentation will run, limit your audio to WAV files and your video to AVI files.

For your kiosk presentation, you want music to play continuously while the presentation runs. You will use a short music sound clip that you located and saved on your computer.

1

● **Display slide 1 and open the Insert tab.**

● **Click** **in the Media group and choose Audio from File.**

● **Select** pp04_ Background1 **from your data file location and click** **Insert** ▾.

Additional Information

Use the Clip Art task pane to search Audio to locate and preview short sound files and music.

Your screen should be similar to Figure 4.41

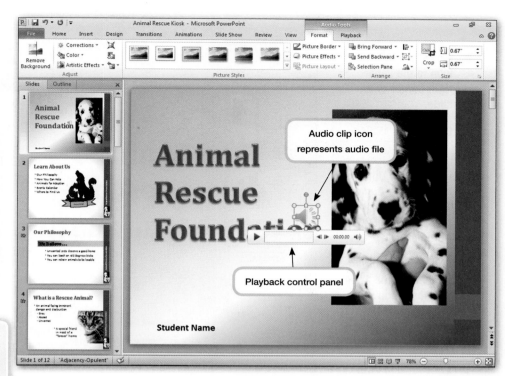

Figure 4.41

An audio clip icon representing the audio file appears in the center of the slide above a playback control panel. This panel has a Play/Pause, Time Line, Move Back/Move Forward, elapsed time in seconds, and volume control. When the audio icon is selected, the Audio Tools Playback and Format tabs are also available. Because the audio file plays only 35 seconds, you need to repeat the sound so it will play the length of the presentation.

2

● Move the audio clip icon to the lower right corner of the slide.

● Click

in the Audio Options group of the Audio Tools Playback tab and choose Automatically.

● Choose Hide During Show from the Audio Options group so the audio icon is not displayed during a slide show.

● Choose Loop until Stopped so the audio will repeat.

● Click ▶ on the playback control panel to preview the music.

● When you are finished listening to the music, click ❚❚ on the playback control panel.

Figure 4.42

The settings you specified will function only when the slide show begins with slide 1. Now you need to control when the music will stop playing. You want the music to play continuously while the slide show runs and then stop after the last slide is viewed.

Having Trouble?

You need speakers and a sound card on your computer system to hear the sound.

Another Method

You can also click ▶ Play in the Preview group to test the music.

Your screen should be similar to Figure 4.42

Additional Information

If you need to use a hidden playback control during a presentation, point to where the audio clip icon is hidden and the playback control will appear.

3

● Open the Animations tab and click .

● Open the pp04_ Background1 drop-down list of options and choose Effect Options.

● If necessary, open the Effect tab.

Your screen should be similar to Figure 4.43

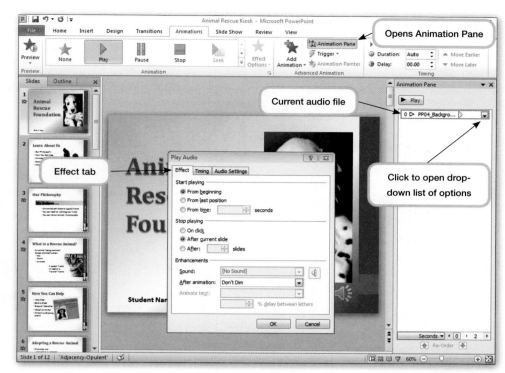

Figure 4.43

You have set the audio to start playing automatically when slide 1 appears. Now you will set the ending for the last slide (12) in the presentation. Now, regardless of how long you display each slide, the audio will loop continuously and end after the last slide.

4

● Under Stop Playing, choose After: and enter **12** in the text box.

● Click OK.

● Close the Animation Pane.

● Run the slide show from the beginning.

● Press Esc after viewing slide 12 to end the slide show.

The music played continuously as you moved from slide to slide and stopped at the end of the presentation.

MODIFYING SLIDE TRANSITIONS

Currently most slides in the presentation use either the Clock or Gallery transition effect. You want to add transition effects to the slides that do not have any and to have the slides automatically advance to the next slide after a set time has elapsed.

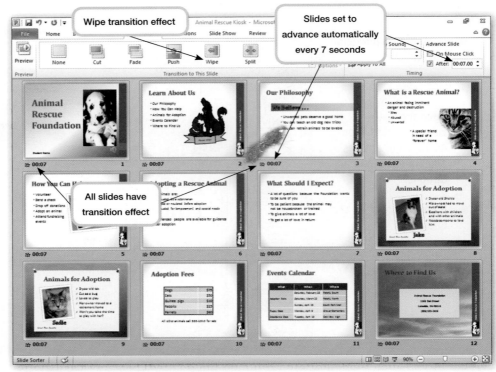

1

- Switch to Slide Sorter view.

- Select slides 1, 2, and 12.

- Open the Transitions tab.

- Choose Wipe from the Transitions gallery and set the effect option to From Top-Left.

- Select all the slides.

- If necessary, clear the On Mouse Click option in the Timing group.

- Choose After and set the timing to advance the slides automatically every 7 seconds (00:07:00).

Your screen should be similar to Figure 4.44

Figure 4.44

You will run the slide show next to confirm that the changes you made to the transitions are appropriate.

2

- Run the slide show from the beginning.

- Press Esc when you are finished viewing the presentation.

MAKING THE PRESENTATION SELF-RUNNING

Now you will make the slide show self-running so that it will restart automatically when it has finished.

Opens Set Up Show dialog box

Open the Slide Show tab.

Click 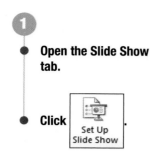 .

Your screen should be similar to Figure 4.45

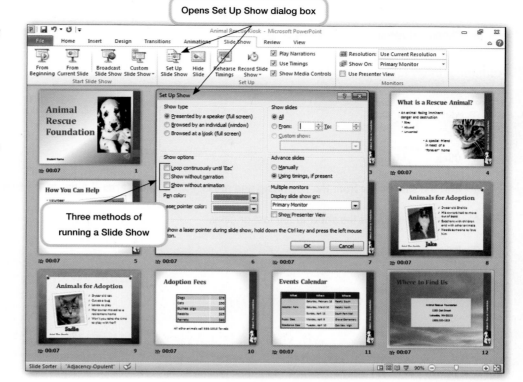

Figure 4.45

The Set Up Show dialog box allows you to choose from three ways of running a show. The first option, Presented by a speaker (full screen), is the default and most frequently used style. As you have seen, this method requires that a speaker run the presentation. The second option, Browsed by an individual (window), is used when one person views the presentation, and how it displays is based on the viewer's window. It could be in a small window on a desktop computer or even on a portable device. The third option, Browsed at a kiosk (full screen), is the option you will use to create a self-running presentation that is displayed full screen showing the entire presentation or selected slides.

You will set up the presentation so that it will show at full-screen size, slides will advance using timings, and the slide show will restart automatically.

2

● **Choose Browsed at a kiosk (full screen).**

Additional Information

The Loop continuously until 'Esc' option is automatically selected when you choose Browsed at a kiosk.

● **Click** ⸤ OK ⸥.

● **Run the slide show from the beginning and press** ⸤Esc⸥ **to end it after it loops to the beginning again.**

● **Adjust the timing if the show is too fast or slow.**

● **Save the presentation.**

Setting Up a Presentation for Individual Browsing

The Animal Rescue Foundation main shelter has a computer in the lobby that they want to use to show this same presentation. Rather than have the presentation loop continuously, you will change it to a presentation that can be run by an individual using mouse control. This gives the viewer the ability to control the slide and go back to review a slide immediately or go forward more quickly to see other slides. Then, to make it easier to run the presentation, you will add hyperlinks and navigation controls to the presentation.

CHANGING THE PRESENTATION SETUP

You will first need to change the slide show setup from self-running on a kiosk to self-running by an individual. Then you will turn back on the capability to allow advancing slides by clicking the mouse. Because this change may affect the number of slides displayed by the individual, you also will adjust the music settings to play longer.

1

- Click **Set Up Slide Show** in the Slide Show tab.

- Choose **Browsed by an individual (window)** and click **OK**.

- In Slide Sorter view, select all slides.

- Choose **On Mouse Click** from the Timing group of the Transition tab.

Your screen should be similar to Figure 4.46

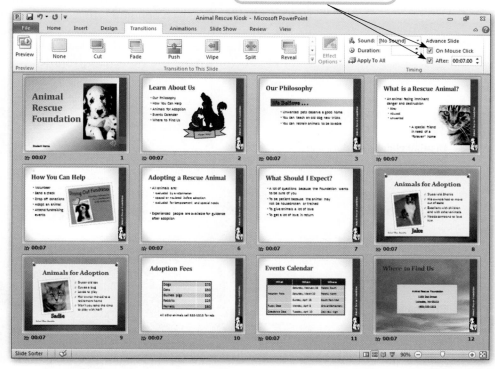

Figure 4.46

Now the presentation can be run by an individual and will advance on clicking the mouse or after 7 seconds have elapsed. Next, you will adjust the music settings.

2

- In Normal view, select the audio clip icon on slide 1.

- Open the Animations tab and click **Animation Pane**.

- Open the pp04_Background1 drop-down list and select Effect Options.

- Increase the number of slides to stop playing after to **25**.

- Click **OK**.

- Close the Animation pane.

- Click **Start: On Click** in the Timing group and choose After Previous.

- Run the first few slides of the presentation to confirm your setting changes.

- Save the revised presentation as Animal Rescue Browsing.

Now you are ready to add features to make it easier for an individual to run the presentation.

ASSIGNING ACTION TO OBJECTS

The next change you want to make is to convert the bulleted list of topics on slide 2 to a SmartArt graphic so the list looks different from other slide content with bulleted lists. Then you will assign an action to the individual shapes in the SmartArt graphic to allow the viewer to click on the shape to jump directly to the slide containing the selected topic.

First you will create the SmartArt graphic.

- Display slide 2 in Normal view.

- Select the content placeholder.

- Click  Convert to SmartArt Graphic in the Home tab.

- Choose More SmartArt Graphics.

- From the List category, choose Vertical Bullet List.

- Click ___OK___.

- Open the SmartArt Tools Design tab.

- Choose the Cartoon SmartArt Style from the 3-D category.

- Resize the SmartArt graphic and reposition it as shown in Figure 4.47.

Figure 4.47

Additional Information
The SmartArt graphic height and width should be about 4" with a 28-point font size.

Your screen should be similar to Figure 4.47

Now you want to modify each of the SmartArt graphic shapes to perform an action when clicked.

Concept 5 Action

Action is the capability of an object to perform a task when you click on or pass the mouse over the object. The most common type of action is a hyperlink to other slides, custom shows, presentations, other files, or Web pages. Other actions you can assign are to run programs, play audio clips, or run a prerecorded set of instructions called a **macro.**

An action can be assigned to the text in a SmartArt graphic, and to any shape, clip art, or picture. Additionally, PowerPoint includes a special set of **action buttons** designed specifically for self-running presentations. They include shapes such as right- and left-facing arrows that are used to navigate through a presentation that you can insert on a slide and assign an action.

You want to add action to each SmartArt shape to jump to another slide in the presentation. Although you can create a hyperlink to the text in the shape, assigning the hyperlink action to the shape will be convenient for viewers because they can click anywhere on the shape instead of being required to click directly on the text.

2

- Select the first SmartArt shape, Our Philosophy.

- Open the Insert tab.

- Click [Action] in the Links group.

Your screen should be similar to Figure 4.48

Figure 4.48

The two tabs in the Action Settings dialog box allow you to specify the action that is associated with this shape. During a slide show, Mouse Click performs an action when the viewer clicks the shape such as hyperlinking, running a program or macro, or playing a sound. Mouse Over performs the action when the mouse pointer rests or passes over the shape. Generally, it is best to use Mouse Click for hyperlinks so that you do not accidentally go to a location because you passed the mouse pointer over the hyperlink. Mouse Over is commonly used to play sounds.

You will create a mouse click hyperlink to slide 3 and use the mouse over feature to highlight the object when the mouse points to it.

3

- On the Mouse Click tab, choose Hyperlink to.

- Open the Hyperlink to drop-down menu and choose Slide. . . .

- From the Hyperlink to Slide dialog box, choose 3. Our Philosophy, and click OK .

Your screen should be similar to Figure 4.49

Figure 4.49

The destination for the hyperlink action has been set to the Our Philosophy slide. Next you will add a second action that will highlight the object when the mouse passes over it to show that the object will perform an action when clicked.

4

● Open the Mouse Over tab and choose Highlight when mouse over.

● Click [OK].

● Select each of the remaining shapes and repeat the process including Highlight when mouse over, linking to these slides:

How You Can Help	slide 5
Animals for Adoption	slide 8
Events Calendar	slide 11
Where to Find Us	slide 12

● Save the presentation.

● Display slide 2 in Slide Show view and point to the Animals for Adoption shape.

Your screen should be similar to Figure 4.50

Figure 4.50

Additional Information

The music did not play because you did not start the slide show from the beginning.

Now when you point to one of the shapes during the slide show, it appears highlighted and the mouse pointer changes to a pointing hand to show that action is available.

5

● Click on Animals for Adoption.

● Press Esc to end the show.

The action was performed and the presentation jumped from slide 2 to slide 8.

ADDING BUILT-IN ACTION BUTTONS

To help the viewer navigate through the presentation, you decide to add action buttons to the slides. Action buttons are special buttons in the Shapes gallery. Most of these shapes have an icon on them that helps to communicate what the button will do. When you insert an action button, the Action Settings dialog box automatically opens.

You want the first slide to display continuously until the viewer clicks on a button to start the presentation. Once in the presentation, each slide will have a home button that will take the viewer back to the **agenda slide**, a forward button that will go to the next slide, and a backward button that will return to the previous slide.

1

- **Display slide 1 in Normal view and open the Insert tab.**

- **Click .**

- **Click ☐ Action Button: Custom (last row, last button).**

- **Click below the slide title to create a default size button.**

Additional Information

The default size button is 1.14 inches square. You also can drag to create a button of any size.

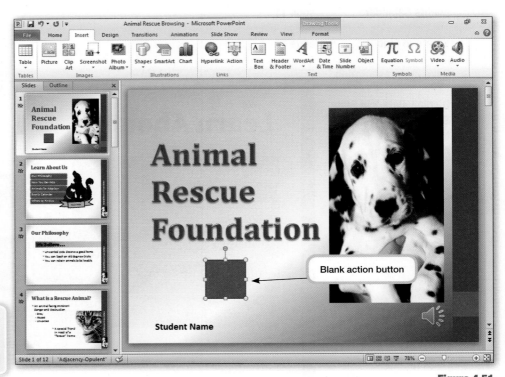

Figure 4.51

- **Choose Hyperlink to Next Slide from the Mouse Click tab of the Action Settings dialog box.**

- **Click 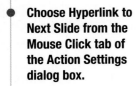.**

Your screen should be similar to Figure 4.51

Next you need to add text to the button that contains the instructions for the viewer. You add button text just as you add text to a text box.

2

- In the shape type **Click Here to Learn More**

- **Open the Drawing Tools Format tab.**

- **Click** Shape Effects ▾, select Bevel and choose Circle.

- **Position and size the button as in Figure 4.52.**

- **Click outside the action button to deselect it.**

Your screen should be similar to Figure 4.52

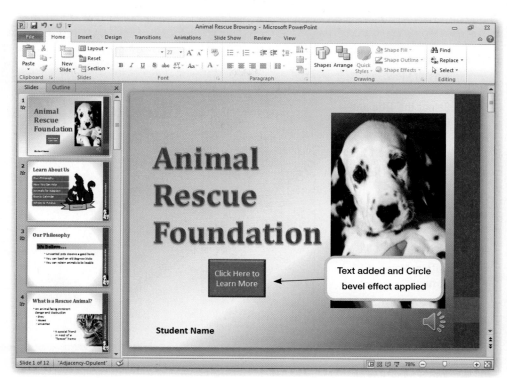

Figure 4.52

You will follow the same procedure to insert three other action buttons: home, forward, and backward. Because these buttons already contain icons that represent the action they perform, you will not need text. Since you want these buttons to appear on all slides other than title slides, you will add them to the Slide Master. Do not be concerned with the location of these buttons as you insert them and apply action. You will later resize and position them.

3

- Switch to Slide Master view.

- Select the Title and Content Layout.

- Open the Insert tab and click [Shapes].

- Click [🏠] Action Button: Home (fifth button).

- Click in the lower part of the slide to create the button.

- Add a hyperlink to slide 2. Learn About Us.

- Click [OK] twice.

Your screen should be similar to Figure 4.53

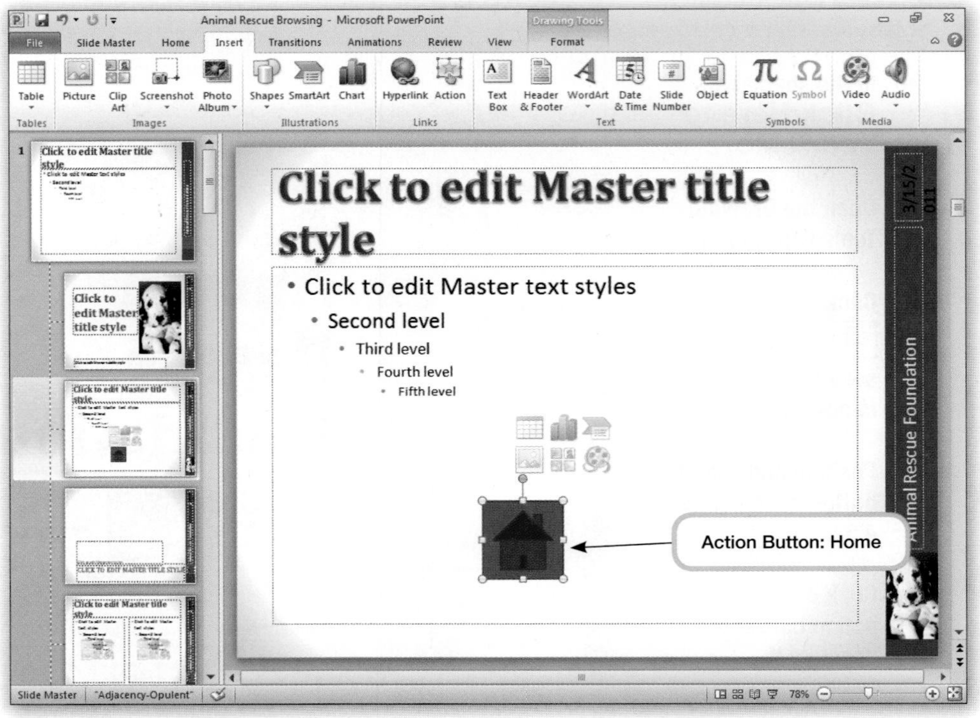

Figure 4.53

You will repeat this process to add forward and backward buttons. Then you will apply a bevel effect to all buttons.

4

- Insert a Action Button: Back or Previous (first button) that hyperlinks to the previous slide.

- Insert a ▷ Action Button: Forward or Next (second button) that hyperlinks to the next slide.

- Select the three buttons and open the Drawing Tools Format tab.

Additional Information

Hold down (Shift) while clicking each button to select multiple objects.

- Click Shape Effects ▾, select Bevel and choose Circle.

Your screen should be similar to Figure 4.54

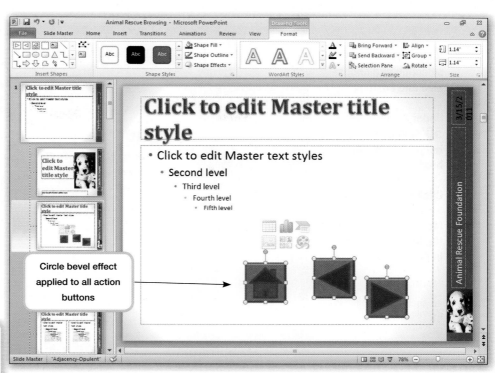

Figure 4.54

SCALING AND ALIGNING OBJECTS

Now you want to reduce the size of the buttons by about half. In addition to changing the size of an object by dragging to an approximate size, you can change the size by entering an exact measurement for the object's height and width. You can also **scale** an object's size by increasing or decreasing it using a percentage value of the object's original size. Since you want to make the buttons about half their original size, you will reduce their size by 50 percent.

1

- **Right-click on the selection and choose Size and Position.**

- **Under Scale enter 50% in both the Height and Width boxes.**

- **Click** Close .

- **Move the buttons to the locations shown in Figure 4.55.**

Your screen should be similar to Figure 4.55

Figure 4.55

At this point, spacing between the buttons and their alignment may not be even. Now you will fix the alignment of the buttons.

2

- **Select the three buttons.**

- **Click** Align ▾ **and choose Align Top.**

Additional Information

There must be at least three objects selected to align and distribute objects.

- **Click** Align ▾ **and choose Distribute Horizontally.**

- **Reposition the buttons as shown in Figure 4.56.**

Additional Information

The outside buttons do not move; only the middle button moves to equalize the spacing.

Figure 4.56

Your screen should be similar to Figure 4.56

The three buttons are evenly aligned by their top edges and are an equal distance apart horizontally. Because the buttons were added to the Title and Content layout on the slide master, they will appear in the same location on each slide with that layout. You need to copy the buttons and add them to slide master layouts that are used by other slides in the presentation. Then you will check the slides to make sure that text or objects on the slide do not interfere with the buttons.

3

- Copy the three buttons and paste them on the Title Only Layout of the Adjacency-Opulent master and the Two Content Layout of the Pushpin slide master.

- If necessary, move the buttons to align with the bottom of the white rectangle in the Pushpin Two Content Layout.

- Delete the three footer placeholders from the Pushpin Two Content Layout.

- Switch to Slide Sorter view and check the placement of the navigation buttons on all slides.

Your screen should be similar to Figure 4.57

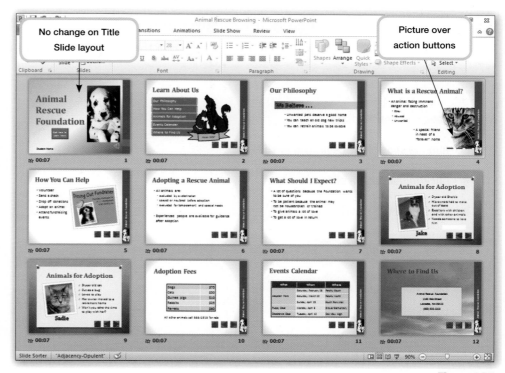

Figure 4.57

Navigation buttons correctly appear on all slides except the Title slide. Additionally, when you copied the buttons, the placement of the buttons on the slide also was copied, giving the presentation a consistent appearance. You notice, however, that the cat picture on slide 4 overlaps the buttons.

4

- On slide 4, move the cat picture up so it does not overlap the buttons.

- Make other adjustments if necessary.

ADDING ACTION TO PICTURES

When viewers are looking at pictures of available pets, they may want to immediately know what the adoption fees are. Therefore, you decide to add action to the pictures of Jake and Sadie that will hyperlink to the adoption fee slide.

1

- On slide 8, select the picture of Jake.

- Add action to hyperlink to slide 10, Adoption Fees, with a mouse-over highlight.

- Repeat this process for slide 9 with the picture of Sadie.

USING ACTION BUTTONS

Now you are ready to run the revised presentation using the action buttons.

1

- Save the presentation.

- Run the slide show beginning at slide 1.

- Click the button on slide 1.

- Click How You can Help on slide 2.

- Click Home.

- Click Animals for Adoption.

- Click on Jake's picture.

- Click Back.

- Press ⎡Esc⎤ to end the show.

Saving a Presentation as a PowerPoint Template

You have invested a lot of time setting up navigation and design elements for the self-running presentation. To make it easier to create similar presentations in the future, you decided to save the presentation as a template. **Templates** provide a convenient way to save presentation themes, placeholder positioning, reusable content, and other features such as navigation controls that you can quickly apply to other presentations in the future. Templates that you save are available to use when you start a new presentation.

Rather than save the entire presentation as a template, you will save selected slides that contain navigation and design features you may use in another presentation designed for self-browsing. The default location to save a design template is the Templates folder on your computer's hard drive. Then, when you start a new presentation, the template will be available when you click My templates. However, because you will save it to your solution file location, it will not display in the Personal Templates list.

1

- **Switch to Slide Sorter view.**

- **Select slides 3, 4, 6, 7, 9, and 10 and delete them.**

- **Open the File tab and choose Save As.**

- **From the Save As Type box, choose PowerPoint Template.**

- **Change the file location to the location of your solution files.**

- **Name the template** Self Browsing Presentation.

- **Click** Save .

Your screen should be similar to Figure 4.58

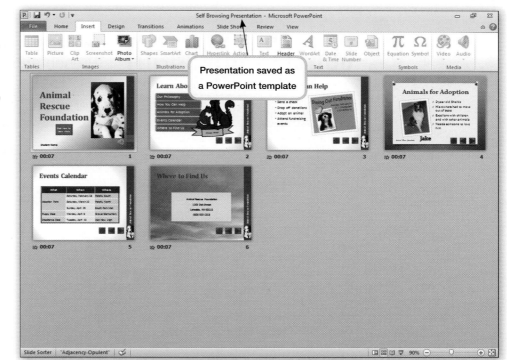

Figure 4.58

The presentation is saved with a .potx file extension in your solution file folder. Depending on how your computer is configured, you may not see the extension. The template can be opened and modified to create a new presentation. When you save the modified presentation, you can give it a new file name, thereby preserving the template file for future use.

2

- **Print the template slides as handouts six per page horizontal.**

- **Close the presentation and exit PowerPoint.**

FOCUS ON CAREERS

EXPLORE YOUR CAREER OPTIONS

Public Relations Specialist

The responsibilities of a public relations specialist, sometimes called media specialist or communication specialist, are varied. Informing the general public of an organization's products and services as well as their policies, activities, and accomplishments is very important. Public relations work is often combined with advertising efforts.

Public relations specialists have many speaking engagements such as press conferences and conventions. They also may lead fundraising campaigns and prepare materials for radio, print, and televised media. Strong communication skills, both writing and speaking, are extremely important. PowerPoint can be used to create presentations that can be distributed or viewed in public places, such as a kiosk. The position of public relations specialist usually requires a college degree and commands salaries from $39,000 to over $75,000 depending on experience and skill.

Lab 4 CONCEPT SUMMARY Creating a Self-Running Presentation

Stacking Order (PP4.23)

Stacking order is the order in which objects are inserted in the different layers of a slide. As each object is added to the slide, it is added to the top, creating a new layer.

Group (PP4.26)

A group is two of more objects that are treated as a single object. This allows you to easily move, resize, flip, or rotate all pieces of the group as a single unit.

Object Alignment (PP4.28)

Object alignment refers to the position of objects relative to each other or to the slide. Objects are aligned horizontally by their left, center, or right edges; objects are aligned vertically by their top, middle, or bottom edges.

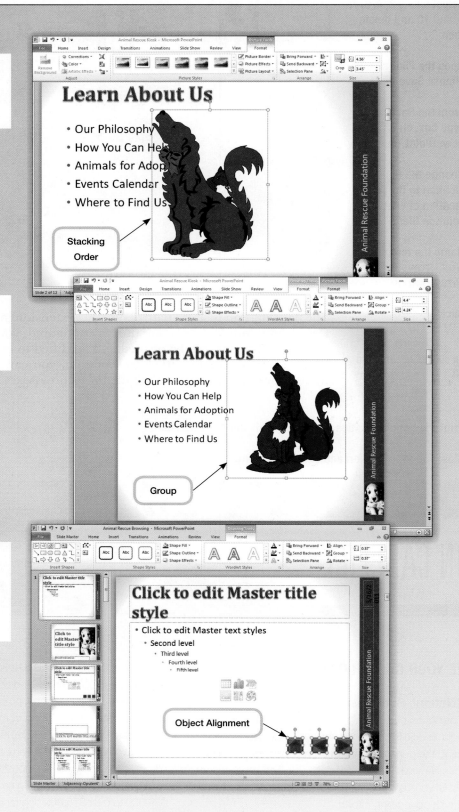

Audio and Video Files (PP4.42)

Almost all PCs today are equipped with multimedia capabilities, which means they can play the most commonly used audio and video files. An audio file is a type of file that plays sounds or music, and a video file plays a motion picture with sound.

Action (PP4.51)

Action is the capability of an object to perform a task when you click on or pass the mouse over the object.

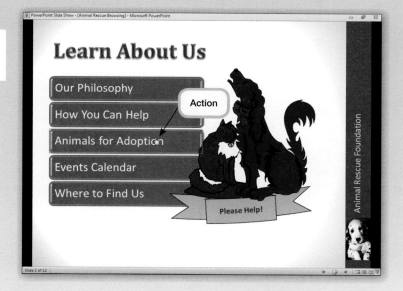

LAB REVIEW Lab 4 Creating a Self-Running Presentation

KEY TERMS

action PP4.51
action button PP4.51
agenda slide PP4.54
audio file PP4.42
gradient PP4.7
group PP4.26
kiosk PP4.41
object alignment PP4.28
scale PP4.57
Screen Clipping PP4.33
Screenshot PP4.32
stacking order PP4.23
template PP4.60
ungroup PP4.26
video file PP4.42

COMMAND SUMMARY

Command	Shortcut	Action
File tab		
Save As	F12	Saves a presentation using a different file name or file type
Insert tab		
Tables group		
Table /Draw table		Creates a table by first drawing table boundaries and then drawing rows and columns
Images group		
Screenshot		Inserts a copy of any open application window
Screenshot /Screen Clipping		Used to capture a portion of any open application window
Illustrations group		
Shapes /Action Buttons		Adds navigation buttons to a slide
Links group		
Action		Used to assign hyperlink action and mouse click or mouse over commands
Media group		
Audio		Inserts audio files from file or from clip art audio
Drawing Tools Format tab		
Arrange group		
Bring Forward ▾		Brings objects forward or to the front
Send Backward ▾		Sends objects backward or to the back
Align ▾ Align		Aligns the edges of multiple selected objects
Group ▾ Group		Combines objects in to one group so they can be treated as a single object and also ungroups

COMMAND SUMMARY (CONTINUED)

Command	Shortcut	Action
Picture Tools Format tab		
Adjust group		
☼ Corrections ▾		Adjusts picture brightness and contrast
Color ▾		Recolors picture to grayscale shades or accent colors
Reset Picture		Resets a picture to its original size and color
Picture Styles group		
▾ More		Opens Picture Styles gallery
Arrange group		
Align ▾ Align		Aligns the edges of multiple selected objects
Group ▾ Group		Combines objects into a single group or ungroups them
Table Tools Design tab		
Table Style Options group		
Header Row		Turns of or off display of header row in table
Banded Row		Applies shading to alternate rows
Banded Columns		Applies shading to alternate columns
Table Styles group		
▾ More		Opens the Table Styles gallery
Borders		Customize the border of selected cells
Effects		Applies visual effects to tables such as bevel, shadow, or reflection
Draw Borders group		
Pen Style		Changes the style of the line used to draw borders
1 pt Pen Weight		Changes the line thicknesses used to draw borders
Pen Color ▾		Changes the line color used to draw borders
Draw Table		Draws a table plus row and column borders
Eraser		Removes table lines

COMMAND SUMMARY (CONTINUED)

Command	Shortcut	Action
Table Tools Layout tab		
Table group		
Select		Selects different areas of a table
Cell Size group		
Distribute Rows		Distributes the row height of selected rows equally between them
Transitions tab		
Transition to This Slide group		
More		Opens the Transition gallery
Timing group		
Advance Slide		Controls slide advancing on mouse click or after seconds
Animations tab		
Animation group		
More		Opens the Animation gallery
Advanced Animation group		
Animation Pane		Opens the Animation Pane
Slide Show tab		
Set Up group		
Set Up Slide Show		Sets up advanced options for the slide show
Audio Tools Playback tab		
Preview group		
Play		Plays the inserted audio clip
Audio Options group		
Start: On Click		Controls audio playback on mouse click or automatically
Hide During Show		Hides audio clip icon during slide show

LAB EXERCISES

MATCHING

Match the numbered item with the correct lettered description.

1. guide   _____ a. removes table border lines
2. agenda slide   _____ b. two or more objects treated as a single object
3. Screenshot   _____ c. a series of vertical and horizontal lines that help to position objects on a slide
4. mpeg   _____ d. audio file extension
5. action buttons   _____ e. an effect applied to text and objects
6. group   _____ f. contains a list of items or main topics for a presentation
7. grid   _____ g. moving picture file extension
8. bevel   _____ h. shapes that are used to navigate through a presentation
9. eraser   _____ i. a single vertical and horizontal line that helps to position objects on a slide
10. WAV   _____ j. captures an image of any open application window

MULTIPLE CHOICE

Circle the letter of the correct response to the questions below.

1. Many illustrated image graphics are made up of multiple parts that are _____ together.
   a. applied
   b. arranged
   c. grouped
   d. ungrouped

2. _____ means to position objects relative to each other by their left, right, top, or bottom edges.
   a. Branch arrangement
   b. Object alignment
   c. Stacking order
   d. Group distribution

3. A(n) _____ is a vertical or horizontal line that helps align objects on a slide.
   a. align gauge
   b. form gauge
   c. grid
   d. guide

4. The _____ feature is most useful for creating complex tables that contain cells of different heights or varying number of columns per row.
   a. Create Table
   b. Draw Table
   c. Insert Table
   d. Table Slide Layout

5. If you do not have control over what computer your presentation will run on, use _____ and _____ files for audio and video.
   a. WAV, MPEG
   b. MIDI, AVI
   c. WAV, AVI
   d. MIDI, MOV

6. _____ refers to the overall lightness or darkness of a picture.
   a. Brightness
   b. Clarity
   c. Contrast
   d. Transparency

7. The _____ feature is used to capture a portion of any open window.
   a. Cut Special
   b. Extract
   c. Screen Clipping
   d. Slicer

8. An inserted audio file is represented on a slide by a(n) _____ icon.
   a. CD
   b. headset
   c. musical note
   d. audio

9. The _____ controls the order of drawing layers on a slide.
   a. stacking order
   b. grouping order
   c. alignment order
   d. object order

10. Scaling means to _____.
    a. change the size of an object by a percentage amount.
    b. change object layers.
    c. remove selected parts of an object.
    d. stack objects in a particular order.

LAB EXERCISES

TRUE/FALSE

Check the correct answer to the following statements.

1. A slide master title layout defines the format and placement of titles and text for slides that use the title layout.   **True**   **False**

2. You must have at least three objects selected to distribute them.   **True**   **False**

3. .bmp, jpg, .gif, and .png file types can be converted to drawing objects and ungrouped.   **True**   **False**

4. Only one slide master can be used in a presentation.   **True**   **False**

5. When a table is created in PowerPoint, it must have an equal number of columns and rows.   **True**   **False**

6. A picture can be used as a background for one or more slides.   **True**   **False**

7. When a presentation is run on a kiosk, it requires user interaction to repeat itself.   **True**   **False**

8. Topics on an agenda slide can be linked to other slides in the presentation.   **True**   **False**

9. Action buttons can be added to the slide master and appear on all slides in the presentation.   **True**   **False**

10. Effect Options are the same for all Transition effects.   **True**   **False**

FILL-IN

Complete the following statements by filling in the blanks with the correct terms.

1. To work with separate parts of a graphic, you must _____ the elements.

2. The _____ ensures that as each object is added to the slide, it is added to the top layer.

3. _____ allows you to capture a portion of an open window.

4. Changing the _____ percentage only affects the onscreen display of the slide; it does not change the actual font or object size.

5. PowerPoint includes predefined slide layouts in a(n) _____ that are used to control the placement of objects on a slide.

6. Saving a presentation as a(n) _____ provides a means to save customized themes, content, and navigation for future use when developing a new presentation.

7. When a presentation automatically restarts, it is considered _____.

8. _____ files do not require any special hardware, but they produce the lowest quality video.

9. A _____ is a set of intersecting lines that form small squares on a slide that help with object alignment.

10. _____ buttons can be added to a presentation so the viewer can click them to move to other slides in the presentation.

STEP-BY-STEP

WALDEN ZOO ★

1. The director of Walden Zoo, Randy Griffin, has asked you to help him prepare a promotional presentation for the zoo. It will be picture-based with very little text for use at a convention center kiosk to let out-of-town visitors know about the zoo and all it has to offer. The text needs to be large so people can read it from a distance. He will continue to add more information to this presentation, including video, but it now contains pictures of some zoo animals in habitats that visitors enjoy. Randy wants you to design a dark green background that will reflect the outdoor environment of the zoo and arrange some of the text so it is more interesting. Also, he wants the presentation to be self-running, with rapid slide transitions and automatic restart. Some of the completed slides are shown here.

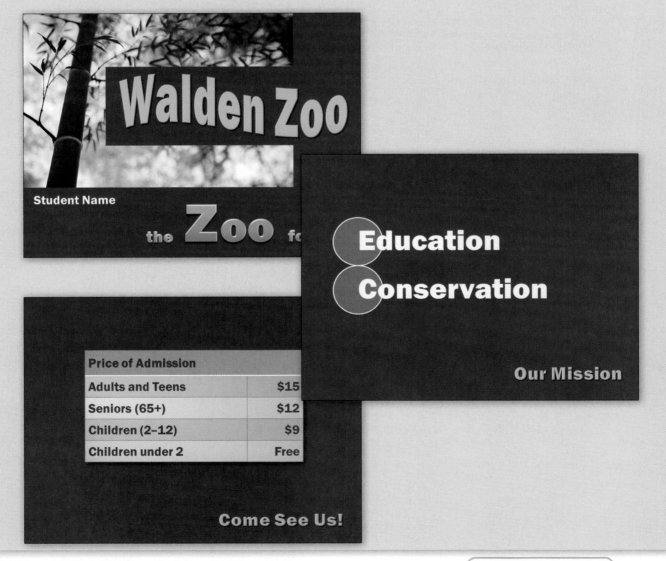

a. Start PowerPoint 2010 and open the presentation pp04_WaldenZoo.

b. Create a custom color theme named **Zoo** that changes the dark background color to a dark green. Change to a solid background style.

c. On slide 1, make the following changes:

- Insert your name in the subtitle.
- Change the rectangle shape behind the title to match the slide background.
- To the title, apply a Transform shape effect of Wave 1 and adjust the text position so it fits on the rectangle.
- To the grouped text at the bottom, apply the WordArt style of Fill - Olive Green, Accent 2, Warm Matte Bevel. Adjust the size of the group so the text does not word wrap.

d. On slide 2, convert the text to the SmartArt Vertical Circle List. Change the font to Franklin Gothic Heavy to match the other text in the presentation. Move the SmartArt up slightly.

e. On slide 17, draw a table and copy the slide text into appropriate columns and rows of the table. Apply an appropriate table style. Change the font to Franklin Gothic Demi font at 28 points and make all text Olive Green. Make the right column right-aligned. Distribute row spacing evenly. Resize and position the table for a pleasing design.

f. Repeat this process on slide 18 to arrange the text in a table with the same settings.

g. Search for animal sounds (frog, lion, and monkey) and insert the audio files on slides 3, 10, and 12. Set them to start automatically and hide the audio clip icon.

h. Apply the Box transition to all slides and make them advance automatically after 3 seconds. On slides 17 and 18, make them advance after 7 seconds. Change the show type to a kiosk so the slide show will loop automatically.

i. Save the presentation as Walden Zoo Promotion.

SUMMER IN EUROPE ★ ★

2. The college MBA office where you work offers classes in Europe for graduate students. They are held at different locations each summer where university facilities are made available to American students. While there, students have opportunities to travel in small groups and independently to other locations of interest. Some students extend their stay beyond the weeks of the course. You have been asked to set up a self-running presentation for display in the MBA office so those students thinking about going will have some more information. Some of the completed slides are shown on the next page.

a. Start PowerPoint and open the file pp04_Europe. Include your name on the title slide.

b. Apply the design theme of Module. Change the color theme to Elemental and choose Style 2 (light blue) for the background style. Save these changes as a new design theme called **Europe theme** and apply it to all slides.

c. On the title slide, search clip art for pictures of Holland and insert an appropriate picture. Use Format Painter to copy the effects from another picture already in the presentation and apply them to this picture.

LAB EXERCISES

d. Move the subtitle and title text up so they appear above the picture. Apply bold to the subtitle and your name; increase the size of the title to 54 points. Left-align the text.

e. Adjust the size and position of slide placeholders so bulleted text fits with the pictures. Use varied positions to add interest, with text sometimes on the right.

f. On slide 3, search for **Euro** to replace the out-of-date picture. Apply the same effects.

g. On slide 7, add a WordArt object with the text **Off the beaten path** in a style of your choice. Apply the Cascade Up Transform effect. Position the WordArt object over the bulleted text.

h. On slide 10, since the dollar amounts are all even, delete the decimal point and zeros. Add an illustrated graphic of a dollar sign so it is clear that these numbers are expressed in United States currency.

i. After slide 10, insert a new slide with the title **Get More Information**. Open the Word file pp04_Netherlands and make a Screen Clipping of the top of this flyer. Apply an Offset Bottom shadow effect.

j. On slide 12, move the title above the picture. Increase the size of the picture slightly. Increase the size of the text at the bottom, then resize the text box so the text fits on one line. Remove the fill color. Left-align both text boxes.

k. Apply the Ripple transition effect to all slides. Set the slides to advance automatically after 8 seconds and on mouse click. Set the presentation to be browsed by an individual.

l. Insert a new slide with the Title and Content layout after slide 1. Create a SmartArt list diagram with four sections and apply action to link to the appropriate slides:

Clothing and Currency, slide 3

Food Options, slide 6

Travel Opportunities, slide 9

Costs and More Information, slide 11

m. Apply an appropriate style and resize as needed. Add the slide title **Click to Learn More**.

n. On the slide master, insert Action buttons Home, Next, and Previous on the Title and Content layout. Reduce their default size by scaling them to 40% and place them on the lower right. Align and distribute space as needed.

o. Copy the Action buttons and paste them on the Title Slide layout.

p. Check slide content and make any needed adjustments so the Action buttons are not hidden.

q. On the title slide, insert an audio of your choice to run while the presentation runs. Hide the audio speaker icon.

r. Save the presentation as Europe Study. Print the presentation with six slides per page.

REGAL THEATER ★★

3. You work at the Regal Theater in the media and customer relations department. The Theater is one of several businesses being featured on campus during freshman orientation, so you have been asked to create a presentation about the theater that will run as a kiosk presentation. You want to use colors of black, gold, and red to convey the atmosphere of this beautifully restored theater. It has a unique Art Deco architectural design and interior décor. To encourage new students to visit the theater, you are offering reduced matinee prices. Some of the completed slides from your presentation are shown here.

a. Open the presentation pp04_Regal Theater and apply the Perspective design theme. Create a new color theme named **Regal** and change the Text/Background—Light 2 color to Gold from the Standard colors. Change the background style to a solid black.

b. Customize the slide master. On the Perspective Slide Master layout (first slide layout), change the title placeholder text to Harlow Solid Italic. Increase the size of the first bulleted line to 28 points. Delete the gold shapes in the upper right. Close Master View. Save the current theme with the name **Regal**. Reset slide layouts.

c. On slide 1, center the title, then apply a bevel effect and the transform effect of Inflate Top. Resize the text so it has a height of 3" and width of 8" and position it in the center of the slide. Move the student name to the lower left.

d. Insert the graphic pp04_Art Deco and send it backward so it is behind the title.

e. On slide 2, insert the picture pp04_Curtain1. Resize the image proportionally so it fills the slide (7.5" height). Position it on the right of the slide.

f. On slide 3, insert pp04_Interior as a picture background using Background Styles on the Design tab. Resize the text placeholder (text should be 28 points) and move it and the slide title to the lower part of the picture where the colors are darker and the text will be most readable.

g. On slide 4, draw a table and insert the content of the list into the cells using a font size of 24 points. Delete the bulleted list placeholder.

h. Apply a table style with red and white colors. Add headings for **Group** and **Price**. Apply a cell bevel to the column heading row.

i. Distribute row spacing and vertically center all table text. Right-align the Price column. Position the table appropriately.

j. On slide 6, resize the bulleted list placeholder so each item fits on one line.

k. Copy slide 1 and paste the copy after slide 6. Insert pp04_Curtain2 as a picture background. Delete the Art Deco2 picture and move the title up.

l. Create a text box and type this text: **For a limited time, we have discounted matinee prices. Come and enjoy a movie for the low cost of only $4.00!** Change the font size to 22 points, bold, then resize the text box so the text fits on two lines. Apply a black fill color.

m. On slide 1, add the sound file pp04_Film and select the automatic start option and hide during show.

n. Apply the Vortex transition effect to all slides. Set the slides to advance automatically after 5 seconds. Set the presentation to run on a kiosk as a continuous loop.

o. Print slides 1, 3, and 4 as handouts, three per page.

p. Save the presentation as Regal Theater Promotion.

q. Delete slides 3–6, then save the remaining slides as a PowerPoint template with the name Regal Template in your solution files location.

LAB EXERCISES

LIFESTYLE FITNESS PROMOTION ★ ★ ★

4. The Lifestyle Fitness Club would like you to create a presentation that prospective clients can view while visiting the club. The outline containing the text for the presentation has already been created, so you will use that content and add more information and graphic enhancements. You will design a custom theme and add navigation features. Then you will save the presentation as a template for future use. Several slides of the completed presentation are shown here.

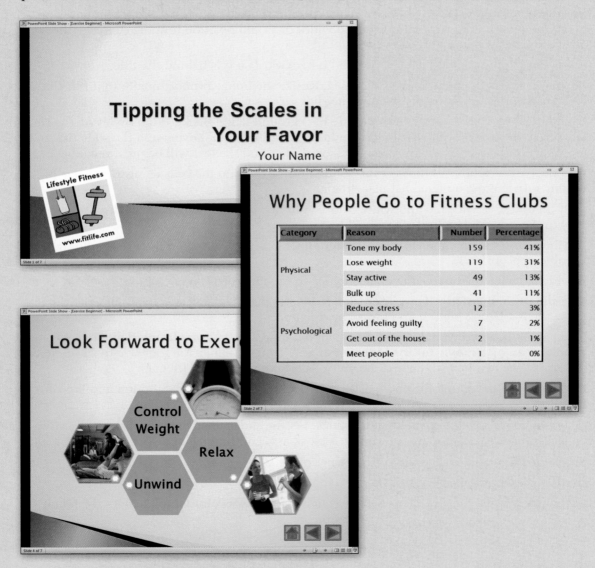

a. Create a new presentation using the Concourse design template. Add slides to the presentation using the Word outline pp04_Exercise Outline.

b. Delete the blank first slide. Apply the Title slide layout to the first slide. Add your name as a subtitle on the title slide. Insert the Lifestyle Fitness logo, pp04_LF Logo. Rotate the logo and position it on the lower left.

c. Apply the Trek color theme and change the Background Style to Style 6, a yellow gradient color. Reset all slide layouts.

d. On slide 2, insert the animated file pp04_Exercise. Increase its size to about 3.5" wide.

e. On slide 3, delete the first line of the bulleted list and increase the list level of the remaining three items. Convert this text to a SmartArt graphic. Use the Hexagon Cluster in the Picture category. Click each of the shapes with a picture icon and insert these pictures in their respective places: pp04_Unwind, pp04_Relax, and pp04_Weight. Change the text to black and apply bold.

f. On slide 7, insert the picture pp04_Stretch and apply the picture style of Moderate Frame, Black so it blends with the animated image.

g. On slides 4 and 5, use the numbered bullet style to consecutively number the tips.

h. After slide 1, insert a new slide with the Title and Content layout. Title the slide **Why People Go to Fitness Clubs**.

j. Use Draw Table to create a table with 4 columns and 9 rows. Draw the rows so four items are in each category in the first column. Enter the following information. Include appropriate formatting.

Category	Reason	Number	Percentage
Physical	Tone my body	159	41%
	Lose weight	119	31%
	Stay active	49	13%
	Bulk up	41	11%
Psychological	Reduce stress	12	3%
	Avoid feeling guilty	7	2%
	Get out of house	2	1%
	Meet people	1	0%

j. Set up the presentation for individual browsing.

k. Add home, previous, and next action buttons to the slide master. Make the home button return to the first slide. Add a custom action button to the title slide master with the text **Click to Start** that links to the next slide. Appropriately size, align, and position the buttons.

l. Apply a transition to all slides.

m. Add an audio clip of your choice to the title slide so music will start automatically and will play throughout the presentation. Hide the audio icon.

n. Save the presentation as Exercise Beginner. Print the presentation four slides per page.

o. Delete slides 2–6 and save the remaining two slides as a PowerPoint template named Exercise Template in your student files location.

LAB EXERCISES

SPORTS COMPANY KIOSK ★ ★ ★

5. The Sports Company is expanding its advertising by preparing an in-store kiosk presentation to feature some special products in the stores. You have been asked to develop this presentation with a custom theme that blends well with the sports topic. Several slides of the completed presentation are shown here.

a. Create a presentation using the News Print design theme. Add slides to the presentation by inserting the Word file pp04_Sports Company Outline.

b. Delete the blank slide 1. Apply the Title slide layout to slide 1. Enter your name as a subtitle on the title slide.

c. Change the background on slide 1 to solid fill, Blue-Gray Accent 4, Darker 25%.

d. Change two slide master layouts. On the first slide master, align the red rectangle to the top left of the slide. Duplicate this rectangle; change the fill to Blue-Gray, Accent 4, Darker 25%; and align it on the top right of the slide. For the body text placeholder, change the font to Tahoma.

e. Copy the blue rectangle and paste it on the Title slide layout just below the red rectangle. Change its fill to Blue-Gray, Accent 4, Darker 50%. Move the title placeholder up to fit on the red rectangle. Apply the WordArt style of Fill—Brown, Accent 2, Warm Matte Bevel. Make the subtitle placeholder bold. Close Slide Master View.

f. Insert the picture pp04_WeightLifter. Increase its size to a height of 5.5" and position the picture on the right.

g. On slide 2, insert four pictures: pp04_Football, pp04_Soccer, pp04_Baseball, and pp04_Tennis. Position the pictures on the right of the slide in an overlapping arrangement. Resize as needed.

h. On slide 4, insert the picture pp04_Mountain Bike. Size and position the picture and adjust the text placeholder as needed.

i. On slide 6, insert the file pp04_Tennis Racquet.

j. On slide 7, change the text to three bulleted items.

k. Move slide 3 after slide 6.

l. Apply the Reveal transition to all slides and set the slide show to automatically change after 3 seconds. Set the slide show to run on a kiosk.

m. Save the presentation as Sports Company Self Running.

n. Insert a new slide after slide 1 to create an agenda slide. Delete the title placeholder. Insert a SmartArt graphic of your choice showing two parts. Label those parts **Products** and **Services**. Change the font to Tahoma at 40 points and resize the shapes to better fit the text. Apply action to those shapes to link to the appropriate slides on mouse click and highlight on mouse over.

o. Add home, previous, and next action buttons to the slide master. Color, size, and position the buttons appropriately.

p. Run the presentation to test the hyperlinks. Print the presentation with six slides per page.

q. Save the presentation as Sports Company Browse.

LAB EXERCISES

ON YOUR OWN

HOME GYM KIOSK ★

1. The response to your home gym presentation (Lab 3, On Your Own 2) at the Sports Connection has been positive with several sales as a result of the information you provided. New customer interest has been significant, too. Your manager now wants you to update the presentation for viewer browsing. Prepare the presentation as a kiosk so it automatically loops and use action buttons for navigation. Apply automatic slide transitions, preset timings, and an audio clip that plays music continuously with the slide show. Save the presentation as Home Gym Kiosk and print the presentation with six slides per page.

TIME MANAGEMENT ★ ★

2. The manager of your campus advising office learned about the time management presentation (Lab 3, On Your Own 4) you recently gave for one of the student organizations at your college. They have asked you to update the presentation to make it a self-running presentation they can show to students who need to improve their study skills. It will be available for students to view with an adviser or to view independently, so the navigation must be easily understandable. Create an agenda slide and apply action to hyperlink to slides. Insert action buttons for forward, next, and home on the slide master. Save the presentation as Time Management and print the presentation with six slides per page.

CARPOOLING KIOSK ★ ★ ★

3. As cities surrounding Seattle get larger, rush hour traffic to the business district increases. You have been hired by the Washington Department of Transportation to create a presentation for their office lobby and at other places throughout the city to educate people about the benefits of mass transit and carpooling. Use the information in the American Public Transportation Association web site, www.apta.com, and other related Web sites. Prepare the presentation with a unique theme that will grab attention. It should provide information for how to use mass transit and carpooling to save fuel costs and benefit the city. Use the features you learned in Lab 4, including sound and navigation. Include a screenshot or screen clipping and credit the source used. Prepare a reference slide listing all sources used to prepare the presentation. Save the presentation as Carpooling Kiosk and print it with six slides per page.

BIKE SAFETY ★ ★ ★

4. The manager at Sports Connection has asked you to develop a presentation on bicycle safety as a self-running presentation in the bicycle area of the store. Use Web sources to develop the content. Create a unique theme with bright colors and graphics that will be interesting for young children learning to ride. Use as little text as possible to tell the story. Use WordArt and SmartArt as well as features you learned in Lab 4. Include action buttons and audio to gain attention. Prepare a reference slide listing all sources that you used. Save the file as Bike Safety. Print the presentation with six slides per page.

MUSICFIRST KIOSK ★ ★ ★

5. MusicFirst, a large retail chain of stores that sells CDs, concert clothing, and jewelry, would like you to create a presentation featuring a new artist monthly. This presentation will run on a computer displayed in each store. Spotlight your favorite musician and his or her latest release. Create a presentation with the features you have learned in PowerPoint. Include music and an agenda slide with navigation to enable browsing by the customers. Prepare a reference slide listing all sources used to prepare the presentation. Save your file as MusicFirst Kiosk. Print the presentation with six slides per page.

CASE STUDY

Animal Rescue Foundation

Now that the presentation to promote the Animal Rescue Foundation is nearly complete, you need feedback from Steve Dow, the agency director, before distributing the presentation for use at shopping malls. To do this, you will send him a copy of the presentation by e-mail and ask him to add comments and make changes directly in the presentation and return it to you. When you receive the reviewed presentation, you will combine it with the original presentation and review all his comments and suggestions for changes to improve the presentation.

Once the kiosk presentation is finalized, you will send a copy to the local shopping malls that provide a kiosk for use by local volunteer organizations. You will prepare the presentation for distribution to mall directors by packaging it for a CD.

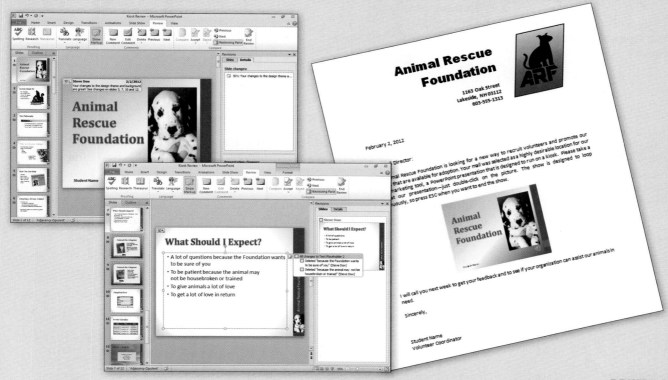

Reviewing a Presentation

The kiosk presentation is almost complete and you want to send it to the agency director, Steve Dow, to review. The review process consists of several steps: prepare the presentation to send to a reviewer, send the presentation, receive the reviewed presentation, compare the reviewed presentation with the original, consider comments as well as accept or reject changes, and end the review.

ADDING A COMMENT

Before you send the presentation for review, you want to add a comment for the reviewer. A **comment** is a note that is displayed in a separate box and attached to a text or an object on a slide or to the entire slide. You will add a general comment that you will attach to the first slide in the presentation.

1

- **Start PowerPoint 2010.**

- **Open the file** ppwt2_ Animal Rescue Kiosk**.**

- **Display slide 1 in Normal view.**

- **Open the Review tab**

  and click **.**

Your screen should be similar to Figure 1

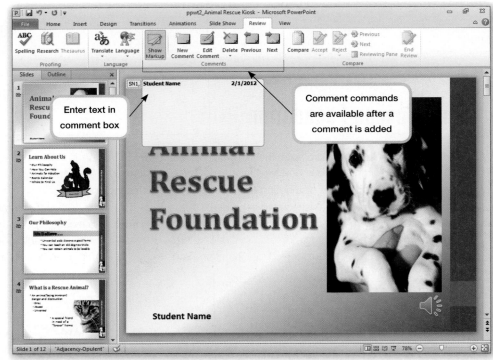

Figure 1

Additional Information

Comments can also be attached to slide placeholders by selecting the placeholder before adding the comment.

A comment box is displayed in which the text of the comment is entered. The name of the user inserting the comment appears on the first line followed by the system date. Because you did not select text or an object on the slide, the comment is attached to the entire slide. When you add a comment, the commands in the Comments group of the Review tab become active. You will use these commands when you review the comments sent back to you by the reviewer.

2

Type the following comment text:
Please add your comments and changes directly in the presentation and return it to me. Thank you for your help.

Your screen should be similar to Figure 2

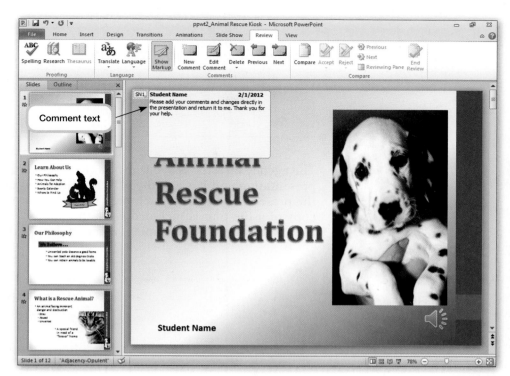

Figure 2

After entering comment text, clicking outside the comment closes it and displays an icon called a **review comment thumbnail** that indicates a comment has been added to the slide. The review comment thumbnail generally contains the initials of the person who added the comment To see the comment text again, simply point to the review comment thumbnail. The Show Markup option must be on for comments to be displayed in the presentation.

3

Click outside the comment.

Point to the review comment thumbnail.

Your screen should be similar to Figure 3

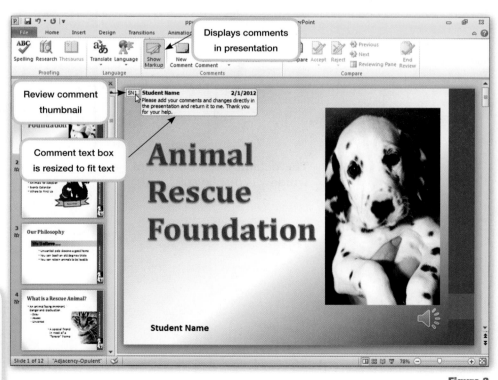

Figure 3

Additional Information

You can revise a comment by editing the existing text or adding more information. Click the review comment thumbnail

and click [Edit Comment] or simply double-click

the review comment thumbnail.

The comment is displayed in a text box that is sized to fit the contents.

4 Save the presentation as Kiosk Review to your solution file location.

E-mailing a Presentation

The agency director, Steve Dow, wants to review the changes you made to the presentation and has asked you to send it by e-mail. To do this, you will send the presentation as an attachment to an e-mail message. An **attachment** is a copy of a file that is included with an e-mail message. The attached file can then be opened by the recipient using the application in which it was created.

1

Open the File tab and choose Save & Send.

Choose Send Using E-mail, then click

Send as Attachment

Having Trouble?

If you do not have an e-mail program installed, you will receive an error message and you will need to skip this section.

Your screen should be similar to Figure 4

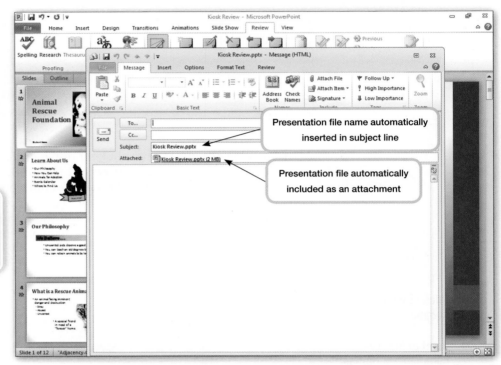

Presentation file name automatically inserted in subject line

Presentation file automatically included as an attachment

Figure 4

Having Trouble?

If your default e-mail program is other than Microsoft Outlook, your e-mail window will look different.

The default e-mail program on your system is started, and a new message window is displayed.

You need to specify the recipient's e-mail address, the e-mail address of anyone to whom you want to send a courtesy copy (CC:) of this message, and the subject and body of the message. You can select recipient names from your e-mail address book, attach a file to the message, set the message priority (high or low importance), include a follow-up message flag, and set other e-mail options. The file name of the presentation appears in the Subject box. The Attached box also displays the file name of the presentation file that will be sent with the e-mail message.

2

● In the To field, enter your e-mail address.

● Enter the following in the message text area:
Attached is the presentation I have been working on for the shopping mall kiosk. Please add your comments and changes in the presentation and return it to me. Thanks!

● Press Enter twice and type your name.

Your screen should be similar to Figure 5

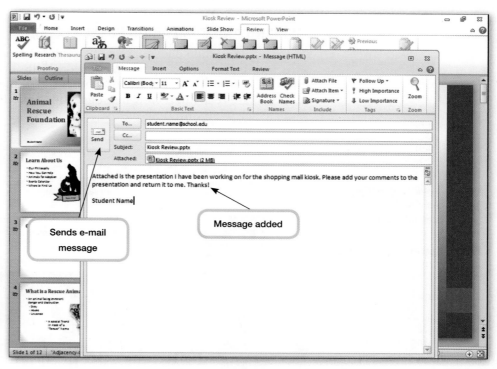

Figure 5

You are now ready to send the e-mail message. If you have an Internet connection, you could click [Send] to send the e-mail message. When the message is received, the recipient can open the attachment and view the presentation using PowerPoint. Instead, you will save it as a text file to be sent at a later time.

3

● Open the File tab and choose Save As.

● From the Save as type drop-down menu, chose Text Only.

● Save the message as Kiosk Review E-mail to your solution file location.

● Close the e-mail window.

MERGING AND COMPARING PRESENTATIONS

The next day, while checking your e-mail for new messages, you see that the director has returned the presentation with his comments and suggested changes. You have saved the attachment as a file on your computer system. Now you are ready to review his suggestions and to compare the two presentations to see what differences exist.

1

● If necessary, open the Kiosk Review presentation.

● Open the Review tab.

● Click **Compare**.

● Change to your data file location and select the reviewed presentation, ppwt2_Kiosk Review Dow.

● Click **Merge** ⏷.

● Display slide 1.

Your screen should be similar to Figure 6

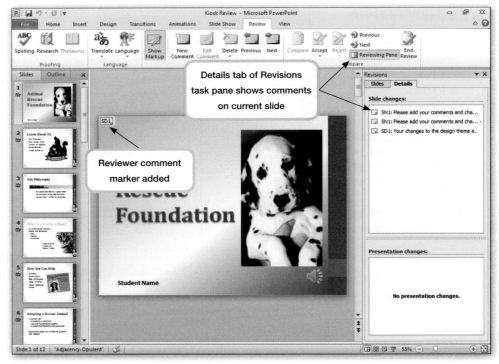

Figure 6

The changes and comments from Steve Dow have been merged with your original presentation. The Revisions task pane is automatically opened and consists of the Slides tab that displays a thumbnail of the current slide showing the changes made by another reviewer to the slide and a Details tab that displays all the comments and changes for the current slide.

VIEWING AND RESPONDING TO COMMENTS AND REVISIONS

The comment you added when you sent the presentation for review appears twice in the Revisions pane, once from the original file and once from the reviewer's file. The third comment is a new comment from Steve Dow. Review comment thumbnails appear in a stack in the upper-left corner of the slide and are listed in the Revisions task pane. Review comment thumbnails for each person appear in different colors. You can read the comments by clicking on the review comment thumbnail or by clicking on the comment in the Details tab.

First you will remove the comment you added when you sent the presentation for review and its duplicate, then you will read Steve's comment. Once you have reviewed Steve's comments and made any changes you agree are necessary, the comment also can be removed.

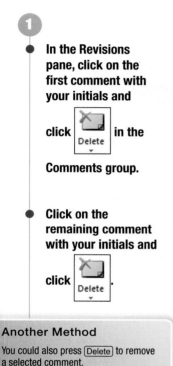

1

- In the Revisions pane, click on the first comment with your initials and

    click ☒ **Delete** in the

    Comments group.

- Click on the remaining comment with your initials and

    click ☒ **Delete**.

Another Method

You could also press Delete to remove a selected comment.

- Click on the comment from Steve Dow.

Your screen should be similar to Figure 7

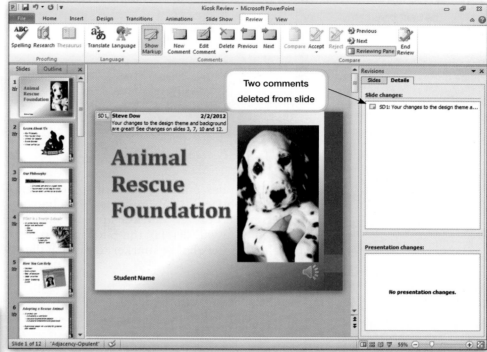

Figure 7

Your comments were removed from the slide and the Revisions pane. Now, all the remaining comments and changes in the presentation have been made by the director.

After reading Steve's comment on slide 1, you decide to check the comments on the other slides before deleting his comment.

Click  **in the Comments group to advance to the next comment.**

Delete the comment on slide 5.

Click ▢ **to see the next comment.**

Your screen should be similar to Figure 8

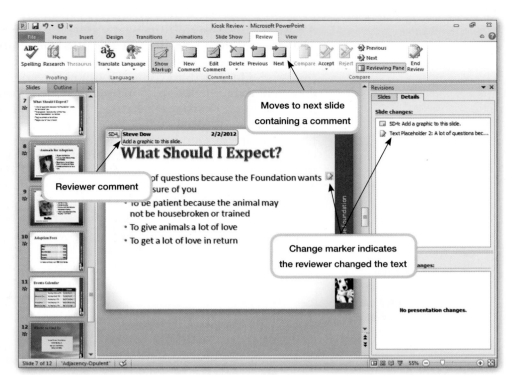

Figure 8

Slide 7 includes both a comment to add a graphic and changes to the slide content. The Details tab indicates the changes were made in the text placeholder and a **change marker** appears next to the text placeholder that was changed. You will display the Slides tab to see the changes made in the slide and click on the change marker to display the specific details.

3

Click on the Slides tab in the Revisions pane.

Click ▢.

Your screen should be similar to Figure 9

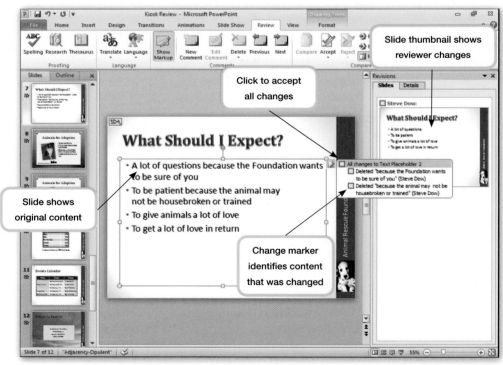

Figure 9

Additional Information

Clicking the box next to the individual change in the change marker accepts that change only.

The slide thumbnail in the Slides tab shows how the slide will look if the changes are accepted. The change marker identifies the content that was changed—in this case, deleted. You will accept both changes and insert an animated graphic on the slide as suggested in the comment.

4

- **Click the top box in the change marker list to accept all changes to the text placeholder.**

- **Insert the graphic** ppwt2_Dog Wagging **from your data file location.**

- **Size, flip, and position the graphic as in Figure 10.**

- **Delete the comment.**

- **Display the Details tab again.**

Your screen should be similar to Figure 10

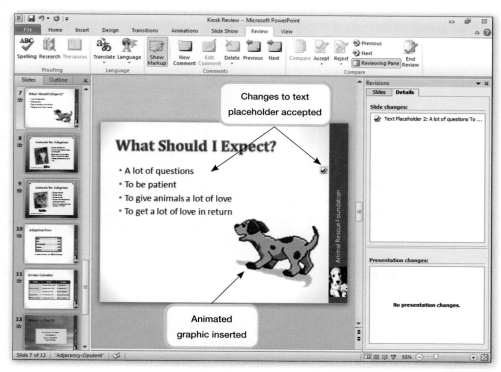

Figure 10

Additional Information

You can refuse a change using 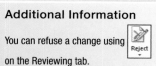 on the Reviewing tab.

The change marker displays a checkmark indicating that the text changes were added to the slide. The addition of the graphic greatly improves the slide. You will advance to the next slide containing a comment and make the suggested changes.

5

● Click  to see the next comment.

● Accept all changes to the text box.

● Insert the graphic ppwt2_ARF Logo from your data file location and size and position it as in Figure 11.

● Copy the graphic.

● Switch to Slide Master view and replace the Dalmatian graphic in the footer bar with the logo graphic.

● Size and position the logo graphic as in Figure 11.

● Copy the small logo graphic again and repeat this process in all slide layouts displaying the Dalmatian graphic in the footer bar.

● Display Normal view and delete the comment from slide 12.

Your screen should be similar to Figure 11

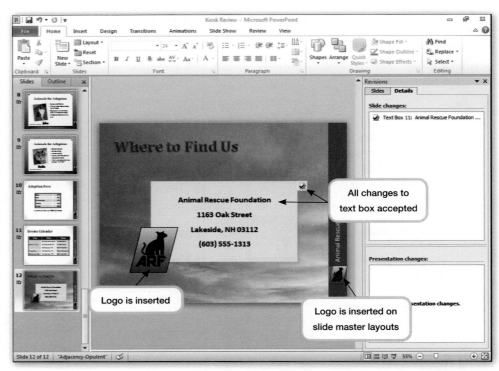

Figure 11

You have navigated to and read all the comments in the presentation. Next, you will check to see if there are revisions on any slides that did not include comments. Since you are on the last slide in the presentation, you will move backward to locate the revisions. Because the change markers are still present, all revisions, regardless of their status, will be identified.

6

- Click 🔁 Previous in the Compare group twice to see the revision on slide 10.

- Open the Slides tab to see the changes.

- Click ✍ Accept in the Compare group to accept the changes.

Your screen should be similar to Figure 12

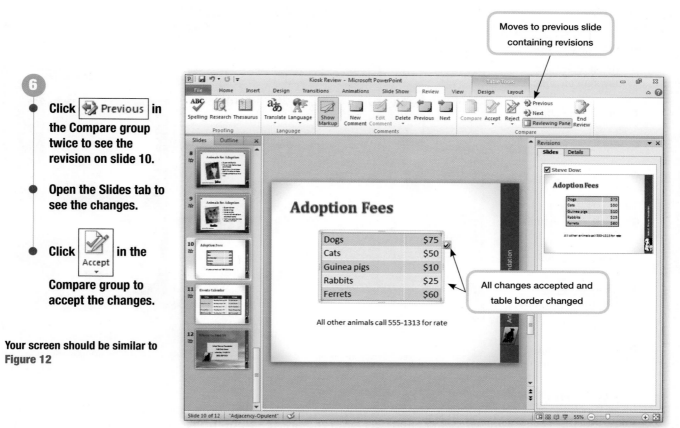

Figure 12

ENDING THE REVIEW

You will continue checking for additional revisions and accept the changes. Then you will end the review, which will permanently apply the revision changes you accepted. Any unapplied changes will be discarded.

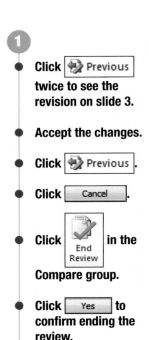

1

• Click 🔄 Previous twice to see the revision on slide 3.

• Accept the changes.

• Click 🔄 Previous.

• Click Cancel.

• Click 📋 End Review in the Compare group.

• Click Yes to confirm ending the review.

• Locate and delete any remaining comments.

• Save the presentation as Kiosk Final.

Your screen should be similar to Figure 13

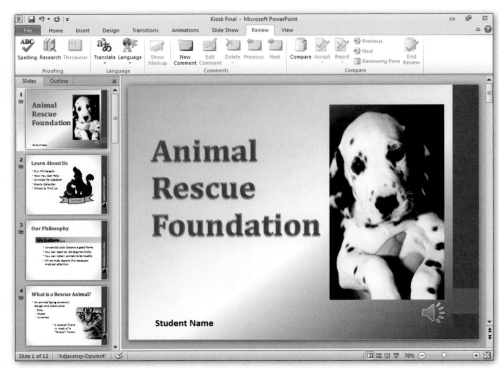

Figure 13

Ending the review permanently applies the changes you accepted and removes all change markers from the presentation. It does not remove comments. The Revisions pane closes automatically once the presentation no longer includes change markers or comments.

Collaborating Online

As suggested by the agency director, you looked into other methods you can use to have the presentation reviewed by directors of other animal shelters and members of the Animal Protection Association.

In addition to using e-mail to send a presentation as an editable file, PowerPoint also can create and send PDF or XPS copies that would not be as easily changed.

PowerPoint provides other ways to collaborate when the necessary network access is available. If you have a Windows Live account, presentations can be made available for other people to view from any computer. By using Power-Point's Broadcast Service, which also requires a Windows Live account, you can invite people to view the presentation in a Web browser.

You could subscribe to Microsoft SharePoint Online service. SharePoint provides a server location where multiple people can work together on a presentation saved there. Reviewers can edit and their comments and suggested changes are merged into the presentation. This can make your job as the presentation developer much easier. You can see all the comments made by the reviewers, and they can too, which means that if there is a question about a comment, the reviewers can discuss it among themselves.

Distributing a Presentation

The agency director is very pleased with the final kiosk presentation and asks you to send a copy by e-mail to the directors of the local malls for their evaluation. Before sending a file for distribution to others, it is a good idea to inspect the presentation for hidden data and personal information that may not be appropriate to send. Hidden information might include your name, the company name, and other confidential information that is stored with the file properties. Other items may be objects or hidden slides that are formatted as invisible that you would not want distributed.

INSPECTING A DOCUMENT

To locate and remove this information, you use the Document Inspector feature.

1
> Open the File tab and
> click 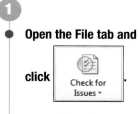 .
>
> Choose Inspect Document.
>
> Your screen should be similar to Figure 14

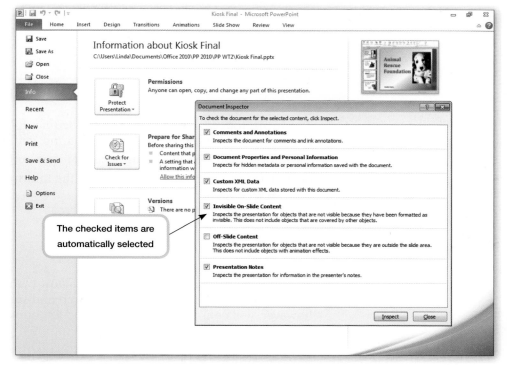

Figure 14

Using the Document Inspector dialog box, you can specify the type of content you want inspected by checking each of the types described in the following table.

Type	Removes
Comments and Annotations	Comments and ink annotations
Document Properties and Personal Information	All document properties, including statistical information, e-mail headers, routing slips, send-to-review information, document server properties, content type information, user name, template name
Custom XML Data	All custom XML data that was stored within the document
Invisible On-Slide Content	All content that has been formatted as invisible
Off-Slide Content	Objects outside the slide area that are not visible
Presentation Notes	Any information that was added in presenter notes

You will inspect the presentation for all types of information.

If necessary, select all six types of content to check.

Click Inspect .

Your screen should be similar to Figure 15

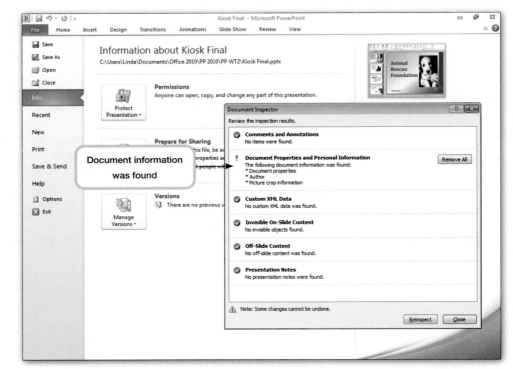

Figure 15

The Inspector results show that only Document Properties and Personal Information were located. For any located items, you have the option of removing the information. To remove any located information, you would click Remove All next to each item in the list; otherwise, the information is maintained. You will remove all document properties.

3

Click Remove All and then click Close .

The information in the file properties is now blank and all past statistical data maintained with the file has been cleared and started fresh. This information, however, will continue to be maintained as you work with the file.

4

Save the presentation.

Now the presentation is ready to send as an e-mail attachment.

Embedding a Presentation

You have already created a letter to the mall directors and just need to insert the presentation file in the letter document file. Then you will send the letter as an e-mail attachment.

To insert the presentation in the letter, you will open the letter in Word and embed the PowerPoint presentation file in the document. When you embed a PowerPoint presentation, the first slide of the presentation is displayed in the document.

Having Trouble?

See Working Together 1 to review embedding objects.

1

- **Start Word 2010 and, if necessary, maximize the application window.**

- **Open the file** ppwt2_Mall Letter **from your data file location.**

- **Move to the middle blank line below the first paragraph.**

- **Open the Insert tab.**

- **Click** Object ▾ **in the Text group and choose Object.**

- **Open the Create from File tab.**

- **Click** Browse... **.**

- **Change to your solution file location and select** Kiosk Final**.**

- **Click** Insert ▾ **.**

- **Click** OK **.**

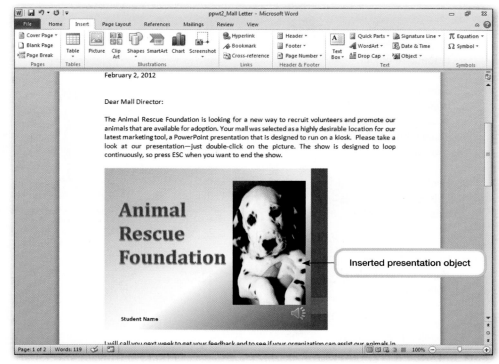

Figure 16

Your screen should be similar to Figure 16

The opening slide of the presentation is inserted as an embedded object in the letter. You will later reduce the object's size so the letter fits on one page. Before you send the letter, you want to run the slide show to make sure that it looks good and runs correctly. The directions to run the presentation from within the Word document file are included in the first paragraph of the letter.

2

- **Double-click on the embedded object.**

- **View the entire presentation and press [Esc] to end the show when it starts over again.**

- **Center the embedded object and reduce its size until the letter fits on one page.**

- **Replace Student Name in the closing with your name.**

- **Save the letter as** Kiosk Presentation Letter **to your solution file location.**

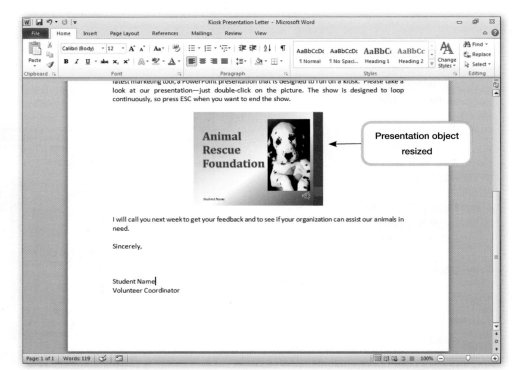

Figure 17

Your screen should be similar to Figure 17

3

- **Preview and print the letter.**

- **Exit Word.**

Additional Information

Most e-mail programs include the capability to create a distribution list that consists of the e-mail addresses of a group of people. The list is then assigned a name that is entered in the To box when you send the message. All addresses in the list receive the message.

Now that the letter is complete, you want to send the letter via e-mail to the list of local malls. This is only one way to distribute your presentation. You also could just send an e-mail with the presentation as an attachment or you could send a CD in the mail containing the presentation along with a letter of introduction. By embedding the presentation in the letter, you create both an e-mail distribution method and a letter that could be printed containing the first slide in your presentation as a graphic.

Packaging a Presentation for CD

Then, in preparation for providing a copy of the presentation to the mall directors to install on their kiosks, you will copy it to a CD. To do this you use the Package Presentation for CD feature, which copies all the files and fonts in your presentation to either a CD or a folder on your local computer or network.

● **Choose Save & Send from the File tab.**

● **Under File Types, choose Package Presentation for CD.**

● **Click** [Package for CD].

Your screen should be similar to Figure 18

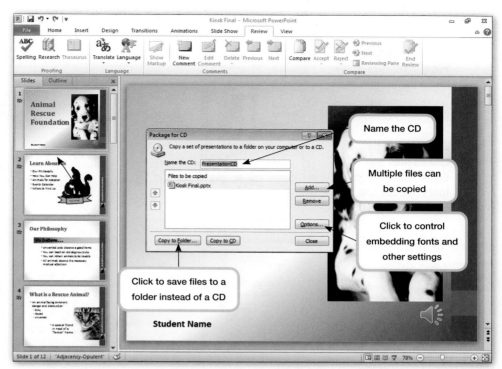

Figure 18

From the Package for CD dialog box you can select the active presentation or select additional presentations to copy directly to a CD or to a folder on your computer to be copied to a CD at a later time. You decide to copy to a folder so you can create multiple CDs later. Because you have an audio file in your presentation, you also need to copy linked files so they can be opened on the destination computer. Additionally, you want to include TrueType fonts with the presentation. **TrueType Fonts** are scalable fonts that appear on screen exactly as they will appear when printed. Embedded TrueType fonts ensure that the text will display correctly even if the font is not installed on the destination computer.

Finally, you will add a **password,** a private code, to the presentation that will prevent changes to its content. It is important to use strong passwords consisting of a combination of upper- and lowercase characters, numbers, and symbols. The longer the password, the more difficult it is to break. Because passwords cannot be retrieved, write them down and put them in a secure place or enter a strong password you can remember.

2

- Enter **Animal Rescue CD** in the Name the CD text box.

- Click [Options...].

- Confirm that the Linked files and Embedded TrueType fonts options are both checked.

Additional Information

Choosing the Inspect presentations option will run the Document Inspector. Since you just inspected the presentation, you do not need to include this option.

- Enter the password **Ma86Er** in the Password to modify each presentation text box.

Additional Information

The password will appear as dots to ensure the privacy of the password.

- Click [OK].

- Reenter the password and click [OK].

- Click [Copy to Folder...] and change to the location where you save your files.

- Click [Select].

- Click [OK].

- Click [Yes] in response to the message about copying linked files.

Additional Information

You could leave the Include Linked Files option selected even if the presentation does not include linked files.

Your screen should be similar to Figure 19

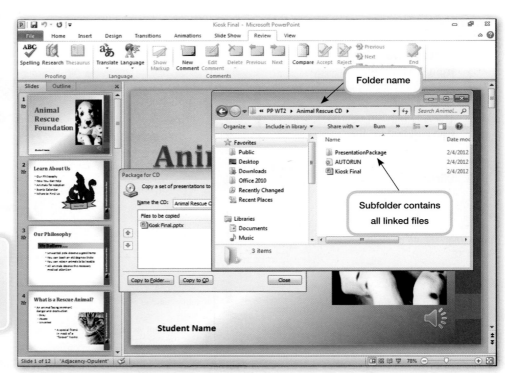

Figure 19

A folder named Animal Rescue CD has been created in your solution file location. It contains a copy of the presentation file and a subfolder called PresentationPackage. The subfolder contains all the linked files. The Animal Rescue CD folder can be transferred to another computer or copied to a CD when convenient.

3

- **Close the folder window.**

- **Click** [Close] **to close the Package for CD dialog box.**

- **Close the presentation and exit PowerPoint 2010.**

Additional Information

If you need to show a presentation on a computer that does not have PowerPoint installed, you can download a free PowerPoint Viewer from Microsoft. com. You can open, view, and print presentations with PowerPoint Viewer, but you cannot edit them.

KEY TERMS

attachment PPWT2.4
change marker PPWT2.8
comment PPWT2.2

password PPWT2.17
review comment thumbnail PPWT2.3
TrueType font PPWT2.17

COMMAND SUMMARY

Command	Action
File tab	
Send as Attachment	Attaches a copy of the current presentation to an e-mail
Info/ Check for Issues /Inspect Document	Checks for hidden properties, personal information, accessibility issues, or compatibility with earlier versions of PowerPoint
Save & Send/Package Presentation for CD/ Package for CD	Saves a presentation with linked or embedded items to a CD or folder
Review tab	
Comments group	
New Comment	Inserts a comment into a presentation
Edit Comment	Opens a comment for revisions
Delete	Removes the selected comment
Next	Moves to the slide with the next comment
Compare group	
Compare	Compares a reviewed presentation with the original
Accept	Accepts a reviewer's change
Reject	Rejects a reviewer's change
Previous	Moves to the previous comment
End Review	Ends the review

STEP-BY-STEP

DISTRIBUTING THE STUDY IN EUROPE PRESENTATION ★

1. To make more students aware of the class offered in Europe (Step-by-Step Exercise 2, Lab 4) by your MBA program, you have been asked to distribute the presentation to other graduate programs on campus. Marjorie Thomas, the MBA director, reviewed the presentation. You will first consider her comments and include the changes she made. Then you will embed the revised presentation in a Word document and send it via e-mail. The completed memo is displayed here.

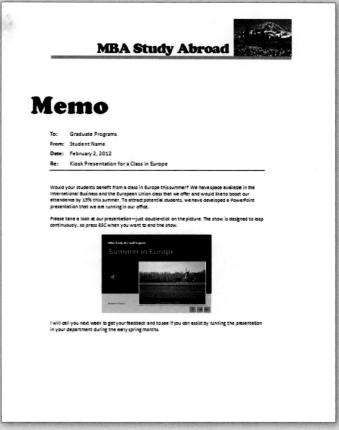

   a. Open the Europe Study presentation from your solution file location (or ppwt2_Europe Study from your data file location).

   b. Compare this presentation to ppwt2_Europe Study Review Thomas from your data file location.

   c. Review each of the comments and make the changes that Marjorie Thomas requested. Accept the changes she made, including the new slide she added at the end of the presentation.

   d. Inspect the presentation and remove all document properties.

   e. Save the revised presentation as Europe Study2 to your solution file location.

   f. Start Word 2010 and open the ppwt2_Europe Study Promotion file from your data file location.

   g. Insert the revised Europe study presentation file, Europe Study2, below the second paragraph.

   h. Reduce the size of the object and center it.

   i. Replace the "From" name with your name.

   j. Save the document as Europe Study Promotion Graduate to your solution file location.

   k. E-mail the document to your instructor for review.

   l. Print the letter.

LAB EXERCISES

PROMOTING AN EXERCISE PROGRAM ★ ★

2. The Lifestyle Fitness Club exercise presentation you created (Step-by-Step Exercise 4, Lab 4) has received positive feedback from the members. You want to share this presentation with affiliated clubs in other states and provide suggestions for how they can customize the content for their clubs. You decide to do this by embedding the presentation in a Word document and sending it via e-mail. The completed letter is displayed here.

    a. Open the Exercise Beginner presentation file from your solution file location (or ppwt2_Exercise Beginner from your data file location).

    b. Edit the presentation to include the following comments suggesting changes they might make to customize the presentation for their own use.

    Slide 1, title slide **Include your business name.**

    Slide 4, Looking Forward to Exercising **You could include pictures from your facility here.**

    Slide 6, Tips (cont.) **Your personal trainers could revise these tips if they want to make changes.**

    Slide 7, Three Key Points **After this slide, you could provide a list of upcoming classes or other activities clients could attend. Encourage them to become involved--and have fun, too!**

    c. Save the revised presentation as Exercise Beginner2 to your solution file location.

    d. Use the Package Presentation for CD feature to create a backup copy of the presentation and linked files in a folder named Exercise CD. Your comments will not be included for this backup version.

    e. Start Word 2010 and open the file ppwt2_LF Fitness from your data file location.

    f. Embed the Exercise Beginner2 presentation file in the letter.

    g. Reduce the size of the object and center it. Be sure the letter fits on one page.

    h. Insert your name in the closing of the letter.

    i. Save the document as Exercise Presentation Letter to your solution file location. E-mail the document as an attachment to your instructor for review.

    j. Print the letter.

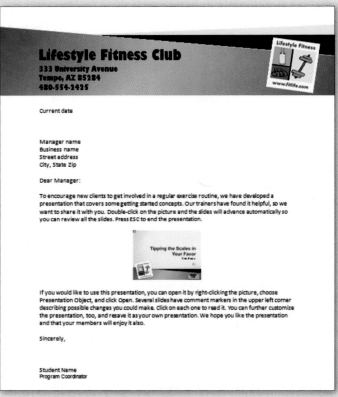

DISTRIBUTING THE SPORTS COMPANY KIOSK ★★

3. The Sports Company's kiosk presentation has worked out well. The store manager would like you to send the presentation you created (Step-by-Step Exercise 5, Lab 4) to the store managers of the other stores in the state. He wants you to include comments for how the managers might customize the presentation for their use. The completed letter is shown here.

a. Open your presentation file Sports Company Self Running from your solution file location (or ppwt2_Sports Company Self Running from your data file location).

b. Edit the presentation to include the following comments suggesting changes they might make to customize the presentation for their own use.

Slide 1, title slide **Include a welcome comment.**

Slide 2, Products **These products will change seasonally.**

Slide 3, Mountain Bikes **You could include other brands if you have inventory you need to move.**

Slide 7, Customer Service **Change the phone number and e-mail address for your local store.**

c. Save the revised presentation as Sports Company Self Running2 to your solution file location.

d. Use the Package Presentation for CD feature to create a backup copy of the presentation files in a folder named Sports CD. Your comments will not be included for this backup version.

e. Start Word 2010 and open the file ppwt2_New Products from your data file location. Use this file to create a letter by replacing the date and address information.

f. Compose the paragraphs of the letter to explain the purpose of the presentation and to let the managers know how to view the presentation.

g. Reduce the size of the embedded object and center it.

h. Insert your name in the closing of the letter.

i. Save the document as Sports Company Letter to your solution file location.

j. E-mail the document to your instructor for review.

k. Print the letter.

POWERPOINT 2010 COMMAND SUMMARY

COMMAND	SHORTCUT	ACTION
Quick Access Toolbar		
💾 Save	Ctrl + **S**	Saves presentation
↶ ▾ Undo	Ctrl + **Z**	Reverses last action
File Tab		
Save	Ctrl + **S**	Saves presentation
Save As	F12	Saves presentation using new file name and/or location
Open	Ctrl + **O**	Opens existing presentation
Close		Closes presentation
Info		Document properties
New	Ctrl + **N**	Opens New Presentation dialog box
New/New from existing		Inserts an existing presentation as a new unnamed presentation
Print	Ctrl + **P**	Opens print settings and a preview pane
☒ Exit		Closes PowerPoint
Save & Send Group		
Send as Attachment		Attaches a copy of the current presentation to an e-mail
Home Tab		
Clipboard Group		
Paste ▾	Ctrl + **V**	Pastes item from Clipboard
Paste ▾ / ▢		Embeds an object from another application
Paste ▾ / **A** Keep Text Only		Keeps the format associated with the destination format

POWERPOINT 2010 COMMAND SUMMARY

COMMAND	SHORTCUT	ACTION
Paste /Paste Special/Paste Link		Inserts an object as a linked object
✂ Cut	Ctrl + **X**	Cuts selection to Clipboard
📋 Copy ▾	Ctrl + **C**	Copies selection to Clipboard
▫ Dialog box launcher		Turns on Office Clipboard
Slides Group		
New Slide ▾	Ctrl + **M**	Inserts new slide with selected layout
New Slide ▾ /Slides from Outline		Inserts new slides using a Word outline
New Slide ▾ /Reuse Slides		Inserts new slides from another presentation
📑 Layout ▾		Changes layout of a slide
📑 Reset		Converts all the slides' content to match the presentation's theme
📑 Section ▾		Inserts an untitled section that can be renamed
Font Group		
Trebuchet MS (Bo ▾ Font		Changes font type
44 ▾ Size		Changes font size

POWERPOINT 2010 COMMAND SUMMARY

COMMAND	SHORTCUT	ACTION
A Increase Font Size	Ctrl + Shift + >	Increases font size of selected text
A Decrease Font Size		Decreases font size of selected text
I Italic	Ctrl + I	Italicizes text
U Underline	Ctrl + U	Underlines text
S Text Shadow		Applies a shadow effect
A Font Color		Changes font color
Paragraph Group		
Bullets		Formats bulleted list
Numbering		Formats numbered lists
Align Left	Ctrl + F	Aligns text to the left
Align Center	Ctrl + E	Centers text
Align Right	Ctrl + R	Aligns text to the right
Justify	Ctrl + F	Aligns text to both the left and right margins
Align Text		Sets vertical alignment of text
Convert to SmartArt		Converts bulleted text to a SmartArt graphic
Editing Group		
Find	Ctrl + F	Finds specified text
Replace	Ctrl + H	Replaces located text with replacement text
Select / Select All	Ctrl + A	Selects everything in the placeholder box

POWERPOINT 2010 COMMAND SUMMARY

COMMAND	SHORTCUT	ACTION
Insert Tab		
Tables Group		
Table /Draw table		Creates a table by first drawing table boundaries and then drawing rows and columns
Images Group		
Picture		Inserts picture from a file
Clip Art		Inserts clip art
Screenshot		Inserts a copy of any open application window
Screenshot /Screen Clipping		Used to capture a portion of any open application window
Illustrations Group		
Shapes		Inserts a shape
Shapes /Action Buttons		Adds navigation buttons to a slide
SmartArt		Inserts a SmartArt graphic
Chart		Inserts a chart

POWERPOINT 2010 COMMAND SUMMARY

COMMAND	SHORTCUT	ACTION
Links group		
Hyperlink	Ctrl + K	Creates a link to a slide, custom show, other file, or Web page
Action		Used to assign hyperlink action and mouse click or mouse over commands
Text Group		
Text Box		Inserts text box or adds text to selected shape
Header & Footer		Inserts a header and footer
WordArt		Inserts a WordArt graphic object
Media Group		
Audio		Inserts audio files from file or from clip art audio
Design Tab		
Themes Group		
More		Opens gallery of document themes
Colors		Changes the color for the current theme
Transitions Tab		
Preview Group		
Preview		Displays the transition effect

POWERPOINT 2010 COMMAND SUMMARY

COMMAND	SHORTCUT	ACTION
Transition to This Slide Group		
⊽ More		Opens the Transition gallery
Apply to All		Applies transitions in current slide to all slides
Effect Options ▾		Opens a gallery of effect options
Timing Group		
Advance Slide		Controls slide advancing on mouse click or after seconds
Animations Tab		
Preview Group		
Preview		Displays the animation effect
Animation Group		
⊽ More		Opens the Animation gallery
Advanced Animation Group		
Animation Pane		Opens the Animation pane
Animation Painter		Copies animation effect to another object
Timing Group		
Start:		Sets the trigger for the animation
Slide Show Tab		
Start Slide Show Group		
From Beginning	F5	Displays presentation starting with the first slide

WWW.MHHE.COM/OLEARY

POWERPOINT 2010 COMMAND SUMMARY

COMMAND	SHORTCUT	ACTION
From Current Slide	Shift + F5	Displays presentation starting with the current slide
Custom Slide Show		Creates or plays a custom slide show
Set Up group		
Set Up Slide Show		Sets up presentation to run for specific situations; specifies advanced options for a slide show
Hide Slide		Marks a slide so it will be hidden during a presentation
Rehearse Timings		Practices timing or pace of a presentation
Review Tab		
Proofing Group		
Spelling	F7	Spell-checks presentation
Comments Group		
New Comment		Inserts a comment into a presentation
Edit Comment		Opens a comment for revisions
Delete		Removes the selected comment

POWERPOINT 2010 COMMAND SUMMARY

COMMAND	SHORTCUT	ACTION
Next		Moves to the slide with the next comment
Compare Group		
Compare		Combines a reviewed presentation with the original
Accept		Accepts a reviewer's change
Reject		Rejects a reviewer's change
End Review		Ends the review
View Tab		
Presentation Views Group		
Normal		Switches to Normal view
Slide Sorter		Switches to Slide Sorter view
Notes Page		Displays current slide in Notes view to edit the speaker notes
Master Views Group		
Slide Master		Opens Slide Master view to change the design and layout of the master slides

POWERPOINT 2010 COMMAND SUMMARY

COMMAND	SHORTCUT	ACTION
Picture Tools Format Tab		
Adjust Group		
☼ Corrections ▾		Adjust picture brightness and contrast
Color ▾		Modifies the color of the picture; recolors picture to gray-scale shades or accent colors
Reset Picture ▾		Resets a picture to its original size and color
Picture Styles Group		
More		Opens Picture Style gallery; applies an overall visual style to picture
Picture Border ▾		Applies a border style to picture
Picture Effects ▾		Applies a visual effect to picture
Picture Layout ▾		Changes layout of a drawing
Arrange Group		
Bring Forward ▾		Brings objects forward or to the front
Send Backward ▾		Sends objects backward or to the back
Align ▾		Opens a list of vertical and horizontal alignment options
Group ▾		Combines objects in one group and also ungroups
Size Group		
Crop ▾		Crops off unwanted section of a picture
Drawing Tools Format Tab		
Shapes Styles Group		
More		Opens the Shape Styles gallery to select a visual style to apply to a shape

POWERPOINT 2010 COMMAND SUMMARY

COMMAND	SHORTCUT	ACTION
Shape Effects ▾		Applies a visual effect to a shape
WordArt Styles Group		
▾ More		Opens the WordArt Style gallery to choose a visual style for the WordArt text
A ▾ Text Effects		Provides many options for special text effects such as bevel, reflection, and more
Arrange Group		
Bring Forward ▾		Brings objects forward or to the front
Send Backward ▾		Sends objects backward or to the back
Align ▾		Opens a list of vertical and horizontal alignment options
Group ▾		Combines objects in one group and also ungroups
Rotate ▾		Rotates or flips the selected object
Table Tools Design Tab		
Table Style Options Group		
Header Row		In Table Styles, emphasizes the first row of a table
Banded Row		In Table Styles, applies shading to alternate rows
Banded Columns		In Table Styles, applies shading to alternate columns
Table Styles Group		
▾ More		Opens Table Styles gallery
Shading ▾		Colors background behind selected text or paragraph
Borders ▾		Applies a border style in different locations
Effects ▾		Applies a visual effect to the table and cells, such as shadows and reflections
Draw Borders Group		
Pen Style ▾		Applies a solid or dashed line
1 pt Pen Weight ▾		Applies different line thicknesses
Pen Color ▾		Changes line colors

WWW.MHHE.COM/OLEARY

PowerPoint 2010

POWERPOINT 2010 COMMAND SUMMARY

COMMAND	SHORTCUT	ACTION
Draw Table		Draws a table plus row and column borders
Eraser		Removes table lines

Table Tools Layout Tab

Table Group

COMMAND	SHORTCUT	ACTION
Properties		Edit table properties within the embedded object
Select		Selects different areas of a table

Cell Size Group

COMMAND	SHORTCUT	ACTION
Distribute Rows		Adjusts row height

Alignment Group

COMMAND	SHORTCUT	ACTION
Center		Centers the text within a cell
Center Vertically		Centers the text vertically within a cell

Arrange Group

COMMAND	SHORTCUT	ACTION
		Opens a gallery of alignment options

Chart Tools Design Tab

COMMAND	SHORTCUT	ACTION
More		Opens the Chart Styles gallery to choose alternative chart styles including chart color and appearance

Chart Tools Layout Tab

Labels Group

COMMAND	SHORTCUT	ACTION
Axis Titles		Adds labels to the vertical and horizontal axes

Chart Tools Format Tab

Shape Styles Group

COMMAND	SHORTCUT	ACTION
More		Opens the Shape Style gallery to choose a visual style for the shape or line

POWERPOINT 2010 COMMAND SUMMARY

COMMAND	SHORTCUT	ACTION
SmartArt Tools Design Tab		
Create Graphic Group		
Add Shape ▾		Adds a shape to SmartArt graphic
➡ Demote		Demotes selected element of SmartArt graphic
Layouts Group		
⯆ More		Opens the Layouts gallery to choose the layout for the SmartArt shape
SmartArt Styles Group		
Change Colors ▾		Changes the color variation of a SmartArt graphic
⯆ More		Opens the SmartArt Styles gallery to choose an overall visual style for the SmartArt graphic
Audio Tools Playback Tab		
Preview Group		
▶ Play		Plays the inserted audio clip
Audio Options group		
Start: On Click ▾		Controls audio playback on mouse click or automatically
Hide During Show		Hides audio speaker icon during slide show

b

Backstage view: Contains commands that allow you to work with your document, unlike the Ribbon that allows you to work in your document; contains commands that apply to the entire document.

Buttons: Graphical elements that perform the associated action when you click on them using the mouse.

c

Clipboard: Where a selection is stored when it is cut or copied.

Commands: Options that carry out a selected action.

Context menu: Also called a shortcut menu; opened by right-clicking on an item on the screen.

Contextual tabs: Also called on-demand tabs; tabs that are displayed only as needed. For example, when you are working with a picture, the Picture Tools tab appears.

Cursor: The blinking vertical bar that marks your location in the document and indicates where text you type will appear; also called the insertion point.

d

Database: A collection of related data.

Default: The standard options used by Office 2010.

Destination: The new location into which a selection that is moved from its original location is inserted.

Dialog box launcher: A button that is displayed in the lower-right corner of a tab group if more commands are available; clicking opens a dialog box or task pane of additional options.

Document window: The large center area of the program window where open application files are displayed.

e

Edit: To revise a document by changing the parts that need to be modified.

Enhanced ScreenTip: Displayed by pointing to a button in the Ribbon; shows the name of the button and the keyboard shortcut.

f

Field: The smallest unit of information about a record; a column in a table.

Font: Type style; also called typeface.

Font size: Size of typeface, given in points.

Format: The appearance of a document.

g

Groups: Part of a tab that contains related items.

h

Hyperlink: Connection to information located in a separate location, such as on a Web site.

i

Insertion point: Also called the cursor; the blinking vertical bar that marks your location in a document and indicates where text you type will appear.

k

Keyboard shortcut: A combination of keys that can be used to execute a command in place of clicking a button.

Keyword: A descriptive word that is associated with the file and can be used to locate a file using a search.

l

Live Preview: A feature that shows you how selected text in a document will appear if a formatting option is chosen.

m

Metadata: Details about the document that describe or identify it, such as title, author name, subject, and keywords; also called document properties.

Mini toolbar: Appears automatically when you select text; displays command buttons for often-used commands from the Font and Paragraph groups that are used to format a document.

o

Office Clipboard: Can store up to 24 items that have been cut or copied.

On-demand tabs: Also called contextual tabs; tabs that are displayed only as needed.

p

Paste Preview: Shows how a Paste Option will affect a selection.

Properties: Shown in a panel along the right side of the Info tab, divided into four groups; information such as author, keywords, document size, number of words, and number of pages.

q

Quick Access Toolbar: Located to the right of the Window button; provides quick access to frequently used commands such as Save, Undo, and Redo.

r

Records: The information about one person, thing, or place; contained in a row of a table.

Ribbon: Below the title bar; provides a centralized location of commands that are used to work in your document.

s

ScreenTip: Also called a tooltip; appears with the command name and the keyboard shortcut.

Scroll bar: Horizontal or vertical, it is used with a mouse to bring additional information into view in a window.

Selection cursor: Cursor that allows you to select an object.

Shortcut menu: A context-sensitive menu, meaning it displays only those commands relevant to the item or screen location; also called a context menu, it is opened by right-clicking on an item on the screen.

Slide: An individual page of a presentation.

Slide shows: Onscreen electronic presentations.

Source: The original location of a selection that is inserted in a new location.

Status bar: At the bottom of the application window; displays information about the open file and features that help you view the file.

t

Tables: A database object consisting of columns and rows.

Tabs: Used to divide the Ribbon into major activity areas.

Tag: A descriptive word that is associated with the file and can be used to locate a file using a search; also called a keyword.

Task pane: A list of additional options opened by clicking the dialog box launcher; also called a dialog box.

Text effects: Enhancements such as bold, italic, and color that are applied to selected text.

Tooltip: Also called a ScreenTip; appears displaying a command name and the keyboard shortcut.

Typeface: A set of characters with a specific design; also commonly referred to as a font.

u

User interface: A set of graphical elements that are designed to help you interact with the program and provide instructions for the actions you want to perform.

v

View buttons: Used to change how the information in the document window is displayed.

w

Worksheet: An electronic spreadsheet, or work-sheet, that is used to organize, manipulate, and graph numeric data.

z

Zoom slider: Located at the far right end of the status bar; used to change the amount of information displayed in the document window by "zooming in" to get a close-up view or "zooming out" to see more of the document at a reduced view.

a

Action: The capability of a graphic object to perform a task when you click on or pass the mouse over the object.

Action button: Special buttons in the Shapes gallery that provide a place for the presenter to click and initiate an action.

Agenda slide: Slide that contains a list of items or main topics for a presentation.

Alignment: Controls the position of text entries within a space.

Animated GIF: A type of graphic file that has motion.

Animation: Special effects that add action to text and graphics so they move around on the screen during a slide show.

Assistant shape: A shape in an organization chart that represents administrative or managerial assistants to a manager.

Attachment: A copy of a file that is included with an e-mail message.

Audio file: A type of file that plays sounds or music.

AutoCorrect: A feature that makes some basic assumptions about the text you are typing and, based on those assumptions, automatically corrects the entry.

b

Background styles: A set of theme colors and textures that you can apply to the background of your slides.

Branch: A shape and all the shapes that report to it in an organization chart.

c

Cell: The intersection of a row and a column in a table.

Change marker: A notation that indicates where a change has been made to text or a presentation.

Character formatting: Applies changes such as color and size to the selected characters only.

Chart: A visual representation of numeric data.

Clip art: Simple drawings; available in the Clip Organizer, a Microsoft Office tool that arranges and catalogs clip art and other media files stored on the computer's hard disk.

Collecting and pasting: The capability of the program to store multiple copied items in the Office Clipboard and then paste one or more of them into another document.

Comment: A remark that is displayed in a separate box and attached to a slide.

Comment marker: Indicates that a comment has been added to the slide.

Co-worker shape: In an organization chart, shapes that have the same manager.

Cropping: Trimming or removing part of a graphic.

Current slide: The slide that will be affected by any changes you make.

Custom dictionary: The dictionary you can create to hold words you commonly use, such as proper names and technical terms, that are not included in the spelling checker's main dictionary.

Custom show: A presentation that runs within a presentation.

d

Default settings: The most commonly used settings, automatically used in a new blank presentation file.

Demote: Indenting a bulleted point to the right, making it a lower or subordinate topic in the outline hierarchy.

Destination file: The file into which an object is embedded.

Document theme: A predefined set of formatting choices that can be applied to an entire document in one simple step.

Drawing object: A graphic consisting of shapes such as lines and boxes.

e

Embedded object: Graphics that were created from another program and then inserted in a slide. An embedded object becomes part of the presentation file and can be opened and edited using the program in which it was created.

f

Find and Replace: A feature used to find text in a presentation and replace it with other text.

g

Gradient: A gradual progression of colors and shades.

Graph: A visual representation of numeric data.

Graphic: A nontext element or object, such as a drawing or picture, that can be added to a slide.

Group: Two or more objects that are treated as a single object.

h

Hide Slides: A way to hide slides in a presentation without deleting them.

Hierarchical relationship: A ranked interaction.

Hierarchy: A system of ranking, as within a business association.

Hyperlink: A connection to a location in the current document, another document, or a Web site.

k

Keyword: Descriptive words or phrases associated with a graphic or figure that give information about the properties of the object.

Kiosk: A stand-alone application that provides information and services on a computer screen.

l

Layout: Defines the position and format for objects and text that will be added to a slide. A layout contains placeholders for the different items such as bulleted text, titles, charts, and so on.

Linked object: A way to insert information created in one application into a document created by another application. With a linked object, the actual data is stored in the source file.

Live link: Connection that allows changes made in the source file that affect the linked object to be automatically reflected in the destination file when it is opened.

m

Macro: A prerecorded set of instructions.

Main dictionary: The dictionary that is supplied with the spelling checker program.

Manager shape: The top-level shape of a group in an organization chart.

Master: A special slide or page that stores information about the formatting for all slides or pages in a presentation.

Metadata: Additional data saved by PowerPoint as part of the presentation; may include author's name and other personal information.

n

Notes pages: Pages that display notes below a small version of the slide they accompany.

Notes pane: View that includes space for you to enter notes that apply to the current slide.

o

Object alignment: The position of objects relative to each other or to the slide.

Object animations: Used to display each bullet point, text, paragraph, or graphic independently of the other text or objects on the slide.

Office Clipboard: A location that saves clips of material from across all Office applications to use in any Office application.

Organization chart: Graphical representation of the structure of an organization.

Outline tab: Displays the text content of each slide in outline format.

p

Paragraph formatting: Formatting features that affect an entire paragraph.

Password: A private code that will prevent changes to a presentation's content.

Picture: An image such as a graphic illustration or a scanned photograph, created in another program.

Picture style: Effects added to a picture, such as borders and shadows.

Placeholder: Boxes with dotted borders that are used to contain content such as text, graphics and other objects.

Placeholder text: Messages inside placeholders that prompt you to enter text.

Promote: Removes the indentation before a line. Promoting a line moves it to the left, or up a level in the outline hierarchy.

r

Rehearse timings: Feature that records the length of time spent on each slide and the total presentation time while you are rehearsing.

Rotate handle: Allows you to rotate the selected object to any degree in any direction.

s

Sans serif font: A font without a flair at the base of each letter, such as Arial or Helvetica.

Scaling: Increasing or decreasing an object using a percentage value of the object's original size.

Screen Clipping: A feature in which the PowerPoint window is automatically minimized and the window you viewed previously is displayed and available for clipping.

Screenshot: A feature that captures what is currently displayed on the screen.

Section: Tool used to organize and label logical groupings of slides to make it easier to locate specific slides and to navigate through a lengthy presentation.

Serif font: A font that has a flair at the base of each letter, such as Roman or Times New Roman.

Shape styles: Combinations of fill colors, outline colors, and effects used to enhance the appearance of a shape.

Sizing handles: The four circles and squares that appear at the corners and sides of a selected placeholder's border.

Slide: An individual "page" of your presentation.

Slide indicator: Identifies the number of the slide that is displayed in the workspace, along with the total number of slides in the presentation.

Slide Library: A location on an Office SharePoint Server 2010 that stores and maintains updates to presentation files centrally for use by others in an organization.

Slide master layout: A layout that takes effect for a full presentation.

Slide pane: View that displays the selected slide.

Slide show: Displays each slide full screen and in order.

Slides tab: View that displays a miniature version, or thumbnail, of each slide.

SmartArt: Graphic used to create a visual representation of textual information.

Source file: The original file used to create an embedded object.

Source program: The program in which an object was created.

Spelling checker: Locates all misspelled words, duplicate words, and capitalization irregularities as you create and edit a presentation, and proposes possible corrections.

Stacking order: The order in which objects are inserted into different layers of a slide.

Style: A combination of formatting options that can be applied in one easy step.

t

Table: Used to organize information into an easy-to-read format of horizontal rows and vertical columns.

Table reference: A letter and number used to identify cells in a table. Columns are identified from left to right beginning with the letter A, and rows are numbered from top to bottom beginning with the number 1.

Table styles: Combinations of shading colors, borders, and visual effects such as shadows and reflections that can be applied to a table.

Template: A file containing predefined settings that can be used as a pattern to create many common types of presentations.

Text box: A container for text or graphics.

Text effects: Enhancements to the text such as color and shadow.

Thumbnail: A miniature version of a slide, picture, or object.

Transition: Controls the way that the display changes as you move from one slide to the next during a presentation.

TrueType font: Scalable fonts that appear on screen exactly as they will appear when printed.

U

Ungroup: Detach from a previously created group.

V

Video file: A file that plays a motion picture with sound.

View: A way of looking at a presentation that provides the means to interact with the presentation.

W

WordArt: Used to enhance documents by changing the shape of text and adding special effects such as 3-D and shadows.